Introduction to Matter

HOLT, RINEHART AND WINSTON

A Harcourt Education Company

Orlando • **Austin** • New York • San Diego • Toronto • London

Front Cover Burke/Triolo Productions/Getty Images

Printed in the United States of America

ISBN 0-03-030666-3

2 3 4 5   027   09 08 07 06 05 04

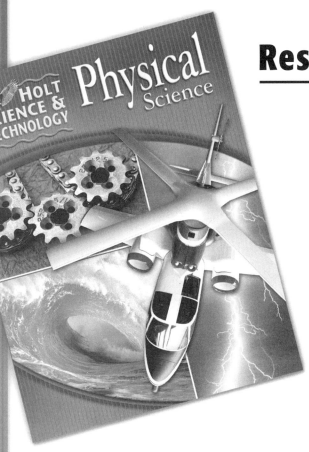

The Properties of Matter

Skills Worksheet

Directed Reading A

Section: What Is Matter?
MATTER

_____ **1.** What unit would you use to measure the amount of water in a lake?
  a. grams (g)   **c.** meters (m)
  b. liters (L)   **d.** milliliters (mL)

_____ **2.** What unit would you use to measure the volume of soda in a can?
  a. centimeters (cm)   **c.** liters (L)
  b. grams (g)   **d.** milliliters (mL)

3. What characteristic do a human, hot soup, the metal wires in a toaster, and the glowing gases in a neon sign have in common?

_____

4. What is matter?

_____

MATTER AND VOLUME

5. What is volume?

_____

6. Things with _____ cannot share the same space at the same time.

7. To measure a volume of water in a graduated cylinder, you should look at the bottom of the curve at the surface of the water called

the _____.

8. The volume of solid objects is commonly expressed

in _____ units.

9. What three dimensions are needed to find the volume of rectangular solid?

_____

VOLUME OF AN IRREGULARLY SHAPED SOLID OBJECT

10. How could the volume of a gold nugget be found using water and a graduated cylinder?

_____

| Directed Reading A *continued*

11. Why can you express the volume of the gold nugget measured by this method in cubic units?

_____

MATTER AND MASS

_____**12.** The amount of matter in an object is its
   a. volume.
   b. length.
   c. meniscus.
   d. mass.

_____**13.** The SI unit of mass is the
   a. newton.
   b. liter.
   c. kilogram.
   d. pound.

_____**14.** The SI unit of weight is the
   a. newton.
   b. liter.
   c. kilogram.
   d. pound.

_____**15.** One newton is equal to the weight of an object that has
   a. a mass of 100 g on the moon.
   b. a volume of 1 m^3 on Earth.
   c. a mass of 1,000 g on Earth.
   d. a mass of 100 g on Earth.

16. What is the only way to change the mass of an object?

_____

_____

THE DIFFERENCE BETWEEN MASS AND WEIGHT

For each description, write whether it applies to mass or to weight.

_____ **17.** is always constant no matter where the object is located.

_____ **18.** is a measure of the gravitational force on an object.

_____ **19.** is measured using a spring scale.

_____ **20.** is expressed in grams (g), kilograms (kg), or milligrams (mg).

_____ **21.** is expressed in newtons (N).

_____ **22.** is less on the moon than on Earth.

_____ **23.** is a measure of the amount of matter in the object.

Directed Reading A *continued*

INERTIA

_____**24.** The tendency of an object to resist a change in motion is known as
- **a.** mass
- **b.** gravitation
- **c.** inertia
- **d.** weight

25. What is needed in order to cause an object at rest to move, or an object in motion to change its direction or speed?

_____

_____

26. How does mass affect the inertia of an object?

_____

_____

_____

27. Why is it harder to get a cart full of potatoes moving than one that is empty?

_____

_____

_____

_____

Skills Worksheet

Directed Reading A

Section: Physical Properties
PHYSICAL PROPERTIES

_____ 1. A characteristic of matter that can be observed or measured without changing the identity of the matter is a
   a. matter property.
   b. physical property.
   c. chemical property.
   d. volume property.

_____ 2. Some examples of physical properties are
   a. color, odor, and age.
   b. color, odor, and speed.
   c. color, odor, and magnetism.
   d. color, odor, and anger.

Match the correct example with the correct physical property. Write the letter in the space provided.

_____ 3. Aluminum can be flattened into sheets of foil.

_____ 4. An ice cube floats in a glass of water.

_____ 5. Copper can be pulled into thin wires.

_____ 6. Plastic foam protects you from hot liquid.

_____ 7. Flavored drink mix dissolves in water.

_____ 8. An onion gives off a very distinctive smell.

_____ 9. A golf ball has more mass than a table tennis ball.

a. state

b. solubility

c. thermal conductivity

d. malleability

e. odor

f. ductility

g. density

10. Density is the _____ that describes the relationship between mass and volume.

11. Objects such as a cotton ball and a small tomato can occupy similar volumes but vary greatly in _____.

12. If you pour different liquids into a graduated cylinder, the liquids will form layers based upon differences in the _____ of each liquid.

13. Which layer of liquid would settle on the bottom?

_____

14. Where will the least dense liquid be found?

_____

15. Why would 1 kg of lead be less awkward to carry around than 1 kg of feathers?

_____

_____

_____

16. What will happen to a solid object made from matter with a greater density than water when it is dropped into water?

_____

_____

_____

17. How will knowing the density of a substance help you determine whether an object made from that material will float in water.

_____

_____

_____

18. What is the equation for density?

_____

19. What do *D*, *V*, and *m* stand for in the equation for density?

_____

_____

_____

20. The units for density take the form of a mass unit divided by a(n)

_____ unit.

21. What are two reasons why density is a useful property for identifying substances?

_____

_____

PHYSICAL CHANGES DO NOT FORM NEW SUBSTANCES

22. A change that only affects the physical properties of a substance is

known as a(n) _____.

23. What kind of changes are melting and freezing?

_____

_____

_____

Identify which of the following activities represent physical changes by writing PC in the space provided, if they cause only physical changes. Put an X beside any that do not.

_____**24.** sanding a piece of wood

_____**25.** baking bread

_____**26.** crushing an aluminum can

_____**27.** melting an ice cube

_____**28.** dissolving sugar in water

_____**29.** molding a piece of silver

MATTER AND PHYSICAL CHANGES

30. When a substance undergoes a physical change,

its _____ does not change.

31. What is changed when matter undergoes a physical change? Give an example to explain your answer.

_____

_____

_____

_____

_____

Skills Worksheet

Directed Reading A

Section: Chemical Properties
CHEMICAL PROPERTIES
Write the letter of the correct answer in the space provided.

_____ **1.** The property of matter that describes its ability to change into new matter with different properties is known as a(n)
a. chemical change. **c.** chemical property.
b. physical change. **d.** physical property.

_____ **2.** The chemical property that describes the ability of two or more substances to combine to form new substances is called
a. reactivity. **c.** density.
b. flammability. **d.** solubility.

_____ **3.** The ability of a substance to burn is a chemical property known as
a. reactivity. **c.** density.
b. flammability. **d.** solubility.

_____ **4.** An iron nail is reactive with
a. rubbing alcohol.
b. other iron nails.
c. wood in a house.
d. oxygen in the air.

_____ **5.** Which of the following statements is true about characteristic properties of matter?
a. Characteristic properties depend on the size of the sample.
b. Characteristic properties may be either physical or chemical properties.
c. Characteristic properties only involve chemical properties.
d. Characteristic properties only involve the physical nature of the matter.

6. Describe the ways that burning changes the nature of wood.

_____

_____

7. A substance always has _____ properties, even though they are difficult to observe.

8. Scientists use _____ properties to help them identify and classify matter.

CHEMICAL CHANGES AND NEW SUBSTANCES

_____ **9.** Chemical changes are the process by which substances
  a. move from place to place.
  b. change into new substances.
  c. change in their physical properties.
  d. become greater in mass.

_____ **10.** Which of the following would NOT be considered an example of a chemical change?
  a. the bubbling action of effervescent tablets
  b. the green coating on copper statues
  c. the melting of a Popsicle
  d. the burning of rocket fuel

11. How do you know that baking a cake involves chemical changes?

_____

_____

_____

_____

12. List some signs or clues that show that a change you are observing is a chemical change.

_____

_____

_____

_____

13. Because _____ change the identity of the substances involved, they are hard to reverse.

14. How could some chemical changes be reversed? Give an example.

_____

_____

_____

_____

PHYSICAL VERSUS CHEMICAL CHANGES

_____**15.** What is the most important question to ask to determine whether a change is physical or chemical?
  a. Was there a color change?
  b. Did the composition change?
  c. Was there a change in size?
  d. Did the change involve a change in state?

_____**16.** What is the name of the process by which water is broken down into hydrogen and oxygen using an electric current?
  a. electrolysis
  b. decomposition
  c. reactivity
  d. reversibility

17. During _____, the composition of a substance does not change.

Identify whether the following changes are physical changes or chemical changes. Label each change either PC for physical change or CC for chemical change.

_____**18.** Mixing vinegar and baking soda

_____**19.** Grinding baking soda into a powder

_____**20.** Souring milk

_____**21.** Melting an ice cream bar

_____**22.** Burning a wooden match

_____**23.** Shooting off fireworks

_____**24.** Mixing drink mix into water

_____**25.** Bending an iron nail

Skills Worksheet)

Directed Reading B

Section: What Is Matter?
MATTER
Circle the letter of the best answer for each question.

1. What do humans, hot soup, and a neon sign have in common?

   a. They are brightly colored.   **c.** They are made of matter.

   b. They are found in space.   **d.** They have the same volume.

2. What has mass and takes up space?

   a. volume   **c.** weight

   b. matter   **d.** space

MATTER AND VOLUME

3. What does the word *volume* mean?

   a. the amount of matter   **c.** the amount of space

   b. an effect of gravity   **d.** an effect of mass

4. Why can't another CD fit in a rack once it is completely filled?

   a. because all the space taken up

   b. because the CD has mass

   c. because space has three dimensions

   d. because the CD is too large

Liquid Volume

5. What unit is used to measure the volume of water in a lake?

   a. grams (g)   **c.** meters (m)

   b. liters (L)   **d.** milliliters (mL)

6. What unit would you use to measure the volume of soda in a can?

   a. centimeters (cm)   **c.** liters (L)

   b. grams (g)   **d.** milliliters (mL)

Measuring the Volume of Liquids

Read the words in the box. Read the sentences. <u>Fill in each blank</u> with the word or phrase that best completes the sentence.

cubic	irregular solid	volume
meniscus	milliliter (mL)	cubic centimeters

7. To measure volume with a graduated cylinder, look at the

bottom of the _____.

Volume of a Regularly Shaped Solid Object

8. The volume of solid objects is usually expressed

in _____ units.

9. To find the _____ of a regular solid,

multiply its length, width, and height.

10. One cubic centimeter (1 cm^3) is equal to

one _____.

Volume of an Irregularly Shaped Solid Object

11. To find the volume of a(n) _____,

measure the amount of water that the object displaces.

12. To express the volume of the irregular solid, you must change

milliliters to _____.

MATTER AND MASS

<u>Circle the letter</u> of the best answer for each question.

13. What is the amount of matter in an object called?

    a. matter   **c.** volume

    b. mass   **d.** weight

| Directed Reading B *continued*

The Difference Between Mass and Weight
Circle the letter of the best answer for each question.

14. Which of the following is a measure of gravitational force?

    a. inertia   **c.** volume

    b. mass   **d.** weight

15. What is the force called that keeps objects from floating into space?

    a. mass   **c.** gravitational force

    b. inertia   **d.** weight

16. Which of the following is true about the weight of an object?

    a. Weight is measured with a balance.

    b. Weight is the same on the moon.

    c. Weight is the same as mass.

    d. Weight depends on location in the universe.

17. Which of the following is true about the mass of an object?

    a. Mass depends on location.

    b. Mass is a measure of gravity.

    c. Mass is always the same.

    d. Mass depends in part on weight.

18. How could you change the mass of an object?

    a. move it to the moon

    b. take some of its matter away

    c. make Earth spin faster

    d. change the object's weight

Measuring Mass and Weight

19. What is the weight on Earth of an object with a mass of 100 g?

    a. 1 newton   **c.** 1 mL

    b. 1 cm^2 **d.** 1 kilogram

| Directed Reading B *continued*

Read the words in the box. Read the sentences. <u>Fill in each blank</u> with the word or phrase that best completes the sentence.

weight	newton
kilogram	mass

20. If a brick and a sponge have the same volume, the brick has

more _____.

21. The SI Unit for mass is the _____.

22. The unit for weight is the SI Unit for force called

the _____.

23. If you know an object's mass, you can figure out

its _____ on Earth.

INERTIA

<u>Circle the letter</u> of the best answer for each question.

24. What is the tendency of an object to resist changes in motion called?

a. mass   **c.** inertia

b. gravity   **d.** weight

25. What will cause changes in the motion of objects?

a. a shift in the object's color   **c.** a change in volume

b. an outside force   **d.** a change in mass

Mass: The Measure of Inertia

26. Which of the following is the easiest to start moving?

a. a cart loaded with two potatoes

b. a cart loaded with many potatoes

c. an empty cart with no potatoes

d. a cart with one potato

Skills Worksheet

Directed Reading B

SECTION: PHYSICAL PROPERTIES

Circle the letter of the best answer for each question.

1. What are the most useful questions to ask about the identity of objects?

   a. about their properties

   b. about their age

   c. about their weight

   d. about their inertia

PHYSICAL PROPERTIES

2. What is a characteristic of an object that can be observed without changing the object's identity?

   a. chemical property

   b. flexible property

   c. physical property

   d. measurable property

IDENTIFYING MATTER

Read the example. Then, draw a line from the dot to the matching property.

3. aluminum flattened into thin sheets of foil ●

4. an ice cube made of solid water ●

5. copper pulled into thin wires ●

   a. ductility

   b. state

   c. malleability

_____

6. flavored drink mix dissolving in water ●

7. a rose smelling sweet ●

8. a foam cup protecting your hand from a hot drink ●

   a. thermal conductivity

   b. solubility

   c. odor

Density

Circle the letter of the best answer for each question.

9. Which physical property describes the relationship between mass and volume?

   a. density

   b. ductility

   c. inertia

   d. weight

Liquid Layers

10. What causes different liquids to form layers when they are poured into a container?

   a. the amounts of each liquid

   b. the differences in density

   c. the differences in color

   d. the temperatures of the liquids

11. Where is the least dense liquid found when liquids form layers?

   a. in the lightest colored layer

   b. in the middle layer

   c. floating at the top

   d. settled to the bottom

Density of Solids

12. What happens to a solid object in water if its density is greater than water?

   a. The object floats on top.

   b. The object dissolves.

   c. The object floats in the middle.

   d. The object sinks to the bottom.

SOLVING FOR DENSITY

Circle the letter of the best answer for each question.

13. Which units would you to use to give the density of a solid?

    a. g/mL   **c.** N/cm^3

    b. m^3/kg **d.** g/cm^3

Using Density to Identify Substances

14. What kind of density does each substance have?

    a. a density that makes it heavy

    b. a density that differs from the densities of other substances

    c. a density that changes in different temperatures

    d. a density that is greater than the density of water

15. Look at the table of densities of common substances. What is the density of lead?

    a. $1.00 \ g/cm^3$

    b. $0.0001663 \ g/cm^3$

    c. $13.55 \ g/cm^3$

    d. $11.35 \ g/cm^3$

16. Look at the table of densities of common substances. Which liquid substance in the table has a density greater than that of water?

    a. mercury

    b. ice

    c. helium

    d. lead

17. Look at the table of densities of common substances. Which substances have a density less than that of water?

    a. zinc and silver

    b. mercury and lead

    c. oxygen and helium

    d. helium and zinc

Directed Reading B *continued*

PHYSICAL CHANGES DO NOT FORM NEW SUBSTANCES

Read the words in the box. Read the sentences. <u>Fill in each blank</u> with the word or phrase that best completes the sentence.

identity	physical change
state	

18. Any change in matter that changes only its physical form is

called a(n) _____.

19. All changes that cause a change of _____

are considered physical changes.

20. When silver is molded into a pendant,

its _____ is the same.

EXAMPLES OF PHYSICAL CHANGES

<u>Circle the letter</u> of the best answer for each question.

21. Which of the following actions does NOT cause a physical change?

a. bending

b. burning

c. dissolving

d. melting

22. Why is making ice from water a physical change?

a. The ice has some new properties.

b. The ice floats on water.

c. The water changes its state.

d. The water changes its identity.

Circle the letter of the best answer for each question.

23. Why is dissolving sugar in water a physical change?

    a. The sugar disappears forever.

    b. The water tastes sweet.

    c. The sugar changes only its state.

    d. The sugar evaporates.

Matter and Physical Changes

24. Why is making a figure from a lump of clay considered a physical change?

    a. The clay's state has changed.

    b. The clay's identity is the same.

    c. The clay's color is the same.

    d. The clay has aged.

Skills Worksheet

Directed Reading B

Section: Chemical Properties

Read the words in the box. Read the sentences. <u>Fill in each blank</u> with the word or phrase that best completes the sentence.

flammability	nonflammability
reactivity	chemical property

CHEMICAL PROPERTIES

1. A property of matter that describes its ability to change into entirely

   new substances is called a(n) _____.

2. The ability of a substance to burn is a chemical property

   known as _____.

3. Something that cannot burn has the property

   of _____.

4. The ability of two or more substances to join together to
   form new substances is a chemical property

   called _____.

Comparing Physical and Chemical Properties

<u>Circle the letter</u> of the best answer for each question.

5. Which of the following phrases describes only the physical
   properties of a material?

   a. liquid, dense, flammable

   b. solid, ductile, yellow

   c. flammable, malleable, liquid

   d. powdery, reactive, insoluble

6. What chemical property causes rust to form on a nail?

   a. conductivity   **c.** reactivity with oxygen

   b. nonflammability   **d.** flammability

Circle the letter of the best answer for each question.

7. What do physical changes NOT change?

   a. the identity of the matter   **c.** the state of matter

   b. the amount of matter   **d.** the volume of the sample

8. What makes chemical properties so hard to observe?

   a. They cause changes of state.

   b. You can't see them until they produce new materials.

   c. Wearing protective glasses is required.

   d. They happen too quickly.

Characteristic Properties

9. Which of these statements is true about characteristic properties of matter?

   a. They depend on sample size.

   b. They only involve physical properties.

   c. They only involve chemical properties.

   d. They can be physical properties as well as chemical properties.

CHEMICAL CHANGES AND NEW SUBSTANCES

Read the words in the box. Read the sentences. <u>Fill in each blank</u> with the word or phrase that best completes the sentence.

change	property

10. A chemical _____ describes which

    changes are possible for a substance.

11. A chemical _____ is the process by which

    substances actually change into new substances.

| Directed Reading B *continued*

Circle the letter of the best answer for each question.

12. Which of these phrases describes a chemical change?

    a. pouring milk into a glass

    b. melting an ice cube

    c. burning wood, making ash and smoke

    d. bending an iron nail

What Happens During a Chemical Change?

13. Which of the following is an example of a chemical change?

    a. sugar dissolving   **c.** chocolate melting

    b. a cake baking   **d.** water freezing

14. Which description describes what happens to the substances involved in a chemical change?

    a. The substances keep their identities.

    b. The substances change in form.

    c. New substances with different properties are formed.

    d. The substances combine and mix.

Signs of Chemical Changes

15. Which of the following is NOT a sign that a chemical change has taken place?

    a. change in state   **c.** foaming or bubbling

    b. sound or light given off   **d.** production of heat or light

Matter and Chemical Changes

16. Why are chemical changes difficult to reverse?

    a. because they involve physical changes

    b. because they change the matter's form

    c. because they change the identity of the matter

    d. because their products are hard to find

| Directed Reading B *continued*

PHYSICAL VERSUS CHEMICAL CHANGES

Circle the letter of the best answer for each question.

17. What is the type of matter that makes up an object and the way it is arranged?

   a. the physical properties of the object

   b. the reactivity of the object

   c. the flammability of the object

   d. the composition of the object

A Change in Composition

18. Why does a physical change differ from a chemical change?

   a. The change is reversible.

   b. The composition of the matter is unchanged.

   c. New properties of the matter are created.

   d. New materials are produced.

19. How can water be broken down into hydrogen and oxygen?

   a. by reactivity

   b. by electrolysis

   c. by composition

   d. by flammability

Reversing Changes

20. Why are chemical changes difficult to reverse?

   a. because they involve changes in composition

   b. because they involve changes in form

   c. because they involve changes in state

   d. because the temperature increases

Skills Worksheet

Vocabulary and Section Summary

What Is Matter?
VOCABULARY
In your own words, write a definition of the following terms in the space provided.

1. matter

_____

_____

2. volume

_____

_____

3. meniscus

_____

_____

4. mass

_____

_____

5. weight

_____

_____

6. inertia

_____

_____

| Vocabulary and Section Summary *continued*

SECTION SUMMARY

Read the following section summary.

- Two properties of matter are volume and mass.
- Volume is the amount of space taken up by an object.
- The SI unit of volume is the liter (L).
- Mass is the amount of matter in an object.
- The SI unit of mass is the kilogram (kg).
- Weight is a measure of the gravitational force on an object, usually in relation to the Earth.
- Inertia is the tendency of an object to resist being moved or, if the object is moving, to resist a change in speed or direction. The more massive an object is, the greater its inertia.

Skills Worksheet

Vocabulary and Section Summary

Physical Properties

VOCABULARY

In your own words, write a definition of the following terms in the space provided.

1. physical property

_____

_____

2. density

_____

_____

3. physical change

_____

_____

SECTION SUMMARY

Read the following section summary.

- Physical properties of matter can be observed without changing the identity of the matter.
- Examples of physical properties are conductivity, state, malleability, ductility, solubility, and density.
- Density is the amount of matter in a given space.
- Density is used to identify substances because the density of a substance is always the same at a given pressure and temperature.
- When a substance undergoes a physical change, its identity stays the same.
- Examples of physical changes are freezing, cutting, bending, dissolving, and melting.

Vocabulary and Section Summary

Chemical Properties

VOCABULARY

In your own words, write a definition of the following terms in the space provided.

1. chemical property

_____

_____

2. chemical change

_____

_____

SECTION SUMMARY

Read the following section summary.

- Chemical properties describe a substance based on its ability to change into a new substance that has different properties.

- Chemical properties can be observed only when a chemical change is happening.

- Examples of chemical properties are flammability and reactivity.

- New substances form as a result of a chemical change.

- Unlike a chemical change, a physical change does not alter the identity of a substance.

Skills Worksheet

Section Review

What Is Matter?

USING KEY TERMS

1. Use the following terms in the same sentence: *volume* and *meniscus*.

_____

_____

2. In your own words, write a definition for each of the following terms: *mass*, *weight*, and *inertia*.

_____

_____

_____

UNDERSTANDING KEY IDEAS

_____ **3.** Which of the following is matter?
  a. dust   **c.** strand of hair
  b. the moon   **d.** All of the above

_____ **4.** A graduated cylinder is used to measure
  a. volume.   **c.** mass.
  b. weight.   **d.** inertia.

_____ **5.** The volume of a solid is measured in
  a. liters.
  b. grams.
  c. cubic centimeters.
  d. all of the above.

_____ **6.** Mass is measured in
  a. liters.   **c.** newtons.
  b. centimeters.   **d.** kilograms.

7. Explain the relationship between mass and inertia.

_____

_____

_____

_____

_____

| Section Review *continued*

MATH SKILLS

8. A nugget of gold is placed in a graduated cylinder that contains 80 mL of water. The water level rises to 225 mL after the nugget is added to the cylinder. What is the volume of the gold nugget? Show your work below.

9. One newton equals about 100 g on Earth. How many newtons would a football weigh if it had a mass of 400 g? Show your work below.

CRITICAL THINKING

10. Identifying Relationships Do objects with large masses always have large weights? Explain.

_____

_____

_____

_____

11. Applying Concepts Would an elephant weigh more or less on the moon than it would weigh on Earth? Explain your answer.

_____

_____

_____

_____

_____

Skills Worksheet

Section Review

Physical Properties

USING KEY TERMS

1. Use each of the following terms in a separate sentence: *physical property* and *physical change.*

_____

_____

_____

_____

UNDERSTANDING KEY IDEAS

_____ 2. The units of density for a rectangular piece of wood are
   a. grams per milliliter.
   b. cubic centimeters.
   c. kilograms per liter.
   d. grams per cubic centimeter.

3. Explain why a golf ball is heavier than a table-tennis ball even though the balls are the same size.

_____

_____

4. Describe what happens to a substance when it goes through a physical change.

_____

_____

_____

5. Identify six examples of physical properties.

_____

_____

_____

_____

_____

_____

| Section Review *continued*

6. List six physical changes that matter can go through.

_____

_____

_____

_____

_____

_____

MATH SKILLS

7. What is the density of an object that has a mass of 350 g and a volume of 95 cm^3? Would this object float in water? Explain. Show your work below.

8. The density of an object is 5 g/mL, and the volume of the object is 10 mL. What is the mass of the object? Show your work below.

CRITICAL THINKING

9. Applying Concepts How can you determine that a coin is not pure silver if you know the mass and volume of the coin?

_____

_____

10. Identifying Relationships What physical property do the following substances have in common: water, oil, mercury, and alcohol?

_____

_____

11. Analyzing Processes Explain how you would find the density of an unknown liquid if you have all of the laboratory equipment that you need.

_____

_____

Skills Worksheet

Section Review

Chemical Properties

USING KEY TERMS

1. In your own words, write a definition for each of the following terms: *chemical property* and *chemical change*.

_____

_____

UNDERSTANDING KEY IDEAS

_____ **2.** Rusting is an example of a
  a. physical property.
  b. physical change.
  c. chemical property.
  d. chemical change.

_____ **3.** Which of the following is a characteristic property?
  a. density
  b. chemical reactivity
  c. solubility in water
  d. All of the above

4. What are chemical properties? List two examples of chemical properties.

_____

_____

_____

5. The Statue of Liberty was originally a copper color. After being exposed to the air, she turned a greenish color. What kind of change happened? Explain your answer.

_____

_____

_____

6. Explain how to tell the difference between a physical and a chemical property.

_____

_____

_____

| Section Review *continued*

MATH SKILLS

7. The temperature of an acid solution is 25°C. A strip of magnesium is added, and the temperature rises 2°C each minute for the first 3 min. After another 5 min, the temperature has risen two more degrees. What is the final temperature? Show your work below.

CRITICAL THINKING

8. Making Comparisons Describe the difference between physical and chemical changes in terms of what happens to the matter involved in each kind of change.

_____

_____

_____

_____

_____

_____

9. Applying Concepts Identify two physical properties and two chemical properties of a bag of uncooked popcorn.

_____

_____

_____

_____

_____

_____

_____

Name _____ Class _____ Date _____

Chapter Review

USING KEY TERMS

1. Use each of the following terms in a separate sentence: *physical property, chemical property, physical change,* and *chemical change.*

_____

_____

_____

_____

For each pair of terms, explain how the meanings of the terms differ.

2. *mass* and *weight*

_____

_____

3. *inertia* and *mass*

_____

_____

4. *volume* and *density*

_____

_____

UNDERSTANDING KEY IDEAS

Multiple Choice

_____ **5.** Which of the following properties is NOT a chemical property?
   a. reactivity with oxygen   **c.** flammability
   b. malleability   **d.** reactivity with acid

_____ **6.** The volume of a liquid can be measured in all of the following units EXCEPT
   a. grams.   **c.** milliliters.
   b. liters.   **d.** cubic centimeters.

_____ **7.** The SI unit for the mass of a substance is the
   a. gram.   **c.** milliliter.
   b. liter.   **d.** kilogram.

_____ **8.** The best way to measure the volume of an irregularly shaped
solid is to
  a. use a ruler to measure the length of each side of the object.
  b. weigh the solid on a balance.
  c. use the water displacement method.
  d. use a spring scale.

_____ **9.** Which of the following statements about weight is true?
  a. Weight is a measure of the gravitational force on an object.
  b. Weight varies depending on where the object is located in relation
  to the Earth.
  c. Weight is measured by using a spring scale.
  d. All of the above

_____ **10.** Which of the following statements does NOT describe a physical
property of a piece of chalk?
  a. Chalk is a solid.
  b. Chalk can be broken into pieces.
  c. Chalk is white.
  d. Chalk will bubble in vinegar.

_____ **11.** Which of the following statements about density is true?
  a. Density is measured in grams.
  b. Density is mass per unit volume.
  c. Density is measured in milliliters.
  d. Density is a chemical property.

Short Answer

12. In one or two sentences, explain how the process of measuring the volume of
a liquid differs from the process of measuring the volume of a solid.

_____

_____

_____

13. What is the formula for calculating density?

_____

_____

14. List three characteristic properties of matter.

_____

_____

_____

| Chapter Review *continued*

Math Skills

15. What is the volume of a book that has a width of 10 cm, a length that is 2 times the width, and a height that is half the width? Remember to express your answer in cubic units. Show your work below.

16. A jar contains 30 mL of glycerin (whose mass is 37.8 g) and 60 mL of corn syrup (whose mass is 82.8 g). Which liquid is on top? Show your work below, and explain your answer.

CRITICAL THINKING

17. Concept Mapping Use the following terms to create a concept map: *matter, mass, inertia, volume, milliliters, cubic centimeters, weight,* and *gravity.*

| Chapter Review *continued*

18. Applying Concepts Develop a set of questions that would be useful when identifying an unknown substance. The substance may be a liquid, a gas, or a solid.

_____

_____

_____

_____

19. Analyzing Processes You are making breakfast for your friend Filbert. When you take the scrambled eggs to the table, he asks, "Would you please poach these eggs instead?" What scientific reason do you give Filbert for not changing his eggs?

_____

_____

_____

20. Identifying Relationships You look out your bedroom window and see your new neighbor moving in. Your neighbor bends over to pick up a small cardboard box, but he cannot lift it. What can you conclude about the item(s) in the box? Use the terms *mass* and *inertia* to explain how you came to your conclusion.

_____

_____

_____

_____

21. Analyzing Ideas You may sometimes hear on the radio or on TV that astronauts are weightless in space. Explain why this statement is not true.

_____

_____

_____

_____

Chapter Review *continued*

INTERPRETING GRAPHICS

Use the drawing of the crushed aluminum soft drink can below to answer the questions that follow.

22. List three physical properties of this aluminum can.

_____

_____

_____

23. When this can was crushed, did it undergo a physical change or a chemical change?

_____

_____

_____

24. How does the density of the metal in the crushed can compare with the density of the metal before the can was crushed?

_____

_____

_____

25. Can you tell what the chemical properties of the can are by looking at the picture? Explain your answer.

_____

_____

_____

_____

Reinforcement

A Matter of Density

Complete this worksheet after you finish reading the section "Physical Properties."

Imagine that you work at a chemical plant. This morning, four different liquid chemicals accidentally spilled into the same tank. Luckily, none of the liquids reacted with one another! Also, you know the liquids do not dissolve in one another, so they must have settled in the tank in four separate layers. The sides of the tank are made of steel, so you can only see the surface of what's inside. But you need to remove the red chemical to use in a reaction later this afternoon.

How will you find and remove the red chemical? By finding the chemicals' different densities, of course!

The following liquids were spilled into the tank:

- a green liquid that has a volume of 48 L and a mass of 36 kg
- a blue liquid that has a volume of 144 L and a mass of 129.6 kg
- a red liquid that has a volume of 96 L and a mass of 115.2 kg
- a black liquid that has a volume of 120 L and a mass of 96 kg

1. Calculate the density of each liquid.

Green liquid: _____

Blue liquid: _____

Red liquid: _____

Black liquid: _____

2. Determine the order in which the liquids have settled in the tank.

First (bottom): _____

Second: _____

Third: _____

Fourth (top): _____

_____ **3.** What kind of property did you use to distinguish among these four chemicals?
   a. a chemical property   **c.** a liquid property
   b. a physical property   **d.** a natural property

| Reinforcement *continued*

4. Use colored pencils to sketch and label the position of the liquid layers in the tank on the diagram shown below.

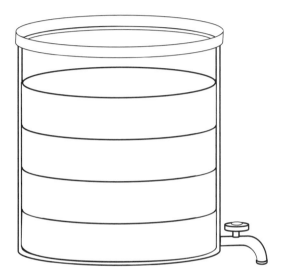

5. Now that you know where the red chemical is inside the tank, how would you remove it?

_____

_____

_____

_____

_____

Name _____ Class _____ Date _____

Critical Thinking

As a Matter of Fact!

From the Journal of Captain Jane P. Fleet

LOG 2551

I have sent two of my best science officers to explore the planet Xerxes. Their mission is to collect samples of matter from the planet's surface.

LOG 2552

The science officers brought back a small cube of space matter from Xerxes. The cube is white, odorless, and grapefruit-sized, and it glows in the dark. We will observe the cube for a few days.

LOG 2553

Last night, the space cube expanded to three times its normal size. It is now about the size of a packing box. Its mass did not change.

LOG 2554

Today the cube divided into four smaller cubes. Each new cube has more mass than the original cube.

LOG 2555

Lab officers applied electricity to one of the cubes. The cube burst into flames and exploded, covering the room and our science officers with a green paste. The paste reacted with the surfaces, and now the walls and the science officers are permanently green.

COMPREHENDING IDEAS

1. What changes in the properties of the space cube were recorded in Log entry 2553?

_____

_____

2. Explain how the changes recorded in Log entry 2553 affected the space cube's density.

_____

_____

_____

ANALYZING INFORMATION

3. List the properties of the cube that changed between Log 2551—2555.

_____

_____

4. Describe whether each change was chemical or physical.

_____

_____

_____

_____

COMPARE AND CONTRAST

5. Which of the cubes changes are not commonly observed in matter found on Earth? Explain your answer.

_____

_____

_____

_____

_____

6. Which of the cube's changes are possible to observe in matter on Earth? Explain your answer.

_____

_____

_____

_____

_____

Section Quiz

Section: What Is Matter?

Match the correct definition with the correct term. Write the letter in the space provided.

_____ **1.** a measure of the amount of matter in objects

_____ **2.** a measure of the gravitational force on objects

_____ **3.** the curve at a liquid's surface

_____ **4.** anything that has mass and takes up space

_____ **5.** the amount of space occupied by an object

_____ **6.** the tendency of matter to resist changes in motion

a. volume

b. mass

c. inertia

d. matter

e. meniscus

f. weight

Write the letter of the correct answer in the space provided.

_____ **7.** What equation would you use to find the volume of a rectangular box?
a. $volume = length + width + height$
b. $volume = length \times width \times height$
c. $volume = length \times width$
d. $volume = length + height$

_____ **8.** Which of the following units would you use to express the volume of an irregular solid such as a rock?
a. liters (L)
b. cubic centimeters (cm^3)
c. milliliters (mL)
d. newtons (N)

_____ **9.** Which of the following statements is true about an object's weight but NOT about its mass?
a. It may vary depending on the object's location.
b. It is a measure of the amount of matter in the object.
c. It is measured in kilograms (kg) or grams (g).
d. It would be the same on the moon as it is on Earth.

_____ **10.** The larger an object's mass, the
a. smaller its inertia.
b. larger its volume.
c. larger its inertia.
d. smaller its volume.

Section Quiz

Section: Physical Properties

Match the correct definition with the correct term. Write the letter in the space provided.

_____ **1.** the ability to be made into thin sheets

_____ **2.** a change in the form of a substance that does not change its identity

_____ **3.** the ability to conduct electric current

_____ **4.** the relationship between mass and volume

_____ **5.** the ability of a substance to dissolve

_____ **6.** characteristic that can be observed or measured such as color, state, or hardness

a. density

b. physical property

c. solubility

d. physical change

e. malleability

f. electrical conductivity

Write the letter of the correct answer in the space provided.

_____ **7.** If you poured three liquids (that do not mix completely) into a beaker, how could you tell which one is the densest liquid?
   a. The liquid that is floating on top is the densest liquid.
   b. The liquid that settles to the bottom is the densest liquid
   c. The liquid with the deep red color is the densest liquid.
   d. There is no way to tell which liquid is densest from the description.

_____ **8.** What happens to a solid object with a density that is less than water when it is placed in water?
   a. The object sinks about halfway into the water.
   b. The object displaces an quantity of water greater than its volume.
   c. The object settles to the bottom of the water.
   d. The object floats on top of the water.

_____ **9.** Which of the following is NOT an example of a physical change?
   a. the shaping of a gold bar
   b. the melting of a Popsicle
   c. the explosion of fireworks
   d. the sanding of a piece of wood

_____ **10.** What kinds of changes in substances are always physical changes?
   a. changes of state from solid to liquid to gas and back
   b. changes that result in new substances being formed
   c. changes that change the identity of the substances
   d. changes that change the density of the substances

Assessment

Section Quiz

Section: Chemical Properties

Match the correct definition with the correct term. Write the letter in the space provided.

_____ **1.** the type of matter and its arrangement in an object

_____ **2.** the ability of a substance to burn

_____ **3.** the process of changing into entirely new substances

_____ **4.** changes in matter that do not change the composition of the substance

_____ **5.** the ability of two or more substances to combine to form other substances

a. reactivity

b. chemical change

c. flammability

d. composition

e. physical change

Write the letter of the correct answer in the space provided.

_____ **6.** Why are chemical properties harder to observe than physical properties?
 a. Chemical properties change the substance's identity.
 b. Chemical properties depend on the size of the sample.
 c. Physical properties can be observed and measured.
 d. Physical properties change the identity of a substance.

_____ **7.** What is the best way to tell if a chemical change has taken place?
 a. The matter changes color.
 b. The change is reversible.
 c. A mixture separates into layers.
 d. The composition changes.

_____ **8.** Which of the following is NOT the result of a chemical change?
 a. soured milk
 b. rusted metal
 c. ground flour
 d. digested food

_____ **9.** Which of the following is a chemical property of matter?
 a. solubility
 b. volume
 c. density
 d. reactivity

_____ **10.** What makes characteristic properties useful to scientists?
 a. They can be either physical or chemical.
 b. They can be used to identify matter.
 c. They are easy to observe and measure.
 d. Sample size does not matter.

Assessment

Chapter Test A

The Properties of Matter
MULTIPLE CHOICE
Write the letter of the correct answer in the space provided.

_____ **1.** Which property of matter is a measure of the gravitational force?
  a. density
  b. mass
  c. volume
  d. weight

_____ **2.** In a graduated cylinder containing several liquid layers, the least dense liquid is found
  a. floating at the top.
  c. in the lightest colored layer.
  b. in the middle layer.
  d. settled on the bottom.

_____ **3.** How does a physical change differ from a chemical change?
  a. New volumes are created in a physical change.
  b. New materials are produced in a physical change.
  c. The composition is unchanged in a physical change.
  d. The change is reversible in a physical change.

_____ **4.** Melting crayons is an example of a
  a. physical property.
  b. physical change.
  c. chemical property.
  d. chemical change.

_____ **5.** Which of the following units would be best for describing the volume of mercury (liquid) used in an experiment?
  a. grams or kilograms
  c. liters or milliliters
  b. meters or centimeters
  d. newtons

_____ **6.** Which of the following events is NOT a common sign that a chemical change has taken place?
  a. change in color or odor
  b. change in state
  c. foaming or bubbling
  d. production of heat or light

_____ **7.** What chemical property is responsible for iron rusting?
   a. flammability
   b. conductivity
   c. nonflammability
   d. reactivity with oxygen

_____ **8.** The motion of a 150 g ball is more difficult to change than the motion of a 50 g ball because the 150 g ball has
   a. less weight than the 50 g ball has.
   b. greater density than the 50 g ball has.
   c. more mass than the 50 g ball has.
   d. larger volume than the 50 g ball has.

_____ **9.** What unit of density would be appropriate to describe a solid bar of silver?
   a. g/mL
   b. g/cm^3
   c. oz/ft^3
   d. kg/L

_____ **10.** Which physical property of matter describes the relationship between mass and volume?
   a. density
   b. ductility
   c. reactivity
   d. weight

_____ **11.** Souring milk is an example of a
   a. physical property.
   b. physical change.
   c. chemical property.
   d. chemical change.

_____ **12.** Malleability is an example of a
   a. physical property.
   b. physical change.
   c. chemical property.
   d. chemical change.

| Chapter Test A *continued*

MATCHING

Match the correct description with the correct term. Write the letter in the space provided. Some terms will not be used.

_____**13.** the saltiness of seawater is the result of this property

_____**14.** objects float or sink as a result of this property

_____**15.** the physical form in which a substance exists

_____**16.** the type of matter that makes up an object and the way it is arranged

_____**17.** the breakdown of water to form two gases is the result of this process

_____**18.** the ability of a substance to resist burning

_____**19.** the tendency of a substance to resist changes in its motion

_____**20.** the rate at which a substance conducts heat

a. thermal conductivity

b. composition

c. nonflammability

d. inertia

e. state of matter

f. solubility

g. reactivity

h. electrolysis

i. ductility

j. density

Chapter Test A *continued*

MULTIPLE CHOICE

The table below shows the density of some common substances. Use the table below to answer questions 21–25.

SUBSTANCE	DENSITY (g/cm³)	SUBSTANCE	DENSITY (g/cm³)
Aluminum (solid)	2.7	Ice (solid)	0.93
Iron pyrite (solid)	5.02	Water (liquid)	1.00
Mercury (liquid)	13.55	Zinc (solid)	7.13
Silver (solid)	10.50	Wood (oak)	0.85

_____21. A cube has a density of 2.7 g/cm³. What substance is the cube made of?
    a. aluminum   **c.** iron pyrite
    b. ice   **d.** wood

_____22. What substance has a density more than 13 times greater than water?
    a. ice   **c.** aluminum
    b. silver   **d.** mercury

_____23. Why will ice float on top of liquid water?
    a. Ice has a lower density than water.
    b. Ice has a higher density than water.
    c. Ice is a solid.
    d. Ice is colder than water.

_____24. What is the density of oak wood?
    a. 85 g/cm³   **c.** 0.85 g/cm³
    b. 5.02 g/cm³   **d.** 0.93 g/cm³

_____25. What is the densest solid shown in the table?
    a. mercury   **c.** zinc
    b. silver   **d.** iron pyrite

Assessment

Chapter Test B

The Properties of Matter
USING KEY TERMS

Use the terms from the following list to complete the sentences below. Each term may be used only once. Some terms may not be used.

weight	mass	density
volume	physical change	inertia
chemical change	chemical	physical

1. Because of _____ all objects tend to resist a change in motion.

2. The physical property of matter that describes the relationship between mass and volume is _____.

3. Water evaporating from a puddle is an example of a(n)

_____.

4. One way to learn about the _____ properties of a substance is to observe what new substances form during a reaction.

5. An object's _____ is affected by the gravitational force.

6. A copper penny can turn green if it reacts with carbon dioxide and water.

This is an example of a(n) _____.

UNDERSTANDING KEY IDEAS

Write the letter of the correct answer in the space provided.

_____ **7.** In scientific experiments, the amount of a liquid used is expressed in
    a. centimeters or meters.   **c.** liters or milliliters.
    b. grams or milligrams.   **d.** ounces or gallons.

_____ **8.** Which of the following is not a physical property of matter?
    a. ductility   **c.** thermal conductivity
    b. color   **d.** reactivity with water

_____ **9.** Which of the following has more inertia than a 100 g object on Earth?
    a. an object that weighs one newton on Earth
    b. a 50 g object on Earth
    c. a 10 g object on Earth
    d. an object that weighs two newtons on Earth

| Chapter Test B *continued*

_____**10.** During physical changes, matter always retains its
      a. size.
      b. identity.
      c. state.
      d. texture.

_____**11.** To compare the densities of oil and water, pour the liquids into a
     container and observe how they
      a. change color.
      b. evaporate quickly.
      c. separate into layers.
      d. create an odor.

12. Explain why volume and mass are not characteristic properties of matter.

_____

_____

_____

13. Describe two ways to compare the densities of unknown substances. Why is
density a useful property for identifying matter?

_____

_____

_____

_____

_____

14. Why could an astronaut carry more massive equipment around on the moon
than on Earth?

_____

_____

_____

_____

| **Chapter Test B** *continued*

CRITICAL THINKING

15. After a tree is cut with a chain saw, it is impossible to put the tiny wood chips back together. The process cannot be reversed. Does this mean that cutting trees with a chain saw causes a chemical change in the wood? Explain why or why not.

_____

_____

_____

_____

_____

_____

16. Summarize the differences between mass and weight. Why do you think people tend to confuse these terms?

_____

_____

_____

_____

_____

17. A glass cylinder contains four liquids in four separate layers. One liquid is water. The purple liquid has a density 1.62 g/cm^3. The yellow liquid has a density of 0.46 g/cm^3. The red has a density of 0.91 g/cm^3. What is the order of the liquids in the cylinder? Explain your answer. What will happen if you slip a small, flat, chip of wood (density 0.85 g/cm^3) into the cylinder?

_____

_____

_____

_____

_____

_____

INTERPRETING GRAPHICS

Cibwa salt is prepared from a kind of grass found in Zambia, Africa.

Examine the diagram below showing the steps in this process. Use the diagram to answer questions 18 and 19.

Production of Cibwa Salt

Grass turns brown as it dries.	Grass burns and turns to ash.	Ashes mix with water.	Salt from ash dissolves in water.
A.	B.	C.	D.

Undissolved ashes are removed from water.	Water is heated until it evaporates.	Salt remains.
E.	F.	G.

18. Does step A involve a chemical or a physical change? Explain.

_____

_____

_____

_____

19. In step B, the grass burns and turns into ash. However, the salt remains in the ashes and dissolves in Step D. What does this tell you about the properties of the salt?

_____

_____

_____

_____

Chapter Test C

The Properties of Matter
MULTIPLE CHOICE
Circle the letter of the best answer for each question.

1. What has mass and takes up space?

   a. weight

   b. volume

   c. space

   d. matter

2. How does a physical change differ from a chemical change?

   a. New properties of the matter are observed.

   b. New materials are produced.

   c. The change always involves heat or light.

   d. The composition of the matter is unchanged.

3. Which of the following would be the easiest to start moving?

   a. a cart loaded with two potatoes

   b. an empty cart with no potatoes

   c. a cart loaded with many sacks of potatoes

   d. a cart with one potato

4. Which of the following signs does NOT indicate that a chemical change has happened?

   a. change in state

   b. change in color or odor

   c. foaming or bubbling

   d. production of heat or light

MATCHING

Read the description. Then, <u>draw a line</u> from the dot to the matching word.

5. aluminum made into thin sheets ●
of foil

  a. ductility

6. an ice cube made of solid water ●

  b. reactivity

7. rust forming on metals ●

  c. state of matter

8. copper pulled into thin wires ●

  d. malleability

---

9. flavored drink mix dissolving ●
in water

  a. density

10. objects floating or sinking ●
in water

  b. solubility

  c. odor

11. wood burning in a fireplace ●

  d. flammability

12. a flower smelling sweet ●

Chapter Test C *continued*

FILL-IN-THE-BLANK

Read the words in the box. Read the sentences. <u>Fill in each blank</u> with the word or phrase that best completes each sentence.

mass	volume
property	change

13. Things with _____ cannot share the same

place at the same time.

14. A chemical _____ describes which

changes are possible for a substance.

15. A chemical _____ describes the process

by which new substances are formed.

16. The amount of matter in an object is

its _____.

Read the words in the box. Read the sentences. <u>Fill in each blank</u> with the word or phrase that best completes each sentence.

milliliters	weight
kilogram	inertia

17. The SI unit for mass is the _____.

18. If you know an object's mass, you can figure out

its _____ on Earth.

19. The tendency of an object to resist a change in its motion

is _____.

20. You could use _____ to measure the

volume of a soft drink can.

| Chapter Test C *continued*

INTERPRETING GRAPHICS

**Use the table of common densities below to answer questions 21 and 22.
Circle the letter of the best answer for each question.**

Table 1 Densities of Common Substances*

Substance	Density (g/cm^3)	Substance	Density (g/cm^3)
Helium (gas)	0.0001663	Zinc (solid)	7.13
Oxygen (gas)	0.001331	Silver (solid)	10.50
Water (liquid)	1.00	Lead (solid)	11.35
Iron pyrite (solid)	5.02	Mercury (liquid)	13.55

*at 20°C and 1.0 atm

21. Look at the table. Which substance is the least dense?

a. lead

b. helium

c. oxygen

d. iron pyrite

22. Look at the table. Which two substances are the densest?

a. oxygen and water

b. silver and mercury

c. water and iron pyrite

d. mercury and lead

Performance-Based Assessment

OBJECTIVE

Every metal has a unique density. You will measure these densities to find out what metals coins are made of.

KNOW THE SCORE!

As you work through the activity, keep in mind that you will be earning a grade for the following:

- how well you work with the materials and equipment (30%)
- how well you make observations and test the hypothesis (40%)
- how accurately you identify test objects (30%)

Using Scientific Methods

ASK A QUESTION

How can I determine which metal I have?

MATERIALS AND EQUIPMENT

- 10 pennies
- 10 nickels
- 10 dimes
- 5 quarters
- graduated cylinder (1.0 mL increments)

- copper sample
- zinc sample
- balance
- 1 L of water
- calculator

SAFETY INFORMATION

- Clean up water spills immediately. Spilled water is a slipping hazard.
- Notify your teacher if a graduated cylinder breaks or if you cut yourself on broken glass.

MAKE OBSERVATIONS

1. Compare the luster and appearance of the coins with the luster and appearance of the copper and zinc samples.

_____

_____

_____

| Performance-Based Assessment *continued*

FORM A HYPOTHESIS

2. Which metals do you think the coins are mostly made of? Support your hypothesis with observations.

_____

_____

_____

_____

TEST THE HYPOTHESIS

3. Place the copper sample on the balance. Measure and record the mass in the table.

4. Pour water into the graduated cylinder until it is half full. Record the starting volume of the water in the table.

5. Place the copper sample in the cylinder. Record the ending volume of the water in the table.

6. Subtract the starting volume from the ending volume to find the volume of the metal. Record this value in the table below.

7. Repeat steps 3–6, with the zinc sample. Record your measurements.

8. Repeat steps 3–6, with the 10 pennies. Record your measurements. Continue to repeat steps 3–6 until all of the sets of coins have been tested.

MATERIALS DATA

Metal sample	Starting volume (mL)	Ending volume (mL)	Volume of metal (mL)	Mass of metal (mL)	Density of metal (g/mL)
Copper					
Zinc					
Penny					
Nickel					
Dime					

| Performance-Based Assessment *continued*

ANALYZE THE RESULTS

9. Calculate the density of each metal by dividing the mass of the metal by the volume of the metal. Record the density in the table above. Show your work below.

DRAW CONCLUSIONS

10. Compare the densities of the coins with the densities of the known metals. What are the coins mostly made of? Support your answer.

_____

_____

_____

_____

Standardized Test Preparation

READING

Read each of the passages below. Then, answer the questions that follow each passage.

Passage 1 Astronomers were studying the motions of galaxies in space when they noticed something odd. They thought that the large gravitational force, which causes the galaxies to rotate rapidly, was due to a large amount of mass in the galaxies. Then, they discovered that the mass of the galaxies was not great enough to explain this large gravitational force. So, what was causing the additional gravitational force? One theory is that the universe contains matter that we cannot see with our eyes or our telescopes. Astronomers call this invisible matter <u>dark matter</u>.

_____ **1.** According to this passage, what did astronomers originally think caused the rotation of the galaxies?
   A a lack of inertia
   B a large gravitational force
   C a small amount of mass in the galaxies
   D a small gravitational force

_____ **2.** Why do you think astronomers use the term *dark matter*?
   F Dark matter refers to dark objects.
   G Dark matter refers to matter that we can't see.
   H You need a telescope to see dark matter.
   I All large objects are dark.

_____ **3.** Which statement is the best summary of the passage?
   A The enormous amount of mass in the galaxies explains why the galaxies rotate.
   B Dark matter may be responsible for the gravitational force that causes the rotation of galaxies.
   C Invisible matter is called dark matter.
   D Galaxies rotate as they move through the universe.

Standardized Test Preparation *continued*

Passage 2 Blimps and dirigibles are types of airships. An airship consists of an engine, a large balloon that contains gas, and a gondola that carries passengers and crew. Airships float in air because the gases that the airships contain are less dense than air. In the early 1900s, airships were commonly used for travel, including transatlantic flights. Airships were less frequently used after the 1937 explosion and crash of the *Hindenburg* in New Jersey. The *Hindenburg* was filled with <u>flammable</u> hydrogen gas instead of helium gas, which is nonflammable.

_____ **1.** In this passage, what does *flammable* mean?
  A able to burn
  B able to float
  C able to sink
  D not able to burn

_____ **2.** Which of the following statements is true according to the passage?
  F Hydrogen gas is nonflammable.
  G Airships float because they contain gases that are less dense than air.
  H Helium gas was used in the *Hindenburg*.
  I The gondola contains gas.

_____ **3.** Which of the following statements about airships is true?
  A Airships are still a major mode of transportation.
  B Airships now contain nonflammable, hydrogen gas.
  C Airships consist of an engine, a gondola, and a large balloon.
  D Airships traveled only in the United States.

❙ Standardized Test Preparation *continued*

INTERPRETING GRAPHICS

The table below shows the properties of different substances. Use the table below to answer the questions that follow.

Properties of Some Substances*		
Substance	**State**	**Density (g/cm^3)**
Helium	Gas	0.0001663
Iron Pyrite	Solid	5.02
Mercury	Liquid	13.55
Gold	Solid	19.32

*at room temperature and pressure

_____ **1.** What could you use to tell iron pyrite (fool's gold) and gold apart?
    A volume
    B density
    C mass
    D state

_____ **2.** What do you think would happen if you placed a nugget of iron pyrite into a beaker of mercury?
    F The iron pyrite would sink.
    G The iron pyrite would dissolve.
    H The mercury and the iron pyrite would react.
    I The iron pyrite would float.

_____ **3.** If a nugget of iron pyrite and a nugget of gold each have a mass of 50 g, what can you conclude about the volume of each nugget?
    A The volume of iron pyrite is greater than the volume of gold.
    B The volume of iron pyrite is less than the volume of gold.
    C The volumes of the substances are equal.
    D There is not enough information to determine the answer.

_____ **4.** Which substance has the lowest density?
    F helium
    G iron pyrite
    H mercury
    I gold

| **Standardized Test Preparation** *continued*

MATH

Read each question below, and choose the best answer.

_____ 1. Imagine that you have discovered a new element, and you want to find its density. It has a mass of 78.8 g and a volume of 8 cm^3. To find the density of the element, you much divide the element's mass by its volume. What is the density of the element?
A 0.102 g/cm^3
B 0.98 g/cm^3
C 9.85 g/cm^3
D 630.4 g/cm^3

_____ 2. Many soft drinks come in bottles that contain about 590 mL. If the density of a soft drink is 1.05 g/mL, what is the mass of the drink?
F 0.0018 g
G 498.2 g
H 561.9 g
I 619.5 g

_____ 3. If you have 150 g of pure gold and the density of gold is 19.32 g/cm^3, what is the volume of your gold nugget?
A 2,898 cm^3
B 7.76 cm^3
C 0.98 cm^3
D 0.13 cm^3

_____ 4. Three objects have a mass of 16 g each. But their volumes differ. Object A, a liquid, has a volume of 1.2 mL. Object B, a solid, has a volume of 3.2 cm^3. Object C, another solid, has a volume of 1.9 cm^3. Which object is the least dense?
F object A
G object B
H object C
I There is not enough information to determine the answer.

Skills Practice

White Before Your Eyes

You have learned how to describe matter based on its physical and chemical properties. You have also learned some signs that can help you determine whether a change in matter is a physical change or a chemical change. In this lab, you'll use what you have learned to describe four substances based on their properties and the changes that they undergo.

OBJECTIVES

Describe the physical properties of four substances.

Identify physical and chemical changes.

Classify four substances by their chemical properties.

MATERIALS

- baking powder
- baking soda
- carton, egg, plastic-foam
- cornstarch
- eyedroppers (3)
- iodine solution
- spatulas (4)
- stirring rod
- sugar
- vinegar
- water

SAFETY INFORMATION

PROCEDURE

1. Use Table 1 to describe the appearance of four substances and write down your observations.

2. Using a spatula, place a small amount of baking powder into three cups of your egg carton. Use just enough baking powder to cover the bottom of each cup. Record your observations about the baking powder's appearance, such as color and texture, in the "Unmixed" column of Table 1.

3. Use an eyedropper to add 60 drops of water to the baking powder in the first cup. Stir with the stirring rod. Record your observations in Table 1 in the column labeled "Mixed with water." Clean your stirring rod.

Name _____ Class _____ Date _____

Table 1: Observations

Substance	Unmixed	Mixed with water	Mixed with vinegar	Mixed with iodine solution
baking powder				
baking soda				
cornstarch				
sugar				

4. Use a clean dropper to add 20 drops of vinegar to the second cup of baking powder. Stir. Record your observations in Table 1 in the column labeled "Mixed with vinegar." Clean your stirring rod.

5. Use a clean dropper to add five drops of iodine solution to the third cup of baking powder. Stir. Record your observations in Table 1 in the column labeled "Mixed with iodine solution." Clean your stirring rod. **Caution:** Be careful when using iodine. Iodine will stain your skin and clothes.

6. Repeat steps 2–5 for each of the other substances (baking soda, cornstarch, and sugar). Use a clean spatula for each substance.

ANALYZE THE RESULTS

1. Examining Data What physical properties do all four substances share?

_____

2. Analyzing Data In Table 2, write the type of change—physical or chemical—that you observed for each substance. State the property that the change demonstrates.

Table 2: Analyzing Data

Substance	Mixed with water		Mixed (vinegar)		Mixed (iodine solution)	
	Change	Property	Change	Property	Change	Property
baking powder						
baking soda						
cornstarch						
sugar						

DRAW CONCLUSIONS

3. Evaluating Results Classify the four substances by the chemical property of reactivity. For example, which substances are reactive with vinegar (acid)?

_____

_____

_____

Quick Lab

Space Case

MATERIALS

- beaker or bucket
- cup, clear plastic
- paper, sheet
- pencil
- water

SAFETY INFORMATION

PROCEDURE

1. Crumple a **piece of paper**. Fit it tightly in the bottom of a **clear plastic cup** so that it won't fall out.

2. Turn the cup upside down. Lower the cup straight down into a **bucket** half-filled with **water.** Be sure that the cup is completely underwater.

3. Lift the cup straight out of the water. Turn the cup upright, and observe the paper. Record your observations.

_____

_____

_____

4. Use the point of a **pencil** to punch a small hole in the bottom of the cup. Repeat steps 2 and 3.

5. How do the results show that air has volume? Explain your answer.

_____

_____

_____

_____

_____

Name _____ Class _____ Date _____

Changing Change

MATERIALS AND EQUIPMENT

- pennies, 3 shiny
- pie plate, metal
- towel, paper
- vinegar

SAFETY INFORMATION

PROCEDURE

1. Place a folded **paper towel** in a **small pie plate**.

2. Pour **vinegar** into the pie plate until the entire paper towel is damp.

3. Place **three shiny pennies** on top of the paper towel.

4. Put the pie plate in a safe place. Wait 24 hours.

5. Describe and explain the change that took place.

_____

_____

_____

_____

_____

Name _____ Class _____ Date _____

Physical or Chemical Change?

MATERIALS

- bar magnet
- beaker
- effervescent tablet
- iron filings
- paper, sheet
- powdered sulfur
- test tube
- water
- wooden stick

SAFETY INFORMATION

PROCEDURE

1. Watch as your teacher places a burning **wooden stick** into a **test tube**. Record your observations.

2. Place a mixture of **powdered sulfur** and **iron filings** on a sheet of **paper**. Place a **bar magnet** underneath the paper, and try to separate the iron from the sulfur.

3. Drop an **effervescent tablet** into a **beaker** of **water**. Record your observations.

_____

_____

4. Identify whether each change is a physical change or a chemical change. Explain your answers.

_____

_____

_____

_____

_____

_____

Skills Practice Lab

Volumania!

You have learned how to measure the volume of a solid object that has square or rectangular sides. But there are lots of objects in the world that have irregular shapes. In this lab activity, you'll learn some ways to find the volume of objects that have irregular shapes.

MATERIALS

Part A
- graduated cylinder
- water
- various small objects supplied by your teacher

Part B
- bottle, plastic (or similar container), 2 L, bottom half
- funnel
- graduated cylinder
- pan, aluminum pie
- paper towels
- water

SAFETY INFORMATION

Part A: Finding the Volume of Small Objects
PROCEDURE

1. Fill a graduated cylinder half full with water. Read and record the volume of the water in a separate notebook. Be sure to look at the surface of the water at eye level and to read the volume at the bottom of the meniscus.

2. Carefully slide one of the objects into the tilted graduated cylinder.

3. Read the new volume, and record it.

4. Subtract the old volume from the new volume. The resulting amount is equal to the volume of the solid object.

5. Use the same method to find the volume of the other objects. Record your results.

ANALYZE THE RESULTS

6. What changes do you have to make to the volumes you determine in order to express them correctly?

_____

_____

7. Do the heaviest objects always have the largest volumes? Why or why not?

_____

_____

| Volumania *continued*

Part B: Finding the Volume of Your Hand
PROCEDURE

1. Completely fill the container with water. Put the container in the center of the pie pan. Be sure not to spill any of the water into the pie pan.

2. Make a fist, and put your hand into the container up to your wrist.

3. Remove your hand, and let the excess water drip into the container, not the pie pan. Dry your hand with a paper towel.

4. Use the funnel to pour the overflow water into the graduated cylinder. Measure the volume. This measurement is the volume of your hand. Record the volume. (Remember to use the correct unit of volume for a solid object.)

5. Repeat this procedure with your other hand.

ANALYZE THE RESULTS

1. Was the volume the same for both of your hands? If not, were you surprised? What might account for a person's hands having different volumes?

_____

_____

2. Would it have made a difference if you had placed your open hand into the container instead of your fist? Explain your reasoning.

_____

_____

3. Compare the volume of your right hand with the volume of your classmates' right hands. Create a class graph of right-hand volumes. What is the average right-hand volume for your class?

_____

_____

APPLYING YOUR DATA

Design an experiment to determine the volume of a person's body. In your plans, be sure to include the materials needed for the experiment and the procedures that must be followed. Include a sketch that shows how your materials and methods would be used in this experiment.

Using an encyclopedia, the Internet, or other reference materials, find out how the volumes of very large samples of matter—such as an entire planet—are determined.

Name _____ Class _____ Date _____

Determining Density

The density of an object is its mass divided by its volume. But how does the density of a small amount of a substance relate to the density of a larger amount of the same substance? In this lab, you will calculate the density of one marble and of a group of marbles. Then, you will confirm the relationship between the mass and volume of a substance.

MATERIALS

- balance, metric
- graduated cylinder, 100 mL
- marbles, glass (8–10)
- paper, graph
- paper towels
- water

SAFETY INFORMATION

PROCEDURE

1. Use the table below to record your data.

Mass of marble (g)	Total mass of marbles (g)	Total volume (mL)	Volume of marbles (mL)(total volume minus 50.0 mL)	Density of marbles (g/mL) (total mass divided by volume)

2. Fill the graduated cylinder with 50 mL of water. If you put in too much water, twist one of the paper towels, and use it to absorb excess water.

3. Measure the mass of a marble as accurately as you can (to at least .01 g). Record the mass in the table.

4. Carefully drop the marble in the tilted cylinder, and measure the total volume. Record the volume in the third column.

5. Measure and record the mass of another marble. Add the masses of the marbles together, and record this value in the second column of the table.

6. Carefully drop the second marble in the graduated cylinder. Complete the row of information in the table.

7. Repeat steps 5 and 6. Add one marble at a time. Stop when you run out of marbles, the water no longer completely covers the marbles, or the graduated cylinder is full.

Determining Density *continued*

ANALYZE THE RESULTS

1. Examine the data in your table. As the number of marbles increases, what happens to the total mass of the marbles? What happens to the volume of the marbles? What happens to the density of the marbles?

_____

_____

2. Graph the total mass of the marbles (*y*-axis) versus the volume of the marbles (*x*-axis). Is the graph a straight line?

DRAW CONCLUSIONS

3. Does the density of a substance depend on the amount of substance present? Explain how your results support your answer.

_____

_____

APPLYING YOUR DATA

Calculate the slope of the graph. How does the slope compare with the values in the column entitled "Density of marbles"? Explain.

_____

_____

_____

_____

_____

Name _____ Class _____ Date _____

Layering Liquids

You have learned that liquids form layers according to the densities of the liquids. In this lab, you'll discover whether it matters in which order you add the liquids.

MATERIALS

- beaker (or other small, clear container)
- funnel (3)
- graduated cylinder, 10 mL (3)

- liquid A
- liquid B
- liquid C

SAFETY INFORMATION

ASK A QUESTION

1. Does the order in which you add liquids of different densities to a container affect the order of the layers formed by those liquids?

FORM A HYPOTHESIS

2. Write a possible answer to the question above.

_____

TEST THE HYPOTHESIS

3. Using the graduated cylinders, add 10 mL of each liquid to the clear container. Remember to read the volume at the bottom of the meniscus. Record the order in which you added the liquids.

_____

4. Observe the liquids in the container. Sketch what you see. Be sure to label the layers and the colors.

5. Add 10 mL more of liquid C. Observe what happens, and record your observations.

_____

6. Add 20 mL more of liquid A. Observe what happens, and record your observations.

_____

│ Layering Liquids *continued*

ANALYZE YOUR RESULTS

1. Which of the liquids has the greatest density? Which has the least density? How can you tell?

_____

_____

_____

2. Did the layers change position when you added more of liquid C? Explain your answer.

_____

_____

_____

3. Did the layers change position when you added more of liquid A? Explain your answer.

_____

_____

_____

4. Find out in what order your classmates added the liquids to the container. Compare your results with those of a classmate who added the liquids in a different order. Were your results different? Explain why or why not.

_____

_____

_____

DRAW CONCLUSIONS

5. Based on your results, evaluate your hypothesis from step 2.

_____

_____

_____

_____

Activity

Vocabulary Activity

Search for Matter

After you finish reading the chapter, try this puzzle! Complete each statement by filling in the blanks with the correct word. Then, find the words in the puzzle. Words can be spelled forward or backward and can be vertical, horizontal, or diagonal. Some words may be used more than once.

1. The tendency of an object to resist any change in motion is

   called _____.

2. When water is in a container, the surface of the water is curved. This curve is

   called the _____.

3. The amount of space taken up or occupied by an object is

   its _____.

4. A measure of the amount of matter in an object is

   its _____. The SI unit for expressing this quantity is

   the _____.

5. The force which keeps objects from floating off into space is known as

   the _____ force.

6. The measure of how much gravitational force is exerted on an object is called

   its _____. The SI unit for expressing this force is

   the _____.

7. Anything that has mass and occupies space is called

   _____.

8. The amount of matter in a given volume of space is

   its _____. Units for this quantity are commonly

   expressed as a(n) _____ unit divided by

   a(n) _____ unit.

9. A property of matter that can be observed and measured, without changing

   its identity is known as a(n) _____.

10. A change in matter from one form to another without a change in its

    chemical properties is called a(n) _____.

Name _____ Class _____ Date _____

Vocabulary Activity continued

11. The ability of matter to change into new matter with completely new

properties is called a(n) _____.

12. The process by which matter actually changes into new substances is

called a(n) _____.

13. A property of matter that is always the same, no matter what size the sample,

is a(n) _____ property. Scientists often use these

properties to help them identify substances.

14. The _____ of an object is the type of matter that makes

up the object and the way that the matter is arranged.

Now see if you can find the vocabulary words in the word search puzzle. Some terms may be used more than once.

D	Y	B	G	R	A	V	I	T	I	O	N	A	L	P	W	R	T
X	T	A	R	F	G	E	X	J	O	L	M	E	W	K	M	I	J
B	R	V	Q	U	I	T	E	M	U	L	O	V	E	W	T	O	N
F	E	P	H	Y	S	I	C	A	L	P	R	O	P	E	R	T	Y
K	P	C	J	H	W	N	D	S	K	I	L	O	G	R	A	M	T
V	O	L	U	M	E	E	I	S	P	O	D	N	I	I	C	N	I
J	R	O	K	A	I	R	A	M	T	B	A	W	E	I	W	R	S
P	P	V	O	S	G	T	V	O	L	H	T	E	G	I	N	W	N
T	L	D	T	S	H	I	M	A	C	B	H	I	D	E	E	Y	E
X	A	G	R	A	T	A	S	L	R	I	M	G	H	O	W	C	D
N	C	R	M	R	A	W	A	K	I	L	O	H	F	A	T	N	R
A	I	A	D	A	W	C	O	M	P	O	S	I	T	I	O	N	H
C	M	P	M	B	I	M	M	P	V	Q	U	A	O	N	N	M	T
I	E	P	V	M	A	T	T	E	R	G	R	A	V	I	T	E	R
S	H	L	E	R	I	T	E	L	T	R	A	W	A	I	T	O	R
Y	C	H	A	R	A	C	T	E	R	I	S	T	I	C	B	Y	C
H	C	E	G	N	A	H	C	L	A	C	I	S	Y	H	P	R	O
P	T	Z	B	C	N	M	E	N	I	S	C	U	S	R	P	O	Y

Name _____ Class _____ Date _____

SciLinks Activity

DESCRIBING MATTER

Go to www.scilinks.org. To find links related to Describing Matter, type in the keyword HSM0391. Use the links to answer the following questions about Describing Matter.

$SC\!i$
$L\!INKS$®

NSTA
Developed and maintained by the
National Science Teachers Association

Go to www.scilinks.org

Topic: Describing Matter
SciLinks code: HSM0391

1. What are materials scientists and what do they do?

_____

_____

_____

_____

2. List five broad categories of materials studied by materials scientists. Describe their properties and how their uses relate to their properties.

_____

_____

_____

_____

3. Find a description of some science activities with eggs. Explain how the property of inertia could be used to separate a raw egg from a hardboiled one without cracking the egg.

_____

_____

_____

4. Describe two chemical and two physical properties of water. How do its properties help explain why water is such a unique substance?

_____

_____

_____

Performance-Based Assessment

Teacher Notes and Answer Key

PURPOSE

Students will measure the mass and volume of copper and zinc to calculate their densities. They will use this information to determine which coins are made of copper and which are made of zinc.

Terry Rakes
Elmwood Junior High
Rogers, AK

TIME REQUIRED

One 45-minute class period
Students will need 30 minutes at the activity station and 15 minutes to answer the analysis questions.

RATING

Easy ←—1——2——3——4—→ Hard

Teacher Prep–2
Student Set-up–1
Concept Level–2
Clean Up–1

ADVANCE PREPARATION

Make sure you use graduated cylinders that measure in 1.0 mL increments. The diameter of the cylinder should be wide enough so that the largest coin that you will test can easily fall in and out. (You don't want it to get stuck!)
Cover each activity station with a tarp or a drop cloth. Equip each activity station with the necessary materials.

SAFETY INFORMATION

Spilled water is a slipping hazard. Clean up water spills immediately. Students should immediately notify the teacher if a graduated cylinder breaks or if a student cuts himself or herself. Have a sharps container nearby in case of glass breakage.

TEACHING STRATEGIES

This activity works best in groups of 4–5 students. Before the activity, review how to calculate density. Show students how to correctly read a water level in a graduated cylinder. Point out that for students to get an accurate reading, they must read at the water level.

Pennies minted before 1982 were made of 95 percent copper and 5 percent zinc. From 1982 and thereafter, pennies were made of copper-plated zinc. Nickels are 75 percent copper and 25 percent nickel. Dimes and quarters are manufactured with a pure copper core and a face that is 75 percent copper and 25 percent nickel.

Performance-Based Assessment Teacher Notes *continued*

Although none of the coins will have precisely the same density as the pure metals, students should be able to distinguish whether the coins consist mostly of copper or zinc.

The pennies used in this activity should all be minted either before or after 1982. This will ensure consistency in the measurement of density.

Evaluation Strategies

Use the following rubric to help evaluate student performance.

Rubric for Assessment

Possible points	Appropriate use of materials and equipment (30 points possible)
30–20	Successful completion of activity; safe and careful handling of materials and equipment; attention to detail; superior lab skills
19–10	Activity is generally complete; successful use of materials and equipment; sound knowledge of lab techniques; somewhat unfocused performance; mild neglect of safety measures
9–1	Attempts to complete activity yield inadequate results; unsafe lab technique; apparent lack of skill
	Making observations and testing hypotheses (40 points possible)
40–27	Superior analysis stated clearly and accurately; high level of detail; correct usage of scientific terminology
26–14	Complete analysis; moderate level of detail, but expressed in unclear manner; minor inaccuracies; some errors or inconsistencies
13–1	Erroneous, incomplete, or unclear analysis; complete lack of accuracy and detail
	Drawing conclusions (30 points possible)
30–20	Clear, detailed explanation shows good understanding of density; use of examples support explanations
19–10	Adequate understanding of density with minor difficulty in expression
9–1	Poor understanding of density; explanation unclear or not relevant to the activity; substantial factual errors

Performance-Based Assessment

OBJECTIVE

Every metal has a unique density. You will measure these densities to find out what metals coins are made of.

KNOW THE SCORE!

As you work through the activity, keep in mind that you will be earning a grade for the following:

- how well you work with the materials and equipment (30%)
- how well you make observations and test the hypothesis (40%)
- how accurately you identify test objects (30%)

Using Scientific Methods

ASK A QUESTION

How can I determine which metal I have?

MATERIALS AND EQUIPMENT

- 10 pennies
- 10 nickels
- 10 dimes
- 5 quarters
- graduated cylinder (1.0 mL increments)

- copper sample
- zinc sample
- balance
- 1 L of water
- calculator

SAFETY INFORMATION

- Clean up water spills immediately. Spilled water is a slipping hazard.
- Notify your teacher if a graduated cylinder breaks or if you cut yourself on broken glass.

MAKE OBSERVATIONS

1. Compare the luster and appearance of the coins with the luster and appearance of the copper and zinc samples.

   Sample answer: The luster and appearance of the pennies resembles the

   copper sample and the luster and appearance of the nickels, dimes, and

   quarters resembles the zinc sample.

Performance-Based Assessment *continued*

FORM A HYPOTHESIS

2. Which metals do you think the coins are mostly made of? Support your hypothesis with observations.

Sample hypothesis: I think the penny is made of copper because it is the

same color as the copper sample. I think the nickel, dime, and quarter are

mostly made of zinc because they are almost the same color as the zinc

sample.

TEST THE HYPOTHESIS

3. Place the copper sample on the balance. Measure and record the mass in the table.

4. Pour water into the graduated cylinder until it is half full. Record the starting volume of the water in the table.

5. Place the copper sample in the cylinder. Record the ending volume of the water in the table.

6. Subtract the starting volume from the ending volume to find the volume of the metal. Record this value in the table below.

7. Repeat steps 3–6, with the zinc sample. Record your measurements.

8. Repeat steps 3–6, with the 10 pennies. Record your measurements. Continue to repeat steps 3–6 until all of the sets of coins have been tested.

MATERIALS DATA

Metal sample	Starting volume (mL)	Ending volume (mL)	Volume of metal (mL)	Mass of metal (mL)	Density of metal (g/mL)
Copper					8.96
Zinc					7.14
Penny					
Nickel					
Dime					

| Performance-Based Assessment *continued*

ANALYZE THE RESULTS

9. Calculate the density of each metal by dividing the mass of the metal by the volume of the metal. Record the density in the table above. Show your work below.

DRAW CONCLUSIONS

10. Compare the densities of the coins with the densities of the known metals. What are the coins mostly made of? Support your answer.

The penny was made mostly of zinc (unless the penny was made before 1982;

then it is mostly copper). The nickel, dime, and quarter are made mostly of

copper. The densities of the coins are very close to the densities of the pure

metals that primarily compose the coins.

White Before Your Eyes

TIME REQUIRED

One or two 45-minute class periods

Joseph Price
H.M. Browne Junior High
Washington, D.C.

LAB RATINGS

Teacher Prep–2
Student Set-Up–1
Concept Level–2
Clean Up–2

MATERIALS

Use an iodine solution that contains no more than 1.0% iodine in water. You may wish to use a 24-well spot plate or test tubes. A small test tube taped to the bottle makes a great holder for a dropper or pipette and decreases the chance of contamination. A drinking straw cut in half at an angle works well as a spatula the pointed end is a great scoop, and its large size makes it easy to handle.

SAFETY CAUTION

When iodine is being used, be certain that a functioning eyewash is available in case of a splash. Caution students that iodine can stain skin and clothes. Students should wash their face and hands when finished. Clean up any spills immediately to avoid slips and falls.

White Before Your Eyes

You have learned how to describe matter based on its physical and chemical properties. You have also learned some signs that can help you determine whether a change in matter is a physical change or a chemical change. In this lab, you'll use what you have learned to describe four substances based on their properties and the changes that they undergo.

OBJECTIVES

Describe the physical properties of four substances.

Identify physical and chemical changes.

Classify four substances by their chemical properties.

MATERIALS

- baking powder
- baking soda
- carton, egg, plastic-foam
- cornstarch
- eyedroppers (3)
- iodine solution
- spatulas (4)
- stirring rod
- sugar
- vinegar
- water

SAFETY INFORMATION

PROCEDURE

1. Use Table 1 to describe the appearance of four substances and write down your observations.

2. Using a spatula, place a small amount of baking powder into three cups of your egg carton. Use just enough baking powder to cover the bottom of each cup. Record your observations about the baking powder's appearance, such as color and texture, in the "Unmixed" column of Table 1.

3. Use an eyedropper to add 60 drops of water to the baking powder in the first cup. Stir with the stirring rod. Record your observations in Table 1 in the column labeled "Mixed with water." Clean your stirring rod.

White Before Your Eyes *continued*

Table 1: Observations				
Substance	**Unmixed**	**Mixed with water**	**Mixed with vinegar**	**Mixed with iodine solution**
baking powder				
baking soda				
cornstarch				
sugar				

4. Use a clean dropper to add 20 drops of vinegar to the second cup of baking powder. Stir. Record your observations in Table 1 in the column labeled "Mixed with vinegar." Clean your stirring rod.

5. Use a clean dropper to add five drops of iodine solution to the third cup of baking powder. Stir. Record your observations in Table 1 in the column labeled "Mixed with iodine solution." Clean your stirring rod. **Caution:** Be careful when using iodine. Iodine will stain your skin and clothes.

6. Repeat steps 2–5 for each of the other substances (baking soda, cornstarch, and sugar). Use a clean spatula for each substance.

ANALYZE THE RESULTS

1. Examining Data What physical properties do all four substances share?

All four substances are white solids, and are granular or powdery.

2. Analyzing Data In Table 2, write the type of change—physical or chemical—that you observed for each substance. State the property that the change demonstrates.

Table 2: Analyzing Data						
Substance	**Mixed with water**		**Mixed (vinegar)**		**Mixed (iodine solution)**	
	Change	**Property**	**Change**	**Property**	**Change**	**Property**
baking powder	chemical	reactivity with water	chemical	reactivity with acid	physical	solubility
baking soda	physical	solubility	chemical	reactivity with acid	physical	solubility
cornstarch	physical	solubility	physical	solubility	chemical	reactivity with iodine
sugar	physical	solubility	physical	solubility	physical	solubility

DRAW CONCLUSIONS

3. Evaluating Results Classify the four substances by the chemical property of reactivity. For example, which substances are reactive with vinegar (acid)?

reactive with water–baking powder; reactive with vinegar–baking powder,

baking soda; reactive with iodine–cornstarch

_____

_____

Quick Lab

Space Case

MATERIALS

- beaker or bucket
- cup, clear plastic
- paper, sheet
- pencil
- water

SAFETY INFORMATION

PROCEDURE

1. Crumple a **piece of paper**. Fit it tightly in the bottom of a **clear plastic cup** so that it won't fall out.

2. Turn the cup upside down. Lower the cup straight down into a **bucket** half-filled with **water.** Be sure that the cup is completely underwater.

3. Lift the cup straight out of the water. Turn the cup upright, and observe the paper. Record your observations.

_____

_____

_____

4. Use the point of a **pencil** to punch a small hole in the bottom of the cup. Repeat steps 2 and 3.

5. How do the results show that air has volume? Explain your answer.

The water could not enter the cup because air occupied the space. Once the

hole was punched, the water could force the air out of the cup and occupy

the space in the cup.

_____

_____

Teacher Notes Students can feel the air being "moved out of the way" by the water if they hold a finger above the hole while they submerge the cup.

Name _____ Class _____ Date _____

Changing Change

MATERIALS AND EQUIPMENT

• pennies, 3 shiny

• pie plate, metal

• towel, paper

• vinegar

SAFETY INFORMATION

PROCEDURE

1. Place a folded **paper towel** in a **small pie plate**.

2. Pour **vinegar** into the pie plate until the entire paper towel is damp.

3. Place **three shiny pennies** on top of the paper towel.

4. Put the pie plate in a safe place. Wait 24 hours.

5. Describe and explain the change that took place.

The shiny copper surface became coated with a dull, green substance. The

color change and change in the appearance of the coin indicated that a

chemical change took place.

_____

_____

Safety Caution: Have students wear goggles, gloves, and an apron for this activity.

Name _____ Class _____ Date _____

Physical or Chemical Change?

MATERIALS
- bar magnet
- beaker
- effervescent tablet
- iron filings
- paper, sheet
- powdered sulfur
- test tube
- water
- wooden stick

SAFETY INFORMATION

PROCEDURE

1. Watch as your teacher places a burning **wooden stick** into a **test tube**. Record your observations.

2. Place a mixture of **powdered sulfur** and **iron filings** on a sheet of **paper**. Place a **bar magnet** underneath the paper, and try to separate the iron from the sulfur.

3. Drop an **effervescent tablet** into a **beaker** of **water**. Record your observations.

_____

_____

4. Identify whether each change is a physical change or a chemical change. Explain your answers.

The burning wooden stick is undergoing a chemical change because the wood

is being changed into a new substance with different properties. Separating

the iron filings and the powdered sulfur is a physical change because the

components of the mixture did not change into new substances. The effer-

vescent tablet undergoes a chemical change when it is dropped in the water

because it forms a new substance with different properties.

Volumania!

Teacher Notes and Answer Key

TIME REQUIRED

One 45-minute class period

Alyson Mike
Radley Middle School
East Helena, Montana

LAB RATINGS

Easy ←—1——2——3——4——→ Hard

Teacher Prep–1
Student Set-Up–1
Concept Level–2
Clean Up–1

Part A: Finding the Volume of Small Objects

MATERIALS

The materials listed are for each group of 2–3 students. The objects used must be small enough to fit in the graduated cylinders but still be large enough to make a measurable change in the volume of the water. Rock or mineral samples, hardware (such as bolts or screws), and fishing weights work well.

SAFETY CAUTION

Caution students to tilt the graduated cylinder so objects can slide in gently to avoid breaking glass graduated cylinders. Remind students to read the volume when the meniscus is at eye level. Caution students to wear goggles during this lab.

Part B: Finding the Volume of Your Hand

MATERIALS

Plastic containers from whipped toppings and the like can also be used. Containers should be deep enough so students' fists can be submerged. Remind students that their containers must be completely filled with water so that they overflow as their hands enter. The pie pan should be dry at the start. When students remove their hands from the containers, they should allow the water cupped in their hands to drip back into the containers and not into the pie pan. This water was not displaced and should not be measured.

Name _____ Class _____ Date _____

Volumania!

You have learned how to measure the volume of a solid object that has square or rectangular sides. But there are lots of objects in the world that have irregular shapes. In this lab activity, you'll learn some ways to find the volume of objects that have irregular shapes.

MATERIALS

Part A
- graduated cylinder
- water
- various small objects supplied by your teacher

Part B
- bottle, plastic (or similar container), 2 L, bottom half
- funnel
- graduated cylinder
- pan, aluminum pie
- paper towels
- water

SAFETY INFORMATION

Part A: Finding the Volume of Small Objects

PROCEDURE

1. Fill a graduated cylinder half full with water. Read and record the volume of the water in a separate notebook. Be sure to look at the surface of the water at eye level and to read the volume at the bottom of the meniscus.

2. Carefully slide one of the objects into the tilted graduated cylinder.

3. Read the new volume, and record it.

4. Subtract the old volume from the new volume. The resulting amount is equal to the volume of the solid object.

5. Use the same method to find the volume of the other objects. Record your results.

ANALYZE THE RESULTS

6. What changes do you have to make to the volumes you determine in order to express them correctly?

   Sample answer: The units of milliliters should be changed to cubic

   centimeters because you are measuring the volume of a solid object.

7. Do the heaviest objects always have the largest volumes? Why or why not?

   Sample answer: no; Sometimes a heavier object will have a smaller volume

   than a lighter object because the matter is more tightly packed.

Part B: Finding the Volume of Your Hand
PROCEDURE

1. Completely fill the container with water. Put the container in the center of the pie pan. Be sure not to spill any of the water into the pie pan.

2. Make a fist, and put your hand into the container up to your wrist.

3. Remove your hand, and let the excess water drip into the container, not the pie pan. Dry your hand with a paper towel.

4. Use the funnel to pour the overflow water into the graduated cylinder. Measure the volume. This measurement is the volume of your hand. Record the volume. (Remember to use the correct unit of volume for a solid object.)

5. Repeat this procedure with your other hand.

ANALYZE THE RESULTS

1. Was the volume the same for both of your hands? If not, were you surprised? What might account for a person's hands having different volumes?

   Answers may vary. Often, the preferred hand will be slightly larger due to

   greater muscle development.

2. Would it have made a difference if you had placed your open hand into the container instead of your fist? Explain your reasoning.

   Sample answer: It would not make a difference; A hand's volume remains the

   same regardless of its shape.

3. Compare the volume of your right hand with the volume of your classmates' right hands. Create a class graph of right-hand volumes. What is the average right-hand volume for your class?

   Answers may vary by class. Check for correct graphing technique and

   interpretation.

APPLYING YOUR DATA

Design an experiment to determine the volume of a person's body. In your plans, be sure to include the materials needed for the experiment and the procedures that must be followed. Include a sketch that shows how your materials and methods would be used in this experiment.

Using an encyclopedia, the Internet, or other reference materials, find out how the volumes of very large samples of matter—such as an entire planet—are determined.

   Designs should center on finding the volume of the body through water
   displacement. The equipment designed should be large enough to perform
   the experiment and allow for overflow. Accept all reasonable answers and
   findings.

Determining Density

Teacher Notes and Answer Key

TIME REQUIRED

One 45-minute class period

Alyson Mike
Radley Middle School
East Helena, Montana

LAB RATINGS

Easy ◄——— 1 —— 2 —— 3 —— 4 ———► Hard

Teacher Prep–1
Student Set-Up–1
Concept Level–2
Clean Up–1

SAFETY CAUTION

Caution students to tilt the graduated cylinder so marbles can slide in gently.

Name _____ Class _____ Date _____

Skills Practice Lab

Determining Density

DATASHEET FOR LABBOOK

The density of an object is its mass divided by its volume. But how does the density of a small amount of a substance relate to the density of a larger amount of the same substance? In this lab, you will calculate the density of one marble and of a group of marbles. Then, you will confirm the relationship between the mass and volume of a substance.

MATERIALS

- balance, metric
- graduated cylinder, 100 mL
- marbles, glass (8–10)
- paper, graph
- paper towels
- water

SAFETY INFORMATION

PROCEDURE

1. Use the table below to record your data.

Mass of marble (g)	Total mass of marbles (g)	Total volume (mL)	Volume of marbles (mL)(total volume minus 50.0 mL)	Density of marbles (g/mL) (total mass divided by volume)

2. Fill the graduated cylinder with 50 mL of water. If you put in too much water, twist one of the paper towels, and use it to absorb excess water.

3. Measure the mass of a marble as accurately as you can (to at least .01 g). Record the mass in the table.

4. Carefully drop the marble in the tilted cylinder, and measure the total volume. Record the volume in the third column.

5. Measure and record the mass of another marble. Add the masses of the marbles together, and record this value in the second column of the table.

6. Carefully drop the second marble in the graduated cylinder. Complete the row of information in the table.

7. Repeat steps 5 and 6. Add one marble at a time. Stop when you run out of marbles, the water no longer completely covers the marbles, or the graduated cylinder is full.

| Determining Density *continued*

ANALYZE THE RESULTS

1. Examine the data in your table. As the number of marbles increases, what happens to the total mass of the marbles? What happens to the volume of the marbles? What happens to the density of the marbles?

The mass and the volume of the marbles increases, but the marbles' density

remains the same.

2. Graph the total mass of the marbles (*y*-axis) versus the volume of the marbles (*x*-axis). Is the graph a straight line?

The graph is a straight line (see graph below).

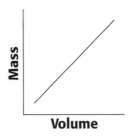

DRAW CONCLUSIONS

3. Does the density of a substance depend on the amount of substance present? Explain how your results support your answer.

The density is the same for one marble as it is for several marbles.

APPLYING YOUR DATA

Calculate the slope of the graph. How does the slope compare with the values in the column entitled "Density of marbles"? Explain.

To find the slope of the graph, pick two points on the line. The slope is the

difference between the *y*-values of the points divided by the difference

between the *x* values of the points. The slope of the graph should be equal to

the density of the marbles because the graph shows mass versus volume,

which means the slope is mass divided by volume—in other words, density.

Skills Practice Lab

Layering Liquids

Teacher Notes and Answer Key

TIME REQUIRED

One 45-minute class period

Alyson Mike
Radley Middle School
East Helena, Montana

LAB RATINGS

Easy ◄——1——2——3——4——► Hard

Teacher Prep–3
Student Set-Up–1
Concept Level–2
Clean Up–2

PREPARATION NOTES

Liquid A is red-colored water, liquid B is vegetable oil, and liquid C is dark corn syrup.

DISPOSAL INFORMATION

Have students empty their containers into several disposable containers to keep the oil out of the drains. These can be capped, refrigerated, and thrown in the trash. It might be interesting to let these waste bottles stand overnight to see if the layers are visible the following day.

Name _____ Class _____ Date _____

DATASHEET FOR LABBOOK

Layering Liquids

You have learned that liquids form layers according to the densities of the liquids. In this lab, you'll discover whether it matters in which order you add the liquids.

MATERIALS

- beaker (or other small, clear container)
- funnel (3)
- graduated cylinder, 10 mL (3)

- liquid A
- liquid B
- liquid C

SAFETY INFORMATION

ASK A QUESTION

1. Does the order in which you add liquids of different densities to a container affect the order of the layers formed by those liquids?

FORM A HYPOTHESIS

2. Write a possible answer to the question above.

_____

TEST THE HYPOTHESIS

3. Using the graduated cylinders, add 10 mL of each liquid to the clear container. Remember to read the volume at the bottom of the meniscus. Record the order in which you added the liquids.

_____

4. Observe the liquids in the container. Sketch what you see. Be sure to label the layers and the colors.

5. Add 10 mL more of liquid C. Observe what happens, and record your observations.

_____

6. Add 20 mL more of liquid A. Observe what happens, and record your observations.

_____

Layering Liquids *continued*

ANALYZE YOUR RESULTS

1. Which of the liquids has the greatest density? Which has the least density?
How can you tell?

Liquid C has the greatest density; Liquid B has the least density; The liquids

form layers with the least dense on top and the most dense on bottom.

_____

2. Did the layers change position when you added more of liquid C? Explain
your answer.

The position of the layers did not change; Adding more of liquid C does not

change its density, so its position stays the same.

_____

3. Did the layers change position when you added more of liquid A? Explain
your answer.

The position of the layers did not change; Adding more of liquid A does not

change its density, so its position stays the same.

_____

4. Find out in what order your classmates added the liquids to the container.
Compare your results with those of a classmate who added the liquids in a
different order. Were your results different? Explain why or why not.

All results should be identical; Liquid B is the top layer, liquid A is the

middle layer, and liquid C is the bottom layer.

_____

DRAW CONCLUSIONS

5. Based on your results, evaluate your hypothesis from step 2.

Answers may vary, depending on the original prediction. The order in which

the liquids are added does not affect the order of the layers formed.

_____

_____

Answer Key

Directed Reading A

SECTION: WHAT IS MATTER?

1. B
2. D
3. They are all made of matter.
4. Matter is anything that has mass and takes up space.
5. Volume is the amount of space taken up by an object.
6. volume
7. meniscus
8. length, width, and height
9. cubic
10. Answers will vary. Sample answer: The volume could be measured by placing the nugget in a graduated cylinder with water. The volume of water displaced is the volume of the nugget.
11. Because 1 milliliter of water is equal to 1 cubic centimeter.
12. D
13. C
14. A
15. D
16. The only way to change the mass is to change the amount of matter it contains.
17. mass
18. weight
19. weight
20. mass
21. weight
22. weight
23. mass
24. C
25. An outside force is needed to change the motion of an object.
26. The more mass an object has, the greater its inertia.
27. Answers will vary. Sample answer: A full cart has more mass than an empty one. More mass means the cart has more inertia. Because it has more inertia, a full cart is harder to put into motion.

SECTION: PHYSICAL PROPERTIES

1. B
2. C
3. D
4. A
5. F
6. C
7. B
8. E
9. G
10. physical property
11. density
12. density
13. The densest layer will settle on the bottom.
14. The least dense layer will be found on top.
15. because 1 kg of lead would take up less space than 1 kg of feathers
16. The object will sink.
17. Answers will vary. Sample answer: If you know the density of the substance, you could compare it with the density of water. If the density of the object is less than water it will float.
18. $D = m/V$
19. density; volume; mass
20. volume
21. Answers will vary. Sample answers: Because a substance's density is always the same at a given temperature and pressure and because most substances have different densities.
22. physical change
23. changes in state
24. PC
25. X
26. PC
27. PC
28. PC
29. PC
30. identity

31. Answers will vary. Sample answer: When matter undergoes a physical change, one or more physical properties are changed. For example, if a lump of copper is drawn out into a thin wire, only its shape is changed, not its identity.

SECTION: CHEMICAL PROPERTIES

1. C
2. A
3. B
4. D
5. B
6. Answers will vary. Sample answer: The burning changes wood to smoke and ashes.
7. chemical
8. characteristic
9. B
10. C
11. Answers will vary. Sample answer: Baking a cake involves chemical changes because the cake has completely different properties than its original ingredients. It is impossible reverse the results of those changes.
12. Answers will vary. Sample answer: The creation of new substances with new properties shows that a change is chemical. Other signs include fizzing or foaming, a change in color or odor, the production of heat, sounds, or light being given off.
13. chemical changes
14. Answers will vary. Sample answer: Some chemical changes can be reversed with more chemical changes. For example: The water formed in a space shuttle's rockets can later be split back into hydrogen and oxygen using an electric current.
15. B
16. A
17. physical changes
18. CC
19. PC
20. CC
21. PC
22. CC
23. CC
24. PC
25. PC

Directed Reading B

SECTION: WHAT IS MATTER?

1. C
2. B
3. C
4. A
5. B
6. D
7. meniscus
8. cubic
9. volume
10. milliliter
11. irregular solid
12. cubic centimeters
13. B
14. D
15. C
16. D
17. C
18. B
19. A
20. A
21. kilogram
22. newton
23. weight
24. C
25. B
26. C

SECTION: PHYSICAL PROPERTIES

1. A	10. B
2. C	11. C
3. C	12. D
4. B	13. D
5. A	14. B
6. B	15. D
7. C	16. A
8. A	17. C
9. A	

18. physical change
19. state
20. identity
21. B
22. C
23. C
24. B

SECTION: CHEMICAL PROPERTIES

1. chemical property
2. flammability
3. nonflammability
4. reactivity
5. B

6. C
7. A
8. B
9. D
10. property
11. change
12. C   **17.** D
13. B   **18.** B
14. C   **19.** B
15. A   **20.** A
16. C

Vocabulary and Section Summary

SECTION: WHAT IS MATTER?

1. matter: anything that has mass and takes up space
2. volume: a measure of the size of a body or region in three-dimensional space
3. meniscus: the curve at a liquid's surface by which one measures the volume of the liquid
4. mass: a measure of the amount of matter in an object
5. weight: a measure of the gravitational force exerted on an object; value can change with the location of the object in the universe
6. inertia: the tendency of an object to resist being moved or, if the object is moving, to resist a change in speed or direction until an outside force acts on the object

SECTION: PHYSICAL PROPERTIES

1. physical property: a characteristic of a substance that does not involve a chemical change, such as density color, or hardness
2. density: the ratio of the mass of a substance to the volume of the substance
3. physical change: a change of matter from one form to another without a change in chemical properties

SECTION: CHEMICAL PROPERTIES

1. chemical property: a property of matter that describes a substance's ability to participate in chemical reactions

2. chemical change: a change that occurs when one or more substances change into entirely new substances with different properties

Section Review

SECTION: WHAT IS MATTER?

1. Answers will vary. Sample answer: You can measure the volume of a liquid by pouring it into a graduated cylinder and reading the scale at the bottom of the meniscus.
2. Answers will vary. Sample answers: Mass is a measurement of how much matter is in an object. Weight is a measurement of how much gravitational force is exerted on an object's mass. Inertia is what causes an object to remain at rest or remain in motion. The more mass an object has, the greater its inertia.
3. D
4. A
5. C
6. D
7. Mass is a measure of inertia. The more massive an object is, the more inertia it has.
8. 145 mL
9. 4 N
10. Not all objects with large masses have large weights because the weight of an object can change depending on where it is located in the universe. Mass remains the same everywhere in the universe. So a massive object in space may not have a large weight.
11. The elephant's weight on the moon would be only one-sixth of its weight on Earth. This is due to the moon having only one-sixth the gravitational force of the earth.

SECTION: PHYSICAL PROPERTIES

1. Answers will vary. Sample answer: A physical property can be observed without changing the identity of the matter. When matter undergoes a physical change, its shape or form changes, but its identity remains the same.
2. D

3. A golf ball feels heavier than a table-tennis ball because it is more dense; that is, it has more mass in a similar volume.

4. A physical change changes the shape or form of the matter without changing its identity. It is still the same matter as before the change and has most of the same properties.

5. Some physical properties include color, shape, odor, volume, weight, and density.

6. Some physical changes that matter can go through are breaking, melting, freezing, cutting, crushing and dissolving.

7. 3.68 g/cm^3; this object would not float in water because its density is greater than the density of water.

8. 50 g

9. Answers will vary. Sample answer: Measure the mass and volume of the coin. Calculate the coin's density. Compare this density with the known density of silver.

10. All of these substances are liquid.

11. Answers will vary. Sample answer: Obtain equal volumes of several immiscible liquids of known density. One at a time, carefully pour each liquid, including the unknown, into a graduated cylinder. Note where each liquid settles in relation to the other liquids. The liquids will separate into layers from top to bottom in order of increasing density. The density of the unknown liquid can be estimated based on the densities of the liquids adjacent to it.

SECTION: CHEMICAL PROPERTIES

1. Answers will vary. Sample answer: A chemical property determines whether or not a substance will react with another substance. A chemical change is a change to a substance that causes it to form a new substance or substances with different properties.

2. D

3. D

4. Answers will vary. Sample answer: Two chemical properties are reactivity and flammability. Reactivity tells you whether or not a substance will react with another substance and form new products with new properties. Flammability tells you whether or not a substance will burn.

5. Answers will vary. Sample answer: A chemical change occurred. The copper in the Statue of Liberty combined with oxygen in the air and formed new copper compounds with different properties.

6. Answers will vary. Sample answer: You can tell the difference between a chemical change and a physical change by determining if the starting material is the same or different in composition after the change occurs.

7. The final temperature is 33°C.

8. Answers will vary. Sample answers: When matter undergoes a physical change, its shape or form changes, but its identity remains the same. When matter undergoes a chemical change, its identity and properties change.

9. Answers will vary. Sample answers: Physical properties of uncooked bag: almost flat, cool to the touch, kernels feel like small pebbles, smells like salt or butter. Chemical properties of uncooked bag: bag is flammable, popcorn kernels will pop and change into fluffy popcorn when heated. Physical properties of cooked bag: hot to the touch, volume has increased, smells like cooked popcorn. Chemical properties of cooked bag: kernels have changed into fluffy popcorn, bag may be scorched or burned inside.

Chapter Review

1. Answers will vary. Sample answers: Physical properties of a substance include color, shape and density. Flammability is a chemical property of matter. Sugar dissolving in water is an example of a physical change. When a piece of iron metal rusts it is undergoing a chemical change.

2. Answers will vary. Sample answers: Mass is the amount of matter in an object and is always constant. Weight is a measure of the gravitational force, and it will change, depending on the object's distance from the earth or other bodies.

3. Answers will vary. Sample answers: Mass is a measure of inertia. The more massive an object is, the more inertia it has.

4. Answers will vary. Sample answers: Volume is the amount of space occupied by an object, and density is the amount of mass in a given volume of the substance.

5. B

6. A

7. A

8. C

9. D

10. D

11. B

12. Answers will vary. Sample answer: The volume of a liquid can be measured by pouring it into a graduated cylinder and reading the scale at the bottom of the meniscus. The volume of a regular solid is determined by multiplying the objects length, width, and height.

13. density = mass/volume

14. Characteristic properties include density, solubility, reactivity with acid, melting point, and boiling point.

15. volume = length × width × height = 20 cm × 10 cm × 5 cm = 1,000 cm^3

16. Density of glycerin = 37.8 g/30 mL = 1.26 g/mL. Density of corn syrup = 82.8 g/60mL = 1.38 g/mL. The glycerin will be on top because it is less dense than corn syrup.

17. An answer to the concept mapping exercise can be found in the end of the textbook.

18. Answers will vary. Questions can ask about the size, shape color, weight, density, state, odor, etc.

19. Answers will vary. Sample answer: Cooking eggs involves a chemical change. I cannot change the cooked eggs back into raw eggs in order to poach them.

20. Answers will vary. Sample answer: If my neighbor has trouble lifting a small box, I would conclude that the box's inertia is large. The box resists my neighbor's attempt to move it. A large inertia means that the item(s) in the box has a large mass.

21. Answers will vary. Sample answer: An astronaut weighs less in orbit than on Earth because of the astronaut's increased distance from Earth. However, an astronaut is not weightless because there are still gravitational forces between the astronaut and all other objects in the universe.

22. Answers will vary. Sample answers: crushed shape, somewhat shiny, metallic

23. physical change

24. The density before and after the change is the same because density is a characteristic property of matter.

25. No; chemical properties cannot be determined simply by looking at a substance. Chemical properties can only be observed when a chemical change occurs.

Reinforcement

A MATTER OF DENSITY

1. Green liquid: 0.75 kg/L; Blue liquid: 0.9 kg/L; Red liquid: 1.2 kg/L; Black liquid: 0.8 kg/L

2. First (bottom): red; Second layer: blue; Third layer: black; Fourth (top): green

3. B

4. The layers of the diagram should be shaded/labeled in the following order from the top: green, black, blue, red.

5. Accept all reasonable answers. Sample answer: I could open the spigot at the bottom of the tank and let the red liquid out.

Critical Thinking

1. The cube's volume increased, and its mass remained the same.
2. Answers will vary. Sample answer: Because the cube's volume increased and its mass remained the same, the larger cube has less mass per unit volume. As a result, the cube's density decreased.
3. The cube changed in volume, density, composition, and number.
4. Answers will vary. Sample answer: The changes in volume, density and number are physical changes because the composition of the cube remained the same. The cube's transformation into a green paste is a chemical change because a new substance was formed.
5. Answers will vary. Sample answer: An object's mass or volume cannot spontaneously change on Earth without a recognizable cause. An object's density remains the same at a given temperature and pressure.
6. Answers will vary. Sample answer: An explosion caused by electricity could happen on Earth. Applying an electric current causes some chemical changes such as splitting water into the gases that make it up.

Section Quizzes

SECTION: WHAT IS MATTER?

1. B	6. C
2. F	7. B
3. E	8. B
4. D	9. A
5. A	10. A

SECTION: PHYSICAL PROPERTIES

1. E	6. B
2. D	7. B
3. F	8. D
4. A	9. C
5. C	10. A

SECTION: CHEMICAL PROPERTIES

1. D	6. A
2. C	7. D
3. B	8. C
4. E	9. D
5. A	10. B

Chapter Test A

1. D	14. J
2. A	15. E
3. C	16. B
4. B	17. H
5. C	18. C
6. B	19. D
7. D	20. A
8. C	21. A
9. B	22. D
10. A	23. A
11. D	24. C
12. A	25. B
13. F	

Chapter Test B

1. inertia
2. density
3. physical change
4. chemical
5. weight
6. chemical change
7. C
8. D
9. D
10. B
11. C
12. Answers will vary. Sample answer: Characteristic properties such as density, reactivity, or solubility do not depend on the amount of the substance. Volume and mass cannot be characteristic properties because they are defined by measurements that depend on the size or amount of the substance in a sample.

13. Answers will vary. Sample answer: If the two substances are liquids, you could observe how they separate into layers as a result of differences in -density. If the two substances are solids, you could observe whether they float or sink in water. Density is a useful property for identifying substances because most substances have different densities that are constant at a given temperature and pressure.

14. Answers will vary. Sample answer: The astronauts should be able to carry more mass on the moon because the gravitational force acting on the objects is less there. Thus, the equipment will weigh less than it does on Earth.

15. Answers will vary. Sample answer: No; even though it would be nearly impossible to put the wood chips back together, this is still a physical change. The chips, log, and stump keep their identity as wood. Only their size and shape changes.

16. Mass is a measure of the amount of matter, while weight is a measure of gravitational force. Mass is constant no matter where the object is located while weight depends on where it is found in space. Mass is measured with a balance and expressed in grams, while weight is measured with a spring scale and measured in newtons. People tend to confuse the two concepts because both mass and weight remain constant on Earth, and weight does give you a fairly good estimate of the mass of an object.

17. The purple liquid will form the bottom layer, followed by the water and the red liquid. The yellow liquid will be on top. The greater the density, the lower the layer. Water has a density of 1.00 g/cm^3, which means it will float on the liquid with a density of 1.62 g/cm^3. The wood chip should sink through the yellow liquid and float on the red.

18. Step A involves a chemical change because the leaves turn brown. The color change signals a chemical change.

19. The salt did not burn, which shows that it has the chemical property of nonflammability. It has the physical property of solubility in water as well.

Chapter Test C

1. D	**12.** C
2. D	**13.** volume
3. B	**14.** property
4. A	**15.** change
5. D	**16.** mass
6. C	**17.** kilogram
7. B	**18.** weight
8. A	**19.** inertia
9. B	**20.** milliliters
10. A	**21.** B
11. D	**22.** D

Standardized Test Preparation

READING

Passage 1
 1. B
 2. G
 3. B

Passage 2
 1. A
 2. G
 3. C

INTERPRETING GRAPHICS
 1. B
 2. I
 3. A
 4. F

MATH
 1. C
 2. I
 3. B
 4. F

Vocabulary Activity

SEARCH FOR MATTER
 1. inertia
 2. meniscus
 3. volume
 4. mass; kilogram
 5. gravitational
 6. weight; newton

7. matter

8. density; mass; volume

9. physical property

10. physical change

11. chemical property

12. chemical change

13. characteristic

14. composition

```
D Y B G R A V I T I O N A L P W R T
X T A R F G E X J O L M E W K M I J
B R V Q U I T E M U L O V E W T O N
F E P H Y S I C A L P R O P E R T Y
K P C J H W N D S K I L O G R A M T
V O L U M E E I S P O D N I I C N I
J R O K A I R A M T B A W E I W R S
P P V O S G T V O L H T E G I N W N
T L D T S H I M A C B H I D E E Y E
X A G R A T A S L R I M G H O W C D
N C R M R A W A K I L O H F A T N R
A I A D A W C O M P O S I T I O N H
C M P M B I M M P V Q U A O N N M T
I E P V M A T T E R G R A V I T E R
S H L E R I T E L T R A W A I T O R
Y C H A R A C T E R I S T I C B Y C
H C E G N A H C L A C I S Y H P R O
P T Z B C N M E N I S C U S R P O Y
```

SciLinks Activity

1. Answers will vary. Sample answer: Materials science covers a broad range of activities and touches on many scientific fields such as chemistry, biology, and physics. Materials scientists are sometimes considered engineers or metalurgists. Their job is to manipulate or change materials based on our understanding of how the materials are put together.

2. Answers will vary. Sample answers: *Polymers* are long-repeating chains of smaller molecules linked together. Rubber bands, paints, and plastics are made from polymers. *Composites* are combinations of different kinds of materials. A bicycle might be made from an ultralight carbon fiber. *Semiconductors* conduct electricity. They are often used in electronic computer chips. *Metals* were among the first substances to be engineered. They can be drawn into wires and molded and they conduct electricity very well. *Biomaterials* are found in every part of your body from your bones to your fingernails and hair. Their properties can be used to protect you from heat or cold or to cut and grind food.

3. Answers will vary. Sample answer: If you spin the egg and it spins well, it's a hardboiled egg. But if you spin a raw egg and try to stop it by touching it with your finger, the egg will continue spinning due to the inertia of the liquid inside.

4. Answers will vary. Sample answers: Water has a high surface tension. It has the ability to form drops. Water expands and gets less dense when it freezes and will actually float on its liquid form. Many things can be dissolved in liquid water. Because of its hydrogen bonds, water boils at an extremely high temperature and freezes at a much higher temperature than might be expected for the size of its particles. Also, because of its bonding, water has a very high specific heat, which means that it takes a long time to cool off.

Lesson Plan

Section: What Is Matter?

Pacing

Regular Schedule: **with Lab(s):** N/A **without Lab(s):** 1 day

Block Schedule: **with Lab(s):** N/A **without Lab(s):** 0.5 day

Objectives

1. Describe the two properties of all matter.

2. Identify the units used to measure volume and mass.

3. Compare mass and weight.

4. Explain the relationship between mass and inertia.

National Science Education Standards Covered

ST 1: Abilities of technological design

ST 2: Understandings about science and technology

SPSP 1: Personal health

SPSP 5: Science and technology in society

PS 1a: A substance has characteristic properties, such as density, a boiling point, and solubility, all of which are independent of the amount of the sample. A mixture of substances often can be separated into the original substances using one or more of the characteristic properties.

PS 1c: Chemical elements do not break down during normal laboratory reactions involving such treatments as heating, exposure to electric current, or reaction with acids. There are more than 100 known elements that combine in a multitude of ways to produce compounds, which account for the living and nonliving substances that we encounter.

KEY
SE = Student Edition   **TE** = Teacher's Edition
CRF = Student Resource file

FOCUS (*5 minutes*)

_ **Chapter Starter Transparency** Use this transparency to introduce the chapter.

_ **Bellringer, TE** Have students write what they think are the components of several common items. (**GENERAL**)

_ **Bellringer Transparency** Use this transparency as students enter the classroom and find their seats.

_ **Reading Strategy, SE** Have students write the headings for each section in a notebook and predict what they think they will learn.

MOTIVATE *(10 minutes)*

_ **Demonstration, TE** Display a variety of objects, compare their size, and discuss the connection between volume and taking up space. **(GENERAL)**

TEACH *(20 minutes)*

_ **Discussion, TE** Have students list the characteristics of matter and give examples. **(GENERAL)**

_ **Teaching Transparency, Growth Chart, TE** Use this transparency to help students understand how humans grow and add mass.

_ **Group Activity, TE** Have students measure the volume of a variety of containers using the bottom of the meniscus at eye level. **(GENERAL)**

_ **Connection Activity Music, TE** Have students measure the volume of containers and determine the connection between pitch and volume. **(GENERAL)**

_ **Demonstration, Relating Matter, Mass, and Volume, TE** Display classroom objects and have students discuss the relationship between size and mass. **(GENERAL)**

_ **Quick Lab, SE** Students demonstrate that air has volume by placing a cup with crumpled paper inside under water. **(GENERAL)**

_ **Directed Reading A/B, CRF** These worksheets reinforce basic concepts and vocabulary presented in the lesson. **(BASIC/SPECIAL NEEDS)**

_ **Vocabulary and Section Summary, CRF** Students write definitions of key terms and read a summary of section content. **(GENERAL)**

CLOSE *(10 minutes)*

_ **Reteaching, TE** Provide measuring tools and have students explain how they would measure volume and mass. **(BASIC)**

_ **Section Review, CRF** Students answer end-of-section vocabulary, key ideas, math, and critical thinking questions. **(GENERAL)**

_ **Section Quiz, SE** Students answer 10 objective questions about matter. **(GENERAL)**

_ **Quiz, TE** Students answer 3 questions about matter. **(GENERAL)**

_ **Alternative Assessment, TE** Have students write science fiction stories about a universe in which matter does not obey the usual rules. **(GENERAL)**

Lesson Plan

Section: Physical Properties

Pacing

Regular Schedule:	**with Lab(s):** N/A	**without Lab(s):** 1 day
Block Schedule:	**with Lab(s):** N/A	**without Lab(s):** 0.5 day

Objectives

1. Identify six examples of physical properties of matter.

2. Describe how density is used to identify substances.

3. List six examples of physical changes.

4. Explain what happens to matter during a physical change.

National Science Education Standards Covered

SAI 1: Abilities necessary to do scientific inquiry

PS 1a: A substance has characteristic properties, such as density, a boiling point, and solubility, all of which are independent of the amount of the sample. A mixture of substances often can be separated into the original substances using one or more of the characteristic properties.

KEY
SE = Student Edition   **TE** = Teacher's Edition
CRF = Student Resource file

FOCUS (5 minutes)

_ **Bellringer, TE** Have students write how they would describe an orange to someone who had never seen one. (**GENERAL**)

_ **Bellringer Transparency** Use this transparency as students enter the classroom and find their seats.

MOTIVATE (10 minutes)

_ **Demonstration, TE** Have students examine some objects and describe them using a variety of properties. (**GENERAL**)

TEACH (20 minutes)

_ **Reading Strategy, SE** Have students create a mnemonic device to help them remember examples of physical properties. (**GENERAL**)

_ **Discussion, TE** Draw your students' attention to the chart of physical properties and have volunteers give other examples of each property. (**GENERAL**)

_ **Connection Activity, Math, TE** Have students solve math problems related to density as a group. (**GENERAL**)

_ **Activity, TE** Have students examine bottles of vinegar and oil to observe how they separate on the basis of density. **(BASIC)**

_ **Directed Reading A/B, CRF** These worksheets reinforce basic concepts and vocabulary presented in the lesson. **(BASIC/SPECIAL NEEDS)**

_ **Vocabulary and Section Summary, CRF** Students write definitions of key terms and read a summary of section content. **(GENERAL)**

_ **Reinforcement, CRF** This worksheet reinforces key concepts in the chapter. **(BASIC)**

CLOSE *(10 minutes)*

_ **Reteaching, TE** Have groups of students brainstorm ways to change the physical properties of common objects, and demonstrate them in their groups. **(BASIC)**.

_ **Homework, TE** Have students play a guessing game in which they describe a favorite object from home and have classmates identify the object. **(GENERAL)**

_ **Section Review, SE** Students answer end-of-section vocabulary, key ideas, math, and critical thinking questions. **(GENERAL)**

_ **Section Quiz, CRF** Students answer 10 objective questions about physical properties **(GENERAL)**

_ **Quiz, TE** Students answer 2 questions about physical properties. **(GENERAL)**

_ **Alternative Assessment, TE** Have students identify ways that they could change the physical properties of a sugar cube. **(GENERAL)**

Lesson Plan

Section: Chemical Properties

Pacing

Regular Schedule: **with Lab(s):** 2 days   **without Lab(s):** 1 day

Block Schedule: **with Lab(s):** 1 day   **without Lab(s):** 0.5 day

Objectives

1. Describe two examples of chemical properties.

2. Explain what happens during a chemical change.

3. Distinguish between physical and chemical changes.

National Science Education Standards Covered

PS 1a: A substance has characteristic properties, such as density, a boiling point, and solubility, all of which are independent of the amount of the sample. A mixture of substances often can be separated into the original substances using one or more of the characteristic properties.

PS 1b: Substances react chemically in characteristic ways with other substances to form new substances (compounds) with different characteristic properties. In chemical reactions, the total mass is conserved. Substances often are placed in categories or groups if they react in similar ways; metals is an example of such a group.

KEY
SE = Student Edition   **TE** = Teacher's Edition
CRF = Student Resource file

FOCUS *(5 minutes)*

‒ **Bellringer, TE** Have students look at the picture of the car, and share other examples of rusting metals that they have observed. (**GENERAL**)

‒ **Bellringer Transparency** Use this transparency as students enter the classroom and find their seats.

MOTIVATE *(10 minutes)*

‒ **Demonstration, TE** Use such common items as a candle, match, and a stick to demonstrate the difference between a physical and chemical changes. (**BASIC**)

TEACH *(65 minutes)*

_ **Reading Strategy, SE** Have students create an outline of this section using the section headings.

_ **Connection Activity Life Science, TE** Students use library or internet resources to learn about the importance of water to living things. (**GENERAL**)

_ **Directed Reading A/B, CRF** These worksheets reinforce basic concepts and vocabulary presented in the lesson. (**BASIC/SPECIAL NEEDS**)

_ **Vocabulary and Section Summary, SE** Students write definitions of key terms and read a summary of section content. (**GENERAL**)

_ **Quick Lab, Changing Change, CRF** Students observe how vinegar reacts with copper to produce a green coating on shiny pennies. (**GENERAL**)

_ **Quick Lab, Physical or Chemical Change?, SE** Students observe changes in substances and identify whether they are physical or chemical. (**GENERAL**)

_ **Teaching Transparency, Examples of Chemical Changes** Use this transparency to help students understand chemical changes. (**GENERAL**)

_ **Chapter Lab, SE** Students describe four substances, identify physical and chemical changes, and classify them based upon those changes. (**GENERAL**)

_ **Critical Thinking, CRF** Ask students to fill out the worksheet about the unusual properties of a mysterious space cube. (**ADVANCED**)

_ **SciLinks Activity, Describing Matter, SciLinks code HSM0391, CRF** Students research Internet resources related to the properties of polymers. (**GENERAL**)

CLOSE *(10 minutes)*

_ **Reteaching, TE** Have students write down ways chemical changes could occur to a raw egg, a sheet of paper, and a nail chemically. (**BASIC**)

_ **Section Review, SE** Students answer end-of-section vocabulary, key ideas, math, and critical thinking questions. (**GENERAL**)

_ **Section Quiz, CRF** Students answer 10 objective questions about chemical properties (**GENERAL**)

_ **Quiz, TE** Students answer 2 questions about chemical properties. (**GENERAL**)

_ **Alternative Assessment, TE** Have students identify two ways that they could change the chemical properties of a sugar cube. (**GENERAL**)

Lesson Plan

End of Chapter Review and Assessment

Pacing

Regular Schedule: **with Lab(s):** N/A   **without Lab(s):** 2 days

Block Schedule: **with Lab(s):** N/A   **without Lab(s):** 1 day

---

KEY

SE = Student Edition   **TE** = Teacher's Edition

CRF = Student Resource file

_ **Chapter Review, SE** Students review chapter vocabulary terms by filling in completion items and using the clues to solve a word search puzzle.

_ **Vocabulary Activity, CRF** Students review chapter vocabulary terms by filling in blanks with terms and finding them in a puzzle.

_ **Concept Mapping Transparency** Use this graphic top review key concepts.

_ **Chapter Test A/B/C, CRF** Assign questions from the appropriate test for the chapter assessment. (**GENERAL/ADVANCED/SPECIAL NEEDS**)

_ **Performance-Based Assessment, CRF** Assign this activity for general level assessment for the chapter. (**GENERAL**)

_ **Standardized Test Preparation, CRF** Students answer reading comprehension, math, and interpreting graphics questions in the format of a standardized test. (**GENERAL**)

_ **Test Generator, One-Stop Planner** Create a customized homework assignment, quiz, or test using the HRW Test Generator Program.

MULTIPLE CHOICE

1. What equation would you use to find the volume of a rectangular box?
   a. volume = length x width x height
   c. volume = length x width
   b. volume = length + width + height
   d. volume = length + height

   Answer: B   Difficulty: 1   Section: 1   Objective: 2

2. Which of the following units would you use to express the volume of an irregular solid such as a rock?
   a. liters (L)
   c. milliliters (mL)
   b. cubic centimeters (cm3)
   d. newtons (N)

   Answer: B   Difficulty: 1   Section: 1   Objective: 2

3. Which of the following statements is true about an object's weight but NOT about its mass?
   a. It may vary depending on the object's location.
   b. It is a measure of the amount of matter in the object.
   c. It is measured in kilograms (kg) or grams (g).
   d. It would be the same on the moon as it is on Earth.

   Answer: A   Difficulty: 1   Section: 1   Objective: 3

4. The larger an object's mass, the
   a. smaller its inertia.
   c. larger its inertia.
   b. larger its volume.
   d. smaller its volume.

   Answer: A   Difficulty: 1   Section: 1   Objective: 4

5. If you poured three liquids (that do not mix completely) into a beaker, how could you tell which one is the densest liquid?
   a. The liquid that is floating on top is the densest liquid.
   b. The liquid that settles to the bottom is the densest liquid
   c. The liquid with the deep red color is the densest liquid.
   d. There is no way to tell which liquid is densest from the description.

   Answer: B   Difficulty: 2   Section: 2   Objective: 2

6. What happens to a solid object with a density that is less than water when it is placed in water?
   a. The object sinks about halfway into the water.
   b. The object displaces a quantity of water greater than its volume.
   c. The object settles to the bottom of the water.
   d. The object floats on top of the water.

   Answer: D   Difficulty: 2   Section: 2   Objective: 2

7. Which of the following is NOT an example of a physical change?
   a. the shaping of a gold bar
   c. the explosion of fireworks
   b. the melting of a Popsicle
   d. the sanding of a piece of wood

   Answer: C   Difficulty: 1   Section: 2   Objective: 3

8. What kinds of changes in substances are always physical changes?
   a. changes of state from solid to liquid to gas and back
   b. changes that result in new substances being formed
   c. changes that change the identity of the substance
   d. changes that change the density of the substances

   Answer: A   Difficulty: 1   Section: 2   Objective: 4

9. Why are chemical properties harder to observe than physical properties?
   a. Chemical properties change the substance's identity.
   b. Chemical properties depend on the size of the sample.
   c. Physical properties can be observed and measured.
   d. Physical properties change the identity of a substance.

   Answer: A   Difficulty: 2   Section: 3   Objective: 4

10. What is the best way to tell if a chemical change has taken place?
    a. The matter changes color.   c. A mixture separates into layers.
    b. The change is reversible.   d. A composition changes.

    Answer: D   Difficulty: 2   Section: 3   Objective: 2

11. Which of the following is NOT the result of a chemical change?
    a. soured milk   c. ground flour
    b. rusted metal   d. digested food

    Answer: C   Difficulty: 1   Section: 3   Objective: 3

12. Which of the following is a chemical property of matter?
    a. solubility   c. density
    b. volume   d. reactivity

    Answer: D   Difficulty: 2   Section: 3   Objective: 1

13. What makes characteristic properties useful to scientists?
    a. They can be either physical or chemical.   c. They are easy to observe and measure.
    b. They can be used to identify matter.   d. Sample size does not matter.

    Answer: B   Difficulty: 2   Section: 3   Objective: 3

14. Which property of matter is a measure of the gravitational force?
    a. density   c. volume
    b. mass   d. weight

    Answer: D   Difficulty: 1   Section: 1   Objective: 3

15. In a graduated cylinder containing several liquid layers, the least dense liquid is found
    a. floating at the top.   c. in the lightest colored layer.
    b. in the middle layer.   d. settled on the bottom.

    Answer: A   Difficulty: 2   Section: 2   Objective: 2

16. How does a physical change differ from a chemical change?
    a. In a physical change new volumes are created.
    b. In a physical change new materials are produced.
    c. In a physical change the composition is unchanged.
    d. In a physical change the change is reversible.

    Answer: C   Difficulty: 2   Section: a3   Objective: 4

17. Melting crayons is an example of a
    a. physical property.   c. chemical property.
    b. physical change.   d. chemical change.

    Answer: B   Difficulty: 1   Section: 2   Objective: 3

18. Which of the following units would be best for describing the volume of mercury (liquid) used in an experiment?
    a. grams or kilograms   c. liters or milliliters
    b. meters or centimeters   d. newtons

    Answer: C   Difficulty: 1   Section: 1   Objective: 2

19. Which of the following events is NOT a common sign that a chemical change has taken place?
    a. change in color or odor
    b. change in state
    c. foaming or bubbling
    d. production of heat or light
    Answer: B   Difficulty: 2   Section: 3   Objective: 2

20. What chemical property is responsible for iron rusting?
    a. flammability
    b. conductivity
    c. nonflammability
    d. reactivity with oxygen
    Answer: D   Difficulty: 1   Section: 3   Objective: 1

21. The motion of a 150 g ball is more difficult to change than the motion of a 50 g ball because the 150 g ball has
    a. less weight than the 50 g ball.
    b. greater density than the 50 g ball.
    c. more mass than the 50 g ball.
    d. larger volume than the 50 g ball.
    Answer: C   Difficulty: 2   Section: 2   Objective: 4

22. What unit of density would be appropriate to describe a solid bar of silver?
    a. g/mL
    b. g/cm^3
    c. oz/ft^3
    d. kg/L
    Answer: B   Difficulty: 1   Section: 2   Objective: 2

23. Which physical property of matter describes the relationship between mass and volume?
    a. density
    b. ductility
    c. reactivity
    d. weight
    Answer: A   Difficulty: 1   Section: 2   Objective: 2

24. Souring milk is an example of a
    a. physical property.
    b. physical change.
    c. chemical property.
    d. chemical change.
    Answer: D   Difficulty: 1   Section: 3   Objective: 3

25. Malleability is an example of a
    a. physical property.
    b. physical change.
    c. chemical property.
    d. chemical change.
    Answer: A   Difficulty: 1   Section: 2   Objective: 3

26. In scientific experiments, the amount of a liquid used is expressed in
    a. centimeters or meters
    b. grams or milligrams
    c. liters or milliliters
    d. ounces or gallons
    Answer: C   Difficulty: 1   Section: b   Objective: 2

27. Which of the following is not a physical property of matter?
    a. ductility
    b. color
    c. thermal conductivity
    d. reactivity with water
    Answer: D   Difficulty: 1   Section: 3   Objective: 4

28. Which of the following has more inertia than a 100 g object on Earth?
    a. an object that weighs one newton on Earth
    b. a 50 g object on Earth
    c. a 10 g object on Earth
    d. an object that weighs two newtons on Earth
    Answer: D   Difficulty: 2   Section: 1   Objective: 4

29. During physical changes, matter always retains its
    a. size.
    b. identity.
    c. state.
    d. texture.
    Answer: B   Difficulty: 1   Section: b3   Objective: 3

30. To compare the densities of oil and water, pour the liquids into a container and observe how they
    a. change color.
    b. evaporate quickly.
    c. separate into layers.
    d. create an odor.
    Answer: C   Difficulty: 2   Section: 2   Objective: 2

31. What has mass and takes up space?
    a. weight
    b. volume
    c. space
    d. matter
    Answer: D   Difficulty: 1   Section: 1   Objective: 1

32. How does a physical change differ from a chemical change?
    a. New properties of the matter are observed.
    b. New materials are produced.
    c. The change always involves heat or light.
    d. The composition of the matter is unchanged.
    Answer: D   Difficulty: 1   Section: 3   Objective: 3

33. Which of the following would be the easiest to start moving?
    a. a cart loaded with two potatoes
    b. an empty cart with no potatoes
    c. a cart loaded with many sacks of potatoes
    d. a cart with one potato
    Answer: B   Difficulty: 1   Section: 1   Objective: 4

34. Which of the following signs does NOT indicate that a chemical change has happened?
    a. change in state
    b. change in color or odor
    c. foaming or bubbling
    d. production of heat or light
    Answer: A   Difficulty: 2   Section: 3   Objective: 2

35. What units would you use to measure liquid volume in an experiment?
    a. grams or kilograms
    b. meters or centimeters
    c. newtons
    d. liters or milliliters
    Answer: D   Difficulty: 1   Section: 1   Objective: 2

36 Which of these phrases describes the results of a chemical change?
    a. gold nuggets not burning
    b. reactivity with oxygen
    c. charred wood, ash, and smoke
    d. a bent auto fender
    Answer: C   Difficulty: 2   Section: 3   Objective: 3

37. Why is density considered a useful property for identifying matter?
    a. Different substances have the same densities.
    b. Density is unique to each substance.
    c. Density predicts whether objects float.
    d. Density varies at different temperatures
    Answer: B   Difficulty: 2   Section: 2   Objective: 2

38. What property of matter is demonstrated by the fact that you cannot fit any more books onto a bookshelf that is already filled?
    a. inertia
    b. mass
    c. volume
    d. weight
    Answer: C   Difficulty: 1   Section: 1   Objective: 1

39. How could you change the mass of an object?
    a. Move to another large body or moon.
    b. Add or take away some matter.
    c. Make Earth spin faster or slower.
    d. Change the object's temperature.
    Answer: B   Difficulty: 1   Section: 1   Objective: 3

40. Why is freezing water to make ice considered a physical change?
    a. The ice has some new properties.   c. The water changes its state.
    b. The ice floats on water.   d. The water changes its identity
    Answer: C   Difficulty: 2   Section: 2   Objective: 4

41. Why would dissolving salt in water be considered a physical change?
    a. The salt disappears forever.   c. The salt changes its state.
    b. The water tastes salty.   d. The salt returns if the mixture is heated.
    Answer: D   Difficulty: 1   Section: 2   Objective: 4

42. Why would molding clay be considered a physical change?
    a. The clay changes only its shape.   c. The clay changes only its state of matter.
    b. The clay changes in composition.   d. The clay changes its identity.
    Answer: A   Difficulty: 2   Section: 2   Objective: 4

43. What happens to matter during chemical changes?
    a. It retains its identity.   c. The state of matter changes.
    b. Its composition changes.   d. Only the form of the matter changes.
    Answer: B   Difficulty: 1   Section: 3   Objective: 2

44. What makes chemical properties so difficult to observe?
    a. They result in changes of state.   c. Wearing protective glasses is required.
    b. Observing them produces new materials.d. They happen too quickly
    Answer: B   Difficulty: 2   Section: 3   Objective: 2

45. What happens to matter during a physical change?
    a. Its composition changes.   c. Its mass and density may change.
    b. It combines and forms new substances.   d. It keeps its identity.
    Answer: D   Difficulty: 2   Section: 2   Objective: 4

46. How can you tell that baking a cake produces a chemical change?
    a. It produces changes of state in the ingredients.
    b. It combines the ingredients to form new substances.
    c. It causes changes that are not reversible.
    d. It changes physical properties such as color and odor.
    Answer: B   Difficulty: 2   Section: 3   Objective: 2

47. How can you tell that the electrolysis of water produces a chemical change?
    a. It is a reversible reaction.   c. It requires heat to produce changes.
    b. It produces a change of state.   d. It changes the composition of matter.
    Answer: D   Difficulty: 2   Section: 3   Objective: 2

COMPLETION

Use the terms from the following list to complete the sentences below.

    weight   mass
    density   volume
    physical change   inertia
    chemical change   chemical
    physical

48. Because of _____ all objects tend to resist a change in motion.
    Answer: inertia   Difficulty: 1   Section: 1   Objective: 4

49. The physical property of matter that describes the relationship between mass and
    volume is _____.
    Answer: density   Difficulty: 1   Section: 2   Objective: 1

50. Water evaporating from a puddle is an example of a(n) _____.
    Answer: physical change
    Difficulty: 2   Section: 2   Objective: 3

51. One way to learn about the properties of a(n) _____ substance is to observe what new substances form during a reaction.
    Answer: chemical   Difficulty: 1   Section: 3   Objective: 2

52. An object's _____ is affected by the gravitational force.
    Answer: weight   Difficulty: 1   Section: 3   Objective: 3

53. A copper penny can turn green if it reacts with carbon dioxide and water. This is an example of a(n) _____.
    Answer: chemical change
    Difficulty: 1   Section: 3   Objective: 3

Use the terms from the following list to complete the sentences below.

    mass   volume
    property   change

54. Things with _____ cannot share the same place at the same time.
    Answer: volume   Difficulty: 1   Section: 3   Objective: 2

55. A chemical _____ describes which changes are possible for a substance.
    Answer: property   Difficulty: 1   Section: 1   Objective: 1

56. A chemical _____ describes the process by which new substances are formed.
    Answer: change   Difficulty: 1   Section: 3   Objective: 1

57. The amount of matter in an object is its _____.
    Answer: mass   Difficulty: 1   Section: 1   Objective: 1

Use the terms from the following list to complete the sentences below.

    milliliters   weight
    kilograms   inertia

58. The SI unit for mass is the _____.
    Answer: kilogram   Difficulty: 1   Section: 2   Objective: 2

59. If you know an object's mass, you can figure out its _____ on Earth.
    Answer: weight   Difficulty: 1   Section: 1   Objective: 3

60. The tendency of an object to resist a change in its motion is _____.
    Answer: inertia   Difficulty: 1   Section: 1   Objective: 4

61. You could use _____ to measure the volume of a soft drink can.
    Answer: milliliters   Difficulty: 1   Section: 1   Objective: 2

SHORT ANSWER

62. Explain why volume and mass are not characteristic properties of matter.
    Answer:

Answers will vary. Sample answer: Characteristic properties such as density, reactivity, or solubility do not depend on the amount of the substance. Volume and mass cannot be characteristic properties because they are defined by measurements that depend on the size or amount of the substance in a sample.
    Difficulty: 2   Section: 1   Objective: 1

63. Describe two ways to compare the densities of unknown substances. Why is density a useful property for identifying matter?

Answer:
Answers will vary. Sample answer: If the two substances are liquids, you could observe how they separate into layers as a result of differences in density. If the two substances are solids, you could observe whether they float or sink in water. Density is a useful property for identifying substances because most substances have different densities that are constant at a given temperature and pressure.

Difficulty: 2   Section: 2   Objective: 2

64. Why could an astronaut carry more massive equipment around on the moon than on Earth?

Answer:
Answers will vary. Sample answer: The astronauts should be able to carry more mass on the moon because the gravitational force acting on the objects is less there. Thus, the equipment will weigh less than it does on Earth.

Difficulty: 3   Section: 1   Objective: 3

65. Describe some of the signs that a chemical change is taking place. Provide everyday examples for each clue.

Answer:
The production of new products with new properties is the most important sign that a change is chemical in nature. For example, the fizzing and foaming that appear when vinegar and baking soda are mixed shows that gases are being produced. Other signs include a change in color, such as what happens when iron rusts, in odor such as the smell of sour milk, or the production of heat, sounds, or light as with a roaring campfire.

Difficulty: 2   Section: 3   Objective: 2

66 Explain how you would measure the volume of an irregular solid such as a rock.

Answer:
Although you could not use the formula to calculate its volume, you could measure the volume of water the object displaces. Fill a graduated cylinder with water to a level high enough to cover the object. Carefully read the volume of water by looking at the lowest part of the liquid's curve, or meniscus. Record this value in milliliters. Then drop the object into the water. Again read the volume. Subtract the original volume from the new value to obtain the volume of water displaced. Convert the volume in milliliters to cubic centimeters ($1 \text{ mL} = 1 \text{ cm}^3$) to obtain the volume of the solid.

Difficulty: 2   Section: 1   Objective: 2

67. Explain how the concepts of mass and weight are related.

Answer:
Weight, which is actually a measure of the pull of gravitational force on an object, depends on mass. The greater the mass, or amount of matter in an object, the greater is the pull between Earth and the object and the larger is its weight. Weight, however, will vary depending on the object's location in the universe, while mass is constant. On the moon or another smaller body, the same object would weigh less than on Earth.

Difficulty: 2   Section: 1   Objective: 3

68. Suppose you had two bricks with exactly the same volume, one made of clay and the other made from plastic foam (painted to look like stone). Explain how you could use inertia to tell which brick has the most mass.

    Answer:
    There is direct relationship between mass and inertia. The more mass the harder it is to change an object's motion. You could try pushing the two objects with exactly the same force. The brick that has the least mass would move the furthest. Once in motion, the more massive brick would also be the hardest to slow, stop, or change the direction of that motion.

    Difficulty: 2   Section: 1   Objective: 4

69. Describe the two characteristics that all matter has in common.

    Answer:
    Whether it's a solid, a liquid or a gas, all matter shares the properties of mass and volume. Volume is the amount of three-dimensional space occupied by the matter. You know that things have volume because they cannot share the same space. They push other bits of matter aside. Volume is measured in milliliters, liters, or in the case of solids, in cubic measurements (cm^3 or m^3). Mass is a measure of the amount of matter an object contains. Mass remains constant regardless of its location and is measured in grams or kilograms.

    Difficulty: 1   Section: 1   Objective: 1

70 Compare what happens during physical and chemical changes in terms of the reversibility of the changes.

    Answer:
    Physical changes are generally much easier to reverse than chemical changes. Applying or removing heat can reverse changes of state. Changes to the shape of matter (such as molding or drawing out wires) can also be reversed with some effort. Some of these changes seem to be permanent, such as grinding rock to form sand, but the sediment may be deposited and form a rock again under great pressure. Other materials such as paper can be recycled without changing their composition. Chemical changes change the nature of the materials. Some leave permanent changes such as charred wood and gases from burning, which may be difficult to recover. Reversing the chemical reactions, and performing a second chemical change, can reverse some chemical changes.

    Difficulty: 2   Section: 3   Objective: 3

71. Describe two physical and two chemical properties of an ice cube.

    Answer:
    The ice cube is solid and can be shaped or carved. Ice is less dense than water because it will float in water. Chemically, ice is nonflammable and in its liquid form could even be used to put out fires. Ice could also be broken down into the two gases that make it up by melting it and applying an electric current.

    Difficulty: 3   Section: 2 and 3   Objective: 2.1 and 3.1

72. Explain why a bowling ball is much heavier than a soccer ball even though they are roughly the same size.

    Answer:
    The bowling ball is made of denser materials and is solid. It packs more matter into the same amount of space. The more dense and massive the object is the more it will weigh.

    Difficulty: 2   Section: 2   Objective: 2

73. What physical property do a wood block, copper tubing, an ice cube, a bar of silver, and a lead fishing weight have in common? What physical property of matter could you use to tell them apart?

Answer:

These objects have the same state of matter. They are all solids. You can use density to tell them apart. To find density, divide mass by volume. The density will identify what each is made from.

Difficulty: 1   Section: 2   Objective: 2

74. Describe four physical changes that you could perform on a glass of water.

Answer:

To change the state of matter, you could apply heat and cause the water to change into a gas. You could dissolve salt or sugar in the water. To change its density, you could freeze the water in an ice tray. Once frozen, you could change its state of matter again by melting it.

Difficulty: 2   Section: 2   Objective: 3

75 Explain how you could use two physical properties to separate a mixture of salt and iron filings.

Answer:

Iron is a magnetic material and salt is soluble in water. You could use a magnet to collect the bits of iron. Since the iron filings are fairly large, you could also dump the mixture into water to dissolve the salt and filter out the iron filings.

Difficulty: 3   Section: 2   Objective: 1

76. Describe the physical and chemical change that occurs when a birthday candle is lit on a cake?

Answer:

Two things happen when the birthday candle is lit. The wax in the candle melts, which is a physical change involving a change of state. The candlewick and some of the wax also burn. Burning produces heat, light, gases and ash. This is a chemical change because it produces new kinds of matter with different properties and a different composition.

Difficulty: 3   Section: 3   Objective: 3

77. Give each student a sugar cube and ask them to write down what physical properties they observe. Then have them write three things they could do that would cause the sugar cube to undergo a physical change.

Answers:

Physical properties: white, tastes sweet; feels gritty in texture, crystal in shape; regular solid; soluble in water; physical changes: crush it, grind it, dissolve it in water

Difficulty: 2   Section: 3   Objective: 3

78. Give each student a sugar cube and have them write two things they could do to the sugar cube to make it undergo a chemical change and what properties these changes represent. Students may use their books to find examples.

Answer:

Answers will vary. Sample answers: they could burn it (flammability), or they could cause it to react with other chemicals (reactivity), such as using it in a recipe.

Difficulty: 2   Section: 3   Objective: 3

79 Give an example of a chemical change that occurs during the preparation of a meal.

Answers:

burning of gas in an oven or a stove burner; cooking an egg, baking a cake.

Difficulty: 2   Section: 3   Objective: 3

80. List three clues that indicate a chemical change is taking place.

    Answers:
    color change, bubbling, fizzing, or foaming, production of heat, sound, or odors
    Difficulty: 1   Section: 3   Objective: 2

81. List three physical properties of water.

    Answer:
    colorless, liquid at room temperature, density of 1.00, melting point of 0°C and a
    boiling point of 100°C, can dissolve salt and sugar
    Difficulty: 2   Section: 2   Objective: 2

82 You have two objects, both about the size of an orange. Object A has a mass of 1,487g,
   and object B has a mass of 878 g. Which object do you think has the greater density?
   Explain.

    Answer:
    Object A; Both objects have about the same volume so the object with the greater mass
    will have the greater density.
    Difficulty: 2   Section: 2   Objective: 2

ESSAY QUESTIONS

83. After a tree is cut with a chain saw, it is impossible to put the tiny wood chips back
    together. The process cannot be reversed. Does this mean that cutting trees with a chain
    saw causes a chemical change in the wood? Explain why or why not.

    Answer:
    Answers will vary. Sample answer: No; even though it would be nearly impossible to
    put the wood chips back together, this is still a physical change. The chips, log, and
    stump keep their identity as wood. Only their size and shape changes.
    Difficulty: 2   Section: 3   Objective: 3

84. Summarize the differences between mass and weight. Why do you think people tend to
    confuse these terms?

    Answer:
    Mass is a measure of the amount of matter, while weight is a measure of gravitational
    force. Mass is constant no matter where the object is located while weight depends on
    where it is found in space. Mass is measured with a balance and expressed in grams,
    while weight is measured with a spring scale and measured in newtons. People tend
    to confuse the two concepts because both mass and weight remain constant on Earth,
    and weight does give you a fairly good estimate of the mass of an object.
    Difficulty: 1   Section: 1   Objective: 3

85. A glass cylinder contains four liquids in four separate layers. One liquid is water. The
    purple liquid has a density 1.62 g/cm^3. The yellow liquid has a density of 0.46 g/cm^3.
    The red has a density of 0.91 g/cm^3. What is the order of the liquids in the cylinder?
    Explain your answer. What will happen if you slip a small, flat, chip of wood (density
    0.85 g/cm^3) into the cylinder?

    Answer:
    The purple liquid will form the bottom layer, followed by the water and the red liquid.
    The yellow liquid will be on top. The greater the density, the lower the layer. Water
    has a density of 1.00 g/cm^3, which means it will float on the liquid with a density of
    1.62 g/cm^3. The wood chip should sink through the yellow liquid and float on the red.
    Difficulty: 2   Section: 2   Objective: 2

MATCHING

a. volume	d. matter
b. mass	e. meniscus
c. inertia	f. weight

86 ____ a measure of the amount of matter in objects

    Answer: B   Difficulty: 1   Section: 1   Objective: 1

87 ____ a measure of the gravitational force on objects

    Answer: F   Difficulty: 1   Section: 1   Objective: 3

88. ____ the curve at a liquid's surface

    Answer: E   Difficulty: 1   Section: 1   Objective: 1

89. ____ anything that has mass and takes up space

    Answer: D   Difficulty: 1   Section: q1   Objective: 1

90. ____ the amount of space occupied by an object

    Answer: A   Difficulty: 1   Section: 1   Objective: 1

91. ____ the tendency of matter to resist changes in motion

    Answer: C   Difficulty: 1   Section: 1   Objective: 1

a. density	d. physical change
b. physical property	e. malleability
c. solubility	f. electrical conductivity

92. ____ ability to be made into thin sheets

    Answer: E   Difficulty: 1   Section: 2   Objective: 1

93. ____ a change in the form of a substance that does not change its identity

    Answer: D   Difficulty: 1   Section: 2   Objective: 4

94. ____ the ability to conduct electric current

    Answer: F   Difficulty: 1   Section: 2   Objective: 1

95. ____ the relationship between mass and volume

    Answer: A   Difficulty: 1   Section: 2   Objective: 1

96. ____ ability of a substance to dissolve

    Answer: C   Difficulty: 1   Section: 2   Objective: 1

97. ____ characteristic that can be observed or measured such as color, state, or hardness

    Answer: B   Difficulty: 1   Section: 2   Objective: 1

a. reactivity	d. composition
b. chemical change	e. physical change
c. flammability	

98. ____ the type of matter and its arrangement in an object

    Answer: D   Difficulty: 1   Section: 3   Objective: 2

99. ____ the ability of a substance to burn

    Answer: C   Difficulty: 1   Section: 3   Objective: 1

100.____ the process of changing into entirely new substances

    Answer: B   Difficulty: 1   Section: 3   Objective: 2

101.____ changes in matter that do not change the composition of the substance

    Answer: E   Difficulty: 1   Section: 3   Objective: 3

102.____ the ability of two or more substances to combine to form other substances

Answer: A   Difficulty: 1   Section: 3   Objective: 1

a. thermal conductivity	f. solubility

b. composition
c. nonflammability
d. inertia
e. state of matter

g. reactivity
h. electrolysis
i. ductility
j. density

103.____ the saltiness of seawater is the result of this property

| Answer: F | Difficulty: 1 | Section: 2 | Objective: 1 |

104.____ objects float or sink as a result of this property

| Answer: J | Difficulty: 1 | Section: 2 | Objective: 1 |

105.____ the physical form in which a substance exists

| Answer: E | Difficulty: 1 | Section: 2 | Objective: 1 |

106.____ the type of matter that makes up an object and the way it is arranged

| Answer: B | Difficulty: 1 | Section: 3 | Objective: 2 |

107.____ the breakdown of water to form two gases is the result of this process

| Answer: H | Difficulty: 1 | Section: a3 | Objective: 1 |

108.____ the ability of a substance to resist burning

| Answer: C | Difficulty: 1 | Section: 2 | Objective: 1 |

109.____ the tendency of a substance to resist changes in its motion

| Answer: D | Difficulty: 1 | Section: 1 | Objective: 4 |

110.____ the rate at which a substance conducts heat

| Answer: A | Difficulty: 1 | Section: 2 | Objective: 1 |

a. ductility
b. reactivity

c. state of matter
d. malleability

111.____ aluminum made into thin sheets of foil

| Answer: D | Difficulty: 1 | Section: 2 | Objective: 1 |

112.____ an ice cube made of solid water

| Answer: C | Difficulty: 1 | Section: 2 | Objective: 1 |

113.____ rust forming on metals

| Answer: B | Difficulty: 1 | Section: 3 | Objective: 1 |

114.____ copper pulled into thin wires

| Answer: A | Difficulty: 1 | Section: 2 | Objective: 1 |

a. density
b. solubility

c. odor
d. flammability

115.____ flavored drink mix dissolving in water

| Answer: B | Difficulty: 1 | Section: 2 | Objective: 1 |

116.____ objects floating or sinking in water

| Answer: A | Difficulty: 1 | Section: 2 | Objective: 2 |

117.____ wood burning in a fireplace

| Answer: D | Difficulty: 1 | Section: 3 | Objective: 1 |

INTERPRETING GRAPHICS

Use the chart below to answer the following questions.

SUBSTANCE	DENSITY (g/cm^3)	SUBSTANCE	DENSITY (g/cm^3)
Aluminum (solid)	2.7	Ice (solid)	0.93
Iron pyrite (solid)	5.02	Water (liquid)	1.00
Mercury (liquid)	13.55	Zinc (solid)	7.13
Silver (solid)	10.50	Wood (oak)	0.85

118. A cube has a density of 2.7 g/cm³. What substance is the cube made of?
    a. aluminum
    b. ice
    c. iron pyrite
    d. wood
    Answer: A   Difficulty: 2   Section: 2   Objective: 2

119. What substance has a density more than 13 times greater than water?
    a. ice
    b. silver
    c. aluminum
    d. mercury
    Answer: D   Difficulty: 2   Section: 2   Objective: 2

120. Why will ice float on top of liquid water?
    a. Ice has a lower density than water.
    b. Ice has a higher density than water.
    c. Ice is a solid.
    d. Ice is colder than water.
    Answer: A   Difficulty: 2   Section: 2   Objective: 2

121. What is the density of oak wood?
    a. 85 g/cm³
    b. 5.02 g/cm³
    c. 0.85 g/cm³
    d. 0.93 g/cm³
    Answer: C   Difficulty: 2   Section: 2   Objective: 2

122. What is the densest solid shown in the table?
    a. mercury
    b. silver
    c. zinc
    d. iron pyrite
    Answer: B   Difficulty: 2   Section: 2   Objective: 2

Use the figure below to answer the following questions.

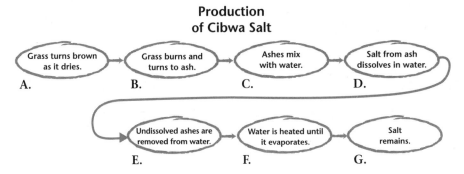

Production of Cibwa Salt

123 Does step A involve a chemical or a physical change? Explain.

Answer:

Step A involves a chemical change because the leaves turn brown. The color change signals a chemical change.

Difficulty: 2   Section: 3   Objective: 3

124. In step B, the grass burns and turns into ash. However, the salt remains in the ashes and dissolves in Step D. What does this tell you about the properties of the salt?

Answer:

The salt did not burn, which shows that it has the chemical property of nonflammability. It has the physical property of solubility in water as well.

Difficulty: 2   Section: 3   Objective: 3

Use the chart below to answer the following questions.

Table 1 Densities of Common Substances*

Substance	Density (g/cm^3)	Substance	Density (g/cm^3)
Helium (gas)	0.0001663	Zinc (solid)	7.13
Oxygen (gas)	0.001331	Silver (solid)	10.50
Water (liquid)	1.00	Lead (solid)	11.35
Iron pyrite (solid)	5.02	Mercury (liquid)	13.55

*at 20 C and 1.0 atm

125. Look at the table. Which substance is the least dense?

Answer: B   Difficulty: 1   Section: 2   Objective: 2

126. Look at the table. Which two substances are the densest?

Answer: D   Difficulty: 1   Section: 2   Objective: 2

TRUE/FALSE

127. ____ The volume of a gas can be measured with a graduated cylinder.

Answer: F   Difficulty: 2   Section: 1   Objective: 1

128. ____ Volumes of solids can be expressed in liters or milliliters

Answer: F   Difficulty: 1   Section: 1   Objective: 2

129. ____ Weight and mass are the same thing.

Answer: F   Difficulty: 2   Section: 1   Objective: 3

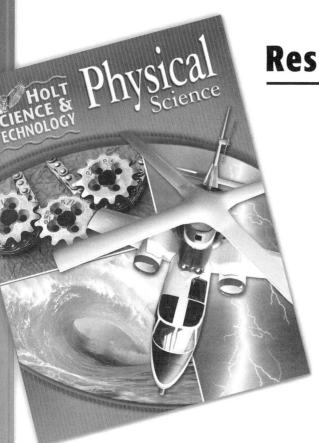

Chapter Resource File

2

States of Matter

CHAPTER 2

Skills Worksheet

Directed Reading A

Section: Three States of Matter

1. What are the three most familiar states of matter?

_____

_____

_____

2. What is a state of matter?

_____

_____

PARTICLES OF MATTER

3. Matter is made up of _____ and

_____.

Match the correct description with the correct state of matter. Write the letter in the space provided.

_____ **4.** Particles have a strong attraction for each other.

_____ **5.** Particles move independently of each other.

_____ **6.** Particles are close together but can slide past one another.

_____ **7.** Particles are close together and vibrate in place.

_____ **8.** Particles move fast enough to overcome nearly all of the attraction between them.

a. solid
b. liquid
c. gas

SOLIDS

_____ **9.** The particles of matter that make up a solid
    a. have a weaker attraction than those of a liquid.
    b. do not move at all.
    c. do not move fast enough to overcome the force of attraction.
    d. vibrate from place to place.

| Directed Reading A *continued*

10. What is a solid?

_____

_____

11. How are the particles in a crystalline solid arranged?

_____

_____

12. How are the particles in an amorphous solid arranged?

_____

_____

LIQUIDS

13. How do the particles of a liquid make it possible to pour juice into a glass?

_____

_____

14. A beaker and a cylinder each contain 350 mL of juice. What does this show you about the properties of a liquid?

_____

_____

15. Liquids tend to form spherical droplets because of _____ tension.

16. Water has a lower _____ than honey.

GASES

17. What is a gas?

_____

_____

18. How is it possible for one tank of helium to fill 700 balloons?

_____

_____

_____

Name _____ Class _____ Date _____

Directed Reading A

Section: Behavior of Gases
DESCRIBING GAS BEHAVIOR

_____ **1.** What state of matter is helium?
a. solid **c.** gas
b. liquid **d.** plasma

2. A measure of how fast the particles in an object are moving

is the _____.

3. Why is more gas needed to fill helium balloons on a cold day?

_____

_____

_____

4. The amount of space that an object takes up is the _____.

5. The volume of any gas depends upon the size of

the _____.

6. The amount of force exerted on a given area is

called _____.

7. Why does the basketball have greater pressure than the beachball?

_____

_____

_____

_____

GAS BEHAVIOR LAWS

_____ **8.** Lifting a piston on a cylinder of gas shows that when the pressure of
the gas
a. increases, the temperature increases.
b. decreases, the volume increases.
c. decreases, the volume decreases.
d. increases, the volume increases.

_____ **9.** All of the following remain constant for Charles's law EXCEPT
    a. the type of piston.
    b. the amount of gas.
    c. the volume of the gas.
    d. the pressure.

10. The relationship between the volume and pressure of a gas is

called _____.

11. Weather balloons are only partially inflated before they're released into the atmosphere. Why is that?

_____

_____

_____

_____

12. Putting a balloon in the freezer is one way to

demonstrate _____.

13. The relationship between the volume and the temperature of a gas when

pressure remains constant is known as _____.

Name _____ Class _____ Date _____

Directed Reading A

Section: Changes of State
ENERGY AND CHANGES OF STATE

_____ 1. Which has the most energy?
    a. particles in steam   **c.** particles in ice
    b. particles in liquid water   **d.** particles in freezing water

2. When a substance changes from one physical form to another, we say the

substance has had a(n) _____.

3. List the five changes of state.

_____

_____

_____

_____

_____

MELTING: SOLID TO LIQUID

4. Could you use gallium to make jewelry? Why or why not?

_____

_____

_____

_____

5. The temperature at which a substance changes from solid to liquid is

the _____ of the substance.

6. Melting is considered a(n) _____ change because energy

is gained by the substance as it changes state.

FREEZING: LIQUID TO SOLID

7. A substance's _____ is the temperature at which it

changes from a liquid to a solid.

8. What happens if energy is added or removed from a glass of ice water?

_____

_____

_____

_____

9. Freezing is considered a(n) _____ change because energy is removed from the substance.

EVAPORATION: LIQUID TO GAS

Match the correct definition with the correct term. Write the letter in the space provided.

_____**10.** the change of a substance from a liquid to a gas

_____**11.** the change of state from a liquid to a gas when the vapor pressure equals the atmospheric pressure

_____**12.** the pressure inside the bubbles of a boiling liquid

_____**13.** temperature at which a liquid boils

a. boiling point

b. vapor pressure

c. evaporation

d. boiling

14. As you go higher above sea level, the _____ decreases and the _____ of a substance gets lower.

CONDENSATION: GAS TO LIQUID

15. The change of state from a gas to a liquid is _____.

16. At a given pressure, the condensation point for a substance is the same as its _____.

17. For a substance to change from a gas to a liquid, particles must _____.

SUBLIMATION: SOLID TO GAS

18. Solid carbon dioxide isn't ice. So why is it called "dry ice"?

_____

_____

_____

19. The change of state from a solid to a gas is called _____.

CHANGE OF TEMPERATURE VS. CHANGE OF STATE

20. The speed of the particles in a substance changes when the

_____ changes.

21. The temperature of a substance does not change before the

_____ is complete.

Skills Worksheet

Directed Reading B

Section: Three States of Matter
Circle the letter of the best answer for each question.

1. What are ice, water, and steam examples of?

    a. solids

    b. states of matter

    c. liquids

    d. gases

PARTICLES OF MATTER

Read the description. Then, draw a line from the dot next to each description to the matching word.

2. particles vibrate in place   ●   **a.** solid

3. particles are far apart   ●   **b.** liquid

4. particles slide past each other   ●   **c.** gas

SOLIDS
Solids Have Definite Shape and Volume
Circle the letter of the best answer for each question.

5. What stays the same in solids?

    a. shape and volume

    b. color and shape

    c. position and shape

    d. state and volume

| Directed Reading B *continued*

There Are Two Kinds of Solids
Circle the letter of the best answer for each question.

6. What are two kinds of solids?

   a. diamond and ice

   b. glass and rubber

   c. with and without fixed shape

   d. crystalline and amorphous

LIQUIDS
Liquids Change Shape but Not Volume

7. Which statement is true of liquids?

   a. They have a fixed shape but not a fixed volume.

   b. They have a fixed shape and a fixed volume.

   c. They have a fixed volume but not a fixed shape.

   d. They do not have a fixed shape or volume.

Liquids Have Unique Characteristics

8. What force acts on particles at the surface of a liquid?

   a. viscosity

   b. moving particles

   c. surface tension

   d. states of matter

Read the words in the box. Read the sentences. <u>Fill in each blank</u> with the word that best completes the sentence.

gas   viscosity

9. The property of liquids that describes their ability to flow is called

_____.

GASES
Gases Change in Both Shape and Volume

10. The state of matter that has no fixed shape or volume is

_____.

<u>Circle the letter</u> of the best answer for each question.

11. What is true of the particles of a gas?

   a. They are very close together.

   b. They are always far apart.

   c. They slide past each other.

   d. They move fast.

Skills Worksheet

Directed Reading B

Section: Behavior of Gases

Read the words in the box. Read the sentences. <u>Fill in each blank</u> with the word that best completes the sentence.

pressure	gas	temperature
volume	particles	

DESCRIBING GAS BEHAVIOR

1. Helium is a _____ .

Temperature

2. A measure of the speed of molecules is the

_____ .

Volume

3. The amount of space matter takes up is its

_____ .

Pressure

4. When the amount of force per unit area increases,

the _____ increases.

5. The pressure in a ball can be increased by adding

more _____ .

Read the words in the box. Read the sentences. <u>Fill in each blank</u> with the word that best completes the sentence.

| gas laws | Boyle's law | Charles's law |

GAS BEHAVIOR LAWS

6. The relationships between temperatures, pressure, and volume are

described by _____ that involve a fixed

amount of gas.

Boyle's Law

7. Volume and pressure of a gas are inversely related. The temperature

must stay the same. This is _____.

Charles's Law

8. The volume of a gas is directly related to its temperature. If the

pressure is constant, _____ says this

is true.

Name _____ Class _____ Date _____

Directed Reading B

Section: Changes of State
ENERGY AND CHANGES OF STATE
Draw a line from each term to the matching number on the picture.

freezing   evaporation   condensation   melting

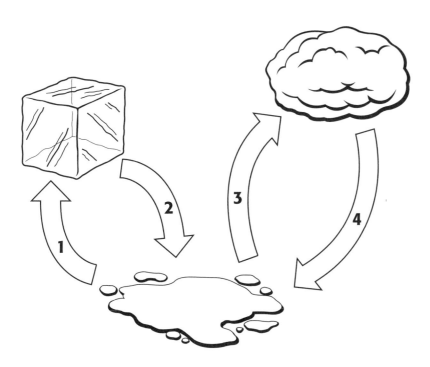

| Directed Reading B *continued*

Read the words in the box. Read the sentences. <u>Fill in each blank</u> with the word or phrase that best completes the sentence.

| change of state | exothermic | evaporation |
| melting | freezing | endothermic |

MELTING: SOLID TO LIQUID

5. A change of state from a solid to a liquid is

called _____.

Adding Energy

6. When energy is gained by something during a change of state,

a(n) _____ change occurs.

FREEZING: LIQUID TO SOLID

7. The melting point of a substance is the same as

its _____ point.

Removing Energy

8. When energy is removed from a substance,

a(n) _____ change may occur.

EVAPORATION: LIQUID TO GAS
Boiling and Evaporation

9. The particles break away from each other during

_____.

10. When water boils, a(n) _____ occurs.

Read the words in the box. Read the sentences. <u>Fill in each blank</u> with the word or phrase that best completes the sentence.

| temperature | boiling point | endothermic |
| sublimation | condensation | |

Effects of Pressure on Boiling Point

11. As you go higher above sea level, the

_____ of a substance gets lower.

CONDENSATION: GAS TO LIQUID

12. The change of state from a gas to a liquid is

_____.

SUBLIMATION: SOLID TO GAS

13. Dry ice changes from a solid to a gas during

_____.

14. Sublimation is a(n) _____ change.

CHANGE OF TEMPERATURE VS. CHANGE OF STATE

15. When the _____ of a substance changes,

the speed of the particles also changes.

Name _____ Class _____ Date _____

Skills Worksheet

Vocabulary and Section Summary

Three States of Matter

VOCABULARY

In your own words, write a definition of the following terms in the space provided.

1. states of matter

_____

_____

2. solid

_____

_____

3. liquid

_____

_____

4. surface tension

_____

_____

5. viscosity

_____

_____

6. gas

_____

_____

SECTION SUMMARY

Read the following section summary.

- The three most familiar states of matter are solid, liquid, and gas.

- All matter is made of tiny particles called atoms and molecules that attract each other and move constantly.

- A solid has a definite shape and volume.

- A liquid has a definite volume but not a definite shape.

- A gas does not have a definite shape or volume.

Skills Worksheet

Vocabulary and Section Summary

Behavior of Gases

VOCABULARY

In your own words, write a definition of the following terms in the space provided.

1. temperature

_____

_____

2. volume

_____

_____

3. pressure

_____

_____

4. Boyle's law

_____

_____

5. Charles's law

_____

_____

SECTION SUMMARY

Read the following section summary.

• Temperature measures how fast the particles in an object are moving.

• Gas pressure increases as the number of collisions of gas particles increases.

• Boyle's law states that the volume of a gas increases as the pressure decreases, if the temperature doesn't change.

• Charles's law states that the volume of a gas increases as the temperature increases, if the pressure doesn't change.

Skills Worksheet

Vocabulary and Section Summary

Changes of State
VOCABULARY

In your own words, write a definition of the following terms in the space provided.

1. change of state

_____

_____

2. melting

_____

_____

3. evaporation

_____

_____

4. boiling

_____

_____

5. condensation

_____

_____

6. sublimation

_____

_____

▌Vocabulary and Section Summary *continued*

SECTION SUMMARY

Read the following section summary.

- A change of state is the conversion of a substance from one physical form to another.

- Energy is added during endothermic changes. Energy is removed during exothermic changes.

- The freezing point and the melting point of a substance are the same temperature.

- Boiling and evaporation both result in a liquid changing to a gas.

- Condensation is the change of a gas to a liquid. It is the reverse of evaporation.

- Sublimation changes a solid directly to a gas.

- The temperature of a substance does not change during a change of state.

Name _____ Class _____ Date _____

Section Review

Three States of Matter

USING KEY TERMS

1. Use each of the following terms in a separate sentence: *viscosity* and *surface tension*.

_____

_____

UNDERSTANDING KEY IDEAS

_____ **2.** One property that all particles of matter have in common is they
  a. never move in solids.
  b. only move in gases.
  c. move constantly.
  d. None of the above

3. Describe solids, liquids, and gases in terms of shape and volume.

_____

_____

_____

CRITICAL THINKING

4. Applying Concepts Classify each substance according to its state of matter: apple juice, bread, a textbook, and steam.

_____

_____

_____

5. Identifying Relationships The volume of a gas can change, but the volume of a solid cannot. Explain why this is true.

_____

_____

Name _____ Class _____ Date _____

INTERPRETING GRAPHICS

Use the drawing below to answer the questions that follow.

6. Identify the state of matter shown in the jar.

_____

_____

7. Discuss how the particles in the jar are attracted to each other.

_____

_____

_____

_____

_____

_____

Skills Worksheet

Section Review

Behavior of Gases
USING KEY TERMS

1. Use each of the following terms in the same sentence: *temperature, pressure, volume,* and *Charles's law.*

_____

_____

_____

_____

UNDERSTANDING KEY IDEAS

_____ **2.** Boyle's law describes the relationship between
    a. volume and pressure.
    b. temperature and pressure.
    c. temperature and volume.
    d. All of the above

3. What are the effects of a warm temperature on gas particles?

_____

_____

_____

_____

MATH SKILLS

4. You have 3 L of gas at a certain temperature and pressure. What would the volume of the gas be if the temperature doubled and the pressure stayed the same? Show your work below.

CRITICAL THINKING

5. Applying Concepts What happens to the volume of a balloon that is taken outside on a cold winter day? Explain.

_____

_____

_____

_____

6. Making Inferences When scientists record the volume of a gas, they also record the temperature and the pressure of the gas. Why?

_____

_____

_____

_____

7. Analyzing Ideas Explain what happens to the pressure of a gas if the volume of gas is tripled.

_____

_____

_____

_____

Name _____ Class _____ Date _____

Section Review

Changes of State
USING KEY TERMS
For each pair of terms, explain how the meanings of the terms differ.

1. *melting* and *freezing*

_____

_____

2. *condensation* and *evaporation*

_____

_____

UNDERSTANDING KEY IDEAS

_____ 3. The change from a solid directly to a gas is called
    a. evaporation.
    b. boiling.
    c. melting.
    d. sublimation.

4. Describe how the motion and arrangement of particles in a substance change as the substance freezes.

_____

_____

_____

5. Explain what happens to the temperature of an ice cube as it melts.

_____

_____

_____

6. How are evaporation and boiling different? How are they similar?

_____

_____

_____

_____

MATH SKILLS

7. The volume of a substance in the gaseous state is about 1,000 times the volume of the same substance in the liquid state. How much space would 18 mL of water take up if it evaporated? Show your work below.

CRITICAL THINKING

8. Evaluating Data The temperature of a beaker of water is 25°C. After adding a piece of magnesium, the temperature is 28°C. Is this an exothermic or endothermic reaction? Explain your answer.

_____

_____

_____

_____

9. Applying Concepts Solid crystals of iodine were placed in a flask. The top of the flask was covered with aluminum foil. The flask was gently heated. Soon, the flask was filled with a reddish gas. What change of state took place? Explain your answer.

_____

_____

_____

_____

10. Predicting Consequences Would using dry ice in your holiday punch cause it to become watery after several hours? Why or why not?

_____

_____

_____

_____

_____

Skills Worksheet

Chapter Review

USING KEY TERMS

For each pair of terms, explain how the meanings of the terms differ.

1. *solid* and *liquid*

_____

_____

2. *Boyle's law* and *Charles's law*

_____

_____

3. *evaporation* and *boiling*

_____

_____

4. *condensation* and *sublimation*

_____

_____

UNDERSTANDING KEY IDEAS

Multiple Choice

_____ **5.** Which of the following statements best describes the particles of a liquid?
   a. The particles are far apart and moving fast.
   b. The particles are close together but moving past each other.
   c. The particles are far apart and moving slowly.
   d. The particles are closely packed and vibrating in place.

_____ **6.** Which of the following statements describes what happens as the temperature of a gas in a balloon increases?
   a. The speed of the particles decreases.
   b. The volume of the gas increases, and the speed of the particles increases.
   c. The volume of the gas decreases.
   d. The pressure of the gas decreases.

_____ **7.** Boiling points and freezing points are examples of
   a. chemical properties.   **c.** energy.
   b. physical properties.   **d.** matter.

Chapter Review *continued*

_____ **8.** Dew collecting on a spider web in the early morning is an example of
  a. condensation.   **c.** sublimation.
  b. evaporation.   **d.** melting.

_____ **9.** During which change of state do atoms or molecules become more ordered?
  a. boiling   **c.** melting
  b. condensation   **d.** sublimation

_____ **10.** Which of the following changes of state is exothermic?
  a. evaporation   **c.** freezing
  b. melting   **d.** All of the above

_____ **11.** What happens to the volume of a gas inside a cylinder if the temperature does not change but the pressure is reduced?
  a. The volume of the gas increases.
  b. The volume of the gas stays the same.
  c. The volume of the gas decreases.
  d. There is not enough information to determine the answer.

_____ **12.** The atoms and molecules in matter
  a. are attracted to one another.
  b. are constantly moving.
  c. move faster at higher temperatures.
  d. All of the above

Short Answer

13. Explain why liquid water takes the shape of its container but an ice cube does not.

_____

_____

_____

_____

14. Rank solids, liquids, and gases in order of particle speed from the highest speed to the lowest speed.

_____

_____

_____

_____

MATH SKILLS

15. Kate placed 100 mL of water in five different pans, placed the pans on a windowsill for a week, and measured how much water evaporated from each pan. Draw a graph of her data, which is shown below. Place surface area on the x-axis and volume evaporated on the y-axis. Is the graph linear or nonlinear? What does this information tell you?

Pan number	1	2	3	4	5
Surface area (cm^2)	44	82	20	30	65
Volume evaporated (mL)	42	79	19	29	62

CRITICAL THINKING

16. Concept Mapping Use the following terms to create a concept map:

states of matter   solid   liquid
gas   changes of state   freezing
vaporization   condensation   melting

Chapter Review *continued*

17. Analyzing Ideas Water can be split to form two new substances, hydrogen and oxygen. Is this a change of state? Explain your answer.

_____

_____

_____

_____

18. Applying Concepts After taking a shower, you notice that small droplets of water cover the mirror. Explain how this happens. Be sure to describe where the water comes from and the changes it goes through.

_____

_____

_____

_____

_____

19. Analyzing Methods To protect their crops during freezing temperatures, orange growers spray water onto the trees and allow it to freeze. In terms of energy lost and energy gained, explain why this practice protects the oranges from damage.

_____

_____

_____

_____

20. Making Inferences At sea level, water boils at 100°C, while methane boils at −161°C. Which of these substances has a stronger force of attraction between its particles? Explain your reasoning.

_____

_____

_____

_____

_____

| Chapter Review *continued*

INTERPRETING GRAPHICS

Use the graph below to answer the questions that follow.

21. What is the boiling point of the substance? What is the melting point?

_____

_____

_____

_____

22. Which state is present at 30°C?

_____

_____

_____

_____

23. How will the substance change if energy is added to the liquid at 20°C?

_____

_____

_____

_____

Name _____ Class _____ Date _____

Reinforcement

Make a State-ment

Complete this worksheet after you finish reading the section "Behavior of Gases."

Each figure below shows a container that is meant to hold one state of matter. Identify the state of matter, and write the state on the line below the corresponding figure. Then write each of the descriptions listed below in the correct boxes. Some descriptions may go in more than one box.

Particles are close together.

Particles are held tightly in place by other particles.

Particles break away completely from one another.

changes volume to fill its container

changes shape when placed in a different container

has viscosity

obeys Boyle's law

amount of empty space can change

has definite shape

Particles vibrate in place.

does not change in volume

has surface tension

State of matter	Description
Liquid	
Gas	
Solid	

Name _____ Class _____ Date _____

Critical Thinking

What a State!

From the *Journal of Galactic Research:*

Amazing Discovery of New Planet

Nobel Prize–winning astrophysicist Dr. Philo Philosophus has announced the discovery of a new planet, named Phazon. Dr. Philosophus reports that although Phazon resembles Earth from a distance, it is really quite different. Matter on Phazon exists in three states—liquid, solid, and gas—as it does on Earth. On Phazon, however, each of these states of matter has one unique property.

Unique Properties of Matter on Planet Phazon

Solid	At high temperatures, solids always sublime from solid to gas.
Liquid	Liquids have no fixed volumes and must be stored in pressurized containers.
Gas	Gases have fixed volumes, as liquids on Earth do.

APPLYING CONCEPTS

1. Imagine that you have been chosen to visit Phazon. Do you think you will need special equipment to be able to breathe on the planet's surface? Explain your reasoning.

_____

_____

_____

_____

_____

2. Temperatures on Phazon can be quite low. If wood were available, would it be possible to make a fire for warmth? Explain.

HELPFUL HINT
A fire needs oxygen in order to burn.

_____

_____

_____

_____

_____

Critical Thinking *continued*

DEMONSTRATING REASONED JUDGMENT

3. The human body is composed mainly of liquids. Considering this fact, do you think it would be safe to visit planet Phazon without protective clothing? Explain your answer.

_____

_____

_____

_____

_____

_____

4. Give two examples of how cars on Phazon would differ from cars on Earth. Explain your reasoning.

_____

_____

_____

_____

_____

_____

_____

AGREE OR DISAGREE

5. Dr. Philosophus is considering a new project: finding Phazon's energy sources. On Phazon, some solids will sublime into gas and then change directly back into solids. Do you think the conversion of a gas to a solid would be an exothermic process? Explain.

_____

_____

_____

_____

_____

Assessment

Section Quiz

Section: Three States of Matter

Write the letter of the correct answer in the space provided.

_____ **1.** Which of the following statements is NOT true of atoms and molecules?
   a. They are tiny particles.
   b. They are always in motion.
   c. They are found in all matter.
   d. They never bump into each other.

_____ **2.** In a solid, the particles
   a. overcome the strong attraction between them.
   b. vibrate in place.
   c. slide past one another.
   d. move independently of one another.

_____ **3.** Crystalline solids
   a. include glass and rubber.
   b. may also be liquids.
   c. have particles that are not in a special arrangement.
   d. have particles in a repeating pattern of rows.

_____ **4.** Orange juice
   a. has a surface tension that is different from gasoline.
   b. changes volume when poured into a different container.
   c. has the same viscosity as other liquids.
   d. has a definite shape.

_____ **5.** A gas
   a. has a definite volume but no definite shape.
   b. has a definite shape but no definite volume.
   c. has fast-moving particles.
   d. has particles that are always close together.

Assessment

Section Quiz

Section: Behavior of Gases

Write the letter of the correct answer in the space provided.

_____ **1.** At higher temperatures
  a. particles in an object move faster.
  b. gas particles bump into walls less often.
  c. a gas contracts.
  d. particles in an object have less energy.

_____ **2.** Balloons can be twisted into shapes because
  a. the volume of a gas is constant.
  b. particles of gas can be compressed.
  c. volume is measured in two dimensions.
  d. the force exerted changes the number of particles.

_____ **3.** How does a basketball under high pressure compare to a basketball under low pressure?
  a. The particles of gas are farther apart.
  b. The particles of gas collide only with each other.
  c. The force exerted on the inside of the ball is lower.
  d. There are more particles of gas.

_____ **4.** Boyle's law states that for a fixed amount of gas
  a. at a constant temperature, the volume of the gas is inversely related to pressure.
  b. at a constant temperature, the volume of the gas is directly related to pressure.
  c. at a constant pressure, the volume of the gas is directly related to temperature.
  d. at a constant pressure, the volume of the gas is inversely related to temperature.

_____ **5.** According to Charles's law
  a. decreasing the temperature of a gas causes the pressure on the molecules to decrease.
  b. decreasing the temperature of a gas causes the volume of a gas to increase.
  c. increasing the temperature of a gas causes the volume of a gas to increase.
  d. increasing the temperature of a gas causes the pressure on the molecules to increase.

Assessment

Section Quiz

Section: Changes of State

Match the correct definition with the correct term. Write the letter in the space provided.

_____ **1.** a change in which energy is gained by a substance as it changes state

_____ **2.** the change of state from a solid to a liquid

_____ **3.** the change of a substance from one physical form to another

_____ **4.** the pressure inside the bubbles of a boiling liquid

_____ **5.** the change of state from a solid directly to a gas

_____ **6.** the change of state from a liquid to a gas

_____ **7.** the change of a liquid to a vapor throughout the liquid

_____ **8.** a change in which energy is removed from the substance as it changes state

_____ **9.** the change of state from a gas to a liquid

_____**10.** the change of state from a liquid to a solid

a. change of state

b. melting

c. evaporation

d. boiling

e. condensation

f. sublimation

g. freezing

h. vapor pressure

i. exothermic

j. endothermic

Assessment

Chapter Test A

States of Matter
MULTIPLE CHOICE
Write the letter of the correct answer in the space provided.

_____ 1. Boyle's law explains the relationship between volume and pressure for a fixed amount of
    a. a solid.
    b. a liquid.
    c. a gas.
    d. any type of matter.

_____ 2. Which of these factors could affect the temperature at which water boils?
    a. the volume of water in the pot
    b. the atmospheric pressure at which the water is heated
    c. the amount of energy added to the water
    d. the type of fuel used to heat the water

_____ 3. How do the particles of water that evaporate from an open container differ from the particles that remain?
    a. The evaporated particles only have more speed.
    b. The evaporated particles have greater order.
    c. The evaporated particles only have higher energy.
    d. The evaporated particles have more speed and higher energy.

_____ 4. Which of the following occurs when a liquid becomes a gas?
    a. The particles give off energy.
    b. The particles break away from one another.
    c. The particles move closer together.
    d. The particles slow down.

_____ 5. According to Charles's law,
    a. heating a balloon will cause it to expand.
    b. crushing a closed container of gas will increase the pressure.
    c. pumping more air into a basketball will increase the pressure.
    d. filling a balloon with helium will cause it to rise.

_____ **6.** If you open a bottle of perfume, after a period of time, the people on the opposite side of the room will be able to smell it due to the process of
   a. condensation.
   b. evaporation.
   c. sublimation.
   d. vapor pressure.

_____ **7.** A drop of vinegar will flow and spread out but a drop of vegetable oil will form a bead. This is evidence that
   a. vegetable oil has a lower surface tension and lower viscosity than vinegar.
   b. vinegar has a lower surface tension and lower viscosity than vegetable oil.
   c. vegetable oil has a lower surface tension and higher viscosity than vinegar.
   d. vinegar has a lower surface tension and higher viscosity than vegetable oil.

_____ **8.** The melting point of salt is the same as its
   a. boiling point.
   b. condensation point.
   c. freezing point.
   d. sublimation point.

_____ **9.** A liter of gasoline will boil at
   a. a higher temperature than a milliliter of gasoline.
   b. a lower temperature than a milliliter of gasoline.
   c. the same temperature as a milliliter of gasoline.
   d. the same temperature as a milliliter of water.

_____**10.** In order for carbon dioxide gas to enter the air from dry ice, the dry ice must
   a. gain energy.
   b. boil.
   c. increase in pressure.
   d. undergo an exothermic change.

_____**11.** Which of the following statements is NOT true of all different types of matter?
   a. They are made up of atoms and molecules.
   b. The particles that make them up are always in motion.
   c. They are made up of extremely small particles.
   d. The particles that make them up move at the same speed.

| Chapter Test A *continued*

_____12. A graph that shows the change in temperature of a substance as it is
heated will show
a. a straight line as the substance melts.
b. a straight line as the substance freezes.
c. a rising line as the substance melts.
d. a falling line as the substance melts.

_____13. The reverse of condensation is
a. boiling.   **c.** freezing.
b. evaporation.   **d.** sublimation.

MATCHING

**Match the correct description with the correct term. Write the letter in the space
provided.**

_____14. It can be determined by measuring the speed
of molecules.

_____15. This happens when tomato soup boils.

_____16. Ice, water, and steam are all examples.

_____17. This is a state of matter in which atoms and
molecules are close together but can slide
past each other.

_____18. It has no definite volume.

_____19. It may be either crystalline or
amorphous.

_____20. It increases when the amount of force per
unit area increases.

_____21. This force acts on the particles of milk at the
surface of a glass of milk.

_____22. This can only be measured in three
dimensions.

_____23. This property of liquids is affected by the
strength of the attraction between the
molecules.

a. states of matter

b. viscosity

c. solid

d. liquid

e. surface tension

f. gas

g. temperature

h. volume

i. pressure

j. change of state

❚ Chapter Test A *continued*

Use the figure below to answer questions 24 and 25. Write the letter of the correct answer in the space provided.

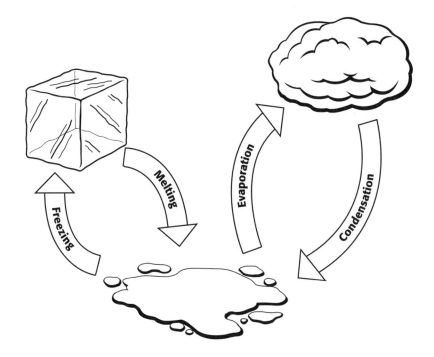

_____**24.** Which of the changes of state shown in the drawing are endothermic changes?
   a. freezing and evaporation
   b. freezing and condensation
   c. evaporation and melting
   d. condensation and melting

_____**25.** Which of the changes of state shown in the drawing are exothermic changes?
   a. freezing and evaporation
   b. condensation and freezing
   c. evaporation and condensation
   d. melting and evaporation

Assessment

Chapter Test B

States of Matter
USING KEY TERMS

Use the terms from the following list to complete the sentences below. Each term may be used only once. Some terms may not be used.

Charles's law	condensation	endothermic
evaporation	gas	liquid
sublimation	viscosity	Boyle's law

1. The drops of water that appear on the outside of a glass of cold juice on a

warm day are an example of _____.

2. The way a balloon decreases in volume when the temperature is decreased

illustrates _____.

3. The change of state from a liquid to a gas is _____.

4. Sublimation is a change of state from a solid directly to

a(n) _____.

5. In a(n) _____ change, energy is added to a substance.

6. One property of liquids is _____.

UNDERSTANDING KEY IDEAS

Write the letter of the correct answer in the space provided.

_____ **7.** Boyle's law explains the relationship between volume and pressure for
    a. a small amount of a gas.   **c.** a fixed amount of a gas.
    b. a large amount of a liquid.   **d.** a fixed amount of a liquid.

_____ **8.** Which of the following examples involves an exothermic change?
    a. ice melting in a glass of lemonade
    b. water boiling in a large pot
    c. gaseous water particles coming together to form droplets on a cup
    d. air in a bicycle tire gaining pressure on a hot day

_____ **9.** Which of these factors could affect the temperature at which water
    boils?
    a. the size and shape of the pot in which the water is heated
    b. the atmospheric pressure at which the water is heated
    c. the amount of heat added to the water
    d. the temperature of the water before it is heated

_____**10.** How do the particles of water that evaporate from an open container differ from the particles that remain?

a. The evaporated particles have less speed.

b. The evaporated particles have greater order and more speed.

c. The evaporated particles have less energy.

d. The evaporated particles have more speed and higher energy.

_____**11.** Hydraulic (liquid) systems, such as the brakes on an automobile, pass on forces because liquids tend to maintain a constant

a. volume. **c.** surface tension.

b. pressure. **d.** viscosity.

_____**12.** Which of the following occurs when a liquid becomes a gas?

a. The particles create energy.

b. The particles break away from one another.

c. The particles clump together.

d. The particles stop moving.

13. What is the relationship between the volume and the pressure of a gas when the temperature is held constant?

_____

_____

_____

14. How will this relationship between volume and pressure affect a long skinny balloon that is twisted into the shape of an animal?

_____

_____

_____

15. What will happen to the temperature of a pot of boiling water as the water evaporates?

_____

_____

_____

16. A container with a mixture of water and ice is at 0°C. What will happen if energy is added to or removed from the water?

_____

_____

_____

_____

CRITICAL THINKING

17. Explain why more time is required to boil pasta in Denver, Colorado, than in New Orleans, Louisiana.

_____

_____

_____

_____

_____

_____

18. To create special effects for movies and television shows, technicians often pour water over solid carbon dioxide, also called dry ice. What effect does this produce? Explain your answer.

_____

_____

_____

_____

_____

_____

19. On Thanksgiving Day a big parade is held in New York City with many giant helium-filled balloons. How will the weather affect the inflating of the balloons? Explain your answer.

_____

_____

_____

_____

_____

_____

INTERPRETING GRAPHICS

The following graph shows the different states of water as it is cooled. Examine the graph, and answer the questions that follow.

Cooling Curve of Water

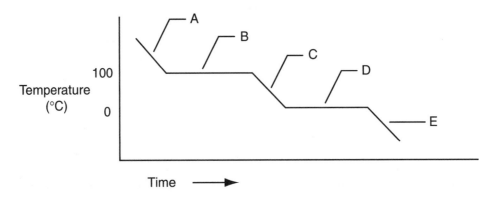

20. Which letters on the graph represent the three states of matter gas, solid, and liquid?

_____

_____

_____

21. Which letters on the graph represent the changes of state of condensation and freezing?

_____

_____

Assessment

Chapter Test C

States of Matter
MULTIPLE CHOICE
Circle the letter of the best answer for each question.

1. What type of matter does Boyle's law tell us about?

   a. solids

   b. liquids

   c. gases

   d. any kind of matter

2. What happens when a liquid becomes a gas?

   a. The particles give off energy.

   b. The particles break away from each other.

   c. The particles move closer together.

   d. The particles slow down.

3. What is the same as the melting point of salt?

   a. its boiling point

   b. its condensation point

   c. its freezing point

   d. its sublimation point

4. Carbon dioxide gas can enter the air from dry ice. What has to happen to the dry ice?

   a. The dry ice must gain energy.

   b. The dry ice must boil.

   c. The dry ice must increase in pressure.

   d. The dry ice must go through an exothermic change.

Chapter Test C *continued*

MATCHING

Read the description. Then, <u>draw a line</u> from the dot next to each description to the matching word.

5. This can be found by measuring the ● speed of molecules.

    a. states of matter

6. This happens when soup boils. ●

    b. temperature

7. Ice, water, and steam are kinds of ● these.

    c. pressure

    d. change of state

8. This increases when the amount of ● force per unit area increases.

| Chapter Test C *continued*

FILL-IN-THE-BLANK

Read the words in the box. Read the sentences. <u>Fill in each blank</u> with the word or phrase that best completes the sentence.

| Charles's law | solid | liquid |
| volume | surface tension | gas |

9. The volume of a gas is related to its temperature. Pressure must be

constant. This is _____.

10. The amount of space that an object takes up is

its _____.

11. The particles of a crystalline _____ have

a three-dimensional pattern.

12. A state of matter with fixed volume, but not a fixed shape,

is a _____.

13. Gasoline has a low _____ and forms

flat drops.

14. The particles of a _____ are far apart.

MATCHING

<u>Draw a line</u> from each term to the matching number on the picture.

condensation   melting   evaporation   freezing

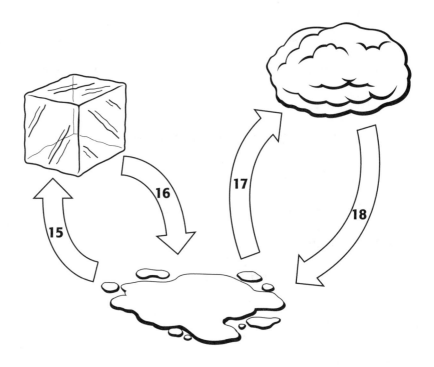

Performance-Based Assessment

OBJECTIVE

Observe the relationship between temperature and pressure.

KNOW THE SCORE!

As you work through the activity, keep in mind that you will be earning a grade for the following:

- how well you work with the materials and equipment (10%)
- the quality and clarity of your observations (50%)
- how well you analyze your observations (40%)

Using Scientific Methods

ASK A QUESTION

How is the volume of air affected by a change in its surrounding temperature?

MATERIALS AND EQUIPMENT

- 1 gal plastic milk container with cap
- heat-resistant gloves
- running hot and cold tap water

SAFETY INFORMATION

- Wipe up spills immediately; spilled water is a slipping hazard.
- Use caution when running hot water over the milk container; hot water is a burn hazard.

FORM A HYPOTHESIS

1. You will partially fill a plastic container with hot water and then cool it. Then you will partially fill the container with cold water and heat it. What do you think will happen to the container?

_____

_____

Effect of Temperature Change on Container of Water	
Container of hot water that is cooled	
Container of cold water that is heated	

| Performance-Based Assessment *continued*

TEST THE HYPOTHESIS

2. CAUTION: Wear heat-resistant gloves. Fill your plastic milk container about one-fourth full of hot water, and cap it.

3. Run a stream of cold water over the container for several minutes. Observe and record what happens to the container.

4. Remove the cap and replace the warm water in the container with cold water. Put the cap back on the container.

5. Run a stream of hot water over the container for several minutes. Observe and record what happens to the container.

ANALYZE THE RESULTS

6. Explain how the container of hot water reacted to the cold tap water.

_____

_____

_____

7. Explain how the container of cold water reacted to the hot tap water.

_____

_____

DRAW CONCLUSIONS

8. Why did the volume of the gas inside the milk container change in step 3?

_____

_____

9. Explain why atmospheric pressure outside the container caused this change in the container.

_____

_____

_____

_____

10. Why do you think water was used in the plastic container instead of just air?

_____

_____

_____

Assessment

Standardized Test Preparation

READING

Read each of the passages below. Then, answer the questions that follow each passage.

Passage 1 Did you know that lightning can turn sand into glass? If lightning strikes sand, the sand can reach temperatures of up to 33,000°C. That temperature is as hot as the surface of the sun! This <u>intense</u> heat melts the sand into a liquid. The liquid quickly cools and hardens into glass. This glass is a rare and beautiful type of natural glass called *fulgurite*.

The same basic process is used to make light bulbs, windows, and bottles. But instead of lightning, glassmakers use hot ovens to melt solid silica (the main ingredient of sand) and other ingredients into liquid glass. Then, before the glass cools and solidifies, the glassmaker forms the glass into the desired shape.

_____ **1.** In the glassmaking process, what happens after the glassmaker forms the material into the desired shape?
   A Solid silica melts in a hot oven.
   B Solid silica is struck by lightning.
   C The glass melts and becomes a liquid.
   D The glass cools and solidifies.

_____ **2.** Which statement is an opinion from the passage?
   F Lightning can form fulgurites.
   G Fulgurites are beautiful.
   H Lightning heats the sand to 33,000°C.
   I Glassmakers use very hot ovens.

_____ **3.** In the passage, what does <u>intense</u> mean?
   A a small amount
   B gaseous
   C a great amount
   D causing something to melt

| Standardized Test Preparation *continued*

Passage 2 For thousands of years, people used wind, water, gravity, dogs, horses, and cattle to do work. But until about 300 years ago, people had little success finding other things to help them do work. Then in 1690, Denis Papin, a French mathematician and physicist, noticed that steam <u>expanding</u> in a cylinder pushed a piston up. As the steam then cooled and contracted, the piston fell. Watching the motion of the piston, Papin had an idea. He connected a water-pump handle to the piston. As the pump handle rose and fell with the piston, water was pumped.

Throughout the next hundred years, other scientists and inventors improved upon Papin's design. In 1764, James Watt turned the steam pump into a true steam engine that could drive a locomotive. Watt's engine helped start the Industrial Revolution.

_____ **1.** In the passage, what does <u>expanding</u> mean?
   A enlarging
   B enhancing
   C enforcing
   D disappearing

_____ **2.** According to the passage, how was steam used?
   F as a source of power for thousands of years
   G by Denis Papin only in France
   H to pump water in the late 1600s
   I in the steam engine first

_____ **3.** Which of the following statements is a fact from the passage?
   A Steam expands and causes a piston to fall.
   B When steam cools, it expands.
   C The invention of the water pump started the Industrial Revolution.
   D People began using steam as a source of power 300 years ago.

INTERPRETING GRAPHICS

Use the chart below to answer the questions that follow.

Freezing Points of Different Brands of Antifreeze	
Brand	**Freezing Point °C**
Ice-B-Gone	-5
Freeze Free	-7
Liqui-Freeze	-9
Aunti Freeze	-11

_____ **1.** Phillip wants to purchase antifreeze for his car. Antifreeze is added to the water in a car's radiator to lower the water's freezing point. The temperature in his area never falls below –10°C. Given the information in the chart above, which of the following brands of antifreeze would be the best for Phillip's car?
   A Ice-B-Gone
   B Freeze Free
   C Liqui-Freeze
   D Aunti Freeze

_____ **2.** Phillip wants to make a bar graph that compares the brands of antifreeze. If he puts the brand name of each antifreeze on the x-axis, what variable belongs on the y-axis?
   F Freezing point of water
   G Freezing point of water with antifreeze in it
   H Freezing point of the antifreeze only
   I Freezing point of the radiator

_____ **3.** Phillip's cousin lives in an area where it rarely freezes. The record low temperature for winter is –2°C. Which brand should Phillip's cousin purchase?
   A Ice-B-Gone
   B Freeze Free
   C Liqui-Freeze
   D Aunti Freeze

| Standardized Test Preparation *continued*

MATH

Read each question below, and choose the best answer.

_____ **1.** Gerard and three of his friends each want to buy a kite. The kites regularly cost $7.95, but they are on sale for $4.50. How much will their total savings be if they all purchase their kites on sale?

A $13.80

B $18.00

C $10.35

D $23.85

_____ **2.** Francis bought a 2 L bottle of juice. How many milliliters of juice does this bottle hold?

F 0.002 mL

G 0.2 mL

H 200 mL

I 2,000 mL

_____ **3.** Which of the following lists contains ratios that are all equivalent to 3/4?

A 3/4, 6/8, 15/22

B 6/10, 15/20, 20/25

C 3/4, 15/20, 20/25

D 3/4, 6/8, 15/20

_____ **4.** The Liu family went to the state fair in their home state. They purchased five tickets, which cost $6.50 each. Tickets for the rides cost $1.25 each, and all five family members rode six rides. Two daughters bought souvenirs that cost $5.25 each. Snacks cost a total of $12.00. What is the total amount of money the family spent on their outing?

F $61.25

G $140.50

H $62.50

I $92.50

Name _____ Class _____ Date _____

A Hot and Cool Lab

When you add energy to a substance through heating, does the substance's temperature always go up? When you remove energy from a substance through cooling, does the substance's temperature always go down? In this lab you'll investigate these important questions with a very common substance—water.

OBJECTIVES

Measure and record time and temperature accurately.

Graph the temperature change of water as it changes state.

Analyze and interpret graphs of phase changes.

MATERIALS

- beaker, 250 or 400 mL
- coffee can, large
- gloves, heat-resistant
- graduated cylinder, 100 mL
- graph paper
- hot plate
- ice, crushed
- rock salt
- stopwatch
- thermometer
- water
- wire-loop stirring device

SAFETY

PROCEDURE

1. Fill the beaker about one-third to one-half full with water.

2. Put on heat-resistant gloves. Turn on the hot plate, and put the beaker on the burner. Put the thermometer in the beaker. **Caution:** Be careful not to touch the burner.

3. Record the temperature of the water every 30 seconds in the table below. Continue doing this until about one-fourth of the water boils away. Note the first temperature reading at which the water is steadily boiling.

Table 1							
Time (s)	30	60	90	120	150	180	210	240
Temperature (°C)								
Time (s)	270	300	330	360	390	420	450	480
Temperature (°C)								

4. Turn off the hot plate.

5. While the beaker is cooling, make a graph of temperature (*y*-axis) versus time (*x*-axis). Draw an arrow pointing to the first temperature at which the water was steadily boiling.

6. After you finish the graph, use heat-resistant gloves to pick up the beaker. Pour the warm water out, and rinse the warm beaker with cool water.

Caution: Even after cooling, the beaker is still too warm to handle without gloves.

7. Put approximately 20 mL of water in the graduated cylinder.

8. Put the graduated cylinder in the coffee can, and fill in around the graduated cylinder with crushed ice. Pour rock salt on the ice around the graduated cylinder. Place the thermometer and the wire-loop stirring device in the graduated cylinder.

9. As the ice melts and mixes with the rock salt, the level of ice will decrease. Add ice and rock salt to the can as needed.

10. Make another copy of Table I. Record the temperature of the water in the graduated cylinder every 30 seconds. Stir the water with the stirring device.

Caution: Do not stir with the thermometer.

11. Once the water begins to freeze, stop stirring. Do not try to pull the thermometer out of the solid ice in the cylinder.

12. Note the temperature when you first notice ice crystals forming in the water. Continue taking readings until the water in the graduated cylinder is completely frozen.

13. Make a graph of temperature (*y*-axis) versus time (*x*-axis). Draw an arrow to the temperature reading at which the first ice crystals form in the water in the graduated cylinder.

ANALYZE THE RESULTS

1. Describing Events What happens to the temperature of boiling water when you continue to add energy through heating?

_____

_____

2. Describing Events What happens to the temperature of freezing water when you continue to remove energy through cooling?

_____

_____

_____

A Hot and Cool Lab *continued*

3. Analyzing Data What does the slope of each graph represent?

_____

_____

4. Analyzing Results How does the slope of the graph that shows water boiling compare with the slope of the graph before the water starts to boil? Why is the slope different for the two periods?

_____

_____

_____

_____

5. Analyzing Results How does the slope of the graph showing water freezing compare with the slope of the graph before the water starts to freeze? Why is the slope different for the two periods?

_____

_____

_____

_____

DRAW CONCLUSIONS

6. Evaluating Data The particles that make up solids, liquids, and gases are in constant motion. Adding or removing energy causes changes in the movement of these particles. Using this idea, explain why the temperature graphs of the two experiments look the way they do.

_____

_____

_____

_____

_____

_____

_____

_____

Name _____ Class _____ Date _____

Boiling Water Is Cool

MATERIALS

- syringe
- warm water

PROCEDURE

1. Remove the cap from a **syringe**.
2. Place the tip of the syringe in the **warm water** that is provided by your teacher. Pull the plunger out until you have 10 mL of water in the syringe.
3. Tighten the cap on the syringe.
4. Hold the syringe, and slowly pull the plunger out.
5. Observe any changes you see in the water. Record your observations.

_____

_____

_____

_____

_____

_____

_____

6. Why are you not burned by the boiling water in the syringe?

_____

_____

_____

_____

_____

Skills Practice Lab

DATASHEET FOR LABBOOK

Full of Hot Air!

Why do hot-air balloons float gracefully above Earth, but balloons you blow up fall to the ground? The answer has to do with the density of the air inside the balloon. *Density* is mass per unit volume, and volume is affected by changes in temperature. In this experiment, you will investigate the relationship between the temperature of a gas and its volume. Then, you will be able to determine how the temperature of a gas affects its density.

MATERIALS

- balloon
- beaker, 250 mL
- gloves, heat-resistant
- hot plate
- ice water
- pan, aluminum (2)
- ruler, metric
- water

SAFETY INFORMATION

Using Scientific Methods

ASK A QUESTION

1. How does an increase or decrease in temperature affect the volume of a balloon?

FORM A HYPOTHESIS

2. Write a hypothesis that answers the question above.

_____

_____

TEST THE HYPOTHESIS

3. Fill an aluminum pan with water about 4 cm to 5 cm deep. Put the pan on the hot plate, and turn the hot plate on.

4. Fill the other pan 4 cm to 5 cm deep with ice water.

5. Blow up a balloon inside the 500 mL beaker, as shown in your textbook. The balloon should fill the beaker but should not extend outside the beaker. Tie the balloon at its opening.

6. Place the beaker and balloon in the ice water. Observe what happens. Record your observations.

_____

_____

Full of Hot Air! *continued*

7. Remove the balloon and beaker from the ice water. Observe the balloon for several minutes. Record any changes.

_____

_____

8. Put on heat-resistant gloves. When the hot water begins to boil, put the beaker and balloon in the hot water. Observe the balloon for several minutes, and record your observations.

_____

_____

9. Turn off the hot plate. When the water has cooled, carefully pour it into a sink.

ANALYZE THE RESULTS

1. Summarize your observations of the balloon. Relate your observations to Charles's law.

_____

_____

_____

2. Was your hypothesis from step 2 supported? If not, revise your hypothesis.

_____

_____

_____

DRAW CONCLUSIONS

3. Based on your observations, how is the density of a gas affected by an increase or decrease in temperature?

_____

_____

_____

_____

Skills Practice Lab

Can Crusher

Condensation can occur when gas particles come near the surface of a liquid. The gas particles slow down because they are attracted to the liquid. This reduction in speed causes the gas particles to condense into a liquid. In this lab, you'll see that particles that have condensed into a liquid don't take up as much space and therefore don't exert as much pressure as they did in the gaseous state.

MATERIALS

- beaker, 1 L
- can, aluminum (2)
- gloves, heat-resistant
- hot plate
- tongs
- water

SAFETY INFORMATION

PROCEDURE

1. Fill the beaker with room-temperature water.

2. Place just enough water in an aluminum can to slightly cover the bottom.

3. Put on heat-resistant gloves. Place the aluminum can on a hot plate turned to the highest temperature setting.

4. Heat the can until the water is boiling. Steam should be rising vigorously from the top of the can.

5. Using tongs, quickly pick up the can, and place the top 2 cm of the can upside down in the 1 L beaker filled with water.

6. Describe your observations.

ANALYZE THE RESULTS

1. The can was crushed because the atmospheric pressure outside the can became greater than the pressure inside the can. Explain what happened inside the can to cause the difference in pressure.

_____

_____

_____

_____

Can Crusher *continued*

DRAW CONCLUSIONS

2. Inside every popcorn kernel is a small amount of water. When you make popcorn, the water inside the kernels is heated until it becomes steam. Explain how the popping of the kernels is the opposite of what you saw in this lab. Be sure to address the effects of pressure in your explanation.

_____

_____

_____

_____

_____

ANALYZING YOUR DATA

Try the experiment again, but use ice water instead of room-temperature water.

_____

_____

_____

_____

_____

_____

_____

_____

_____

_____

_____

_____

_____

_____

Activity

Vocabulary Activity

Know Your States

After you finish reading the chapter, try the crossword puzzle using the clues provided.

ACROSS

1. He said that as the volume of a gas increases, its pressure decreases.

5. change of state from a gas to a liquid

6. If a substance pours very slowly, it has a high _____.

7. change of state from a solid to a gas

11. this property is affected by the number of times particles of gas hit the inside of a container

13. changes shape and volume to fit container

14. changes shape but doesn't change volume

15. the law that describes the relationship between volume and temperature of a gas when pressure is constant

DOWN

1. during this process hot water changes to steam

2. how your body is cooled when you perspire

3. to change state from a solid to a liquid

4. can only be measured in three dimensions

7. a change of _____ occurs during both freezing and melting

8. exists in three physical states

9. a measure of the movement of particles in a substance

10. Liquids form spherical drops because of this property.

12. does not change shape when placed in a different container

Vocabulary Activity *continued*

Activity

SciLinks Activity

SOLIDS, LIQUIDS, AND GASES

Go to www.scilinks.org. To find links related to solids, liquids, and gases, type the keyword HSM1420. Then use the links to answer the following questions about solids, liquids, and gases.

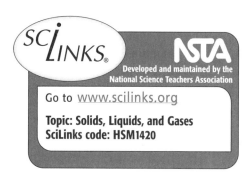

Go to www.scilinks.org

Topic: Solids, Liquids, and Gases
SciLinks code: HSM1420

1. What are some characteristics of solids?

_____

_____

2. What are some characteristics of liquids?

_____

_____

3. What are some characteristics of gases?

_____

_____

In the diagram below, compare solids, liquids, and gases. Where one or more circles overlap, draw an arrow to the area of overlap and list the ways that those states of matter are alike. Where the circles do not overlap, list the ways that each of these states of matter is unique.

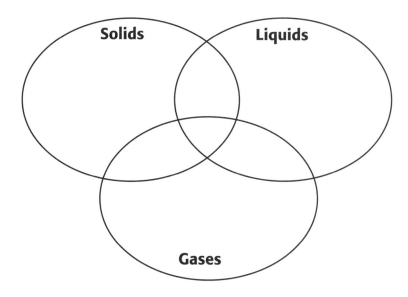

Performance-Based Assessment

Teacher Notes and Answer Key

PURPOSE

Students will observe Charles's law in action. Students then use their knowledge of the relationship between temperature and pressure to answer questions.

Rebecca Ferguson
Northridge Middle School
North Richland Hills, Texas

TIME REQUIRED

One 45-minute class period. Students will need 15 minutes at the activity station and 30 minutes to answer the analysis questions.

RATING

Easy ◄──── 1 2 3 4 ────► Hard

Teacher Prep–1
Student Set-Up–1
Concept Level–2
Clean Up–1

ADVANCE PREPARATION

Equip each activity station with the necessary materials.

SAFETY INFORMATION

Spilled water is a slipping hazard. Wipe up spills immediately. Hot water is a burn hazard. Have students use caution when running hot water over the milk container.

TEACHING STRATEGIES

This activity works best in groups of 2–3 students. The changes in volume of the milk containers in this activity demonstrate the effects of Charles's law.

BACKGROUND INFORMATION

Charles's law states that for a fixed amount of gas at a constant pressure, the volume of the gas increases as its temperature increases.

Performance-Based Assessment *continued*

Evaluation Strategies

Use the following rubric to help evaluate student performance.

Rubric for Assessment

Possible points	Appropriate use of materials and equipment (10 points possible)
10–7	Successful completion of activity; safe and careful handling of materials and equipment; attention to detail; superior lab skills
6–4	Activity is generally complete; successful use of materials and equipment; sound knowledge of lab techniques; somewhat unfocused performance
3–1	Attempts to complete activity yield inadequate results; sloppy lab technique; apparent lack of skill
	Quality and clarity of observations (50 points possible)
50–40	Superior observations stated clearly and accurately; high level of detail; correct usage of units of measurement
39–20	Accurate observations; moderate level of detail; correct usage of units of measurement
19–10	Complete observations but expressed in unclear manner; may include minor inaccuracies; attempts to use units of measurement include inconsistencies
9–1	Erroneous, incomplete, or unclear observations; lack of accuracy, details, units of measurement
	Analysis of observations (40 points possible)
40–25	Clear, detailed explanation shows superior knowledge of Charles's law
24–15	Adequate understanding of Charles's law with minor difficulty in expression
14–1	Poor understanding of Charles's law; explanation unclear or not relevant to activity; substantial factual errors

Name _____ Class _____ Date _____

Performance-Based Assessment

OBJECTIVE

Observe the relationship between temperature and pressure.

KNOW THE SCORE!

As you work through the activity, keep in mind that you will be earning a grade for the following:

• how well you work with the materials and equipment (10%)

• the quality and clarity of your observations (50%)

• how well you analyze your observations (40%)

Using Scientific Methods

ASK A QUESTION

How is the volume of air affected by a change in its surrounding temperature?

MATERIALS AND EQUIPMENT

• 1 gal plastic milk container with cap   • running hot and cold tap water

• heat-resistant gloves

SAFETY INFORMATION

• Wipe up spills immediately; spilled water is a slipping hazard.

• Use caution when running hot water over the milk container; hot water is a burn hazard.

FORM A HYPOTHESIS

1. You will partially fill a plastic container with hot water and then cool it. Then you will partially fill the container with cold water and heat it. What do you think will happen to the container?

Answers will vary. Sample answer: I think it will shrink when the hot water

in it is cooled and expand when the cold water in it is heated.

Effect of Temperature Change on Container of Water	
Container of hot water that is cooled	**The milk container caved in as the cold water ran over it.**
Container of cold water that is heated	**The milk container swelled up as the warm water ran over it.**

Name _____ Class _____ Date _____

Performance-Based Assessment *continued*

TEST THE HYPOTHESIS

2. CAUTION: Wear heat-resistant gloves. Fill your plastic milk container about one-fourth full of hot water, and cap it.

3. Run a stream of cold water over the container for several minutes. Observe and record what happens to the container.

4. Remove the cap and replace the warm water in the container with cold water. Put the cap back on the container.

5. Run a stream of hot water over the container for several minutes. Observe and record what happens to the container.

ANALYZE THE RESULTS

6. Explain how the container of hot water reacted to the cold tap water.

The cold tap water cooled the air inside the milk container, and the volume

of the air inside decreased. Steam in the milk container also condensed into

water.

7. Explain how the container of cold water reacted to the hot tap water.

The stream of hot tap water warmed the air inside the milk container, and

the volume of air increased.

DRAW CONCLUSIONS

8. Why did the volume of the gas inside the milk container change in step 3?

Gas takes up less volume in colder temperatures. Also, water takes up less

volume than steam.

9. Explain why atmospheric pressure outside the container caused this change in the container.

Air inside the container was cooled by the stream of cold water. The cooled

air inside the container created less pressure against the container than the

warmer air. Because the atmospheric pressure outside the container was

greater than the atmospheric pressure inside, the container caved in.

10. Why do you think water was used in the plastic container instead of just air?

Answers will vary. Sample answer: The water was used to hold the heat

because air loses heat much more quickly than water does.

Skills Practice Lab

A Hot and Cool Lab

Teacher Notes
TIME REQUIRED

One or two 45-minute class periods

C. John Graves
Monforton Middle School
Boseman, Montana

RATING

Easy ◄——1——2——3——4——► Hard

Teacher Prep–3
Student Set-Up–2
Concept Level–3
Clean Up–2

MATERIALS

The materials listed are for a group of 3–4 students.

SAFETY INFORMATION

Remind students to review all safety cautions and icons before beginning this lab activity.

PREPARATION NOTES

To construct the wire-loop stirring device, make a small loop at one end of a 25 cm piece of copper wire. The loop should easily fit into the graduated cylinder with the thermometer in place. Angle the loop so that it is perpendicular to the rest of the wire. At the other end of the wire, make a handle that extends in the opposite direction of the loop. Place the loop around the thermometer and using the handle to move the device up and down.

Name _____ Class _____ Date _____

Skills Practice Lab

DATASHEET FOR CHAPTER LAB

A Hot and Cool Lab

When you add energy to a substance through heating, does the substance's temperature always go up? When you remove energy from a substance through cooling, does the substance's temperature always go down? In this lab you'll investigate these important questions with a very common substance—water.

OBJECTIVES

Measure and record time and temperature accurately.

Graph the temperature change of water as it changes state.

Analyze and interpret graphs of phase changes.

MATERIALS

- beaker, 250 or 400 mL
- coffee can, large
- gloves, heat-resistant
- graduated cylinder, 100 mL
- graph paper
- hot plate
- ice, crushed
- rock salt
- stopwatch
- thermometer
- water
- wire-loop stirring device

SAFETY ◈ ◈ ◈ ◈ ◈

PROCEDURE

1. Fill the beaker about one-third to one-half full with water.

2. Put on heat-resistant gloves. Turn on the hot plate, and put the beaker on the burner. Put the thermometer in the beaker. **Caution:** Be careful not to touch the burner.

3. Record the temperature of the water every 30 seconds in the table below. Continue doing this until about one-fourth of the water boils away. Note the first temperature reading at which the water is steadily boiling.

Table 1							
Time (s)	30	60	90	120	150	180	210	240
Temperature (°C)								
Time (s)	270	300	330	360	390	420	450	480
Temperature (°C)								

Name _____ Class _____ Date _____

A Hot and Cool Lab *continued*

4. Turn off the hot plate.

5. While the beaker is cooling, make a graph of temperature (y-axis) versus time (x-axis). Draw an arrow pointing to the first temperature at which the water was steadily boiling.

6. After you finish the graph, use heat-resistant gloves to pick up the beaker. Pour the warm water out, and rinse the warm beaker with cool water.

    Caution: Even after cooling, the beaker is still too warm to handle without gloves.

7. Put approximately 20 mL of water in the graduated cylinder.

8. Put the graduated cylinder in the coffee can, and fill in around the graduated cylinder with crushed ice. Pour rock salt on the ice around the graduated cylinder. Place the thermometer and the wire-loop stirring device in the graduated cylinder.

9. As the ice melts and mixes with the rock salt, the level of ice will decrease. Add ice and rock salt to the can as needed.

10. Make another copy of Table I. Record the temperature of the water in the graduated cylinder every 30 seconds. Stir the water with the stirring device.

    Caution: Do not stir with the thermometer.

11. Once the water begins to freeze, stop stirring. Do not try to pull the thermometer out of the solid ice in the cylinder.

12. Note the temperature when you first notice ice crystals forming in the water. Continue taking readings until the water in the graduated cylinder is completely frozen.

13. Make a graph of temperature (y-axis) versus time (x-axis). Draw an arrow to the temperature reading at which the first ice crystals form in the water in the graduated cylinder.

ANALYZE THE RESULTS

1. **Describing Events** What happens to the temperature of boiling water when you continue to add energy through heating?

    Adding energy to liquid water makes the particles speed up, thereby increas-

    ing the temperature.

2. **Describing Events** What happens to the temperature of freezing water when you continue to remove energy through cooling?

    When energy is removed, the temperature stops falling, and the liquid turns

    to solid. At this point, the particles have less energy, but the temperature of

    the water stays the same.

Name _____ Class _____ Date _____

A Hot and Cool Lab *continued*

3. Analyzing Data What does the slope of each graph represent?

The slope of each graph represents the rate of temperature change.

_____

4. Analyzing Results How does the slope of the graph that shows water boiling compare with the slope of the graph before the water starts to boil? Why is the slope different for the two periods?

The slope is less steep (line should be horizontal) when the

water starts to boil. The slope is different because the energy added to the

water through heating is making steam rather than increasing the temperature.

_____

5. Analyzing Results How does the slope of the graph showing water freezing compare with the slope of the graph before the water starts to freeze? Why is the slope different for the two periods?

The slope is less steep (the line should be horizontal) when the water starts

to freeze. The slope is different because the removal of energy from the

water allows crystal structures (ice) to form rather than decreasing the

temperature.

DRAW CONCLUSIONS

6. Evaluating Data The particles that make up solids, liquids, and gases are in constant motion. Adding or removing energy causes changes in the movement of these particles. Using this idea, explain why the temperature graphs of the two experiments look the way they do.

When the particles speed up enough, water can become gas (steam), which

has more energy at the same temperature. Even though energy is being

added the whole time, the temperature stops rising when the liquid starts

changing into a gas. When the particles slow down enough, the water can

become solid ice, which has less energy at the same temperature. Even

though energy is being removed the whole time, the temperature stops

falling when the liquid starts changing to a solid. This explains the parts of

the graphs that level off.

Name _____ Class _____ Date _____

Quick Lab

Boiling Water Is Cool

MATERIALS

- syringe
- warm water

PROCEDURE

1. Remove the cap from a **syringe**.

2. Place the tip of the syringe in the **warm water** that is provided by your teacher. Pull the plunger out until you have 10 mL of water in the syringe.

3. Tighten the cap on the syringe.

4. Hold the syringe, and slowly pull the plunger out.

5. Observe any changes you see in the water. Record your observations.

Bubbles form in the water as the plunger is pulled out.

_____

_____

_____

_____

_____

_____

6. Why are you not burned by the boiling water in the syringe?

The boiling water is not 100°C. The lower pressure causes the water to boil

at a much lower temperature.

_____

_____

_____

_____

Safety Caution: Remind all students to review all safety cautions and icons before beginning this activity. Since the temperature of the water required depends on the size of the syringes used, it would be best to determine the necessary temperature for the syringes your students will be using.

Skills Practice Lab

DATASHEET FOR LABBOOK

Full of Hot Air!

Sharon L. Woolf
Langston Hughes Middle School
Reston, Virginia

Teacher Notes
TIME REQUIRED

One 45-minute class period

RATING

Easy ←——1——2——3——4——→ Hard

Teacher Prep–2
Student Set-Up–2
Concept Level–3
Clean Up–2

SAFETY CAUTION

Keep all power cords away from the beakers and pans of hot water. Be careful—hot plates may stay hot for a long time. Students should wear heat-resistant gloves when handling the hot beaker.

Name _____ Class _____ Date _____

Skills Practice Lab)   **DATASHEET FOR LABBOOK**

Full of Hot Air!

Why do hot-air balloons float gracefully above Earth, but balloons you blow up fall to the ground? The answer has to do with the density of the air inside the balloon. *Density* is mass per unit volume, and volume is affected by changes in temperature. In this experiment, you will investigate the relationship between the temperature of a gas and its volume. Then, you will be able to determine how the temperature of a gas affects its density.

MATERIALS

- balloon
- beaker, 250 mL
- gloves, heat-resistant
- hot plate
- ice water
- pan, aluminum (2)
- ruler, metric
- water

SAFETY INFORMATION

Using Scientific Methods

ASK A QUESTION

1. How does an increase or decrease in temperature affect the volume of a balloon?

FORM A HYPOTHESIS

2. Write a hypothesis that answers the question above.

_____

_____

TEST THE HYPOTHESIS

3. Fill an aluminum pan with water about 4 cm to 5 cm deep. Put the pan on the hot plate, and turn the hot plate on.

4. Fill the other pan 4 cm to 5 cm deep with ice water.

5. Blow up a balloon inside the 500 mL beaker, as shown in your textbook. The balloon should fill the beaker but should not extend outside the beaker. Tie the balloon at its opening.

6. Place the beaker and balloon in the ice water. Observe what happens. Record your observations.

_____

_____

Name _____ Class _____ Date _____

Full of Hot Air! *continued*

---

7. Remove the balloon and beaker from the ice water. Observe the balloon for several minutes. Record any changes.

_____

_____

8. Put on heat-resistant gloves. When the hot water begins to boil, put the beaker and balloon in the hot water. Observe the balloon for several minutes, and record your observations.

_____

_____

9. Turn off the hot plate. When the water has cooled, carefully pour it into a sink.

ANALYZE THE RESULTS

1. Summarize your observations of the balloon. Relate your observations to Charles's law.

Sample answer: When the balloon cooled, it contracted. When heated, it

expanded. These observations confirm Charles's law.

_____

2. Was your hypothesis from step 2 supported? If not, revise your hypothesis.

Answers may vary, depending on the original hypothesis. Sample supported

hypothesis: Increasing temperature increases the volume of a balloon, and

decreasing temperature decreases the volume of a balloon.

DRAW CONCLUSIONS

3. Based on your observations, how is the density of a gas affected by an increase or decrease in temperature?

As the temperature increases, volume increases, and mass remains constant.

Therefore, the density decreases. Conversely, density increases when

temperature decreases.

_____

_____

Skills Practice Lab

DATASHEET FOR LABBOOK

Can Crusher

Teacher Notes

TIME REQUIRED

One 45-minute class period

Lee Yassinski
Sun Valley Middle School
Sun Valley, California

RATING

Easy ◄—— 1   2   3   4 ——► Hard

Teacher Prep–1
Student Set-Up–1
Concept Level–2
Clean Up–1

SAFETY CAUTION

Remind students to review all safety cautions and icons before beginning this lab activity. Caution students to keep all power cords away from beakers and pans of hot water to prevent spills. Heat-resistant gloves may not be necessary if tongs are properly used.

Name _____ Class _____ Date _____

Can Crusher

Condensation can occur when gas particles come near the surface of a liquid. The gas particles slow down because they are attracted to the liquid. This reduction in speed causes the gas particles to condense into a liquid. In this lab, you'll see that particles that have condensed into a liquid don't take up as much space and therefore don't exert as much pressure as they did in the gaseous state.

MATERIALS

- beaker, 1 L
- can, aluminum (2)
- gloves, heat-resistant
- hot plate
- tongs
- water

SAFETY INFORMATION

PROCEDURE

1. Fill the beaker with room-temperature water.

2. Place just enough water in an aluminum can to slightly cover the bottom.

3. Put on heat-resistant gloves. Place the aluminum can on a hot plate turned to the highest temperature setting.

4. Heat the can until the water is boiling. Steam should be rising vigorously from the top of the can.

5. Using tongs, quickly pick up the can, and place the top 2 cm of the can upside down in the 1 L beaker filled with water.

6. Describe your observations.

ANALYZE THE RESULTS

1. The can was crushed because the atmospheric pressure outside the can became greater than the pressure inside the can. Explain what happened inside the can to cause the difference in pressure.

   Sample answer: The steam inside the can cooled and condensed. The volume

   of water (condensed steam) is smaller than the volume of the steam, so the

   pressure inside the can was reduced.

| Can Crusher *continued*

DRAW CONCLUSIONS

2. Inside every popcorn kernel is a small amount of water. When you make popcorn, the water inside the kernels is heated until it becomes steam. Explain how the popping of the kernels is the opposite of what you saw in this lab. Be sure to address the effects of pressure in your explanation.

Sample answer: When the water inside the kernel becomes steam, the water

expands about 100 times. The pressure inside the kernel increases. The

pressure outside is unchanged, so the pressure inside forces the kernel to

"explode."

_____

ANALYZING YOUR DATA

Try the experiment again, but use ice water instead of room-temperature water.

Sample answer: The can was crushed more quickly because the ice water

made the steam condense more quickly. So, the pressure inside the can

decreased further.

_____

_____

_____

_____

_____

_____

_____

_____

_____

_____

_____

_____

Answer Key

Directed Reading A

SECTION: THREE STATES OF MATTER

1. The three most familiar states of matter are solid, liquid, and gas.
2. A state of matter is the physical forms in which a substance can exist.
3. atoms; molecules
4. A
5. C
6. B
7. A
8. C
9. C
10. A solid is the state of matter that has a definite shape.
11. The particles in a crystalline solid are in an orderly, three-dimensional arrangement, in a repeating pattern of rows.
12. The particles in an amorphous solid do not have a special arrangement. Each particle is in one place, but the particles are not arranged in a pattern.
13. The particles in the liquid move quickly and slide past each other until the liquid takes the shape of the glass.
14. It shows that even when liquids change shape, they don't change volume.
15. surface
16. viscosity
17. A gas is the state of matter that has no definite shape or volume.
18. The cylinder contains helium particles that are forced close together. As helium enters the balloon, the atoms spread out, and the amount of empty space in the gas increases.

SECTION: BEHAVIOR OF GASES

1. C
2. temperature
3. The particles of gas in the balloon will have less energy, and the particles of gas will not push as hard on the walls of the balloon.
4. volume
5. container

6. pressure
7. The pressure is greater in the basketball because it contains more particles of gas in the same volume. More particles of gas hit the inside of the basketball. This makes the force on the inside surface increase, which produces greater pressure.
8. B
9. C
10. Boyle's law
11. As the balloon rises, the pressure of the gas decreases as the volume increases. The balloon would pop if it were completely filled before being released.
12. Charles's law
13. Charles's law

SECTION: CHANGES OF STATE

1. A
2. change of state
3. melting, freezing, evaporation, condensation, sublimation
4. No; gallium's melting point is lower than your body temperature. It would melt in your hand.
5. melting point
6. endothermic
7. freezing point
8. If energy is added, melting occurs. If energy is removed, freezing occurs.
9. exothermic
10. C
11. D
12. B
13. A
14. atmospheric pressure; boiling point
15. condensation
16. boiling
17. clump together
18. It's called "dry ice" because it doesn't melt. It changes from a solid directly into a gas through sublimation.
19. sublimation
20. temperature
21. change of state

Directed Reading B

SECTION: THREE STATES OF MATTER

1. B
2. A
3. C
4. B
5. A
6. D
7. C
8. C
9. viscosity
10. gas
11. D

SECTION: BEHAVIOR OF GASES

1. gas
2. temperature
3. volume
4. pressure
5. particles
6. gas laws
7. Boyle's law
8. Charles's law

SECTION: CHANGES OF STATE

1. freezing
2. melting
3. evaporation
4. condensation
5. melting
6. endothermic
7. freezing
8. exothermic
9. evaporation
10. change of state
11. boiling point
12. condensation
13. sublimation
14. endothermic
15. temperature

Vocabulary and Section Summary

SECTION: THREE STATES OF MATTER

1. states of matter: the physical forms of matter, which include solid, liquid, and gas
2. solid: the state of matter in which the volume and shape of a substance are fixed
3. liquid: the state of matter that has a definite volume but not a definite shape
4. surface tension: the force that acts on the surface of a liquid and that tends to minimize the area of the surface

5. viscosity: the resistance of a gas or liquid to flow
6. gas: a form of matter that does not have a definite volume or shape

SECTION: BEHAVIOR OF GASES

1. temperature: a measure of how hot (or cold) something is; specifically, a measure of the movement of particles
2. volume: a measure of the size of a body or region in three-dimensional space
3. pressure: the amount of force exerted per unit area of a surface
4. Boyle's law: the law that states that the volume of a gas is inversely proportional to the pressure of a gas when temperature is constant
5. Charles's law: the law that states that the volume of a gas is directly proportional to the temperature of a gas when pressure is constant

SECTION: CHANGES OF STATE

1. change of state: the change of a substance from one physical state to another
2. melting: the change of state in which a solid becomes a liquid by adding energy
3. evaporation: the change of a substance from a liquid to a gas
4. boiling: the conversion of a liquid to a vapor when the vapor pressure of the liquid equals the atmospheric pressure
5. condensation: the change of state from a gas to a liquid
6. sublimation: the process in which a solid changes directly into a gas

Section Review

SECTION: THREE STATES OF MATTER

1. Answers will vary. Sample answer: A liquid with a high viscosity does not flow very easily. Water can form spherical droplets because of its surface tension.
2. C
3. Answers will vary. Sample answer: The shape and volume of a solid does not change. Liquids take the shape of their container but their volume does not change. Gases completely fill their container and can vary in volume.

4. apple juice is a liquid; bread is a solid; a textbook is a solid; steam is a gas

5. Answers will vary. Sample answer: The particles of a gas are very far apart with empty space between them. If the gas is compressed, the particles are pushed closer together so the volume of the gas decreases. The particles of a solid are very close together and are strongly attracted to each other. Each particle is locked in place by the particles around it so the shape of the solid does not change.

6. The matter shown in the jar represents a solid.

7. Answers will vary. Sample answer: The particles have a strong attractive force between them that keeps them from moving apart from each other.

SECTION: BEHAVIOR OF GASES

1. Answers will vary. Sample answer: Charles's law states that when the temperature of a gas under constant pressure is decreased, the volume of the gas decreases.

2. A

3. Answers will vary. Sample answer: When gas particles become warmer they move more rapidly and hit the sides of their container more often and with greater force, thus increasing the volume of the gas.

4. The volume of the gas will double.

5. Answers will vary. Sample answer: The volume of the balloon will decrease. When the air particles inside the balloon become cooler, they slow down and do not hit the inside of the balloon as often so the balloon's volume decreases.

6. Answers will vary. Sample answer: The volume, pressure and temperature of a gas are all related. The volume of a gas can be changed by changing the temperature and the pressure.

7. Answers will vary. Sample answer: Boyle's law states that the volume of a gas is inversely proportional to its pressure. If the volume is tripled, the pressure of the gas would drop to one-third of the original value.

SECTION: CHANGES OF STATE

1. Melting changes a solid to a liquid. Freezing changes a liquid to a solid.

2. Condensation changes a gas to a liquid. Evaporation changes a liquid to a gas.

3. D

4. As a substance freezes, its particles lose some of their freedom of motion and become more orderly.

5. The temperature of the ice cube remains constant until the change of state is complete.

6. Evaporation occurs only at the surface of a liquid while boiling occurs throughout a liquid. Both evaporation and boiling are endothermic processes that change a liquid to a gas.

7. 18,000 mL

8. Sample answer: This reaction is exothermic; The temperature increased because energy was released during the reaction.

9. Sample answer: sublimation; The solid crystals were heated and turned directly into vapor.

10. Sample answer: no; Dry ice is solid carbon dioxide. It undergoes sublimation and turns into vapor.

Chapter Review

1. Solid is the state of matter in which the substance has a definite shape and volume. Liquid is the state in which the substance takes the shape of its container but has a definite volume.

2. Boyle's law states that when the pressure of a gas increases, its volume decreases. Charles's law states that when the temperature of a gas increases, its volume increases.

3. Evaporation is the change of a liquid to a gas at the surface of a liquid. Boiling is the change of a liquid to a gas throughout a liquid.

4. Condensation is the change of a gas to a liquid. Sublimation is the change of a substance from a solid to a gas without becoming a liquid.

5. B   **9.** B
6. B   **10.** C
7. B   **11.** A
8. A   **12.** D

13. Sample answer: The particles of liquid water can move past one another and take the shape of a container. Particles in an ice cube are locked in place and cannot move past one another. An ice cube holds its shape no matter what container you put it in.

14. gases, liquids, solids

15.

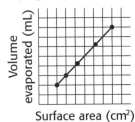

Surface area (cm²)

The graph is linear; both variables (surface area and volume evaporated) increase together.

16. An answer to this exercise can be found at the end of the teacher edition.

17. The splitting of water into hydrogen and oxygen is not a change of state because the substance (water) does not keep its identity during the change. The water is changed into two new substances, hydrogen and oxygen.

18. Sample answer: As you take a shower, some of the liquid water evaporates and becomes a gas. When the gaseous water touches the mirror, the water releases energy to the mirror and condenses into drops of liquid water.

19. Sample answer: Freezing is an exothermic change. As the water freezes, it releases energy. The oranges absorb some of this energy and warm up. (The ice also helps to insulate the oranges from the cold air.)

20. Sample answer: Water has a stronger force of attraction between its particles; A higher temperature, and therefore more energy, is required to separate the water particles from one another than is needed to separate the methane particles from one another.

21. 80°C, 20°C

22. liquid

23. The temperature of the liquid will rise.

Reinforcement

MAKE A STATE-MENT

Liquid: has surface tension; has viscosity; changes shape when placed in a different container; does not change in volume; Particles are close together.

Gas: Particles break away completely from one another; changes shape when placed in a different container; has viscosity; changes volume to fill its container; obeys Boyle's law; amount of empty space can change

Solid: Particles are close together; Particles vibrate in place; Particles are held tightly in place by other particles; does not change in volume; has definite shape

Critical Thinking

1. Answers will vary. Sample answer: It may be necessary to carry oxygen in portable containers because oxygen will probably not surround the planet evenly.

2. Yes; it would be possible to make a fire, but only for a short time. In areas where oxygen is not present, oxygen may have to be supplied to the fire manually. Also, the wood will sublime at high temperatures, leaving no fuel for the fire.

3. It would not be safe to visit without special protective clothing. It would be impossible to maintain liquids inside the human body because it is not a pressurized container.

4. Answers will vary. Sample answer: Phazon's cars would need pressurized gas tanks to keep gasoline inside. Their tires would be designed to hold a fixed volume of air.

5. Yes; the conversion would be an exothermic process. A gas would have to release a large amount of energy to convert directly to solid form.

Section Quizzes

SECTION: THREE STATES OF MATTER

1. D	4. A
2. B	5. C
3. D	

SECTION: BEHAVIOR OF GASES

1. A
2. B
3. D
4. A
5. C

SECTION: CHANGES OF STATE

1. J
2. B
3. A
4. H
5. F
6. C
7. D
8. I
9. E
10. G

Chapter Test A

1. C
2. B
3. D
4. B
5. A
6. B
7. B
8. C
9. C
10. A
11. D
12. A
13. B
14. G
15. J
16. A
17. D
18. F
19. C
20. I
21. E
22. H
23. B
24. C
25. B

Chapter Test B

1. condensation
2. Charles's law
3. evaporation
4. gas
5. endothermic
6. viscosity
7. C
8. C
9. B
10. D
11. A
12. B
13. The volume is inversely proportional to the pressure when the temperature is constant.
14. As the balloon is twisted and the volume of the space in which the air is contained is reduced, the pressure will increase.
15. The temperature of the water will remain the same.
16. If energy is added, the ice will melt, and if energy is removed, the water will freeze.

17. The boiling point of liquids decreases as atmospheric pressure decreases. At higher elevations, atmospheric pressure is reduced, so the boiling point of water will be lower than at sea level. This means that pasta boiled in Denver will cook at a lower temperature than pasta boiled in Louisiana. Pasta will have to cook longer in Denver.

18. Dry ice changes directly from a solid to a gas, producing a smoke like effect. Pouring water over the dry ice causes the carbon dioxide to sublime quickly. As a result, it turns to gas more quickly, producing a more dramatic smoke like effect.

19. The colder the weather is, the more helium will need to be pumped into the balloons for them to inflate to the desired level. This is because the colder the temperature, the slower the particles of gas move and the slower they hit the inside of the balloon. Thus, the colder it is, the lower the pressure. So, if it is cold out, more particles of gas will be needed in order to have the same level of pressure as with fewer particles on a warmer day.

20. A, gas; C, liquid; E, solid
21. B, condensation; D, freezing

Chapter Test C

1. C
2. B
3. C
4. A
5. B
6. D
7. A
8. C
9. Charles's law
10. volume
11. solid
12. liquid
13. surface tension
14. gas
15. freezing
16. melting
17. evaporation
18. condensation

Standardized Test Preparation

READING

Passage 1
1. D
2. G
3. C

Passage 2
1. A
2. H
3. D

INTERPRETING GRAPHICS
1. D
2. H
3. A

MATH
1. C
2. I
3. D
4. I

Vocabulary Activity

Across
1. Boyle
5. condensation
6. viscosity
7. sublimation
11. pressure
13. gas
14. liquid
15. Charles's law

Down
1. boiling
2. evaporation
3. melt
4. volume
7. state
8. matter
9. temperature
10. surface tension
12. solid

SciLinks Activity

1. particles are tightly packed; particles do not move from place to place; keep their shape; do not flow easily
2. Liquids: particles slide past each other
3. Gases: particles move freely; particles move very fast; particles are far apart; volume changes; can be compressed
Venn diagram: Answers will vary.
Sample answer: Solids, Liquids, and Gases: made up of atoms and molecules; particles vibrate;
Solids and Liquids: particles are very close together; keep a fixed volume; not easily compressed;
Liquids and Gases: particles have no regular arrangement; assume the shape of the container; flow easily

Lesson Plan

Section: Three States of Matter

Pacing

Regular Schedule: with Lab(s): N/A   without Lab(s): 1 day

Block Schedule: with Lab(s): N/A   without Lab(s): 0.5 day

Objectives

1. Describe the properties shared by particles of all matter.

2. Describe three states of matter.

3. Explain the differences between the states of matter.

National Science Education Standards Covered

UCP 1: Systems, order, and organization

UCP 2: Evidence, models, and explanation

PS 1a: A substance has characteristic properties, such as density, a boiling point, and solubility, all of which are independent of the amount of the sample. A mixture of substances often can be separated into the original substances using one or more of the characteristic properties.

KEY
SE = Student Edition   TE = Teacher's Edition
CRF = Chapter Resource File

FOCUS (5 minutes)

_ **Chapter Starter Transparency** Use this transparency to introduce the chapter.

_ **Bellringer, TE** Have students answer a question about the forms of water they find in the kitchen.

_ **Bellringer Transparency** Use this transparency as students enter the classroom and find their seats.

MOTIVATE (10 minutes)

_ **Demonstration, Particles in the Air, TE** Spray air freshener into the room and have students discuss possible explanations for why students smelled it at different times. (**GENERAL**)

TEACH (20 minutes)

_ **Reading Strategy, SE** Have students utilize paired summarzing when reading the section. (**BASIC**)

_ **Discussion, TE** Lead a discussion with students about the movement of particles in each of the states of matter. **(GENERAL)**

_ **Teaching Transparency, Models of a Solid, a Liquid, and a Gas** Use this graphic to introduce or review the characteristics of the three states of matter. **(GENERAL)**

_ **Directed Reading A/B, CRF** These worksheets reinforce basic concepts and vocabulary presented in the lesson. **(BASIC/SPECIAL NEEDS)**

_ **Vocabulary and Section Summary, CRF** Students write definitions of key terms and read a summary of section content. **(GENERAL)**

_ **Reinforcement, Make a State-ment, CRF** Students identify the states of matter of substances and their characteristics. **(GENERAL)**

_ **SciLinks Activity, Comparing States of Matter, SciLinks code HSM1420, CRF** Students research Internet resources related to states of matter. **(GENERAL)**

CLOSE (10 minutes)

_ **Reteaching, TE** Provide students with various samples and have them identify each according to its state. **(BASIC)**

_ **Quiz, TE** Students answer 3 questions about states of matter. **(GENERAL)**

_ **Alternative Assessment, TE** Students create a graphic organizer to describe the properties and characteristics of the three states of matter. **(BASIC)**

_ **Section Review, CRF** Students answer end-of-section vocabulary, key ideas, and critical thinking, and interpreting graphics questions. **(GENERAL)**

_ **Section Quiz, CRF** Students answer 5 objective questions about states of matter. **(GENERAL)**

Lesson Plan

Section: Behavior of Gases

Pacing

Regular Schedule:	**with Lab(s):** N/A	**without Lab(s):** 1 day
Block Schedule:	**with Lab(s):** N/A	**without Lab(s):** 0.5 day

Objectives

1. Describe three factors that affect how gases behave.

2. Predict how a change in pressure or temperature will affect the volume of a gas.

National Science Education Standards Covered

UCP 1: Systems, order, and organization

UCP 2: Evidence, models, and explanation

UCP 3: Change, constancy, and measurement

PS 1a: A substance has characteristic properties, such as density, a boiling point, and solubility, all of which are independent of the amount of the sample. A mixture of substances often can be separated into the original substances using one or more of the characteristic properties.

KEY

SE = Student Edition   **TE** = Teacher's Edition

CRF = Chapter Resource File

FOCUS *(5 minutes)*

_ **Bellringer, TE** Read three statements about gases and have student guess if they are true or false.

_ **Bellringer Transparency** Use this transparency as students enter the classroom and find their seats.

MOTIVATE *(10 minutes)*

_ **Demonstration, A Mini Explosion, TE** In two different sizes of containers, each with a plastic lid that can pop off, mix the same amount of baking soda and vinegar and have students compare the results. **(GENERAL)**

TEACH *(20 minutes)*

_ **Reading Strategy, SE** As they read the section, have students make a table to compare the effects of temperature, volume, and pressure on gases. **(BASIC)**

_ **Activity, Changes in Gas Volume, TE** Have students measure the circumference of a balloon after blowing it up, after it sits in the sun, and after it sits in the freezer. (**GENERAL**)

_ **Teaching Transparency, Boyle's Law/Charles's Law** Use this graphic to demonstrate Boyle's law and Charles's law.

_ **Directed Reading A/B, CRF** These worksheets reinforce basic concepts and vocabulary presented in the lesson. (**BASIC/SPECIAL NEEDS**)

_ **Vocabulary and Section Summary, CRF** Students write definitions of key terms and read a summary of section content. (**GENERAL**)

CLOSE *(10 minutes)*

_ **Reteaching, TE** Have students create a table to review the gas laws. (**BASIC**)

_ **Homework, TE** Have students write a research paper discussing the properties of plasma and where plasma is found. (**GENERAL**)

_ **Quiz**, TE Students answer 2 questions about states of matter. (**GENERAL**)

_ **Alternative Assessment, TE** Students create a concept map about Boyle's law and Charles's law. (**GENERAL**)

_ **Section Review, CRF** Students answer end-of-section vocabulary, key ideas, math, and critical thinking questions. (**GENERAL**)

_ **Section Quiz, CRF** Students answer 5 objective questions about behavior of gases. (**GENERAL**)

Lesson Plan

Section: Changes of State

Pacing

Regular Schedule: with Lab(s): 2 days   without Lab(s): 1 day

Block Schedule: with Lab(s): 1 day   without Lab(s): 0.5 day

Objectives

1. Describe how energy is involved in changes of state.

2. Describe what happens during melting and freezing.

3. Compare evaporation and condensation.

4. Explain what happens during sublimation.

5. Identify the two changes that can happen when a substance loses or gains energy.

National Science Education Standards Covered

UCP 3: Change, constancy, and measurement

SAI 1: Abilities necessary to do scientific inquiry

PS 1a: A substance has characteristic properties, such as density, a boiling point, and solubility, all of which are independent of the amount of the sample. A mixture of substances often can be separated into the original substances using one or more of the characteristic properties.

PS 3a: Energy is a property of many substances and is associated with heat, light, electricity, mechanical motion, sound, nuclei, and the nature of a chemical. Energy is transferred in many ways.

KEY
SE = Student Edition   **TE** = Teacher's Edition
CRF = Chapter Resource File

FOCUS (*5 minutes*)

_ **Bellringer, TE** Have students write a statement about how to change liquid water to ice or steam and then make a general prediction about changes of state.

_ **Bellringer Transparency** Use this transparency as students enter the classroom and find their seats.

MOTIVATE (*10 minutes*)

_ **Demonstration, Do Solids Move?, TE** Wrap masking tape around four students and have them model the motion of particles of a solid, as well as how the particles can break apart. (**GENERAL**)

TEACH (*65 minutes*)

_ **Reading Strategy, SE** Have students create a mnemonic device to remember the changes of state as they read the section. (**BASIC**)

_ **Using the Figure, TE** Have students answer questions about the figure and create a concept map to help them understand it. (**GENERAL**)

_ **Chapter Lab, A Hot and Cool Lab, SE** Students investigate what happens to water and its temperature as it is heated. (**GENERAL**)

_ **Guided Practice, TE** Have students work with you to create a sequence of state changes and then use the sequence to create a concept map. (**GENERAL**)

_ **Directed Reading A/B, CRF** These worksheets reinforce basic concepts and vocabulary presented in the lesson. (**BASIC/SPECIAL NEEDS**)

_ **Vocabulary and Section Summary, CRF** Students write definitions of key terms and read a summary of section content. (**GENERAL**)

_ **Critical Thinking, What a State!, CRF** Students read about the states of matter on an imaginary planet and draw conclusions. (**ADVANCED**)

CLOSE (*10 minutes*)

_ **Reteaching, TE** Use the teaching transparency to review changes of state. (**BASIC**)

_ **Homework, TE** Have students research how people in other cultures dress to fit the climate and prepare a poster to present their findings. (**GENERAL**)

_ **Quiz, TE** Students answer questions about states of matter. (**GENERAL**)

_ **Section Review, CRF** Students answer end-of-section vocabulary, key ideas, math, and critical thinking questions. (**GENERAL**)

_ **Section Quiz, CRF** Students answer 10 objective questions about states of matter. (**GENERAL**)

Lesson Plan

End-of-Chapter Review and Assessment

Pacing

Regular Schedule:	**with Lab(s):** N/A	**without Lab(s):** 2 days
Block Schedule:	**with Lab(s):** N/A	**without Lab(s):** 1 day

---

KEY
SE = Student Edition
TE = Teacher's Edition
CRF = Chapter Resource File

_ **Chapter Review, CRF** Students answer end-of-chapter vocabulary, key ideas, math, critical thinking, and interpreting graphics questions. (**GENERAL**)

_ **Vocabulary Activity, CRF** Students review chapter vocabulary terms by completing a crossword puzzle.

_ **Chapter Test A/B/C, CRF** Assign questions from the appropriate test for chapter assessment. (**GENERAL/ADVANCED/SPECIAL NEEDS**)

_ **Performance-Based Assessment, CRF** Assign this activity for general level assessment for the chapter. (**GENERAL**)

_ **Standardized Test Preparation, CRF** Students answer reading comprehension, math, and interpreting graphics questions in the format of a standardized test. (**GENERAL**)

_ **Test Generator, One-Stop Planner** Create a customized homework assignment, quiz, or test using the HRW Test Generator program.

States of Matter

MULTIPLE CHOICE

1. Which of the following statements is NOT true of atoms and molecules?
   a. They are tiny particles.   c. They are found in all matter.
   b. They are always in motion.   d. They never bump into each other.
   Answer: D   Difficulty: 1   Section: 1   Objective: 1

2. In a solid, the particles
   a. overcome the strong attraction between them.
   b. vibrate in place.
   c. slide past one another.
   d. move independently of one another.
   Answer: B   Difficulty: 1   Section: 1   Objective: 2

3. Crystalline solids
   a. include glass and rubber.
   b. may also be liquids.
   c. have particles that are not in a special arrangement.
   d. have particles in a repeating pattern of rows.
   Answer: D   Difficulty: 1   Section: 1   Objective: 2

4. Orange juice
   a. has a surface tension that is different from gasoline.
   b. changes volume when poured into a different container.
   c. has the same viscosity as other liquids.
   d. has a definite shape.
   Answer: A   Difficulty: 1   Section: 1   Objective: 2

5. A gas
   a. has a definite volume but no definite shape.
   b. has a definite shape but no definite volume.
   c. has fast-moving particles.
   d. has particles that are always close together.
   Answer: C   Difficulty: 1   Section: 1   Objective: 2

6. At higher temperatures
   a. particles in an object move faster.
   b. gas particles bump into walls less often.
   c. a gas contracts.
   d. particles in an object have less energy.
   Answer: A   Difficulty: 1   Section: 2   Objective: 1

7. Balloons can be twisted into shapes because
   a. the volume of a gas is constant.
   b. particles of gas can be compressed.
   c. volume is measured in two dimensions.
   d. the force exerted changes the number of particles.
   Answer: B   Difficulty: 2   Section: 2   Objective: 1

8. How does a basketball under high pressure compare to a basketball under low pressure?
   a. The particles of gas are farther apart.
   b. The particles of gas collide only with each other.
   c. The force exerted on the inside of the ball is lower.
   d. There are more particles of gas.
   Answer: D   Difficulty: 1   Section: 2   Objective: 1

9. Boyle's law states that for a fixed amount of gas
   a. at a constant temperature, the volume of the gas is inversely related to pressure.
   b. at a constant temperature, the volume of the gas is directly related to pressure.
   c. at a constant pressure, the volume of the gas is directly related to temperature.
   d. at a constant pressure, the volume of the gas is inversely related to temperature.
   Answer: A   Difficulty: 1   Section: 2   Objective: 2

10. According to Charles's law
    a. decreasing the temperature of a gas causes the pressure on the molecules to decrease.
    b. decreasing the temperature of a gas causes the volume of a gas to increase.
    c. increasing the temperature of a gas causes the volume of a gas to increase.
    d. increasing the temperature of a gas causes the pressure on the molecules to increase.
    Answer: C   Difficulty: 1   Section: 2   Objective: 2

11. Boyle's law explains the relationship between volume and pressure for a fixed amount of
    a. a solid.   c. a gas.
    b. a liquid.   d. any type of matter.
    Answer: C   Difficulty: 1   Section: 2   Objective: 2

12. Which of these factors could affect the temperature at which water boils?
    a. the volume of water in the pot
    b. the atmospheric pressure at which the water is heated
    c. the amount of energy added to the water
    d. the type of fuel used to heat the water
    Answer: B   Difficulty: 2   Section: 3   Objective: 3

13. How do the particles of water that evaporate from an open container differ from the particles that remain?
    a. The evaporated particles only have more speed.
    b. The evaporated particles have greater order.
    c. The evaporated particles only have higher energy.
    d. The evaporated particles have more speed and higher energy.
    Answer: D   Difficulty: 1   Section: 3   Objective: 5

14. Which of the following occurs when a liquid becomes a gas?
    a. The particles give off energy.
    b. The particles break away from one another.
    c. The particles move closer together.
    d. The particles slow down.
    Answer: B   Difficulty: 1   Section: 1   Objective: 3

15. According to Charles's law,
    a. heating a balloon will cause it to expand.
    b. crushing a closed container of gas will increase the pressure.
    c. pumping more air into a basketball will increase the pressure.
    d. filling a balloon with helium will cause it to rise.
    Answer: A   Difficulty: 2   Section: 2   Objective: 2

16. If you open a bottle of perfume, after a period of time, the people on the opposite side of the room will be able to smell it due to the process of
    a. condensation.   c. sublimation.
    b. evaporation.   d. vapor pressure.
    Answer: B   Difficulty: 2   Section: 3   Objective: 3

17. A drop of vinegar will flow and spread out but a drop of vegetable oil will form a bead. This is evidence that
    a. vegetable oil has a lower surface tension and lower viscosity than vinegar.
    b. vinegar has a lower surface tension and lower viscosity than vegetable oil.
    c. vegetable oil has a lower surface tension and higher viscosity than vinegar.
    d. vinegar has a lower surface tension and higher viscosity than vegetable oil.
    Answer: B   Difficulty: 3   Section: 1   Objective: 2

18. The melting point of salt is the same as its
    a. boiling point.   c. freezing point.
    b. condensation point.   d. sublimation point.
    Answer: C   Difficulty: 1   Section: 3   Objective: 2

19. A liter of gasoline will boil at
    a. a higher temperature than a milliliter of gasoline.
    b. a lower temperature than a milliliter of gasoline.
    c. the same temperature as a milliliter of gasoline.
    d. the same temperature as a milliliter of water.
    Answer: C   Difficulty: 2   Section: 3   Objective: 3

20. In order for carbon dioxide gas to enter the air from dry ice, the dry ice must
    a. gain energy.   c. increase in pressure.
    b. boil.   d. undergo an exothermic change.
    Answer: A   Difficulty: 1   Section: 3   Objective: 4

21. Which of the following statement is NOT true of all different types of matter?
    a. They are made up of atoms and molecules.
    b. The particles that make them up are always in motion.
    c. They are made up of extremely small particles.
    d. The particles that make them up move at the same speed.
    Answer: D   Difficulty: 1   Section: 1   Objective: 1

22. A graph that shows the change in temperature of a substance as it is heated will show
    a. a straight line as the substance melts.   c. a rising line as the substance melts.
    b. a straight line as the substance freezes.   d. a falling line as the substance melts.
    Answer: A   Difficulty: 2   Section: 3   Objective: 5

23. The reverse of condensation is
    a. boiling.   c. freezing.
    b. evaporation.   d. sublimation.
    Answer: B   Difficulty: 1   Section: 3   Objective: 3

24. Boyle's law explains the relationship between volume and pressure for
    a. a small amount of a gas.   c. a fixed amount of a gas.
    b. a large amount of a liquid.   d. a fixed amount of a liquid.
    Answer: C   Difficulty: 1   Section: 2   Objective: 2

25. Which of the following examples involves an exothermic change?
    a. ice melting in a glass of lemonade
    b. water boiling in a large pot
    c. gaseous water particles coming together to form droplets on a cup
    d. air in a bicycle tire gaining pressure on a hot day
    Answer: C   Difficulty: 1   Section: 3   Objective: 2

26. Which of these factors could affect the temperature at which water boils?
    a. the size and shape of the pot in which the water is heated
    b. the atmospheric pressure at which the water is heated
    c. the amount of heat added to the water
    d. the temperature of the water before it is heated
    Answer: B   Difficulty: 2   Section: 3   Objective: 3

27. How do the particles of water that evaporate from an open container differ from the particles that remain?
    a. The particles that evaporate have less speed.
    b. The particles that evaporate have greater order and more speed.
    c. The particles that evaporate have less energy.
    d. The particles that evaporate have more speed and higher energy.
    Answer: D   Difficulty: 1   Section: 3   Objective: 3

28. Hydraulic (liquid) systems, such as the brakes on an automobile, pass on forces because liquids tend to maintain a constant
    a. volume.   c. surface tension.
    b. pressure.   d. viscosity.
    Answer: A   Difficulty: 2   Section: 1   Objective: 2

29. Which of the following occurs when a liquid becomes a gas?
    a. The particles create energy.
    b. The particles break away from one another.
    c. The particles clump together.
    d. The particles stop moving.
    Answer: B   Difficulty: 1   Section: 3   Objective: 3

30. What type of matter does Boyle's law tell us about?
    a. solids   c. gases
    b. liquids   d. any kind of matter
    Answer: C   Difficulty: 1   Section: 2   Objective: 2

31. What happens when a liquid becomes a gas?
    a. The particles give off energy.
    b. The particles break away from each other.
    c. The particles move closer together.
    d. The particles slow down.
    Answer: B   Difficulty: 1   Section: 3   Objective: 3

32. What is the same as the melting point of salt?
    a. its boiling point   c. its freezing point
    b. its condensation point   d. its sublimation point
    Answer: C   Difficulty: 1   Section: 3   Objective: 2

33. Carbon dioxide gas can enter the air from dry ice. What has to happen to the dry ice?
    a. The dry ice must gain energy.
    b. The dry ice must boil.
    c. The dry ice must increase in pressure.
    d. The dry ice must go through an exothermic change.
    Answer: A   Difficulty: 1   Section: 3   Objective: 1

COMPLETION

34. The particles of a _____ are far apart and move independently of one another.
    Answer: gas   Difficulty: 1   Section: 1   Objective: 2

35. A liquid's resistance to flow is called _____.
    Answer: viscosity   Difficulty: 1   Section 1   Objective: 2

36. The shape and volume of matter in the _____ state do not change.
    Answer: solid   Difficulty: 1   Section: 1   Objective: 2

Use the terms from the following list to complete the sentences below.

Charles's law	condensation
endothermic	liquid
evaporation	gas
sublimation	viscosity

37. The drops of water that appear on the outside of a glass of cold juice on a warm day are an example of _____.

    Answer: condensation

    Difficulty: 1   Section: 3   Objective: 3

38. The way a balloon decreases in volume when the temperature is decreased illustrates _____.

    Answer: Charles's law

    Difficulty: 1   Section: 2   Objective: 2

39. The change of state from a liquid to a gas is _____.

    Answer: evaporation Difficulty: 1   Section: 3   Objective: 3

40. Sublimation is a change of state from a solid directly to a(n) _____.

    Answer: gas   Difficulty: 1   Section: 3   Objective: 4

41. In a(n) _____ change, energy is added to a substance.

    Answer: endothermic   Difficulty: 2   Section: 3   Objective: 1

42. One property of liquids is _____.

    Answer: viscosity   Difficulty: 1   Section: b1   Objective: 2

Use the terms from the following list to complete the sentences below.

Charles's law	solid
liquid	volume
surface tension	gas

43. The volume of a gas is related to its temperature. Pressure must be constant. This is _____.

    Answer: Charles's law   Difficulty: 1   Section: 2   Objective: 2

44. The amount of space that an object takes up is its _____.

    Answer: volume   Difficulty: 1   Section: 2   Objective: 1

45. The particles of a crystalline _____ have a three-dimensional pattern.

    Answer: solid   Difficulty: 1   Section: 1   Objective: 2

46. A state of matter with fixed volume, but not a fixed shape, is a _____.

    Answer: liquid   Difficulty: 1   Section: 1   Objective: 2

47. Gasoline has a low _____ and forms flat drops.

    Answer: surface tension

    Difficulty: 1   Section: 1   Objective: 2

48. The particles of a _____ are far apart.

    Answer: gas   Difficulty: 1   Section: 1   Objective: 2

SHORT ANSWER

49. What is the relationship between the volume and the pressure of a gas when the temperature is held constant?

   Answer:
   The volume is inversely proportional to the pressure when the temperature is constant.

   Difficulty: 1   Section: 2   Objective: 2

50. How will this relationship between volume and pressure affect a long skinny balloon that is twisted into the shape of an animal?

   Answer:
   As the balloon is twisted and the volume of the space in which the air is contained is reduced, the pressure will increase.

   Difficulty: 2   Section: 2   Objective: 2

51. What will happen to the temperature of a pot of boiling water as the water evaporates?

   Answer:
   The temperature of the water will remain the same until the change of state is complete.

   Difficulty: 1   Section: 3   Objective: 3

52. A container with a mixture of water and ice is at 0°C. What will happen if energy is added to or removed from the water?

   Answer:
   If energy is added, the ice will melt, and if energy is removed, the water will freeze.

   Difficulty: 1   Section: 3   Objective: 2

53. Do models of gases, liquids, and solids help to show the characteristics of these different states of matter? Explain your answer.

   Answer:
   Yes. Models show the relationships of the particles of matter to each other in terms of how far apart they are and whether or not they are moving.

   Difficulty: 3   Section: 1   Objective: 1

54. Students in a science class have been given three unknown solids. They need to find out if any two of them are the same. How could they do this?

   Answer:
   They could heat each one to its melting point and see if two substances have the same melting point. If so, they might be the same substance.

   Difficulty: 3   Section: 3   Objective: 2

55. Which is more like a solid: a liquid with a low viscosity or a liquid with a high viscosity? Explain your answer.

   Answer:
   A liquid with a high viscosity is more like a solid because it does not flow very easily, and solids do not flow.

   Difficulty: 3   Section: 1   Objective: 2

56. What happens to the gas particles in the tires of a bicycle when you sit on the bicycle? Explain why this happens.

   Answer:
   The pressure in the tires increases which causes the molecules of gas to be compressed and to come closer together.

   Difficulty: 2   Section: 2   Objective: 1

57. A solid room air freshener gradually loses mass and volume. How does this happen?
   Answer:
   The solid material turns to a gas through sublimation and the particles enter the air.
   Difficulty: 3   Section: 3   Objective: 4

58. Why is it possible for liquids to flow?
   Answer:
   The particles of a liquid are close together but can slide past each other because they move fast enough to overcome some of the attraction between them. As the particles move past each other, the material moves, or flows.
   Difficulty: 2   Section: 1   Objective: 2

59. If you place a beaker of rubbing alcohol in the freezer along with a thermometer, what would you expect to observe over a period of time?
   Answer:
   The temperature will go down and if the alcohol reaches its freezing point and begins to freeze, the temperature will stabilize. It will then continue to go down until it reaches the temperature of the freezer.
   Difficulty: 2   Section: 3   Objective: 2

60. You are given an unknown substance and asked to prove if it is a solid, a liquid, or a gas. How could you do so?
   Answer:
   Sample answer: You could show whether or not the substance kept its own shape when moved from one container to another, whether or not it could flow, and whether or not it could be compressed under pressure.
   Difficulty: 2   Section: 1   Objective: 3

61. During certain kinds of volcanic eruptions, rock flows out of Earth. What has happened to the rock to make this possible?
   Answer:
   The rock has been heated and has melted and become liquid, making it possible for it to flow.
   Difficulty: 2   Section: 3   Objective: 2

62. How is it possible to make a solid metal container in the shape of a pan?
   Answer:
   The metal is melted so that it will flow and then put into a mold in the shape of a pan. There it cools and freezes so that it holds the shape of the mold.
   Difficulty: 2   Section: 3   Objective: 2

63. A slow leak develops in a basketball. Explain what happens to the gas molecules and the pressure in the ball.
   Answer:
   The gas molecules move out of the ball and into the air so that there are fewer molecules in the same volume of space in the ball. As a result, the pressure inside the ball decreases.
   Difficulty: 2   Section: 2   Objective: 2

64. Is a snowflake a crystalline or an amorphous solid? How can you tell?
   Answer:
   It is an amorphous solid because it has a definite shape that results from the definite pattern of particles in the solid.
   Difficulty: 2   Section: 1   Objective: 2

65. A student wants to slow the motion of particles of a substance as much as possible. What should the student do?

Answer: Cool the substance as much as possible.

Difficulty: 2   Section: 3   Objective: 5

66. Your teacher floats a needle on the surface of a glass of water in a demonstration. What property of water is being demonstrated?

Answer: surface tension

Difficulty: 2   Section: 1   Objective: 2

67. What do you predict will happen to the volume of a gas if the temperature is increased and the pressure is also increased? Why?

Answer:

The temperature increase will cause the volume to increase, but the pressure increase will cause the volume to decrease. Depending on the amount of change of the temperature and the pressure, the volume will probably stay about the same.

Difficulty: 2   Section: 2   Objective: 2

MATCHING

a. change of state
b. melting
c. evaporation
d. boiling
e. condensation

f. sublimation
g. freezing
h. vapor pressure
i. exothermic
j. endothermic

68. ____ a change in which energy is gained by a substance as it changes state

Answer: J   Difficulty: 1   Section: 3   Objective: 1

69. ____ the change of state from a solid to a liquid

Answer: B   Difficulty: 1   Section: 3   Objective: 2

70. ____ the change of a substance from one physical form to another

Answer: A   Difficulty: 1   Section: 3   Objective: 1

71. ____ the pressure inside the bubbles of a boiling liquid

Answer: H   Difficulty: 1   Section: 3   Objective: 3

72. ____ the change of state from a solid directly to a gas

Answer: F   Difficulty: 1   Section: 3   Objective: 4

73. ____ the change of state from a liquid to a gas

Answer: C   Difficulty: 1   Section: 3   Objective: 3

74. ____ the change of a liquid to a vapor throughout the liquid

Answer: D   Difficulty: 1   Section: 3   Objective: 3

75. ____ a change in which energy is removed from the substance as it changes state

Answer: I   Difficulty: 1   Section: 3   Objective: 1

76. ____ the change of state from a gas to a liquid

Answer: E   Difficulty: 1   Section: 3   Objective: 3

77. ____ the change of state from a liquid to a solid

Answer: G   Difficulty: 1   Section: 3   Objective: 2

a. states of matter
b. viscosity
c. solid
d. liquid
e. surface tension

f.   gas
g.   temperature
h.   volume
i.   pressure
j.   change of state

78. ____ It can be determined by measuring the speed of molecules.

Answer: G   Difficulty: 1   Section: 2   Objective: 1

79. ____ This happens when tomato soup boils.

Answer: J   Difficulty: 1   Section: 3   Objective: 1

80. ____ Ice, water, and steam are all examples.

Answer: A   Difficulty: 1   Section: 1   Objective: 1

81. ____ This is a state of matter in which atoms and molecules are close together but can slide past each other.

Answer: D   Difficulty: 1   Section: a1   Objective: 2

82. ____ It has no definite volume.

Answer: F   Difficulty: 1   Section: a1   Objective: 2

83. ____ It may be either crystalline or amorphous.

Answer: C   Difficulty: 1   Section: 1   Objective: 2

84. ____ It increases when the amount of force per unit area increases.

Answer: I   Difficulty: 2   Section: 2   Objective: 2

85. This force acts on the particles of milk at the surface of a glass of milk.

Answer: E   Difficulty: 1   Section: 1   Objective: 2

86. ____ This can only be measured in three dimensions.

Answer: H   Difficulty: 1   Section: 2   Objective: 2

87. ____ This property of liquids is affected by the strength of the attraction between the molecules.

Answer: B   Difficulty: 1   Section: 1   Objective: 2

a. states of matter
b. temperature

c. pressure
d. change of state

88. It can be found by measuring the speed of molecules.

Answer: B   Difficulty: 1   Section: 3   Objective: 1

89. This happens when soup boils.

Answer: D   Difficulty: 1   Section: 3   Objective: 1

90. Ice, water, and steam are kinds of these.

Answer: A   Difficulty: 1   Section: 1   Objective: 1

91. It increases when the amount of force per unit area increases.

Answer: C   Difficulty: 1   Section: 2   Objective: 2

ESSAY

92. Explain why more time is required to boil pasta in Denver, Colorado, than in New Orleans, Louisiana.

    Answer:
    The boiling point of liquids decreases as atmospheric pressure decreases. At higher elevations, atmospheric pressure is reduced, so the boiling point of water will be lower than at sea level. This means that pasta boiled in Denver will cook at a lower temperature than pasta boiled in Louisiana. Pasta will have to cook longer in Denver.

    Difficulty: 3   Section: 3   Objective: 3

93. To create special effects for movies and television shows, technicians often pour water over solid carbon dioxide, also called dry ice. What effect does this produce? Explain your answer.

    Answer:
    Dry ice changes directly from a solid to a gas, producing a smoke like effect. Pouring water over the dry ice causes the carbon dioxide to sublime quickly. As a result, it turns to gas more quickly, producing a more dramatic smoke like effect.

    Difficulty: 2   Section: 3   Objective: 4

94. On Thanksgiving Day a big parade is held in New York City with many giant helium-filled balloons. How will the weather affect the inflation of the balloons? Explain your answer.

    Answer:
    The colder the weather is, the more helium will need to be pumped into the balloons for them to inflate to the desired level. This is because the colder the temperature, the slower the particles of gas move and the slower they hit the inside of the balloon. Thus, the colder it is, the lower the pressure. So, if it is cold out, more particles of gas will be needed in order to have the same level of pressure as with fewer particles on a warmer day.

    Difficulty: 3   Section: 2   Objective: 2

95. Compare and contrast Charles's law and Boyle's law. How are they similar? How are they different?

    Answer:
    Both deal with the behavior of gases under certain conditions of temperature, pressure, and volume. Both deal with a fixed amount of gas under changing circumstances. Boyle's law deals with the relationship between the volume and pressure of a gas at a constant temperature. Charles's law deals with the relationship between the volume of gas and the temperature when the pressure is constant.

    Difficulty: 3   Section: 2   Objective: 2

96. A student analyzed two unknown liquids and determined that they were different materials because one had a boiling point of 30°C and one had a boiling point of 31°C. Do you agree with the student's assessment? What suggestions would you give this student?

    Answer:
    Sample answer: The boiling points are so close that it is unclear whether they are the same substance or not. It would be a good idea to do further tests. The student could observe the viscosity and the surface tension of each liquid and compare them to gain additional information for a better supported determination.

    Difficulty: 3   Section: 3   Objective: 3

97. A scientist has two solids. One is crystalline and has a melting point of 36°C. The other is amorphous and has a melting point of 31°C. What conclusions can the scientist draw about the boiling points of these substances and their behavior as gases?

Answer:

The scientist can conclude that the boiling point of the crystalline solid is over 36°C and the boiling point of the amorphous solid is over 31°C, because the boiling points have to be higher than the melting points. As gases, these substances will behave as other gases do, according to Boyle's law and Charles's law. The fact that one is crystalline and the other is amorphous will have no effect.

Difficulty: 3   Section: 1, 3   Objective: 2, 3

98. Students in a science class have been given several unknown liquids and have been instructed to rank them in terms of their viscosity and the amount of surface tension they have. What should the students do in order to accomplish this task?

Answer:

Students should put a drop of each substance on a sheet of paper and observe the type of drop formed. A flat drop indicates a low surface tension and a rounder drop indicates a higher surface tension. They should pour each liquid and compare the ease with which it flows. A substance that flows easily has a low viscosity and one that is more resistant to flowing has a higher viscosity.

Difficulty: 3   Section: 1   Objective: 2

99. In what ways are the processes of condensation and evaporation similar to the processes of freezing and melting?

Answer:

All of these processes involve a change of state. Condensation and evaporation are opposite processes. Condensation is exothermic and involves a change from a gas to a liquid, while evaporation is endothermic and involves a change from a liquid to a gas. In the same way, freezing is exothermic, but involves the change from a liquid to a solid, while melting is endothermic and involves the change from a solid to a liquid.

Difficulty: 2   Section: 3   Objective: 2, 3

100. If a process opposite to sublimation could occur, what would it involve? Do you think such a process could exist? Why or why not?

Answer:

Sample answer: A process opposite to sublimation would involve a substance changing directly from a gas into a solid, without first condensing into a liquid and then freezing into a solid. I think it could exist because sublimation also exists. However, it would require something being cooled very, very fast so that it was too cold to become a liquid and didn't pass through that state of matter.

Difficulty: 3   Section: 3   Objective: 4, 5

101. A dent in a ping-pong ball that has no holes in it can be removed by placing the ball in boiling water. Explain why this will work.

Answer:

The ping-pong ball contains air, which is a gas. When the ball is placed in the hot water, the gas inside it is heated and expands, as described by Charles's law, which states that, as the temperature increases, the volume of a gas also increases when the pressure is constant for a fixed amount of gas. In this example, the pressure doesn't change and no gas is added to the ball or taken away.

Difficulty: 2   Section: 2   Objective: 2

102. You are sitting in your room and suddenly you smell popcorn. What has happened to enable you to smell the popping corn?

Answer:

The popcorn is heated to get it to pop, and in the process, something in the popcorn changes state from a solid to a gas. The gas leaks out of the container and enters the air. The particles move through the air until they reach you in your room and you smell them.

Difficulty: 2   Section: 1   Objective: 3

103. Have students create a graphic organizer in which they describe the properties and characteristics of the three states of matter discussed in this section. Have them include two examples of matter for each state.

Answer:

Answers will vary, but should show most of the following information. Solids: made up of atoms and molecules, particles vibrate, particles are very close together, keep a fixed volume, not easily compressed, do not flow easily, particles are tightly and regularly packed, particles do not move from place to place, keep their shape; liquids: made up of atoms and molecules, particles vibrate, particles are very close together, keep a fixed volume, not easily compressed, flow easily, particles have no regular arrangement, particles slide past each other, assume the shape of the container; gases: made up of atoms and molecules particles vibrate, particles are far apart, volume changes, can be compressed, flow easily, particles have no regular arrangement, particles move freely, particles move very fast, assume the shape of the container.

Difficulty: 3   Section: 1   Objective: 2,3

INTERPRETING GRAPHICS

Use the art below to answer the following questions.

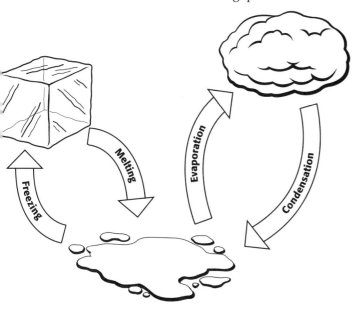

104. Which of the changes of state shown in the drawing are endothermic changes?
    a. freezing and evaporation
    b. freezing and condensation
    c. evaporation and melting
    d. condensation and melting

    Answer: C   Difficulty: 1   Section: 3   Objective: 1

105. Which of the changes of state shown in the drawing are exothermic changes?
    a. freezing and evaporation
    b. condensation and freezing
    c. evaporation and condensation
    d. melting and evaporation

    Answer: B   Difficulty: 1   Section: 3   Objective: 1

Use the art below to answer the following questions

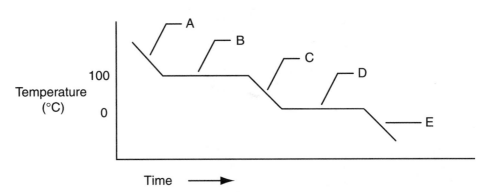

Cooling Curve of Water

106. Which letters on the graph represent the three states of matter: gas, solid, and liquid?
     Answer: A, gas; C, liquid; E, solid   Difficulty: 1   Section: 3   Objective: 3

107. Which letters on the graph represent the changes of state of condensation and freezing?
     Answer: B, condensation; D, freezing   Difficulty: 1   Section: 3   Objective: 3

TRUE/FALSE

108. ____ Changing the temperature of a gas has no effect on the volume of the gas.
     Answer: false   Difficulty: 1   Section: 2   Objective: 2

109. ____ Pressure in a gas-filled container is caused by gas particles hitting the walls of the container.
     Answer: true   Difficulty: 1   Section: 2   Objective: 1

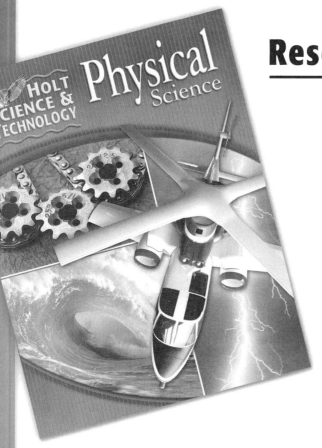

Chapter Resource File

3

Elements, Compounds, and Mixtures

CHAPTER 3

Skills Worksheet

Directed Reading A

Section: Elements

_____ **1.** Which of the following is NOT a physical or chemical change?
  a. crushing
  b. weighing
  c. melting
  d. passing electric current

ELEMENTS, THE SIMPLEST SUBSTANCES

2. A pure substance that cannot be separated into simpler substances by

physical or chemical means is a(n) _____.

3. A substance that contains only one type of particle is

a(n) _____.

PROPERTIES OF ELEMENTS

4. The amount of an element present does not affect the element's

_____.

5. Why does a helium-filled balloon float up when it is released?

_____

_____

Look at each property listed below. If it is a characteristic property of elements, write CP on the line. If it is not a characteristic property, write N.

_____ **6.** size

_____ **7.** melting point

_____ **8.** density

_____ **9.** shape

_____ **10.** mass

_____ **11.** volume

_____ **12.** color

_____ **13.** hardness

_____ **14.** flammability

_____ **15.** weight

_____ **16.** reactivity with acid

CLASSIFYING ELEMENTS BY THEIR PROPERTIES

17. What are some common properties that most terriers share?

_____

_____

18. All elements can be classified as metals, metalloids, or

_____.

19. An element that is shiny and that conducts heat and electric current well is

a(n) _____.

20. An element that conducts heat and electric current poorly, and can be a solid,

liquid, or gas is a(n) _____.

21. Elements that have properties of both metals and nonmetals

are _____.

Indicate whether the description applies to a metal, a nonmetal, or a metalloid. Write the correct letter in the space provided.

_____**22.** malleable

_____**23.** dull or shiny

_____**24.** poor conductors

_____**25.** tend to be brittle and unmalleable as solids

_____**26.** always shiny

_____**27.** also called semiconductors

_____**28.** always dull

_____**29.** somewhat ductile

_____**30.** boron, silicon, antimony

_____**31.** lead, tin, copper

_____**32.** sulfur, iodine, neon

a. metalloids

b. nonmetals

c. metals

Skills Worksheet)

Directed Reading A

Section: Compounds

1. List three examples of compounds you encounter every day.

_____

_____

COMPOUNDS: MADE OF ELEMENTS

_____ **2.** Which of the following is NOT true about compounds?
  a. Compounds join in specific ratios according to their masses.
  b. The mass ratio of a specific compound is always the same.
  c. Compounds are random combinations of elements.
  d. Different mass ratios mean different compounds.

3. When two or more elements are joined by chemical bonds to form a new pure

substance, we call that new substance a(n) _____.

4. A compound is different from the _____ that

reacted to form it.

PROPERTIES OF COMPOUNDS

_____ **5.** Which of the following statements is true about the properties of compounds?
  a. A property of all compounds is to react with acid.
  b. Each compound has its own physical properties.
  c. Compounds cannot be identified by their chemical properties.
  d. A compound has the same properties as the elements that form it.

6. Sodium and chlorine can be extremely dangerous in their elemental form. So how is it possible that we can eat them in a compound?

_____

_____

_____

Match the correct description with the correct term. Write the letter in the space provided.

_____ **7.** a poisonous, greenish yellow gas

_____ **8.** table salt

_____ **9.** a soft, silvery white metal that reacts violently with water

a. sodium chloride

b. chlorine

c. sodium

BREAKING DOWN COMPOUNDS

10. What compound helps give carbonated beverages their "fizz"?

_____

_____

11. Which elements make up the compound that helps give carbonated beverages their "fizz"?

_____

_____

12. The only way to break down a compound is through

a(n) _____.

COMPOUNDS IN YOUR WORLD

_____**13.** What compound is used by plants in photosynthesis to make carbohydrates?
a. nitrogen
b. ammonia
c. hydrogen
d. carbon dioxide

14. Aluminum is produced by breaking down the compound

_____.

Skills Worksheet)

Directed Reading A

Section: Mixtures

1. A pizza is a(n) _____.

PROPERTIES OF MIXTURES

2. A combination of two or more substances that are not chemically

combined is a(n) _____.

3. When two or more materials combine chemically, they form a(n)

_____.

4. How can you tell that a pizza is a mixture?

_____

_____

5. Mixtures are separated through _____ changes.

Match the correct method of separation with the each substance. Write the letter in the space provided. Each method may be used only once.

_____ **6.** crude oil

_____ **7.** aluminum and iron

_____ **8.** parts of blood

_____ **9.** sulfur and salt

a. distillation

b. magnet

c. filter

d. centrifuge

10. Granite can be pink or black, depending on the _____

of feldspar, mica, and quartz.

SOLUTIONS

_____**11.** Which of the following is NOT true of solutions?

    a. They contain a dissolved substance called a solute.

    b. They are composed of two or more evenly distributed substances.

    c. They contain a substance called a solvent, in which another sub-
stance is dissolved.

    d. They appear to be more than one substance.

12. The process in which particles of substances separate and spread evenly

through a mixture is known as _____.

13. In a solution, the _____ is the substance that is dissolved

and the _____ is the substance in which it is dissolved.

14. Salt is _____ in water because it dissolves in water.

15. In a gaseous or liquid solution, the volume of solvent is

greater than the volume of _____.

16. A solid solution of metals or nonmetals dissolved in metals is

a(n) _____.

17. What can particles in solution NOT do because they are so small?

_____

_____

CONCENTRATION OF SOLUTIONS

18. A measure of the amount of solute dissolved in a solvent is called

_____.

19. What is the difference between a dilute solution and a concentrated solution?

_____

_____

20. The ability of a solute to dissolve in a solvent at a certain temperature is

called _____.

21. Solubility is dependent on _____ and

_____.

Name _____ Class _____ Date _____

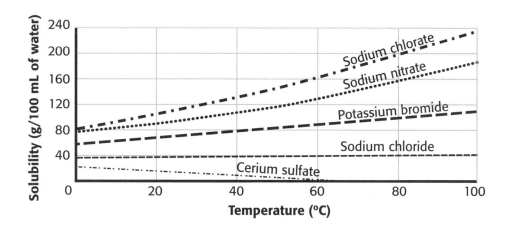

_____**22.** Look at the graph. Which solid is less soluble at higher temperatures than at lower temperatures?
   a. sodium chloride
   b. sodium nitrate
   c. potassium bromide
   d. cerium sulfate

_____**23.** Look at the graph. Which compound's solubility is least affected by temperature changes?
   a. sodium chloride
   b. sodium nitrate
   c. potassium bromide
   d. cerium sulfate

| Directed Reading A *continued*

24. Solubility of solids in liquids tends to _____ with an increase in temperature.

25. Solubility of gases in liquids tends to _____ with an increase in temperature.

26. What are three ways to make a sugar cube dissolve more quickly in water?

_____

_____

SUSPENSIONS

_____**27.** Which of the following does NOT describe a suspension?
   a. Particles are soluble.
   b. Particles settle out over time.
   c. Particles can block light.
   d. Particles scatter light.

28. Why are the particles in a snowglobe considered a suspension?

_____

_____

COLLOIDS

29. What do gelatin, milk, and stick deodorant have in common?

_____

_____

Match the correct description with the correct term. Write the letter in the space provided.

_____**30.** a mixture of two or more uniformly dispersed substances

_____**31.** a mixture of particles that are large enough to scatter or block light

_____**32.** a mixture of particles that are relatively small and well mixed

a. colloid

b. solution

c. suspension

Directed Reading B

Section: Elements
Circle the letter of the best answer for each question.

1. Which process is NOT a physical or chemical change?

    a. crushing

    b. weighing

    c. melting

    d. passing electric current

ELEMENTS, THE SIMPLEST SUBSTANCES

2. What is a pure substance that cannot be broken down into simpler substances?

    a. material

    b. substance

    c. element

    d. chemical

Only One Type of Particle

3. What is a substance with only one type of particle called?

    a. element

    b. pure substance

    c. nugget of gold

    d. bowl of cereal

PROPERTIES OF ELEMENTS

4. What does NOT affect the properties of an element?

    a. the amount of element

    b. the boiling point

    c. the type of element

    d. the density

Circle the letter of the best answer for each question.

5. Why does a helium-filled balloon float up when you let go?

   a. Helium is more dense than air.

   b. Helium is less dense than air.

   c. Krypton is less dense than helium.

   d. Air is less dense than helium.

Identifying Elements by Their Properties

Read the description. Then, draw a line from the dot next to each description to the matching word.

6. a characteristic property of elements   ●

     a. element

7. each has a unique set of properties   ●

     b. hardness

8. combines with oxygen to form rust   ●

     c. iron

     d. cobalt

9. has a melting point of 1,495°C   ●

CLASSIFYING ELEMENTS BY THEIR PROPERTIES

Read the words in the box. Read the sentences. <u>Fill in each blank</u> with the word or phrase that best completes the sentence.

nonmetals	small	metals
elements	metalloids	

10. Most terrier's are _____.

11. All _____ are either metals, metalloids,

or nonmetals.

12. Elements that are shiny and conduct heat and electric current

are _____.

13. Elements that all poor conductors of heat are

_____.

14. Elements with properties of metals and nonmetals are

_____.

Read the description. Then, <u>draw a line</u> from the dot next to each description to the matching word.

Categories Are Similar

15. elements that are malleable   ●   **a.** silicon

16. a type of metalloid   ●   **b.** semiconductor

17. another name for metalloid   ●   **c.** metals

18. elements that are dull   ●   **d.** nonmetals

---

19. iodine, sulfur, neon   ●   **a.** nonmetals

20. lead, copper, tin   ●   **b.** metalloids

21. silicon, boron, antimony   ●   **c.** metals

Directed Reading B

Section: Compounds

Circle the letter of the best answer for each question.

1. Which substance is a compound?

   a. oxygen

   b. salt

   c. magnesium

   d. copper

COMPOUNDS: MADE OF ELEMENTS

2. What kind of substance is composed of two or more elements that are chemically combined?

   a. element

   b. compound

   c. mixture

   d. particle

3. How do the properties of a compound compare with the properties of the elements that form it?

   a. always the same

   b. always different

   c. sometimes the same

   d. sometimes different

The Ratio of Elements in a Compound

4. How do elements join to form compounds?

   a. never in the same ratio

   b. in a specific mass ratio

   c. randomly

   d. in a 1:8 mass ratio

PROPERTIES OF COMPOUNDS

Circle the letter of the best answer for each question.

5. Which is true about compounds?

   a. All react with acid.

   b. Each has its own physical properties.

   c. They are used to identify elements.

   d. Compounds are similar to elements.

Properties: Compounds Versus Elements

6. Why are we able to eat sodium and chlorine in a compound?

   a. Sodium reacts violently with water.

   b. Chlorine is a poisonous gas.

   c. The compound is harmless.

   d. Sodium is a metal.

BREAKING DOWN COMPOUNDS

Read the words in the box. Read the sentences. Fill in each blank with the word or phrase that best completes the sentence.

carbonic acid   chemical change
carbon dioxide

7. The compound that helps give some drinks "fizz" is called

   _____.

8. When you open a soft drink, carbonic acid breaks down into

   _____ and water.

Methods of Breaking Down Compounds

9. The only way to break down compounds is through

   a(n) _____.

COMPOUNDS IN YOUR WORLD
Circle the letter of the best answer for each question.
Compounds in Industry

10. What compound is broken down to make aluminum?

   a. mercury oxide

   b. aluminum oxide

   c. aluminum chloride

   d. magnesium oxide

Compounds in Nature

11. What can form compounds from nitrogen in the air?

   a. bacteria

   b. pea plants

   c. animals

   d. all plants

12. What type of compound do plants and animals use to make proteins?

   a. sugar

   b. ammonia

   c. carbon dioxide

   d. nitrogen compounds

13. What do plants use during photosynthesis to make carbohydrates?

   a. soil

   b. carbon dioxide

   c. carbon monoxide

   d. oxygen

Directed Reading B

Section: Mixtures

Read the words in the box. Read the sentences. <u>Fill in each blank</u> with the word or phrase that best completes the sentence.

mixture	compound	physical	identity

PROPERTIES OF MIXTURES

1. A combination of substances that are not chemically combined is

called a(n) _____.

2. Two or more materials that combine chemically form a(n)

_____.

No Chemical Changes in a Mixture

3. In a mixture, the _____ of the substances

doesn't change.

Separating Mixtures Through Physical Methods

4. Mixtures are separated through _____
changes.

Read the description. Then, <u>draw a line</u> from the dot next to each description to the matching word.

5. used to separate crude oil ●

6. used to separate aluminum and ●   **a.** distillation
iron

    b. centrifuge

7. used to separate the parts of ●
blood   **c.** filter

    d. magnet

8. used to separate sulfur and salt ●

Circle the letter of the best answer for each question.

The Ratio of Components in a Mixture

9. What affects the color of granite?

    a. ratio of minerals

    b. amount of mixture

    c. materials not mixed enough

    d. amount of minerals

SOLUTIONS

10. Which of the following is NOT true of solutions?

    a. They contain a solute.

    b. They contain evenly mixed substances.

    c. They contain a solvent.

    d. They look like two substances.

11. When a substance spreads evenly through a mixture, what is the process called?

    a. solute

    b. dissolving

    c. chemical change

    d. solubility

12. What do you call the substance that is dissolved in a solution?

    a. solute

    b. solvent

    c. compound

    d. mixture

13. In a solution, what do you call the substance in which something dissolves?

    a. solute   **c.** compound

    b. solvent   **d.** mixture

Read the words in the box. Read the sentences. <u>Fill in each blank</u> with the word or phrase that best completes the sentence.

| solvent | particles | alloy | soluble |

14. Salt is _____ in water because it dissolves in water.

15. In a solution of two gases, the substance with the greater amount is called the _____.

Examples of Solutions

16. A solid solution of metals or nonmetals dissolved in metal is called a(n) _____.

Particles in Solutions

17. A solution contains many small _____.

<u>Circle the letter</u> of the best answer for each question.

18. Which is true of particles in solutions?
   a. They scatter light.　　　　**c.** They can't be filtered out.
   b. They settle out.　　　　　**d.** They are large.

CONCENTRATION OF SOLUTIONS

19. What is a measure of the amount of solute dissolved in a solvent?
   a. solution　　　　　　　　**c.** mixture
   b. concentration　　　　　　**d.** solvent

Concentrated or Dilute?

20. How does a concentrated solution differ from a dilute solution?
   a. more solvent　　　　　　**c.** more solute
   b. less solvent　　　　　　 **d.** less solute

| Directed Reading B *continued*

Solubility

Read the words in the box. Read the sentences. <u>Fill in each blank</u> with the word or phrase that best completes the sentence.

temperature   solubility

21. The ability of a solute to dissolve in a solvent is called

_____.

22. In a solution, the _____ usually affects the solubility.

Use the graph below to answer questions 23 and 24. For each question, <u>circle the letter</u> of the best answer for each question.

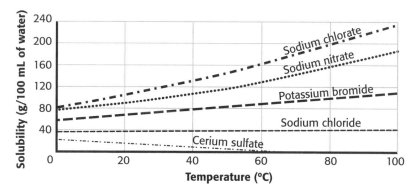

23. Look at the graph. Which solid is less soluble at higher temperatures than at lower temperatures?

a. sodium chloride

b. sodium nitrate

c. potassium bromide

d. cerium sulfate

24. Look at the graph. Which solid's solubility is least affected by temperature changes?

a. sodium chloride   **c.** potassium bromide

b. sodium nitrate   **d.** cerium sulfate

Dissolving Gases in Liquids

Read the words in the box. Read the sentences. <u>Fill in each blank</u> with the word or phrase that best completes the sentence.

increases   decreases

25. Solubility of gases in liquids often _____ as temperatures rise.

26. Solubility of solids in liquids often _____ as temperatures rise.

Dissolving Solids Faster in Liquids

<u>Circle the letter</u> of the best answer for each question.

27. Which method will NOT make a solid dissolve faster?

a. weighing   **c.** heating

b. crushing   **d.** mixing

SUSPENSIONS

28. What is NOT true about particles in a suspension?

a. They are soluble.

b. They settle out over time.

c. They can block light.

d. They scatter light.

COLLOIDS

29. What do gelatin, milk, and stick deodorant have in common?

a. They are colloids.

b. Particles in each can settle out.

c. They are compounds.

d. They are solutions.

Skills Worksheet)

Vocabulary and Section Summary

Elements
VOCABULARY

In your own words, write a definition of the following terms in the space provided.

1. element

_____

_____

2. pure substance

_____

_____

3. metal

_____

_____

4. nonmetal

_____

_____

5. metalloid

_____

_____

SECTION SUMMARY

Read the following section summary.

- A substance in which all of the particles are alike is a pure substance.
- An element is a pure substance that cannot be broken down into anything simpler by physical or chemical means.
- Each element has a unique set of physical and chemical properties.
- Elements are classified as metals, nonmetals, or metalloids, based on their properties.

Vocabulary and Section Summary

Compounds

VOCABULARY

In your own words, write a definition of the following term in the space provided.

1. compound

_____

_____

SECTION SUMMARY

Read the following section summary.

• A compound is a pure substance composed of two or more elements.

• The elements that form a compound always combine in a specific ratio according to their masses.

• Each compound has a unique set of physical and chemical properties that differ from those of the elements that make up the compound.

• Compounds can be broken down into simpler substances only by chemical changes.

Skills Worksheet

Vocabulary and and Section Summary

Mixtures
VOCABULARY

In your own words, write a definition of the following terms in the space provided.

1. mixture

_____

_____

2. solution

_____

_____

3. solute

_____

_____

4. solvent

_____

_____

5. concentration

_____

_____

6. solubility

_____

_____

7. suspension

_____

_____

8. colloid

_____

_____

| Vocabulary and Section Summary *continued*

SECTION SUMMARY

Read the following section summary.

• A mixture is a combination of two or more substances, each of which keeps its own characteristics.

• Mixtures can be separated by physical means, such as filtration and evaporation.

• A solution is a mixture that appears to be a single substance but is composed of a solute dissolved in a solvent.

• Concentration is a measure of the amount of solute dissolved in a solvent.

• The solubility of a solute is the ability of the solute to dissolve in a solvent at a certain temperature.

• Suspensions are mixtures that contain particles large enough to settle out or be filtered and to block or scatter light.

• Colloids are mixtures that contain particles that are too small to settle out or be filtered but are large enough to scatter light.

Skills Worksheet

Section Review

Elements
USING KEY TERMS

1. Use the following terms in the same sentence: *element* and *pure substance*.

_____

_____

UNDERSTANDING KEY IDEAS

_____ **2.** A metalloid
    a. may conduct electric current.
    b. can be ductile.
    c. is also called a semiconductor.
    d. All of the above.

3. What is a pure substance?

_____

_____

MATH SKILLS

4. There are 8 elements that make up 98.5% of the Earth's crust: 46.6% oxygen, 8.1% aluminum, 5.0% iron, 3.6% calcium, 2.8% sodium, 2.6% potassium, and 2.1% magnesium. The rest is silicon. What percentage of Earth's crust is silicon? Show your work below.

| Section Review *continued*

CRITICAL THINKING

5. Applying Concepts From which category of elements would you choose to make a container that wouldn't shatter if dropped? Explain your answer.

_____

_____

_____

_____

6. Making Comparisons Compare the properties of metals, nonmetals, and metalloids.

_____

_____

_____

_____

7. Evaluating Assumptions Your friend tells you that a shiny element has to be a metal. Do you agree? Explain.

_____

_____

_____

_____

_____

Skills Worksheet

Section Review

Compounds

USING KEY TERMS

1. In your own words, write a definition for the term *compound*.

_____

UNDERSTANDING KEY IDEAS

_____ **2.** The elements in a compound

      a. join in a specific ratio according to their masses.

      b. combine by reacting with one another.

      c. can be separated by chemical changes.

      d. All of the above

3. What type of change is needed to break down a compound?

_____

_____

MATH SKILLS

4. Table sugar is a compound made of carbon, hydrogen, and oxygen. If sugar contains 41.86% carbon and 6.98% hydrogen, what percentage of sugar is oxygen? Show your work below.

CRITICAL THINKING

5. Applying Concepts Iron is a solid, gray metal. Oxygen is a colorless gas. When they chemically combine, rust is made. Rust has a reddish brown color. Why is rust different from the iron or oxygen that it is made of?

_____

_____

_____

_____

6. Analyzing Ideas A jar contains samples of the elements carbon and oxygen. Does the jar contain a compound? Explain your answer.

_____

_____

_____

_____

Skills Worksheet

Section Review

Mixtures

USING KEY TERMS

The statements below are false. For each statement, replace the underlined term to make a true statement.

1. The <u>solvent</u> is the substance that is dissolved.

_____

2. A <u>suspension</u> is composed of substances that are spread evenly among each other.

_____

3. A measure of the amount of solute dissolved in a solvent is <u>solubility</u>.

_____

4. A <u>colloid</u> contains particles that will settle out of the mixture if left sitting.

_____

UNDERSTANDING KEY IDEAS

_____ **5.** A mixture
     a. has substances in it that are chemically combined.
     b. can always be separated using filtration.
     c. contains substances that are not mixed in a definite ratio.
     d. All of the above

6. List three ways to dissolve a solid faster.

_____

_____

_____

CRITICAL THINKING

7. Making Comparisons How do solutions, suspensions, and colloids differ?

_____

_____

_____

_____

| **Section Review** *continued*

8. Applying Concepts Suggest a procedure to separate iron filings from sawdust. Explain why this procedure works.

_____

_____

_____

9. Analyzing Ideas Identify the solute and solvent in a solution made of 15 mL of oxygen and 5 mL of helium.

_____

_____

_____

INTERPRETING GRAPHICS

Use the graph below to answer the questions that follow.

Solubility of Different Substances

10. At what temperature is 120 g of sodium nitrate soluble in 100 mL of water?

_____

_____

11. At 60°C, how much more sodium chlorate than sodium chloride will dissolve in 100 mL of water?

_____

_____

Skills Worksheet)

Chapter Review

USING KEY TERMS

Complete each of the following sentences by choosing the correct term from the word bank.

compound	element	suspension	solubility
solution	metal	nonmetal	solute

1. A(n) _____ has a definite ratio of components.

2. The ability of one substance to dissolve in another substance is the

_____ of the solute.

3. A(n) _____ can be separated by filtration.

4. A(n) _____ is a pure substance that cannot be broken

down into simpler substances by chemical means.

5. A(n) _____ is an element that is brittle and dull.

6. The _____ is the substance that dissolves to form a

solution.

UNDERSTANDING KEY IDEAS

Multiple Choice

_____ **7.** Which of the following increases the solubility of a gas in a liquid?
   a. increasing the temperature of the liquid
   b. increasing the amount of gas in the liquid
   c. decreasing the temperature of the liquid
   d. decreasing the amount of liquid

_____ **8.** Which of the following best describes chicken noodle soup?
   a. element   **c.** compound
   b. mixture   **d.** solution

_____ **9.** Which of the following statements describes elements?
   a. All of the particles in the same element are different.
   b. Elements can be broken down into simpler substances.
   c. Elements have unique sets of properties.
   d. Elements cannot be joined together in chemical reactions.

_____ **10.** A solution that contains a large amount of solute is best described as
   a. insoluble.   **c.** dilute.
   b. concentrated.   **d.** weak.

_____**11.** Which of the following substances can be separated into simpler substances only by chemical means?
   a. sodium   **c.** water
   b. salt water   **d.** gold

_____**12.** Which of the following would not increase the rate at which a solid dissolves?
   a. decreasing the temperature
   b. crushing the solid
   c. stirring
   d. increasing the temperature

_____**13.** In which classification of matter are components chemically combined?
   a. a solution   **c.** a compound
   b. a colloid   **d.** a suspension

_____**14.** An element that conducts thermal energy well and is easily shaped is a
   a. metal.
   b. metalloid.
   c. nonmetal.
   d. None of the above

Short Answer

15. What is the difference between an element and a compound?

_____

_____

_____

16. When nail polish is dissolved in acetone, which substance is the solute, and which is the solvent?

_____

_____

_____

Math Skills

17. What is the concentration of a solution prepared by mixing 50 g of salt with 200 mL of water? Show your work below.

18. How many grams of sugar must be dissolved in 150 mL of water to make a solution that has a concentration of 0.6 g/mL? Show your work below.

CRITICAL THINKING

19. Concept Mapping Use the following terms to create a concept map: *matter, element, compound, mixture, solution, suspension,* and *colloid.*

20. **Forming Hypotheses** To keep the "fizz" in carbonated beverages after they have been opened, should you store them in a refrigerator or in a cabinet? Explain.

_____

_____

_____

_____

21. **Making Inferences** A light green powder is heated in a test tube. A gas is given off, and the solid becomes black. In which classification of matter does the green powder belong? Explain your reasoning.

_____

_____

_____

22. **Predicting Consequences** Why is it desirable to know the exact concentration of solutions rather than whether they are concentrated or dilute?

_____

_____

_____

23. **Applying Concepts** Describe a procedure to separate a mixture of salt, finely ground pepper, and pebbles.

_____

_____

_____

_____

Chapter Review *continued*

INTERPRETING GRAPHICS

Dr. Sol Vent did an experiment to find the solubility of a compound. The data below were collected using 100 mL of water. Use the table below to answer the questions that follow.

Temperature (°C)	10	25	40	60	95
Dissolved Solute (g)	150	70	34	25	15

24. Use a computer or graph paper to construct a graph of Dr. Vent's results. Examine the graph. To increase the solubility, would you increase or decrease the temperature? Explain.

_____

_____

_____

_____

25. If 200 mL of water were used instead of 100 mL, how many grams of the compound would dissolve at 40°C?

_____

_____

_____

26. Based on the solubility of this compound, is this compound a solid, liquid, or gas? Explain your answer.

_____

_____

_____

_____

_____

Skills Worksheet

Reinforcement

It's All Mixed Up

Complete this worksheet after you finish reading the section "Mixtures."

Label each figure below with the type of substance it BEST models: colloid, compound, element, solution, or suspension.

1.

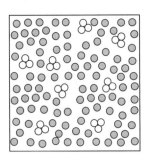

_____

2.

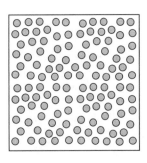

_____

3.

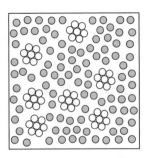

_____

4.

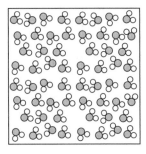

_____

5.

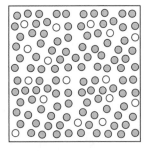

_____

6. Why did you label the figures on the previous page as you did?

_____

_____

_____

_____

_____

_____

PROFESSOR JUMBLE'S CONFUSION

In her lab, Professor Jumble has four shelves labeled "Suspensions," "Solutions," "Compounds," and "Colloids," respectively. Last night, the professor set one beaker of clear liquid on each of the four shelves. When the professor walked into her lab this morning, all four beakers were on the same shelf, and she didn't know which was which. She tested each beaker, and the results are below.

7. Use the test results to help Professor Jumble unjumble the beakers, and write the identity of each liquid in the blanks.

Beaker A: _____

- Light passes right through.
- Particles do not separate in a centrifuge or a filter.
- Upon heating, the liquid evaporates, and a crystal powder remains.

Beaker C: _____

- Liquid scatters light.
- Liquid centrifuged into two different-colored layers.
- Particles were left behind in the filter.

Beaker B: _____

- Light passes right through.
- Particles do not separate in a centrifuge or a filter.
- Upon heating, the liquid evaporates, but no residue remains.
- The particles could not be separated by any other physical changes.

Beaker D: _____

- Liquid scatters light.
- Liquid passes through a filter without leaving a residue.

Name _____ Class _____ Date _____

Critical Thinking

Jet Smart

You receive this letter from a top-secret airplane manufacturer:

Agent X:

We were impressed by your work on our flying saucer project. Your help is now needed in the design of our newest stealth airplane, the FX-2000. We need your help with one simple but important matter—selecting the best metal for the plane's engines. Our team has narrowed the choices to two metals: titanium and platinum. Your mission is to gather facts about titanium and platinum, compare their properties, and recommend the better material. Report your answer within 24 hours.

You immediately turn to your reference books and study the properties of the two metals.

Platinium

- a precious metal
- density: 21.4 g/cm^3
- resists corrosion
- melting point: 1,772°C
- weaker than steel

Titanium

- a metal
- density: 4.51 g/cm^3
- resists corrosion
- melting point: 1,675°C
- as strong as steel

USEFUL TERM

corrosion wearing away gradually by rusting or the action of chemicals

MAKING COMPARISONS

1. How are platinum and titanium similar? How are they different?

_____

_____

_____

_____

_____

_____

| Critical Thinking *continued*

DEMONSTRATING REASONED JUDGMENT

2. Think about the extreme conditions within the engine of a jet. What properties would a metal in this engine need to have?

_____

_____

_____

_____

_____

_____

3. Which material would you recommend? Explain your answer.

_____

_____

_____

_____

_____

_____

PREDICTING CONSEQUENCES

4. Assume that the raw materials will be mined and sent directly to the manufacturing plant without being purified. Predict the possible consequences to the *FX-2000*'s performance. Explain your answer.

_____

_____

_____

_____

_____

Section Quiz

Section: Elements

Match the correct definition with the correct term. Write the letter in the space provided.

_____ **1.** a pure substance that cannot be separated into simpler substances by physical or chemical means

_____ **2.** a sample of matter, either a single element or a single compound, that has definite chemical and physical properties

_____ **3.** an element that is shiny and conducts heat and electric current

_____ **4.** element that conducts heat and electricity poorly and can be a solid, liquid, or gas

_____ **5.** element that has the properties of both metals and nonmetals

a. metal

b. element

c. metalloid

d. nonmetal

e. pure substance

Write the letter of the correct answer in the space provided.

_____ **6.** Boiling point, melting point, and density are some of an element's
a. nonreactive properties.
b. physical properties.
c. chemical properties.
d. pure properties.

_____ **7.** A property of an element that does not depend on the amount of the element is called a
a. electromagnetic property.
b. finite property.
c. unique property.
d. characteristic property.

_____ **8.** An element's ability to react with acid is an example of a
a. pure substance.
b. physical property.
c. chemical property.
d. melting point.

Assessment

Section Quiz

Section: Compounds

Write the letter of the correct answer in the space provided.

_____ **1.** When two or more elements join together chemically,
      a. a compound is formed.
      b. a mixture is formed.
      c. a substance that is the same as the elements is formed.
      d. the physical properties of the substances remain the same.

_____ **2.** The physical properties of compounds do NOT include
      a. melting point.
      b. density.
      c. reaction to light.
      d. color.

_____ **3.** Which of the following will NOT break down compounds?
      a. heat
      b. electric current
      c. a chemical change
      d. filtering

_____ **4.** How do elements join to form compounds?
      a. randomly
      b. in a specific mass ratio
      c. in a ratio of 1 to 8
      d. as the scientist plans it

_____ **5.** Compounds found in all living things include
      a. proteins.
      b. ammonia.
      c. mercury oxides.
      d. carbonic acids.

Assessment

Section Quiz

Section: Mixtures

Match the correct definition with the correct term. Write the letter in the space provided.

_____ **1.** combination of two or more substances that are not chemically combined

_____ **2.** homogeneous mixture of two or more substances uniformly dispersed throughout a single phase

_____ **3.** substance that dissolves in a solvent

_____ **4.** substance in which a solute dissolves

_____ **5.** amount of a substance in a given quantity of a mixture, solution, or ore

_____ **6.** ability of one substance to dissolve in another at a given temperature and pressure

_____ **7.** mixture in which particles of a material are more or less evenly dispersed throughout a liquid or gas

_____ **8.** mixture consisting of tiny particles that are intermediate in size between those in solutions and those in suspensions

_____ **9.** process that separates a mixture based on the boiling points of the components

_____ **10.** machine that separates mixtures by the densities of the components

a. centrifuge

b. solute

c. solvent

d. colloid

e. mixture

f. suspension

g. distillation

h. solution

i. concentration

j. solubility

Assessment

Chapter Test A

Elements, Compounds, and Mixtures
MULTIPLE CHOICE
Write the letter of the correct answer in the space provided.

_____ **1.** What is a pure substance made of two or more elements that are chemically combined?
   a. element
   b. compound
   c. mixture
   d. solution

_____ **2.** If a spoonful of salt is mixed in a glass of water, what is the water called?
   a. solute
   b. solution
   c. solvent
   d. element

_____ **3.** What is a solid solution of a metal or nonmetal dissolved in a metal?
   a. suspension
   b. alloy
   c. colloid
   d. compound

_____ **4.** A colloid has properties of both suspensions and
   a. solutions.
   b. solvents.
   c. solutes.
   d. nonmetals.

_____ **5.** What is formed when particles of two or more substances are distributed evenly among each other?
   a. compound
   b. suspension
   c. solution
   d. element

_____ **6.** The flammability of a substance is
   a. a chemical property.
   b. related to the density.
   c. a physical property.
   d. changeable.

| **Chapter Test A** *continued*

_____ **7.** How is a compound different from a mixture?
   a. Compounds have two or more components.
   b. Each substance in a compound loses its characteristic properties.
   c. Compounds are commonly found in nature.
   d. Solids, liquids, and gases can form compounds.

_____ **8.** The particles in both a solution and a colloid
   a. cannot scatter light.
   b. can settle out.
   c. are soluble.
   d. can pass through a fine filter.

_____ **9.** When elements form mixtures, the elements
   a. keep their original properties.
   b. react to form a new substance with new properties.
   c. combine in a specific mass ratio.
   d. always change their physical state.

_____ **10.** Which of the following is NOT a reason that compounds are considered pure substances?
   a. They are composed of only one type of particle.
   b. The particles are made of atoms of two or more elements that are chemically combined.
   c. Different samples of any compound have the same elements in the same proportion.
   d. They can be separated by physical methods.

_____ **11.** How are metalloids similar to metals?
   a. They have some properties of nonmetals.
   b. Some are shiny, while others are dull.
   c. They are somewhat malleable and ductile.
   d. Some are good conductors of electric current.

_____ **12.** How could a sugar cube be dissolved more quickly in water?
   a. Cool the water.
   b. Crush the sugar cube.
   c. Let the cube sit in the water.
   d. Add more water.

MATCHING

Match the correct definition with the correct term. Write the letter in the space provided.

_____**13.** also known as table salt

_____**14.** used by plants during photosynthesis

_____**15.** a nonmetal

a. carbon dioxide

b. sulfur

c. sodium chloride

Match the correct description with the correct term. Write the letter in the space provided. Some terms may not be used.

_____**16.** an aluminum pie plate

_____**17.** a milkshake

_____**18.** calcium carbonate

_____**19.** potting soil

_____**20.** instant coffee in hot water

_____**21.** a steel crow bar

a. mixture of solids

b. solute

c. element

d. suspension

e. compound

f. alloy

Use the graph below to answer questions 22 and 23. Write the letter of the correct answer in the space provided.

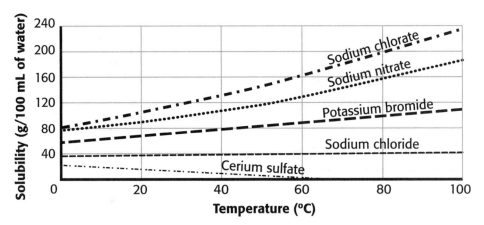

_____**22.** Which solid is the most soluble at lower temperatures than at higher temperatures?

a. sodium chloride

b. sodium nitrate

c. potassium bromide

d. cerium sulfate

_____**23.** Which compound's solubility is least affected by temperature changes?

a. sodium chloride

b. sodium nitrate

c. potassium bromide

d. cerium sulfate

Assessment

Chapter Test B

Elements, Compounds, and Mixtures

USING KEY TERMS

Use the terms from the following list to complete the sentences below. Each term may be used only once. Some terms may not be used.

solvent	solute	alloys
solution	mixture	suspensions
compound	metalloids	

1. A pure substance made of two or more elements that are chemically

combined is called a _____.

2. If a spoonful of salt is mixed in a glass of water, the salt is

the _____.

3. Solid solutions of metals or nonmetals dissolved in metals

are _____.

4. A colloid has the properties of solutions and

_____.

5. Particles of two or more substances that are distributed evenly among

each other form a(n) _____.

UNDERSTANDING KEY IDEAS

Write the letter of the correct answer in the space provided.

_____ **6.** Which of the following is a chemical property?
  a. flammability   **c.** melting point
  b. density   **d.** ductility

_____ **7.** How is a mixture different from a compound?
  a. Mixtures have two or more components.
  b. Each substance in a mixture keeps its characteristic properties.
  c. Mixtures are commonly found in nature.
  d. Solids, liquids, and gases can form mixtures.

_____ **8.** The particles in both a suspension and a colloid can
  a. scatter light.
  b. settle out.
  c. be soluble.
  d. pass through a fine filter.

_____ **9.** When materials combine to form a mixture, they
  a. keep their original properties.
  b. react to form a new substance with new properties.
  c. combine in a specific ratio.
  d. always change their physical state.

10. Explain why compounds are considered pure substances.

_____

_____

_____

11. How are metalloids different from metals?

_____

_____

_____

12. Describe three ways to dissolve solids faster and explain why each works.

_____

_____

_____

CRITICAL THINKING

13. Most fresh water in Saudi Arabia is produced by removing salt from sea water. One method involves distillation. Explain how sea water could be purified by distillation, and tell whether it is a chemical or physical process.

_____

_____

_____

14. Suppose you were given an unknown liquid and asked to determine if it was an element, a compound, or a mixture. What would you do? How would this help you find out what it was?

_____

_____

_____

Name _____ Class _____ Date _____

15. After testing three substances, a scientist has recorded the following data. Are these substances the same or different? How can you tell?

Physical Property	Substance 1	Substance 2	Substance 3
Boiling point		2,750°C	2,467°C
Density	2.702g/cm^3	7.874g/cm^3	
Color	Silvery	Silvery white	
Melting point	660.25°C		660.25°C
Hardness	2.75	4	2.75
Other	Non-magnet		Non-magnet

_____

_____

_____

INTERPRETING GRAPHICS

Use the graph to answer questions 16 and 17.

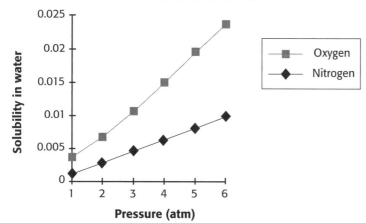

Solubility in Water Versus Pressure for Two Gases at 25°C

16. What is the relationship between pressure and the solubility of oxygen and nitrogen in water?

_____

_____

17. Which gas experiences a greater change in solubility per unit pressure?

_____

_____

| Chapter Test B *continued*

CONCEPT MAPPING

18. Use the following terms to complete the concept map below:

pure substances   physical or chemical   chemical
solutions   suspensions   compounds.

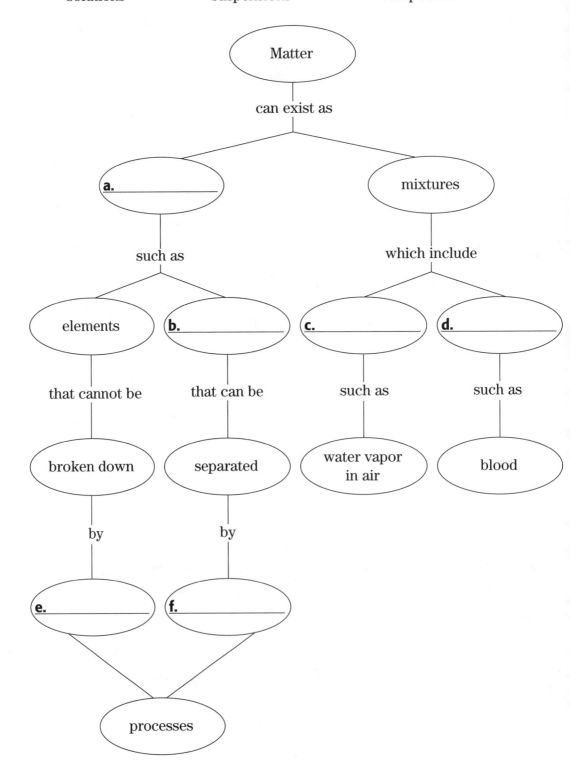

Assessment

Chapter Test C

Elements, Compounds, and Mixtures
MULTIPLE CHOICE
Circle the letter of the best answer for each question.

1. What pure substance forms when two elements chemically combine?

   a. an element

   b. a compound

   c. a mixture

   d. a solution

2. Why can salt dissolve in water?

   a. Salt is the solvent.

   b. Salt is a solution.

   c. Salt is soluble.

   d. Salt is an element.

3. What is a solid solution of a metal dissolved in a metal called?

   a. suspension

   b. alloy

   c. colloid

   d. compound

4. How can a compound be broken down?

   a. by physical changes

   b. by chemical changes

   c. by crushing

   d. by cooling

Circle the letter of the best answer for each question.

5. What forms when particles of two or more substances are evenly mixed?

   a. compound

   b. suspension

   c. solution

   d. element

6. Which of the following is a chemical property?

   a. density

   b. reactivity with acid

   c. boiling point

   d. color

7. What is true about particles in both solutions and colloids?

   a. Particles cannot scatter light.

   b. Particles can settle out.

   c. Particles are soluble.

   d. Particles cannot be filtered.

8. Which of the following is NOT true of compounds?

   a. They contain two or more elements.

   b. They form after a physical change.

   c. They have their own physical properties.

   d. They do not form randomly.

Chapter Test C *continued*

MATCHING

**Read the description. Then, <u>draw a line</u> from the dot next to each
description to the matching word.**

  9. gelatin   ●   **a.** colloid

10. nugget of gold   ●   **b.** solution

11. water   ●   **c.** element

12. salt dissolved in water   ●   **d.** compound

---

13. a solid solution of metals or   ●
nonmetals dissolved in metals

                                   a. alloy

14. an element that shares metal   ●
and nonmetal properties

                                   b. suspension

15. a mixture of large, dispersed   ●
particles

                                   c. solvent

16. the substance in which a solute   ●
dissolves

                                   d. metalloid

FILL-IN-THE-BLANK

Read the words in the box. Read the sentences. <u>Fill in each blank</u> with the word or phrase that best completes the sentence.

distillation	nitrogen	nonmetals	ratio

17. A mixture of liquids can be separated by

_____ .

18. Bacteria make compounds from _____ in

the air.

19. All _____ are poor conductors of heat

and electric current.

20. Elements join in a specific mass _____

to form a compound.

Performance-Based Assessment

OBJECTIVE

You will investigate how solids and gases dissolve in water at different temperatures.

KNOW THE SCORE!

As you work through the activity, keep in mind that you will be earning a grade for the following:

• how well you form and test the hypothesis (30%)

• the quality of your analysis (40%)

• the clarity of your conclusions (30%)

Using Scientific Methods

ASK A QUESTION

Does the temperature of a liquid affect how much salt can dissolve in it?

MATERIALS AND EQUIPMENT

• 240 mL (1 cup) of cold water

• paper towels

• 240 mL beakers (2)

• heat-resistant gloves

• hot plate

• alcohol thermometer

• thermometer holder

• 240 mL of salt

• 5 mL spoon (1 tsp)

• stirring rod or spoon

SAFETY INFORMATION

• Do not eat or drink anything in the laboratory.

• If a thermometer breaks, notify the teacher.

• Use tongs or heatproof gloves to handle heated glassware and other equipment.

• Clean up water spills immediately; spilled water is a slipping hazard.

• Never work with electricity near water; be sure the floor and all work surfaces are dry.

• Wear heat-resistant gloves, goggles, and an apron when using a hot plate to protect your eyes and clothing.

• Never leave a hot plate unattended while it is turned on.

• Tie back long hair, secure loose clothing, and remove loose jewelry.

| Performance-Based Assessment *continued*

FORM A HYPOTHESIS

1. Will the cold water or the hot water dissolve more salt?

_____

_____

2. Will the salt water boil at a lower temperature, the same temperature, or a higher temperature than the plain water?

_____

_____

TEST THE HYPOTHESIS

3. Pour 120 mL of cold water into each empty beaker.

4. Wearing goggles, heat-resistant gloves, and an apron, plug in and turn on the hot plate. Place one of the beakers on the hot plate. When the water begins to boil, place the thermometer in the water. Do not let the thermometer rest on the bottom of the beaker. Write the temperature below. The boiling point for water is _____ °C.

5. Remove the beaker from the hot plate. Set it next to the other beaker.

6. To each beaker, add salt a spoonful at a time while stirring until no more salt dissolves. Record the amount of salt dissolved in the water. (Each spoonful is 5 mL.) You will know when no more salt will dissolve when you see salt fall to the bottom no matter how much you stir.

Amount of Dissolved Salt

Cold water (mL)	Hot water (mL)

7. Place one of the beakers containing salt water on the hot plate. When the water begins to boil, place the thermometer in the water, and write the temperature below. The boiling point for salt water is _____ °C.

8. Turn off and unplug the hot plate.

Performance-Based Assessment *continued*

ANALYZE THE RESULTS

9. Did the salt water boil at a lower temperature, the same temperature, or a higher temperature than the plain water?

_____

_____

10. Did the cold water or the hot water dissolve more salt?

_____

_____

11. Why did you see bubbles in the water when it heated up?

_____

_____

DRAW CONCLUSIONS

12. Compare how easily solids dissolve in hot water with how easily they dissolve in cool water. Write one sentence summarizing your observation.

_____

_____

_____

Standardized Test Preparation

READING

Read each of the passages below. Then, answer the questions that follow each passage.

Passage 1 In 1912, the *Titanic* was the largest ship ever to set sail. This majestic ship was considered to be unsinkable. Yet, on April 15, 1912, the *Titanic* hit a large iceberg. The resulting damage caused the *Titanic* to sink, killing 1,500 of its passengers and crew.

How could an iceberg destroy the 2.5 cm thick steel plates that made up the *Titanic's* hull? Analysis of a recovered piece of steel showed that the steel contained large amounts of sulfur. Sulfur is a normal component of steel. However, the recovered piece has much more sulfur than today's steel does. The excess sulfur may have made the steel <u>brittle</u>, much like glass. Scientists suspect that this brittle steel may have cracked on impact with the iceberg, allowing water to enter the hull.

_____ **1.** In this passage, what does the word *brittle* mean?
   A likely to break or crack
   B very strong
   C clear and easily seen through
   D lightweight

_____ **2.** What is the main idea of the second paragraph of this passage?
   F The *Titanic's* hull was 2.5 cm thick.
   G The steel in the *Titanic's* hull may have been brittle.
   H The large amount of sulfur in the *Titanic's* hull may be responsible for the hull's cracking.
   I Scientists were able to recover a piece of steel from the *Titanic's* hull.

_____ **3.** What was the *Titanic* thought to be in 1912?
   A the fastest ship afloat
   B the smallest ship to set sail
   C a ship not capable of being sunk
   D the most luxurious ship to set sail

Standardized Test Preparation *continued*

Passage 2 Perfume making is an ancient art. It was practiced by the ancient Egyptians, who rubbed their bodies with a substance made by soaking fragrant woods and resins in water and oil. Ancient Israelites also practiced the art of perfume making. This art was also known to the early Chinese, Arabs, Greeks, and Romans.

Over time, perfume making has developed into a fine art. A good perfume may contain more than 100 ingredients. The most familiar ingredients come from fragrant plants, such as sandal-wood or roses. These plants get their pleasant odor from essential oils, which are stored in tiny, baglike parts called *sacs*. The parts of plants that are used for perfumes include the flowers, roots, and leaves. Other perfume ingredients come from animals and from human-made chemicals.

_____ **1.** How did ancient Egyptians make perfume?
   A by using 100 different ingredients
   B by soaking woods and resins in water and oil
   C by using plants or flowers
   D by making tiny, baglike parts called sacs

_____ **2.** What is the main idea of the second paragraph?
   F Perfume making hasn't changed since ancient Egypt.
   G The ancient art of perfume making has been replaced by simple science.
   H Perfume making is a complex procedure involving many ingredients.
   I Natural ingredients are no longer used in perfume.

_____ **3.** How are good perfumes made?
   A from plant oils only
   B by combining one or two ingredients
   C according to early Chinese formulas
   D by blending as many as 100 ingredients

Name _____ Class _____ Date _____

INTERPRETING GRAPHICS

The graph below was constructed from data collected during a laboratory investigation. Use the graph below to answer the questions that follow.

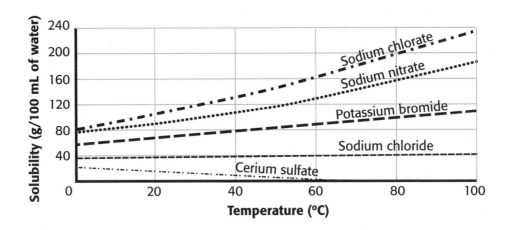

_____ **1.** Which of the following values is the amount of sodium nitrate that can dissolve in 100 mL of water at 40°C?

A 0 g

B 40 g

C 80 g

D 100 g

_____ **2.** How many grams of sodium chloride can dissolve in 100 mL of water at 60°C?

F 40 g

G 80 g

H 125 g

I 160 g

_____ **3.** At what temperature will 80 g of potassium bromide completely dissolve in 100 mL of water?

A approximately 20°C

B approximately 42°C

C approximately 88°C

D approximately 100°C

_____ **4.** At 20°C, which solid is the most soluble?

F sodium chloride

G sodium chlorate

H potassium bromide

I sodium nitrate

Name _____ Class _____ Date _____

MATH

Read each question below, and choose the best answer.

Use the rectangle below to answer questions 1 and 2.

6 cm

12 cm

_____ **1.** What is the perimeter of the rectangle shown above?

A 12 cm

B 18 cm

C 36 cm

D 72 cm

_____ **2.** If the length of all the sides of the rectangle shown above were doubled, what would be the area of the larger rectangle?

F 36 cm^2

G 72 cm^2

H 144 cm^2

I 288 cm^2

_____ **3.** One way to calculate the concentration of a solution is to divide the grams of solute by the milliliters of solvent. What is the concentration of a solution that is made by dissolving 65 g of sugar (the solute) in 500 mL of water (the solvent)?

A 0.13 g•mL

B 0.13 g/mL

C 7.7 g•mL

D 7.7 g/mL

_____ **4.** If 16/n = 1/2, what is the value of n?

F 2

G 8

H 16

I 32

Name _____ Class _____ Date _____

Flame Tests

Fireworks produce fantastic combinations of color when they are ignited. The different colors are the results of burning different compounds. Imagine that you are the head chemist for a fireworks company. The label has fallen off one box, and you must identify the unknown compound inside so that the fireworks may be used in the correct fireworks display. To identify the compound, you will use your knowledge that every compound has a unique set of properties.

OBJECTIVE

Observe flame colors emitted by various compounds.

Determine the composition of an unknown compound.

MATERIALS

- Bunsen burner
- chloride test solutions (4)
- hydrochloric acid, dilute, in a small beaker
- spark igniter

- tape, masking
- test tubes, small (4)
- test-tube rack
- water, distilled, in a small beaker
- wire and holder

SAFETY INFORMATION

Using Scientific Methods

ASK A QUESTION

1. How can you identify an unknown compound by heating it in a flame?

FORM A HYPOTHESIS

2. Write a hypothesis that is a possible answer to the question above. Explain your reasoning.

_____

_____

_____

Flame Tests *continued*

TEST THE HYPOTHESIS

3. Arrange the test tubes in the test-tube rack. Use masking tape to label each tube with one of the following names: calcium chloride, potassium chloride, sodium chloride, and unknown.

4. Use the table below to record your results. Then, ask your teacher for your portions of the solutions. **Caution:** Be very careful in handling all chemicals. Tell your teacher immediately if you spill a chemical.

Test Results	
Compound	**Color of Flame**
Calcium chloride	
Potassium chloride	
Sodium chloride	
Unknown	

5. Light the burner. Clean the wire by dipping it into the dilute hydrochloric acid and then into distilled water. Holding the wooden handle, heat the wire in the blue flame of the burner until the wire is glowing and it no longer colors the flame. Caution: Use extreme care around an open flame.

6. Dip the clean wire into the first test solution. Hold the wire at the tip of the inner cone of the burner flame. Record in the table the color given to the flame.

7. Clean the wire by repeating step 5. Then, repeat steps 5 and 6 for the other solutions.

8. Follow your teacher's instructions for cleanup and disposal.

ANALYZE THE RESULTS

1. Identifying Patterns Is the flame color a test for the metal or for the chloride in each compound? Explain your answer.

_____

_____

_____

_____

_____

Flame Tests *continued*

2. Analyzing Data What is the identity of your unknown solution? How do you know?

_____

_____

_____

_____

DRAW CONCLUSIONS

3. Evaluating Methods Why is it necessary to carefully clean the wire before testing each solution?

_____

_____

_____

4. Making Predictions Would you expect the compound sodium fluoride to produce the same color as sodium chloride in a flame test? Why or why not?

_____

_____

_____

_____

_____

5. Interpreting Information Each of the compounds you tested is made from chlorine, which is a poisonous gas at room temperature. Why is it safe to use these compounds without a gas mask?

_____

_____

_____

Name _____ Class _____ Date _____

Separating Elements

MATERIALS

- magnet, bar
- nails, mixed sample, some iron and some aluminum

SAFETY INFORMATION

PROCEDURE

1. Examine a sample of **nails** provided by your teacher. Record your observations.

_____

_____

_____

2. Your sample has **aluminum nails** and **iron nails.** Try to separate the two kinds of nails. Group similar nails into piles.

3. Pass a **bar magnet** over each pile of nails. Record your results.

_____

_____

_____

4. Were you successful in completely separating the two types of nails? Explain.

_____

_____

_____

5. How could the properties of aluminum and iron be used to separate cans in a recycling plant.

_____

_____

_____

_____

Name _____ Class _____ Date _____

Quick Lab

Compound Confusion

MATERIALS

- baking soda
- cups, clear plastic (2)
- sugar, powdered
- teaspoon
- vinegar

SAFETY INFORMATION

PROCEDURE

1. Measure a **4 g of compound A,** and place it in a **clear plastic cup.**

2. Measure a **4 g of compound B,** and place it in a **second clear plastic cup.**

3. Observe the color and texture of each compound. Record your observations.

_____

_____

_____

4. Add **5 ml of vinegar** to each cup. Record your observations.

_____

_____

_____

5. Baking soda reacts with vinegar. Powdered sugar does not react with vinegar. Which compound is baking soda, and which compound is powdered sugar? Explain your answer.

_____

_____

_____

Name _____ Class _____ Date _____

A Sugar Cube Race!

If you drop a sugar cube into a glass of water, how long will it take to dissolve? What can you do to speed up the rate at which it dissolves? Should you change something about the water, the sugar cube, or the process? In other words, what variable should you change? Before reading further, make a list of variables that could be changed in this situation. Record your list.

MATERIALS

- beakers or other clear containers (2)
- clock or stopwatch
- graduated cylinder
- sugar cubes (2)
- water
- Other materials approved by your teacher

SAFETY INFORMATION

Using Scientific Methods

ASK A QUESTION

1. Write a question you can test about factors that affect the rate sugar dissolves.

_____

FORM A HYPOTHESIS

2. Choose one variable to test. Record your choice, and predict how changing your variable will affect the rate of dissolving.

_____

_____

TEST THE HYPOTHESIS

3. Pour 150 mL of water into one of the beakers. Add one sugar cube, and use the stopwatch to measure how long it takes for the sugar cube to dissolve. You must not disturb the sugar cube in any way! Record this time.

_____

4. Be sure to get your teacher's approval before you begin. You may need additional equipment.

A Sugar Cube Race! *continued*

5. Prepare your materials to test the variable you have picked. When you are ready, start your procedure for speeding up the rate at which the sugar cube dissolves. Use the stopwatch to measure the time. Record this time.

ANALYZE THE RESULTS

1. Compare your results with the prediction you made in step 2. Was your prediction correct? Why or why not?

_____

_____

_____

DRAW CONCLUSIONS

2. Why was it necessary to observe the sugar cube dissolving on its own before you tested the variable?

_____

_____

_____

3. Do you think changing more than one variable would speed up the rate of dissolving even more? Explain your reasoning.

_____

_____

_____

_____

4. Discuss your results with a group that tested a different variable. Which variable had a greater effect on the rate of dissolving?

_____

_____

Skills Practice Lab

DATASHEET FOR LABBOOK

Making Butter

A colloid is an interesting substance. It has properties of both solutions and suspensions. Colloidal particles are not heavy enough to settle out, so they remain evenly dispersed throughout the mixture. In this activity, you will make butter—a very familiar colloid—and observe the characteristics that classify butter as a colloid.

MATERIALS

- clock or stopwatch
- container with lid, small, clear
- heavy cream
- marble

SAFETY INFORMATION

PROCEDURE

1. Place a marble inside the container, and fill the container with heavy cream. Put the lid tightly on the container.

2. Take turns shaking the container vigorously and constantly for 10 min. Record the time when you begin shaking. Every minute, stop shaking the container, and hold it up to the light. Record your observations.

_____

_____

3. Continue shaking the container, taking turns if necessary. When you see, hear, or feel any changes inside the container, note the time and change.

_____

_____

4. After 10 min of shaking, you should have a lump of "butter" surrounded by liquid inside the container. Describe both the butter and the liquid in detail.

_____

_____

| Making Butter *continued*

5. Let the container sit for about 10 min. Observe the butter and liquid again, and record your observations.

_____

_____

_____

_____

_____

ANALYZE THE RESULTS

1. When you noticed the change inside the container, what did you think was happening at that point?

_____

_____

_____

2. Based on your observations, explain why butter is classified as a colloid.

_____

_____

_____

3. What kind of mixture is the liquid that is left behind? Explain.

_____

_____

_____

Name _____ Class _____ Date _____

Unpolluting Water

In many cities, the water supply comes from a river, lake, or reservoir. This water may include several mixtures, including suspensions (with suspended dirt, oil, or living organisms) and solutions (with dissolved chemicals). To make the water safe to drink, your city's water supplier must remove impurities. In this lab, you will model the procedures used in real water treatment plants.

MATERIALS

- beaker, 250 mL (4)
- charcoal, activated, washed
- cup, plastic-foam, 8 oz (2)
- graduated cylinder
- nail, small
- paper, filter (2 pieces)
- rubber band
- ruler, metric
- sand, fine, washed
- scissors
- spoon, plastic (2)
- water, "polluted"

SAFETY INFORMATION

Part A: Untreated Water

PROCEDURE

1. Measure 100 mL of "polluted" water into a graduated cylinder. Be sure to shake the bottle of water before you pour so your sample will include all the impurities.

2. Pour the contents of the graduated cylinder into one of the beakers.

3. In the table below, record your observations of the water in the "Before treatment" row.

	Color	Clearness	Odor	Any layers?	Any solids?	Water volume
Before treatment						
After oil separation						
After sand filtration						
After charcoal						

Unpolluting Water *continued*

Part B: Settling In

If a suspension is left standing, the suspended particles will settle to the top or bottom. You should see a layer of oil at the top.

PROCEDURE

1. Separate the oil by carefully pouring the oil into another beaker. You can use a plastic spoon to get the last bit of oil from the water. Record your observations.

Part C: Filtration

Cloudy water can be a sign of small particles still in suspension. These particles can usually be removed by filtering. Water treatment plants use sand and gravel as filters.

PROCEDURE

1. Make a filter as follows:
   a. Use the nail to poke 5 to 10 small holes in the bottom of one of the cups.
   b. Cut a circle of filter paper to fit inside the bottom of the cup. (This filter will keep the sand in the cup.)
   c. Fill the cup to 2 cm below the rim with wet sand. Pack the sand tightly.
   d. Set the cup inside an empty beaker.
2. Pour the polluted water on top of the sand, and let the water filter through. Do not pour any of the settled mud onto the sand. (Dispose of the mud as instructed by your teacher.) In your table, record your observations of the water collected in the beaker.

Part D: Separating Solutions

Something that has been dissolved in a solvent cannot be separated using filters. Water treatment plants use activated charcoal to absorb many dissolved chemicals.

PROCEDURE

1. Place activated charcoal about 3 cm deep in the unused cup. Pour the water collected from the sand filtration into the cup, and stir with a spoon for 1 min.
2. Place a piece of filter paper over the top of the cup, and fasten it in place with a rubber band. With the paper securely in place, pour the water through the filter paper and back into a clean beaker. Record your observations in your table.

Unpolluting Water *continued*

ANALYZE THE RESULTS

1. Is your unpolluted water safe to drink? Why or why not?

_____

_____

_____

_____

_____

_____

_____

_____

2. When you treat a sample of water, do you get out exactly the same amount of water that you put in? Explain your answer.

_____

_____

3. Some groups may still have cloudy water when they finish. Explain a possible cause for this.

_____

_____

_____

Activity

Vocabulary Activity

An ELEMENTary Word Puzzle

After you finish reading the chapter, identify each term described by the clues. Then find and circle each term in the puzzle on the next page. Words may appear forward or backward, horizontally, vertically, or diagonally.

_____ **1.** amount of solute needed to make a saturated solution using a given amount of solvent at a certain temperature

_____ **2.** mixture in which dispersed particles are too light to settle out

_____ **3.** substance in which another is dissolved

_____ **4.** can be expressed as grams of solute per milliliter of solvent

_____ **5.** pure substance that cannot be separated into simpler substances by physical or chemical means

_____ **6.** two or more substances that are combined physically, not chemically

_____ **7.** pure substance made up of at least two elements that are chemically combined

_____ **8.** characteristic property measured in grams per cubic centimeter that tells a substance's mass per unit volume

_____ **9.** element that has properties of both metals and nonmetals

_____ **10.** solid solution of a metal or a nonmetal dissolved in a metal

_____ **11.** dissolved substance

_____ **12.** shiny element; good conductor of thermal energy and electric current

_____ **13.** mixture in which particles of one substance are large enough to settle out of another substance

_____ **14.** brass, salt water, and air, for example

Name _____ Class _____ Date _____

_____ **15.** element that is a poor conductor of thermal energy and electric current

_____ **16.** a substance in which there is only one type of particle

F	S	O	L	U	B	I	L	I	T	Y	L	O	Z	F
S	J	O	H	E	C	U	F	L	A	M	T	Y	E	C
O	K	I	L	T	N	E	M	E	L	E	B	I	H	O
D	O	P	R	U	N	E	T	R	O	J	I	N	S	N
E	I	M	E	L	T	Z	R	N	I	O	P	M	O	C
N	M	O	N	A	C	E	O	P	C	S	J	D	A	E
S	S	O	L	V	E	N	T	G	O	N	U	N	R	N
I	D	N	E	L	P	S	W	L	L	P	S	U	C	T
T	X	R	S	Y	A	V	U	A	L	M	T	O	A	R
Y	E	U	K	C	S	T	T	A	O	X	D	P	R	A
O	T	P	U	R	I	E	E	P	I	A	E	M	B	T
L	A	M	X	O	M	S	N	M	D	V	J	O	A	I
L	W	K	N	N	K	C	R	E	D	E	M	C	T	O
A	L	O	O	L	S	U	S	P	E	N	S	I	O	N
E	C	N	A	T	S	B	U	S	E	R	U	P	U	Q

Activity

SciLinks Activity

MIXTURES

Go to www.scilinks.org. To find links related to mixtures, type in the keyword HSM0974. Then, use the links to answer the following questions about mixtures.

SCI LINKS®

NSTA
Developed and maintained by the
National Science Teachers Association

Go to www.scilinks.org

Topic: Mixtures
SciLinks code: HSM0974

1. What are three key words or phrases related to solutions?

_____

_____

2. What are three examples of solutions?

_____

_____

3. What are three key words or phrases related to suspensions?

_____

_____

4. What are three examples of suspensions?

_____

_____

5. What are three key words or phrases related to colloids?

_____

_____

6. What are three examples of colloids?

_____

_____

7. Using 10 of the words or phrases you have recorded, create a concept map on a separate sheet of paper about the three different types of mixtures.

Performance-Based Assessment

Teacher Notes and Answer Key

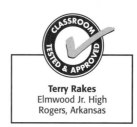

PURPOSE

Students observe the solubility of solids and gases in water at different temperatures.

Terry Rakes
Elmwood Jr. High
Rogers, Arkansas

TIME REQUIRED

One 45-minute class period. Students will need 25 minutes to form and test the hypothesis and 20 minutes to answer the analysis questions.

RATING

Easy  Hard

Teacher Prep–1
Student Set-Up–2
Concept Level–3
Clean Up–1

ADVANCE PREPARATION

Equip each activity station with the necessary materials.

SAFETY INFORMATION

Students should not eat or drink anything in the laboratory. Do not use mercury thermometers. If a thermometer breaks, students should notify the teacher. Students should not heat glassware that is broken, chipped, or cracked. They should use tongs or heatproof gloves to handle heated glassware and other equipment. Clean up water spills immediately; spilled water is a slipping hazard. Never work with electricity near water; be sure the floor and all work surfaces are dry. Students should always wear heat-resistant gloves, goggles, and an apron when using a hot plate to protect their eyes and clothing. Never leave a hot plate unattended while it is turned on. Allow all equipment to cool before storing it. Students should tie back long hair, secure loose clothing, and remove loose jewelry.

TEACHING STRATEGIES

This activity works best in groups of 3–4 students. For this activity, "boiling" is the point at which students first see bubbles form on the bottom of the beaker. Show students how to correctly read a thermometer. In order to get an accurate reading, their eyes should be level with the mark. Ask students how the temperature could be read incorrectly if their eyes are above the level. *If your eyes are above the level, you will read a lower temperature than the actual temperature.* Ask students how the temperature could be read incorrectly if their eyes are below the level. *If your eyes are below the level, you will read a higher temperature than the actual temperature.*

Performance-Based Assessment *continued*

Evaluation Strategies

Use the following rubric to help evaluate student performance.

Rubric for Assessment

Possible points	Forming and testing hypothesis (30 points possible)
30–20	Successful completion of activity; safe and careful handling of materials and equipment; attention to detail; superior lab skills
19–10	Activity is generally complete; successful use of materials and equipment; sound knowledge of lab techniques; somewhat unfocused performance
9–1	Attempts to complete activity yield inadequate results; sloppy lab technique; no attention to detail; apparent lack of skill
	Analyzing results (40 points possible)
40–27	Superior analysis stated clearly and accurately; high level of detail; correct usage of scientific terminology
26–14	Accurate analysis; moderate level of detail; correct usage of scientific terminology
13–1	Erroneous, incomplete, or unclear analysis; incorrect use of scientific terminology
	Drawing conclusions (30 points possible)
30–20	Clear, detailed explanation shows good understanding of solubility of solids and gases in liquids at different temperatures; use of examples to support explanations
19–10	Adequate understanding of solubility of solids and gases in liquids at different temperatures with minor difficulty in expression
9–1	Poor understanding of solubility of solids and gases in liquids at different temperatures; explanation not relevant to the activity; factual errors

Performance-Based Assessment

OBJECTIVE

You will investigate how solids and gases dissolve in water at different temperatures.

KNOW THE SCORE!

As you work through the activity, keep in mind that you will be earning a grade for the following:

• how well you form and test the hypothesis (30%)

• the quality of your analysis (40%)

• the clarity of your conclusions (30%)

Using Scientific Methods

ASK A QUESTION

Does the temperature of a liquid affect how much salt can dissolve in it?

MATERIALS AND EQUIPMENT

• 240 mL (1 cup) of cold water

• paper towels

• 240 mL beakers (2)

• heat-resistant gloves

• hot plate

• alcohol thermometer

• thermometer holder

• 240 mL of salt

• 5 mL spoon (1 tsp)

• stirring rod or spoon

SAFETY INFORMATION

• Do not eat or drink anything in the laboratory.

• If a thermometer breaks, notify the teacher.

• Use tongs or heatproof gloves to handle heated glassware and other equipment.

• Clean up water spills immediately; spilled water is a slipping hazard.

• Never work with electricity near water; be sure the floor and all work surfaces are dry.

• Wear heat-resistant gloves, goggles, and an apron when using a hot plate to protect your eyes and clothing.

• Never leave a hot plate unattended while it is turned on.

• Tie back long hair, secure loose clothing, and remove loose jewelry.

Name _____ Class _____ Date _____

| Performance-Based Assessment *continued*

FORM A HYPOTHESIS

1. Will the cold water or the hot water dissolve more salt?

  Sample hypothesis: The hot water will dissolve more salt.

2. Will the salt water boil at a lower temperature, the same temperature, or a higher temperature than the plain water?

  Sample hypothesis: The salt water will boil at a higher temperature than the

  plain water.

TEST THE HYPOTHESIS

3. Pour 120 mL of cold water into each empty beaker.

4. Wearing goggles, heat-resistant gloves, and an apron, plug in and turn on the hot plate. Place one of the beakers on the hot plate. When the water begins to boil, place the thermometer in the water. Do not let the thermometer rest on the bottom of the beaker. Write the temperature below. The boiling point for water is ____**100**____ °C.

5. Remove the beaker from the hot plate. Set it next to the other beaker.

6. To each beaker, add salt a spoonful at a time while stirring until no more salt dissolves. Record the amount of salt dissolved in the water. (Each spoonful is 5 mL.) You will know when no more salt will dissolve when you see salt fall to the bottom no matter how much you stir.

Amount of Dissolved Salt

Cold water (mL)	Hot water (mL)
10	20

7. Place one of the beakers containing salt water on the hot plate. When the water begins to boil, place the thermometer in the water, and write the temperature below. The boiling point for salt water is ____**104**____ °C.

8. Turn off and unplug the hot plate.

| Performance-Based Assessment *continued*

ANALYZE THE RESULTS

9. Did the salt water boil at a lower temperature, the same temperature, or a higher temperature than the plain water?

The salt water boiled at a higher temperature than the plain water.

_____

10. Did the cold water or the hot water dissolve more salt?

The hot water dissolved more salt.

_____

11. Why did you see bubbles in the water when it heated up?

Air bubbles that had dissolved in the water started to escape.

_____

DRAW CONCLUSIONS

12. Compare how easily solids dissolve in hot water with how easily they dissolve in cool water. Write one sentence summarizing your observation.

Hot water dissolves more solids than cold water dissolves.

_____

_____

Flame Tests

Kenneth J. Horn
Fallston Middle School
Fallston, Maryland

Teacher Notes and Answer Key

TIME REQUIRED

One or two 45-minute class periods

LAB RATINGS

Teacher Prep–3
Student Set-Up–2
Concept Level–4
Clean Up–3

Easy ◄—— 1 ——— 2 ——— 3 ——— 4 ——► Hard

MATERIALS

The materials listed are for each group of 2–3 students. The unknown solution should be clear. Use only dilute hydrochloric acid—concentrations lower than 1.0 M. When diluting an acid, always add the acid to the water.

PREPARATION NOTES

Prepare solutions of KCl, $CaCl_2$, and NaCl in a concentration of 10 g/500mL of solution. Make enough of one of the solutions to serve as the "unknown." You will need 5 to 10 mL of each solution per group. Make the wire holder with Nichrome® wire or paper clips and ice-cream sticks or corks. Bend one end of the wire into a small loop like a bubble wand. Tape the other end of the wire to the stick, or insert it into the cork.

SAFETY CAUTION

Remind students to review all safety cautions and icons before beginning this lab. Students should touch only the wooden handle of the wire holder device because the wire will become hot and could cause burns. Students should be careful with the dilute hydrochloric acid. If contact occurs, they should flush their skin immediately with water. Long hair and loose clothing should be restricted around an open flame. In case of an acid spill, first dilute the spill with water. Then mop up the spill with wet cloths or a wet mop while wearing disposable plastic gloves.

Name _____ Class _____ Date _____

Skills Practice Lab

DATASHEET FOR CHAPTER LAB

Flame Tests

Fireworks produce fantastic combinations of color when they are ignited. The different colors are the results of burning different compounds. Imagine that you are the head chemist for a fireworks company. The label has fallen off one box, and you must identify the unknown compound inside so that the fireworks may be used in the correct fireworks display. To identify the compound, you will use your knowledge that every compound has a unique set of properties.

OBJECTIVE

Observe flame colors emitted by various compounds.

Determine the composition of an unknown compound.

MATERIALS

- Bunsen burner
- chloride test solutions (4)
- hydrochloric acid, dilute, in a small beaker
- spark igniter

- tape, masking
- test tubes, small (4)
- test-tube rack
- water, distilled, in a small beaker
- wire and holder

SAFETY INFORMATION

Using Scientific Methods

ASK A QUESTION

1. How can you identify an unknown compound by heating it in a flame?

FORM A HYPOTHESIS

2. Write a hypothesis that is a possible answer to the question above. Explain your reasoning.

_____

_____

_____

Name _____ Class _____ Date _____

Flame Tests *continued*

TEST THE HYPOTHESIS

3. Arrange the test tubes in the test-tube rack. Use masking tape to label each tube with one of the following names: calcium chloride, potassium chloride, sodium chloride, and unknown.

4. Use the table below to record your results. Then, ask your teacher for your portions of the solutions. **Caution:** Be very careful in handling all chemicals. Tell your teacher immediately if you spill a chemical.

Test Results	
Compound	**Color of Flame**
Calcium chloride	
Potassium chloride	
Sodium chloride	
Unknown	

5. Light the burner. Clean the wire by dipping it into the dilute hydrochloric acid and then into distilled water. Holding the wooden handle, heat the wire in the blue flame of the burner until the wire is glowing and it no longer colors the flame. Caution: Use extreme care around an open flame.

6. Dip the clean wire into the first test solution. Hold the wire at the tip of the inner cone of the burner flame. Record in the table the color given to the flame.

7. Clean the wire by repeating step 5. Then, repeat steps 5 and 6 for the other solutions.

8. Follow your teacher's instructions for cleanup and disposal.

ANALYZE THE RESULTS

1. Identifying Patterns Is the flame color a test for the metal or for the chloride in each compound? Explain your answer.

<u>The flame test is a test for the metal in each compound. Because each com-</u>

<u>pound contains chloride, the color difference must be due to the</u>

<u>different metals. Any color contribution from the chloride would be the same</u>

<u>in each trial.</u>

_____

Name _____ Class _____ Date _____

Flame Tests *continued*

2. Analyzing Data What is the identity of your unknown solution? How do you know?

Answers will depend on the teacher's choice for the unknown compound.

Students will know its identity because it will produce the same color flame

as one of the other three solutions.

DRAW CONCLUSIONS

3. Evaluating Methods Why is it necessary to carefully clean the wire before testing each solution?

The wire must be cleaned so the color observed is from the solution being

tested, not from a mixture of two solutions.

4. Making Predictions Would you expect the compound sodium fluoride to produce the same color as sodium chloride in a flame test? Why or why not?

Yes; the sodium fluoride compound would likely burn the same color as the

sodium chloride compound because the flame test is a test for the metal in a

compound and both compounds contain sodium.

5. Interpreting Information Each of the compounds you tested is made from chlorine, which is a poisonous gas at room temperature. Why is it safe to use these compounds without a gas mask?

Compounds have chemical and physical properties that are different from

those of the elements the compounds are formed from.

Name _____ Class _____ Date _____

Separating Elements

MATERIALS

- magnet, bar
- nails, mixed sample, some iron and some aluminum

SAFETY INFORMATION

PROCEDURE

1. Examine a sample of **nails** provided by your teacher. Record your observations.

_____

_____

_____

2. Your sample has **aluminum nails** and **iron nails.** Try to separate the two kinds of nails. Group similar nails into piles.

3. Pass a **bar magnet** over each pile of nails. Record your results.

_____

_____

_____

4. Were you successful in completely separating the two types of nails? Explain.

The iron nails are attracted to the magnet but the aluminum nails are not.

_____

_____

5. How could the properties of aluminum and iron be used to separate cans in a recycling plant.

Sample answer: A magnet can be used to separate materials that are mag-

netic and non-magnetic. In an aluminum recycling plant, non-aluminum

materials such as iron can be separated by using a magnet.

_____

Name _____ Class _____ Date _____

DATASHEET FOR QUICK LAB

Compound Confusion

MATERIALS

- baking soda
- cups, clear plastic (2)
- sugar, powdered
- teaspoon
- vinegar

SAFETY INFORMATION

PROCEDURE

1. Measure a **4 g of compound A,** and place it in a **clear plastic cup.**

2. Measure a **4 g of compound B,** and place it in a **second clear plastic cup.**

3. Observe the color and texture of each compound. Record your observations.

_____

_____

_____

4. Add **5 ml of vinegar** to each cup. Record your observations.

_____

_____

_____

5. Baking soda reacts with vinegar. Powdered sugar does not react with vinegar. Which compound is baking soda, and which compound is powdered sugar? Explain your answer.

   One compound (baking soda) reacts with vinegar by bubbling, the other

   (powdered sugar) does not react.

_____

A Sugar Cube Race!

Kenneth J. Horn
Fallston Middle School
Fallston, Maryland

Teacher Notes and Answer Key

TIME REQUIRED

One 45-minute class period

LAB RATINGS

Easy ◄——1——2——3——4——► Hard

Teacher Prep–1
Student Set-Up–1
Concept Level–2
Clean Up–1

PREPARATION NOTES

Remind students not to eat the sugar cube. Have hot water or hot plates and heat-resistant gloves ready for students who want to test temperature. Have paper towels on hand for students to wrap their cube in as they crush it.

Name _____ Class _____ Date _____

A Sugar Cube Race!

If you drop a sugar cube into a glass of water, how long will it take to dissolve? What can you do to speed up the rate at which it dissolves? Should you change something about the water, the sugar cube, or the process? In other words, what variable should you change? Before reading further, make a list of variables that could be changed in this situation. Record your list.

MATERIALS

- beakers or other clear containers (2)
- clock or stopwatch
- graduated cylinder
- sugar cubes (2)
- water
- Other materials approved by your teacher

SAFETY INFORMATION

Using Scientific Methods

ASK A QUESTION

1. Write a question you can test about factors that affect the rate sugar dissolves.

_____

FORM A HYPOTHESIS

2. Choose one variable to test. Record your choice, and predict how changing your variable will affect the rate of dissolving.

_____

_____

TEST THE HYPOTHESIS

3. Pour 150 mL of water into one of the beakers. Add one sugar cube, and use the stopwatch to measure how long it takes for the sugar cube to dissolve. You must not disturb the sugar cube in any way! Record this time.

_____

4. Be sure to get your teacher's approval before you begin. You may need additional equipment.

Name _____ Class _____ Date _____

A Sugar Cube Race! *continued*

5. Prepare your materials to test the variable you have picked. When you are ready, start your procedure for speeding up the rate at which the sugar cube dissolves. Use the stopwatch to measure the time. Record this time.

ANALYZE THE RESULTS

1. Compare your results with the prediction you made in step 2. Was your prediction correct? Why or why not?

Answers may vary, depending on the original prediction. Tested variables

may include water temperature, surface area of cube, and stirring.

DRAW CONCLUSIONS

2. Why was it necessary to observe the sugar cube dissolving on its own before you tested the variable?

Observing the sugar cube dissolving on its own provides a control so that

you can measure the effect of the variable.

3. Do you think changing more than one variable would speed up the rate of dissolving even more? Explain your reasoning.

Changing two variables that each increase the dissolving rate should

increase the rate of dissolving even more, but it would be difficult to deter-

mine which variable had the greater effect.

4. Discuss your results with a group that tested a different variable. Which variable had a greater effect on the rate of dissolving?

Accept all reasonable answers based on class data.

Skills Practice Lab

Making Butter

Teacher Notes and Answer Key

Kenneth J. Horn
Fallston Middle School
Fallston, Maryland

TIME REQUIRED

One 45-minute class period

LAB RATINGS

Easy  Hard

Teacher Prep–2
Student Set-Up–1
Concept Level–2
Clean Up–2

MATERIALS

Materials listed are for each pair of students. If using glass containers, students should shake the container vigorously but not violently, because it might break. Be sure each lid fits tightly. A small or medium-sized ball bearing may be substituted for the marble. For best results, the cream should be room temperature, not cold.

SAFETY CAUTION

Caution students to wear safety goggles while performing this activity.

Skills Practice Lab

Making Butter

A colloid is an interesting substance. It has properties of both solutions and suspensions. Colloidal particles are not heavy enough to settle out, so they remain evenly dispersed throughout the mixture. In this activity, you will make butter—a very familiar colloid—and observe the characteristics that classify butter as a colloid.

MATERIALS

- clock or stopwatch
- container with lid, small, clear
- heavy cream
- marble

SAFETY INFORMATION

PROCEDURE

1. Place a marble inside the container, and fill the container with heavy cream. Put the lid tightly on the container.

2. Take turns shaking the container vigorously and constantly for 10 min. Record the time when you begin shaking. Every minute, stop shaking the container, and hold it up to the light. Record your observations.

_____

_____

3. Continue shaking the container, taking turns if necessary. When you see, hear, or feel any changes inside the container, note the time and change.

_____

_____

4. After 10 min of shaking, you should have a lump of "butter" surrounded by liquid inside the container. Describe both the butter and the liquid in detail.

_____

_____

Making Butter *continued*

5. Let the container sit for about 10 min. Observe the butter and liquid again, and record your observations.

_____

_____

_____

_____

_____

ANALYZE THE RESULTS

1. When you noticed the change inside the container, what did you think was happening at that point?

Answers may vary. Students should mention that the suspended materials

were starting to settle out.

_____

2. Based on your observations, explain why butter is classified as a colloid.

The butter appears to have characteristics of both a solution and a

suspension.

_____

3. What kind of mixture is the liquid that is left behind? Explain.

The liquid left behind appears to be a suspension.

_____

_____

Unpolluting Water

Joseph Price
H.M. Browne Junior High
Washington, D.C.

Teacher Notes and Answer Key
TIME REQUIRED
One or two 45-minute class periods

LAB RATINGS
Easy ← 1 2 3 4 → Hard

Teacher Prep–3
Student Set-Up–3
Concept Level–3
Clean Up–2

MATERIALS
Materials listed are for each group of 2–3 students. Use large filter paper for part D, or place filter paper in a funnel.

Special notes on materials:

1. Sand must be thoroughly washed to eliminate as much dust as possible. Put the sand in a bowl, and run water into it while stirring until the water runs clear. The finer the sand, the better the filtering action will be.

2. Use activated charcoal, available from pet-supply stores. This charcoal can be washed by quickly running water through the charcoal in a sieve or colander. Do not allow the charcoal to remain in water too long, or it will lose its absorbing power.

SAFETY CAUTION
Make sure all spills are cleaned up immediately.

PREPARATION NOTES
Make "polluted water" as follows: Put the following into a half-gallon milk jug:

1 cup cooking oil

3⁄4 to 1 cup of dirt

1 or 2 drops of food coloring
(yellow or red works best)

Fill the jug with water, put the cap on, and shake the jug well. It is important that students shake the mixture well before pouring their 100 mL sample. Students can estimate the water volume after Parts B–D using the approximate volume markings on the side of the beaker. Have students use a clean graduated cylinder in Part D to measure the volume of treated water.

Unpolluting Water *continued*

DISPOSAL INFORMATION

1. Solid charcoal should be dried and buried in a landfill that is approved for chemical disposal. You may want to consider drying and reusing the charcoal, although it will eventually lose its absorbing power.

2. Pour cooking oil into disposable containers, refrigerate (if possible) until the oil congeals, and put in the trash.

3. The sand can be reused if it is washed after this activity.

4. Spoon or pour the mud into disposable containers, and put them in the trash.

Name _____ Class _____ Date _____

Unpolluting Water

In many cities, the water supply comes from a river, lake, or reservoir. This water may include several mixtures, including suspensions (with suspended dirt, oil, or living organisms) and solutions (with dissolved chemicals). To make the water safe to drink, your city's water supplier must remove impurities. In this lab, you will model the procedures used in real water treatment plants.

MATERIALS

- beaker, 250 mL (4)
- charcoal, activated, washed
- cup, plastic-foam, 8 oz (2)
- graduated cylinder
- nail, small
- paper, filter (2 pieces)

- rubber band
- ruler, metric
- sand, fine, washed
- scissors
- spoon, plastic (2)
- water, "polluted"

SAFETY INFORMATION

Part A: Untreated Water

PROCEDURE

1. Measure 100 mL of "polluted" water into a graduated cylinder. Be sure to shake the bottle of water before you pour so your sample will include all the impurities.

2. Pour the contents of the graduated cylinder into one of the beakers.

3. In the table below, record your observations of the water in the "Before treatment" row.

	Color	**Clearness**	**Odor**	**Any layers?**	**Any solids?**	**Water volume**
Before treatment						
After oil separation						
After sand filtration						
After charcoal						

Name _____ Class _____ Date _____

| Unpolluting Water *continued*

Part B: Settling In

If a suspension is left standing, the suspended particles will settle to the top or bottom. You should see a layer of oil at the top.

PROCEDURE

1. Separate the oil by carefully pouring the oil into another beaker. You can use a plastic spoon to get the last bit of oil from the water. Record your observations.

Part C: Filtration

Cloudy water can be a sign of small particles still in suspension. These particles can usually be removed by filtering. Water treatment plants use sand and gravel as filters.

PROCEDURE

1. Make a filter as follows:

   a. Use the nail to poke 5 to 10 small holes in the bottom of one of the cups.

   b. Cut a circle of filter paper to fit inside the bottom of the cup. (This filter will keep the sand in the cup.)

   c. Fill the cup to 2 cm below the rim with wet sand. Pack the sand tightly.

   d. Set the cup inside an empty beaker.

2. Pour the polluted water on top of the sand, and let the water filter through. Do not pour any of the settled mud onto the sand. (Dispose of the mud as instructed by your teacher.) In your table, record your observations of the water collected in the beaker.

Part D: Separating Solutions

Something that has been dissolved in a solvent cannot be separated using filters. Water treatment plants use activated charcoal to absorb many dissolved chemicals.

PROCEDURE

1. Place activated charcoal about 3 cm deep in the unused cup. Pour the water collected from the sand filtration into the cup, and stir with a spoon for 1 min.

2. Place a piece of filter paper over the top of the cup, and fasten it in place with a rubber band. With the paper securely in place, pour the water through the filter paper and back into a clean beaker. Record your observations in your table.

Name _____ Class _____ Date _____

Unpolluting Water *continued*

ANALYZE THE RESULTS

1. Is your unpolluted water safe to drink? Why or why not?

Students will have different opinions, depending on their results. Many

will likely say that unpolluted water is safe to drink because it goes

through so many filtering processes, but some may say it is unsafe because

their samples still look cloudy after the experiment. (Note: Students should

be discouraged from tasting the water. This activity does not include

treatment with chlorine that takes place at most water treatment plants to

kill bacteria.)

2. When you treat a sample of water, do you get out exactly the same amount of water that you put in? Explain your answer.

no; Some of the water is lost in the treatment processes.

3. Some groups may still have cloudy water when they finish. Explain a possible cause for this.

Accept all reasonable answers. Sample answer: Dust from the charcoal and

sand made the water cloudy. Bacteria in the water caused it to look cloudy.

Answer Key

Directed Reading A

SECTION: ELEMENTS

1. B
2. element
3. pure substance
4. characteristic properties
5. A helium-filled balloon will float up when released because helium is less dense than air.
6. N
7. CP
8. CP
9. N
10. N
11. N
12. CP
13. CP
14. CP
15. N
16. CP
17. Answers will vary. Sample answer: Terriers are small and they have short hair.
18. nonmetals
19. metal
20. nonmetal
21. metalloid
22. C
23. A
24. B
25. B
26. C
27. A
28. B
29. A
30. A
31. C
32. B

SECTION: COMPOUNDS

1. Answers will vary. Sample answer: salt, water, and sugar
2. C
3. compound
4. elements
5. B

6. Answers will vary. Sample answer: A compound has different properties than the elements that react to form it. Although sodium and chlorine are dangerous individually, they combine to form sodium chloride, a safe substance also known as table salt.
7. B
8. A
9. C
10. carbonic acid
11. carbon, oxygen, and hydrogen
12. chemical change
13. D
14. aluminum oxide

SECTION: MIXTURES

1. mixture
2. mixture
3. compound
4. Answers will vary. Sample answer: You can see each component in the pizza. Each component has the same chemical makeup as it did before the pizza was made.
5. physical
6. A
7. B
8. D
9. C
10. ratio
11. D
12. dissolving
13. solute, solvent
14. soluble
15. solute
16. alloy
17. Answers will vary. Sample answer: Particles in solution are so small that they can never settle out, cannot be removed or filtered out, and cannot scatter light.
18. concentration
19. A dilute solution contains less solute than a concentrated solution does.
20. solubility
21. temperature, pressure
22. D
23. A

24. increase
25. decrease
26. You can heat the solution, mix the solution by stirring or shaking it, or crush the sugar before adding it.
27. A
28. Answers will vary. Sample answer: Unless the globe is shaken, the snow particles will not stay dispersed, and will settle at the bottom.
29. Gelatin, milk, and stick deodorant are all colloids.
30. B
31. C
32. A

Directed Reading B

SECTION: ELEMENTS

1. B
2. C
3. B
4. A
5. B
6. B
7. A
8. C
9. D
10. small
11. elements
12. metals
13. nonmetals
14. metalloids
15. C
16. A
17. B
18. D
19. A
20. C
21. B

SECTION: COMPOUNDS

1. B
2. B
3. B
4. B
5. B
6. C
7. carbonic acid
8. carbon dioxide
9. chemical change
10. B
11. A
12. D
13. B

SECTION: MIXTURES

1. mixture
2. compound
3. identity
4. physical
5. A
6. D
7. B
8. C
9. A
10. D
11. B
12. A
13. B
14. soluble

15. C
16. alloy
17. particles
18. C
19. A
20. C
21. solubility
22. temperature
23. D
24. A
25. decreases
26. increases
27. A
28. A
29. A

Vocabulary and Section Summary

SECTION: ELEMENTS

1. element: a substance that cannot be separated or broken down into simpler substances by chemical means
2. pure substance: a sample of matter, either a single element or a single compound, that has definite chemical and physical properties
3. metal: an element that is shiny and that conducts heat and electric current well
4. nonmetal: an element that conducts heat and electric current poorly; can be solid, liquid, or gas
5. metalloid: elements that have properties of both metals and nonmetals

SECTION: COMPOUNDS

1. compound: a substance made up of atoms of two or more different elements joined by chemical bonds

SECTION: MIXTURES

1. mixture: a combination of two or more substances that are not chemically combined
2. solution: a homogeneous mixture of two or more substances uniformly dispersed throughout a single phase
3. solute: in a solution, the substance that dissolves in the solvent
4. solvent: in a solution, the substance in which the solute dissolves
5. concentration: the amount of a particular substance in a given quantity of a mixture, solution, or ore
6. solubility: the ability of one substance to dissolve in another at a given temperature and pressure

7. suspension: a mixture in which particles of a material are more or less evenly dispersed throughout a liquid or gas

8. colloid: a mixture consisting of tiny particles that are intermediate in size between those in solutions and those in suspensions and that are suspended in a liquid, solid, or gas

Section Review

SECTION: ELEMENTS

1. Sample answer: An element is an example of a pure substance.

2. D

3. A pure substance is a substance in which there is only one type of particle.

4. 98.5% − 46.6% − 8.1% − 5.0% − 3.6% − 2.8% − 2.6% − 2.1% = 27.7% silicon

5. Sample answer: I would make the container with a metal because metals are not brittle, and they are malleable.

6. Metals are shiny, are good conductors of heat and electric current, and are malleable and ductile. Nonmetals are dull, are poor conductors of heat and electric current, and tend to be brittle. Metalloids can be dull or shiny, may conduct heat and electric current, and are somewhat malleable and ductile.

7. Sample answer: I do not agree because the element could be a metalloid. Some metalloids are shiny.

SECTION: COMPOUNDS

1. A compound is something that is made of atoms of two or more elements that are joined by chemical bonds.

2. D

3. A chemical change is needed to break down a compound.

4. 100% − 41.86% − 6.98% = 51.16% oxygen

5. When elements combine to form a compound, the compound's properties are different from the properties of the individual elements.

6. Sample answer: No, the jar does not contain a compound. The jar has carbon and oxygen, but the two elements are not joined by chemical bonds.

SECTION: MIXTURES

1. solute

2. solution

3. concentration

4. suspension

5. C

6. Three ways to dissolve a solid faster are crushing the solid, stirring the solid and liquid, and heating the solid and liquid.

7. A solution appears to be a single substance and contains particles evenly distributed among each other. The particles in a solution are very small and can't be filtered out. A clear solution will not scatter light. A suspension has larger particles that are dispersed but will settle out. The particles in a suspension can be filtered out and are large enough to block or scatter light. Particles in a colloid are smaller than the particles in a suspension, but are still large enough to scatter light.

8. Sample answer: I would use a magnet to separate the iron from the sawdust. The magnet will attract the iron but will not attract the sawdust.

9. The solute is helium and the solvent is oxygen.

10. about 60°C

11. about 120 g more sodium chlorate will dissolve.

Chapter Review

1. compound

2. solubility

3. suspension

4. element

5. nonmetal

6. solute

7. C

8. B

9. C

10. B

11. C

12. A

13. C

14. A

15. Elements cannot be separated into simpler substances, but compounds can be separated by chemical means.

16. Nail polish is the solute, and acetone is the solvent.

17. 50 g/200 mL = 0.25 g/mL

18. 150 mL × 0.6 g/mL = 90 g

19. An answer to this exercise can be found at the end of this book.

20. Carbonated beverages should be stored in a refrigerator. Gases are more soluble at lower temperatures, so more gas will stay dissolved in the beverage if it is kept cold.

21. The powder is a compound. The change in color and the formation of a gas imply that a chemical change took place. Compounds can be broken down by chemical changes.

22. The exact concentration tells you exactly how much solute is dissolved in the solvent. Concentrated and dilute are descriptive terms that do not tell you the amount of solute.

23. Answers will vary. Sample answer: Pass the mixture through a screen that allows the salt and pepper to pass through but traps the pebbles. Mix the salt and pepper with water to dissolve the salt. Filter the mixture to trap the pepper. Evaporate the water to recover the salt.

24. (Teacher note: The graph should have dissolved solute on the y-axis and temperature on the x-axis. The curve will decrease from left to right.) You should decrease the temperature to increase the solubility. As the temperature decreases, more solute can dissolve.

25. 68 g

26. Because the solubility increases as the temperature decreases, the solute is most likely a gas.

Reinforcement

IT'S ALL MIXED UP

1. colloid
2. compound
3. element
4. suspension
5. solution

6. Accept all reasonable answers. Sample answer: In Figure 3, the particles were identical and part of the same substance, so it had to be an element. Figure 2 was a compound because the particles were identical but made of two different substances. The other three figures were mixtures because each contained two different types of particles. Figure 4 had the largest clumps of the solute, so it was a suspension. Figure 1 had the next-largest clumps of the second substance, making it a colloid. Figure 5 had the most homogeneous mix of the two substances, making it a solution.

7. A. solution, B. compound, C. suspension, D. colloid

Critical Thinking

1. They are both metals that resist corrosion, and they have similar melting points. Platinum has a higher density and is a precious metal. Titanium is stronger than platinum.

2. Answers will vary. Sample answer: The metal would have to be lightweight to maximize the jet's speed, yet strong enough to withstand high pressure. It also should have a high melting point and should resist corrosion.

3. Answers will vary. Sample answer: I would choose titanium because it is strong and lightweight. These properties would maximize jet performance and durability. It is probably less expensive because it is not a precious metal.

4. Answers will vary. Sample answer: The jet may be too heavy to fly, or the engine may overheat and melt. Most elements are found in nature as compounds. The properties of a compound are different from the properties of the elements within the compound.

Section Quizzes

SECTION: ELEMENTS

1. B	**5.** C
2. E	**6.** B
3. A	**7.** D
4. D	**8.** C

SECTION: COMPOUNDS

1. A	**4.** B
2. C	**5.** A
3. D	

SECTION: MIXTURES

1. E	**6.** J
2. H	**7.** F
3. B	**8.** D
4. C	**9.** G
5. I	**10.** A

Chapter Test A

1. B	**13.** C
2. C	**14.** A
3. B	**15.** B
4. A	**16.** C
5. C	**17.** D
6. A	**18.** E
7. B	**19.** A
8. D	**20.** B
9. A	**21.** F
10. D	**22.** D
11. D	**23.** A
12. B	

Chapter Test B

1. compound
2. solute
3. alloys
4. suspensions
5. solution
6. A
7. B
8. A
9. A
10. Answers will vary. Sample answer: Compounds are considered pure substances because they are composed of only one type of particle. The particles of a compound are made of atoms of two or more elements that are chemically combined. Different samples of any compound have the same elements in the same proportion.

11. Answers will vary. Sample answer: Metalloids, also called semiconductors, are elements that have properties of both metals and nonmetals. Some metalloids are shiny, while others are dull. They are only somewhat malleable and ductile. Some metalloids, like silicon, are good electrical conductors only when mixed with other elements.

12. Answers will vary. Sample answer: Mixing by stirring or shaking causes the particles to separate from one another and spread out more quickly among the solvent particles. Heating causes particles to move more quickly. The solvent particles can separate the solute particles and spread them out more quickly. Crushing the solute increases the amount of contact it has with the solvent. The particles of the crushed solute mix with the solvent more quickly.

13. Answers will vary. Sample answer: Salt water is a mixture, so its components can be separated by physical methods. Distillation involves heating the water, which changes water into steam. When salt water is distilled, steam is condensed back into water, and salt is left behind.

14. Answers will vary. Sample answer: I would first try to separate it by using distillation and a centrifuge. If I could separate it this way, I would know that it was a mixture. I would also try to separate it by passing an electric current though it. If I could separate it this way, I would know it was a compound. If I could not separate it at all, I might think it was an element, but I might also need to try other methods of separating it to be sure.

15. Answers will vary. Sample answer: Substances 1 and 3 are probably the same because they have the same melting point, the same amount of hardness, and are nonmagnetic. Substance 2 is different because it has a different density and hardness. It is also a slightly different color.

16. As pressure increases, the solubility of oxygen and nitrogen in water increases.

17. Oxygen experiences a greater change in solubility per unit pressure. The slope of the line that represents oxygen is steeper.

18. a. pure substances, **b.** compounds, **c.** solutions, **d.** suspensions, **e.** physical or chemical, **f.** chemical

Chapter Test C

1. B
2. C
3. B
4. B
5. C
6. B
7. D
8. B
9. A
10. C
11. D
12. B
13. A
14. D
15. B
16. C
17. distillation
18. nitrogen
19. nonmetals
20. ratio

Standardized Test Preparation

READING
Passage 1

1. A   3. C
2. H

Passage 2

1. B   3. D
2. H

INTERPRETING GRAPHICS

1. D   3. B
2. F   4. G

MATH

1. C
2. I
3. B
4. I

Vocabulary Activity

1. solubility
2. colloid
3. solvent
4. concentration
5. element
6. mixture
7. compound
8. density
9. metalloid
10. alloy
11. solute
12. metal
13. suspension
14. solution
15. nonmetal
16. pure substance

F	S	O	L	U	B	I	L	I	T	Y	L	O	Z	F
S	J	O	H	E	C	U	F	L	A	M	T	Y	E	C
O	K	I	L	T	N	E	M	E	L	E	B	I	H	O
D	O	P	R	U	N	E	T	R	O	J	I	N	S	N
E	I	M	E	L	T	Z	R	N	I	O	P	M	O	C
N	M	O	N	A	C	E	O	P	C	S	J	D	A	E
S	S	O	L	V	E	N	T	G	O	N	U	N	R	N
I	D	N	E	L	P	S	W	L	L	P	S	U	C	T
T	X	R	S	Y	A	V	U	A	L	M	T	O	A	R
Y	E	U	K	C	S	T	T	A	O	X	D	P	R	A
O	T	P	U	R	I	E	E	P	I	A	E	M	B	T
L	A	M	X	O	M	S	N	M	D	V	J	O	A	I
L	W	K	N	N	K	C	R	E	D	E	M	C	T	O
A	L	O	O	L	S	U	S	P	E	N	S	I	O	N
E	C	N	A	T	S	B	U	S	E	R	U	P	U	Q

SciLinks Activity

1. Answers will vary. Sample answer: dissolve, do not settle out, solute.
2. Answers will vary. Sample answer: sugar in coffee, tea, salt water.
3. Answers will vary. Sample answer: particles distributed, easily settle out filterable particles.
4. Answers will vary. Sample answer: soup, jello, paints.
5. Answers will vary. Sample answer: large particles, settle out very slowly, can not be filtered.
6. Answers will vary. Sample answer: salad dressing, whipping cream, milk.
7. Answer should show the relationships among 10 of the terms listed in answers 1–6.

Lesson Plan

Section: Elements

Pacing

Regular Schedule: **with lab(s):** N/A   **without lab(s):** 1 day

Block Schedule: **with lab(s):** N/A   **without lab(s):** 0.5 day

Objectives

1. Describe pure substances.

2. Describe the characteristics of elements, and give examples.

3. Explain how elements can be identified.

4. Classify elements according to their properties.

National Science Education Standards Covered

UCP 1: Systems, order, and organization

UCP 2: Evidence, models, and explanation

SAI 1: Abilities necessary to do scientific inquiry

PS 1a: A substance has characteristic properties, such as density, a boiling point, and solubility, all of which are independent of the amount of the sample. A mixture of substances often can be separated into the original substances using one or more of the characteristic properties.

PS 1c: Chemical elements do not break down during normal laboratory reactions involving such treatments as heating, exposure to electric current, or reaction with acids. There are more than 100 known elements that combine in a multitude of ways to produce compounds, which account for the living and nonliving substances that we encounter.

KEY

SE = Student Edition   **TE** = Teacher's Edition

CRF = Chapter Resource File

FOCUS (*5 minutes*)

_ **Chapter Starter Transparency** Use this transparency to introduce the chapter.

_ **Bellringer, TE** Have students answer questions about the figure.

_ **Bellringer Transparency** Use this transparency as students enter the classroom and find their seats.

MOTIVATE (*10 minutes*)

_ **Demonstration, TE** Demonstrate the properties of aluminum. (**GENERAL**)

TEACH *(20 minutes)*

_ **Reading Strategy, SE** Have students make a concept map when reading the section. **(BASIC)**

_ **Quick Lab, Separating Elements, SE** Ask students to separate aluminum and iron nails by making use of their properties. **(GENERAL)**

_ **Connection Activity, Math, TE** Have students make a graph to show the percentages of various elements in the human body. **(GENERAL)**

_ **Connection Activity, Real Life, TE** Provide students with information about lead poisoning. **(GENERAL)**

_ **Critical Thinking, Jet Smart, CRF** Ask the students to fill out the worksheet about two different metals. **(ADVANCED)**

_ **Directed Reading A/B, CRF** These worksheets reinforce basic concepts and vocabulary presented in the lesson. **(BASIC/SPECIAL NEEDS)**

_ **Vocabulary and Section Summary, CRF** Students write definitions of key terms and read a summary of section content. **(GENERAL)**

CLOSE *(10 minutes)*

_ **Reteaching, TE** Have students describe and classify various elements. **(BASIC)**

_ **Section Review, SE** Students answer end-of-section vocabulary, key ideas, math, and critical thinking questions. **(GENERAL)**

_ **Section Quiz, CRF** Students answer 8 objective questions about elements. **(GENERAL)**

_ **Quiz, TE** Students answer 4 questions about metals, metalloids, nonmetals, and their properties. **(GENERAL)**

_ **Alternative Assessment, TE** Students make a concept map to compare metals, nonmetals, and metalloids. **(GENERAL)**

Lesson Plan

Section: Compounds

Pacing

Regular Schedule: **with lab(s):** 2 days   **without lab(s):** 1 day

Block Schedule: **with lab(s):** 1 day   **without lab(s):** 0.5 day

Objectives

1. Explain how compounds are made of elements.

2. Describe the properties of compounds.

3. Explain how a compound can be broken down into its elements.

4. Give examples of common compounds.

National Science Education Standards Covered

UCP 1: Systems, order, and organization

UCP 2: Evidence, models, and explanation

SAI 2: Understandings about scientific inquiry

SPSP 5: Science and technology in society

PS 1a: A substance has characteristic properties, such as density, a boiling point, and solubility, all of which are independent of the amount of the sample. A mixture of substances often can be separated into the original substances using one or more of the characteristic properties.

PS 1c: Chemical elements do not break down during normal laboratory reactions involving such treatments as heating, exposure to electric current, or reaction with acids. There are more than 100 known elements that combine in a multitude of ways to produce compounds, which account for the living and nonliving substances that we encounter.

KEY

SE = Student Edition   **TE** = Teacher's Edition
CRF = Chapter Resource File

FOCUS (5 minutes)

_ **Bellringer, TE** Have students write about compounds in their ScienceLog.

_ **Bellringer Transparency** Use this transparency as students enter the classroom and find their seats.

MOTIVATE (10 minutes)

_ **Demonstration, TE** Demonstrate the reaction between magnesium and oxygen. (**GENERAL**)

_ **Reading Strategy, SE** Have students predict what they think they will learn about before reading the section. (**GENERAL**)

TEACH *(65 minutes)*

_ **Activity, TE** Have students compare and contrast the properties of common compounds and the elements in them. (**ADVANCED**)

_ **Chapter Lab, Flame Tests, SE** Have students observe flame colors emitted by various compounds and determine the composition of an unknown compound. (**GENERAL**)

_ **Quick Lab, Compound Confusion, SE** Students observe the reaction between vinegar and two white powders and determine which is baking soda and which is sugar. (**GENERAL**)

_ **Directed Reading A/B, CRF** These worksheets reinforce basic concepts and vocabulary presented in the lesson. (**BASIC/SPECIAL NEEDS**)

_ **Vocabulary and Section Summary, CRF** Students write definitions of key terms and read a summary of section content. (**GENERAL**)

_ **Brainfood, TE** Have students research how salt is produced and present their findings.

CLOSE *(10 minutes)*

_ **Section Review, SE** Students answer end-of-section vocabulary, key ideas, math, and critical thinking questions. (**GENERAL**)

_ **Section Quiz, CRF** Students answer 5 objective questions about physical science. (**GENERAL**)

_ **Reteaching, TE** Students compare letters to elements and words to compounds. (**BASIC**)

_ **Quiz, TE** Students answer 3 questions about compounds. (**GENERAL**)

_ **Alternative Assessment, TE** Students research a specific compound and present their findings. (**GENERAL**)

Lesson Plan

Section: Mixtures

Pacing

Regular Schedule:	**with lab(s):** N/A	**without lab(s):** 1 day
Block Schedule:	**with lab(s):** N/A	**without lab(s):** 0.5 day

Objectives

1. Describe three properties of mixtures.

2. Describe four methods of separating the parts of a mixture.

3. Analyze a solution in terms of its solute and solvent.

4. Explain how concentration affects a solution.

5. Describe the particles in a suspension.

6. Explain how a colloid differs from a solution and a suspension.

National Science Education Standards Covered

UCP 1: Systems, order, and organization

UCP 2: Evidence, models, and explanation

SAI 1: Abilities necessary to do scientific inquiry

SAI 2: Understandings about scientific inquiry

SPSP 3: Natural hazards

SPSP 5: Science and technology in society

PS 1a: A substance has characteristic properties, such as density, a boiling point, and solubility, all of which are independent of the amount of the sample. A mixture of substances often can be separated into the original substances using one or more of the characteristic properties.

KEY

SE = Student Edition   **TE** = Teacher's Edition
CRF = Chapter Resource File

FOCUS (*5 minutes*)

_ **Bellringer, TE** Have students answer a question about mixtures.

_ **Bellringer Transparency** Use this transparency as students enter the classroom and find their seats.

MOTIVATE (*10 minutes*)

_ **Discussion, TE** Have groups discuss pizza as a mixture and create a recipe. (**GENERAL**)

TEACH *(20 minutes)*

_ **Activity, TE** Have teams of students try to separate a mixture of ground coffee and water, and a mixture of sugar and water. (GENERAL)

_ **Demonstration, TE** Demonstrate the separation of salt and sand as described in the text. (GENERAL)

_ **Teaching Transparency, Three Types of Volcanoes,** Use this graphic to make a link to earth science.

_ **Connection Activity, Earth Science, TE** Have students research and report on the three types of volcanoes. (GENERAL)

_ **Activity, TE** Students make and compare concentrated and dilute solutions. (GENERAL)

_ **Connection Activity, Math, TE** Students do math problems related to concentration. (GENERAL)

_ **Connection Activity, Earth Science, TE** Have students research calcium carbonate formations in caves. (GENERAL)

_ **Reinforcement, CRF** This worksheet reinforces key concepts in the chapter. (BASIC)

_ **SciLinks Activity, Mixtures, SciLinks Code HSM0974** Students research Internet resources related to mixtures. (GENERAL)

_ **Directed Reading A/B, CRF** These worksheets reinforce basic concepts and vocabulary presented in the lesson. (BASIC/SPECIAL NEEDS)

_ **Vocabulary and Section Summary, CRF** Students write definitions of key terms and read a summary of section content. (GENERAL)

CLOSE *(10 minutes)*

_ **Reteaching, TE** Students observe oil and vinegar salad dressing and discuss it as a mixture. (BASIC)

_ **Homework, Mixtures in Fabrics, TE** Have students examine clothing labels to get information about mixtures in fabrics.

_ **Section Review, SE** Students answer end-of-section vocabulary, key ideas, critical thinking questions and interpreting graphics. (GENERAL)

_ **Section Quiz, CRF** Students answer 10 objective questions about mixtures. (GENERAL)

_ **Quiz, TE** Students answer 2 questions about mixtures. (GENERAL)

_ **Alternative Assessment, TE** Students answer questions about dissolving solids in liquids and create a concept map. (GENERAL)

Lesson Plan

End-of-Chapter Review and Assessment

Pacing

Regular Schedule: **with lab(s):** N/A   **without lab(s):** 2 days

Block Schedule: **with lab(s):** N/A   **without lab(s):** 1 day

KEY
SE = Student Edition   **TE** = Teacher's Edition **CRF** = Chapter Resource File

_ **Chapter Review, SE** Students answer end-of-chapter vocabulary, key ideas, critical thinking, and graphics questions. **(GENERAL)**

_ **Vocabulary Activity, CRF** Students review chapter vocabulary terms by completing a word search.

_ **Concept Mapping Transparency** Use this graphic to help students review key concepts.

_ **Chapter Test A/B/C, CRF** Assign questions from the appropriate test for chapter assessment. **(GENERAL/ADVANCED/SPECIAL NEEDS)**

_ **Performance-Based Assessment, CRF** Assign this activity for general level assessment for the chapter. **(GENERAL)**

_ **Standardized Test Preparation, CRF** Students answer reading comprehension, math, and interpreting graphics questions in the format of a standardized test. **(GENERAL)**

_ **Test Generator, One-Stop Planner** Create a customized homework assignment, quiz, or test using the HRW Test Generator program.

Elements, Compounds, and Mixtures

MULTIPLE CHOICE

1. Boiling point, melting point, and density are some of an element's
   a. nonreactive properties.
   c. chemical properties.
   b. physical properties.
   d. pure properties.

   Answer: B Difficulty: 1 Section: 1 Objective: 2

2. A property of an element that does not depend on the amount of the element is called a
   a. electromagnetic property.
   c. unique property.
   b. finite property.
   d. characteristic property.

   Answer: D Difficulty: 1 Section: 1 Objective: 2

3. An element's ability to react with acid is an example of a
   a. pure substance.
   c. chemical property.
   b. physical property.
   d. melting point.

   Answer: C Difficulty: 1 Section: 1 Objective: 2

4. When two or more elements join together chemically,
   a. a compound is formed.
   b. a mixture is formed.
   c. a substance that is the same as the elements is formed.
   d. the physical properties of the substances remain the same.

   Answer: A Difficulty: 1 Section: 2 Objective: 1

5. The physical properties of compounds do NOT include
   a. melting point.
   c. reaction to light.
   b. density.
   d. color.

   Answer: C Difficulty: 1 Section: 2 Objective: 2

6. Which of the following will NOT break down compounds?
   a. heat
   c. a chemical change
   b. electric current
   d. filtering

   Answer: D Difficulty: 1 Section: 2 Objective: 3

7. How do elements join to form compounds?
   a. randomly
   c. in a ratio of 1 to 8
   b. in a specific mass ratio
   d. as the scientist plans it

   Answer: B Difficulty: 1 Section: 2 Objective: 1

8. Compounds found in all living things include
   a. proteins.
   c. mercury oxides.
   b. ammonia.
   d. carbonic acids.

   Answer: A Difficulty: 1 Section: 2 Objective: 4

9. What is a pure substance made of two or more elements that are chemically combined?
   a. element
   c. mixture
   b. compound
   d. solution

   Answer: B Difficulty: 1 Section: 2 Objective: 1

10. If a spoonful of salt is mixed in a glass of water, what is the water called?
    a. solute
    c. solvent
    b. solution
    d. element

    Answer: C Difficulty: 1 Section: 3 Objective: 3

11. What is a solid solution of a metal or nonmetal dissolved in a metal?
    a. suspension
    b. alloy
    c. colloid
    d. compound

    Answer: B   Difficulty: 1   Section: 3   Objective: 3

12. A colloid has properties of both suspensions and
    a. solutions.
    b. solvents.
    c. solutes.
    d. nonmetals.

    Answer: A   Difficulty: 1   Section: 3   Objective: 6

13. What is formed when particles of two or more substances are distributed evenly among each other?
    a. compound
    b. suspension
    c. solution
    d. element

    Answer: C   Difficulty: 1   Section: 3   Objective: 3

14. The flammability of a substance is
    a. a chemical property.
    b. related to the density.
    c. a physical property.
    d. changeable.

    Answer: A   Difficulty: 1   Section: 1   Objective: 2

15. How is a compound different from a mixture?
    a. Compounds have two or more components.
    b. Each substance in a compound loses its characteristic properties.
    c. Compounds are commonly found in nature.
    d. Solids, liquids, and gases can form compounds.

    Answer: B   Difficulty: 2   Section: 2, 3   Objective: 1, 1

16. The particles in both a solution and a colloid
    a. cannot scatter light.
    b. can settle out.
    c. are soluble.
    d. can pass through a fine filter.

    Answer: D   Difficulty: 2   Section: 3   Objective: 3, 6

17. When elements form mixtures, the elements
    a. keep their original properties.
    b. react to form a new substance with new properties.
    c. combine in a specific mass ratio.
    d. always change their physical state.

    Answer: A   Difficulty: 1   Section: 3   Objective: 1

18. Which of the following is NOT a reason that compounds are considered pure substances?
    a. They are composed of only one type of particle.
    b. The particles are made of atoms of two or more elements that are chemically combined.
    c. Different samples of any compound have the same elements in the same proportion.
    d. They can be separated by physical methods.

    Answer: D   Difficulty: 1   Section: 2   Objective: 1

19. How are metalloids similar to metals?
    a. They have some properties of nonmetals.
    b. Some are shiny, while others are dull.
    c. They are somewhat malleable and ductile.
    d. Some are good conductors of electric current.

    Answer: D   Difficulty: 2   Section: 1   Objective: 4

20. How could a sugar cube be dissolved more quickly in water?
    a. Cool the water.
    b. Crush the sugar cube.
    c. Let the cube sit in the water.
    d. Add more water.

    Answer: B   Difficulty: 1   Section: 3   Objective: 3

21. What pure substance forms when two elements chemically combine?
    a. an element
    b. a compound
    c. a mixture
    d. a solution
    Answer: B   Difficulty: 1   Section: 2   Objective: 1

22. Why can salt dissolve in water?
    a. Salt is the solvent.
    b. Salt is a solution.
    c. Salt is soluble.
    d. Salt is an element.
    Answer: C   Difficulty: 1   Section: 3   Objective: 3

23. What is a solid solution of a metal dissolved in a metal called?
    a. suspension
    b. alloy
    c. colloid
    d. compound
    Answer: B   Difficulty: 1   Section: 3   Objective: 3

24. How can a compound be broken down?
    a. by physical changes
    b. by chemical changes
    c. by crushing
    d. by cooling
    Answer: B   Difficulty: 1   Section: 2   Objective: 3

25. What forms when particles of two or more substances are evenly mixed?
    a. compound
    b. suspension
    c. solution
    d. element
    Answer: C   Difficulty: 1   Section: 3   Objective: 3

26. Which of the following is a chemical property?
    a. density
    b. reactivity with acid
    c. boiling point
    d. color
    Answer: A   Difficulty: 1   Section: 1   Objective: 2

27. What is true about particles in both solutions and colloids?
    a. Particles cannot scatter light.
    b. Particles can settle out.
    c. Particles are soluble.
    d. Particles cannot be filtered.
    Answer: D   Difficulty: 1   Section: 3   Objective: 5, 6

28. Which of the following is NOT true of compounds?
    a. They contain two or more elements.
    b. They form after a physical change.
    c. They have their own physical properties.
    d. They do not form randomly.
    Answer: B   Difficulty: 1   Section: 2   Objective: 1

COMPLETION

Use the terms from the following list to complete the sentences below.

    brittle   compound
    metalloid   solution
    metal

29. If hydrogen peroxide is exposed to light, a _____ will result.
    Answer: compound   Difficulty: 1   Section: 2   Objective: 2

30. The production of steel involves heating carbon, iron, and other elements to very high heats in order to form a _____.
    Answer: solution   Difficulty: 2   Section: 3   Objective: 3

31. A nonmetal would probably not be good for the frame of a bicycle because it would be too _____.
    Answer: brittle   Difficulty: 2   Section: 1   Objective: 4

32. An element that conducts heat and is dull is probably a _____.
    Answer: metalloid   Difficulty: 2   Section: 1   Objective: 4

33. An unidentified substance is shiny and malleable. It is probably a _____.
    Answer: metal   Difficulty: 2   Section: 1   Objective: 4

Use the terms from the following list to complete the sentences below.

solvent   solute
alloys   solution
mixture   suspensions
compound   metalloids

34. A pure substance made of two or more elements that are chemically combined is called a _____.
    Answer: compound   Difficulty: 1   Section: 2   Objective: 1

35. If a spoonful of salt is mixed in a glass of water, the salt is the _____.
    Answer: solute   Difficulty: 1   Section: 3   Objective: 3

36. Solid solutions of metals or nonmetals dissolved in metals are _____.
    Answer: alloys   Difficulty: 1   Section: 3   Objective: 3

37. A colloid has the properties of solutions and _____.
    Answer: suspensions Difficulty: 1   Section: 1   Objective: 5, 6

38. Particles of two or more substances that are distributed evenly among each other form a(n) _____.
    Answer: solution   Difficulty: 1   Section: 3   Objective: 3

distillation   nitrogen
nonmetals   ratio

39. A mixture of liquids can be separated by _____.
    Answer: distillation Difficulty: 1   Section: 3   Objective: 2

40. Bacteria make compounds from _____ in the air.
    Answer: nitrogen   Difficulty: 1   Section: 2   Objective: 4

41. All _____ are poor conductors of heat and electric current.
    Answer: nonmetals   Difficulty: 1   Section: 1   Objective: 4

42. Elements join in a specific mass _____ to form a compound.
    Answer: ratio   Difficulty: 1   Section: 2   Objective: 1

SHORT ANSWER

43. A student measured the boiling point of a liquid and found that it had two different boiling points. What is the best conclusion the student could draw?
    Answer: The liquid is a mixture of two different liquids with different boiling points.
    Difficulty: 2   Section: 3   Objective: 2

44. Potassium bromide is added to water. The water appears clear. Another ten grams are added. The mixture is stirred, but solid settles to the bottom. What conclusion can be drawn?
    Answer:
       With the addition of the extra 10 grams of potassium bromide, the solution has become saturated, so some solid has settled to the bottom.
    Difficulty: 2   Section: 3   Objective: 3

45. Hydrogen peroxide is can be broken into oxygen and water by yeast and other organisms. What steps would be involved in obtaining hydrogen from hydrogen peroxide?

    Answer:
    First, put the hydrogen peroxide in the presence of yeast to break it into oxygen and water. Then pass an electrical current through the water to break it into hydrogen and oxygen.

    Difficulty: 1   Section: 2   Objective: 3

47. How is the way sodium reacts with water different from the way sodium chloride reacts with water?

    Answer:
    Sodium reacts violently with water to produce a new compound. Sodium chloride dissolves in water to produce a mixture.

    Difficulty: 1   Section: 2   Objective: 2

48. Why can both an element and a compound be considered a pure substance?

    Answer:
    A pure substance is one in which there is only one type of particle. In an element, the particles are particles of the element. In a compound, the particles are made up of one or more elements that are combined chemically. In both cases, there is only one kind of particle.

    Difficulty: 1   Section: 1, 2   Objective: 1-1; 2-1

49. How are chemical changes different from physical changes?

    Answer:
    In a chemical change, the properties of the substance also change, but in a physical change, the properties of the substance remain the same.

    Difficulty: 1   Section: 1   Objective: 2

50. How are lead and iodine similar? How are they different?

    Answer:
    Both lead and iodine are elements and cannot be broken down. However, lead is a metal. It is shiny and a good conductor of heat and electricity. It is malleable and ductile. Iodine is a nonmetal. It is dull and a poor conductor of heat and electricity. It is a liquid, while lead is a solid.

    Difficulty: 1   Section: 1   Objective: 4

51. Compare the particles of oxygen in oxygen gas, water, and carbonic acid.

    Answer: They are all exactly the same.
    Difficulty: 2   Section: 1   Objective: 1

52. Plants use carbon dioxide to build sugars and starches. Explain what is happening in terms of elements and compounds.

    Answer:
    Plants use one compound, carbon dioxide, to make other compounds, sugars and starches, by chemical means.

    Difficulty: 2   Section: 2   Objective: 4

53. How could you separate a mixture of three liquids according to their densities?

    Answer: by using a centrifuge
    Difficulty: 2   Section: 3   Objective: 2

54. Identify the group or groups of elements that are good conductors of electric current.

    Answer: metals, some metalloids
    Difficulty: 1   Section: 1   Objective: 4

55. Identify the group or groups of elements that are brittle and nonmalleable.
    Answer: nonmetals   Difficulty: 1   Section: 1   Objective: 4

56. Identify the group or groups of elements that are shiny.
    Answer: metals, some metalloids
    Difficulty: 1   Section: 1   Objective: 4

57. Identify the group or groups of elements that are poor conductors of thermal energy.
    Answer: nonmetals, some metalloids
    Difficulty: 1   Section: 1   Objective: 4

58. Which of the following is not a solution: air in a scuba tank, muddy water, a soft drink, or salt water?
    Answer: muddy water
    Difficulty: 1   Section: 3   Objective: 3

59. When solid iodine is dissolved in alcohol, which is the solute and which is the solvent?
    Answer: iodine – solute, alcohol – solvent
    Difficulty: 2   Section: 3   Objective: 3

60. Explain why compounds are considered pure substances.
    Answer:
        Answers will vary. Sample answer: Compounds are considered pure substances because they are composed of only one type of particle. The particles of a compound are made of atoms of two or more elements that are chemically combined. Different samples of any compound have the same elements in the same proportion.
    Difficulty: 1   Section: 2   Objective: 1

61. How are metalloids different from metals?
    Answer:
        Answers will vary. Sample answer: Mixing by stirring or shaking causes the particles to separate from one another and spread out more quickly among the solvent particles. Heating causes particles to move more quickly. The solvent particles can separate the solute particles and spread them out more quickly. Crushing the solute increases the amount of contact it has with the solvent. The particles of the crushed solute mix with the solvent more quickly.
    Difficulty: 2   Section: 1   Objective: 4

62. Describe three ways to dissolve solids faster and explain why each works.
    Answer:
        Answers will vary. Sample answer: Mixing by stirring or shaking causes the particles to separate from one another and spread out more quickly among the solvent particles. Heating causes particles to move more quickly. The solvent particles can separate the solute particles and spread them out more quickly. Crushing the solute increases the amount of contact it has with the solvent. The particles of the crushed solute mix with the solvent more quickly.
    Difficulty: 1   Section: 3   Objective: 3

MATCHING

a. aluminum
b. cola drink
c. bubbles in a cola drink
d. protein in a hamburger
e. feldspar

63. ____ broken down by body cells to create new compounds
   Answer: D   Difficulty: 2   Section: 2   Objective: 3
64. ____ a mixture
   Answer: B   Difficulty: 2   Section: 3   Objective: 1
65. ____ cannot be broken down
   Answer: A   Difficulty: 2   Section: 1   Objective: 1
66. ____ can be made from just carbon, oxygen, and hydrogen
   Answer: C   Difficulty: 2   Section: 2   Objective: 3
67. ____ equivalent in granite to cheese on a pizza
   Answer: E   Difficulty: 2   Section: 3   Objective: 2

a. metal
b. element
e. pure substance
c. metalloid
d. nonmetal

68. ____ a pure substance that cannot be separated into simpler substances by physical or
   chemical means
   Answer: B   Difficulty: 1   Section: 1   Objective: 1
69. ____ a sample of matter, either a single element or a single compound, that has definite
   chemical and physical properties
   Answer: E   Difficulty: 1   Section: 1   Objective: 1
70. ____ an element that is shiny and conducts heat and electric current
   Answer: A   Difficulty: 1   Section: 1   Objective: 4
71. ____ element that conducts heat and electricity poorly and can be a solid, liquid, or gas
   Answer: D   Difficulty: 1   Section: 1   Objective: 4
72. ____ element that has the properties of both metals and nonmetals
   Answer: C   Difficulty: 1   Section: 1   Objective: 4

a. centrifuge
b. solute
c. solvent
d. colloid
e. mixture
f. suspension
g. distillation
h. solution
i. concentration
j. solubility

73. ____ combination of two or more substances that are not chemically combined
   Answer: E   Difficulty: 1   Section: 3   Objective: 1
74. ____ homogeneous mixture of two or more substances uniformly dispersed throughout a
   single phase
   Answer: H   Difficulty: 1   Section: 3   Objective: 3
75. ____ substance that dissolves in a solvent
   Answer: B   Difficulty: 1   Section: 3   Objective: 3
76. ____ substance in which a solute dissolves
   Answer: C   Difficulty: 1   Section: 3   Objective: 3
77. ____ amount of a substance in a given quantity of a mixture, solution, or ore
   Answer: I   Difficulty: 1   Section: 3   Objective: 4
78. ____ ability of one substance to dissolve in another at a given temperature and pressure
   Answer: J   Difficulty: 1   Section: 3   Objective: 3
79. ____ mixture in which particles of a material are more or less evenly dispersed
   throughout a liquid or gas
   Answer: F   Difficulty: 1   Section: 3   Objective: 5

80. ____ mixture consisting of tiny particles that are intermediate in size between those in solutions and those in suspensions

    Answer: D   Difficulty: 1   Section: 3   Objective: 6

81. ____ process that separates a mixture based on the boiling points of the components

    Answer: G   Difficulty: 1   Section: 3   Objective: 2

82. ____ machine that separates mixtures by the densities of the components

    Answer: A   Difficulty: 1   Section: 3   Objective: 2

    a. carbon dioxide   c. sodium chloride
    b. sulfur

83. ____ also known as table salt

    Answer: C   Difficulty: 1   Section: 2   Objective: 3

84. ____ used by plants during photosynthesis

    Answer: A   Difficulty: 1   Section: 2   Objective: 4

85. ____ a nonmetal

    Answer: B   Difficulty: 1   Section: 1   Objective: 4

Match the correct description with the correct term. Write the letter in the space provided. Some terms may not be used.

    a. mixture of solids   d. suspension
    b. solute   e. compound
    c. element   f. alloy

86. ____ an aluminum pie plate

    Answer: C   Difficulty: 1   Section: 1   Objective: 4

87. ____ a milkshake

    Answer: D   Difficulty: 1   Section: 3   Objective: 5

88. ____ calcium carbonate

    Answer: E   Difficulty: 1   Section: 2   Objective: 2

89. ____ potting soil

    Answer: A   Difficulty: 1   Section: 3   Objective: 1

90. ____ instant coffee in hot water

    Answer: B   Difficulty: 1   Section: 3   Objective: 3

91. ____ a steel crow bar

    Answer: F   Difficulty: 1   Section: 3   Objective: 3

    a. colloid   c. element
    b. solution   d. compound

92. ____ gelatin

    Answer: A   Difficulty: 1   Section: 3   Objective: 6

93. ____ nugget of gold

    Answer: C   Difficulty: 1   Section: 1   Objective: 1

94. ____ water

    Answer: D   Difficulty: 1   Section: 2   Objective: 1

95. ____ salt dissolved in water

    Answer: B   Difficulty: 1   Section: 3   Objective: 3

    a. alloy   c. solvent
    b. suspension   d. metalloid

96. ____ a solid solution of metals or nonmetals dissolved in metals

    Answer: A   Difficulty: 1   Section: 3   Objective: 3

97. ____ an element that shares metal and nonmetal properties

    Answer: D   Difficulty: 1   Section: 1   Objective: 4

98. ____ a mixture of large, dispersed particles

Answer: B   Difficulty: 1   Section: 3   Objective: 5
99. ____ the substance in which a solute dissolves
      Answer: C   Difficulty: 1   Section: 3   Objective: 5

TRUE/FALSE

100. Compounds cannot be broken down by any means.
      Answer: False   Difficulty: 1   Section: 2   Objective: 3

101. Compounds can be broken down only by chemical means.
      Answer: True   Difficulty: 1   Section: 2   Objective: 3

102. Heating can break down some compounds.
      Answer: True   Difficulty: 1   Section: 2   Objective: 3

ESSAY

103. A student was testing out a substance to try to determine what it was. She pounded it, crumpled it, cut it into bits, found its melting point, and dissolved it in three different solvents. What could she learn about the substance from these tests? What couldn't she learn? Explain your answers.

      Answer:
      Sample answer: Because she only did tests of physical properties, she could find out many of the physical properties of the substance, but none of its chemical properties. Because she didn't do any chemical tests she wouldn't be able to break the substance down if it was a compound. She didn't do any tests to try to separate the substance, so she wouldn't know if it was an element, compound, or mixture.
      Difficulty: 3   Section: 1, 2, 3   Objective: 1, 2, 3, 4; 1, 2, 3; 1, 2, 3

104. A student was given liquid and told that it contained a mixture. How could the student determine whether or not the mixture was a solution, a suspension, or a colloid?

      Answer:
      Sample answer: The student can pass light through the mixture; if it cannot scatter light, it is a solution. The student could put the liquid through a filter. If a solid filtered out, then it is a suspension. If the mixture scatters light and does not have a solid that can be filtered out, it is a colloid.
      Difficulty: 2   Section: 3   Objective: 3, 4, 5

105. A graph shows the solubility of three different substances in water. One substance shows an increasing solubility as temperature increases. A second shows decreasing solubility as temperature increases. The third shows a solubility that barely changes as temperature rises. Which of these substances would be most likely to be useful for filling a balloon? Why?

      Answer:
      Probably the second substance, which is most likely a gas, because generally gases have a decreasing solubility with increasing temperature, as opposed to solids which generally have an increasing solubility with increasing temperature. A solid would be less appropriate than gas for filling a balloon.
      Difficulty: 3   Section: 3   Objective: 3

106. Aluminum oxide is a solid that is insoluble in both water and alcohol. Ammonium ferrous sulphate is a solid that is soluble in water but insoluble in alcohol. How could you separate a mixture of aluminum oxide and ammonium ferrous sulphate?

Answer:

Sample answer: Add alcohol to the mixture and stir thoroughly. Then pour it through a filter. The Ammonium ferrous sulphate will stay on the filter paper and the aluminum oxide will pass through. Then evaporate off the alcohol and the aluminum oxide will be left behind.

Difficulty: 3   Section: 3   Objective: 2

107. The ratio of the mass of oxygen to nitrogen in nine different samples of gases was found. Three samples had a mass ratio of oxygen to nitrogen of 2.28:1. Three had an oxygen to nitrogen mass ratio of 1.14:1, and three had mass ratio of 0.57:1. What could you conclude from this data? Why?

Answer:

These are probably three different compounds containing the elements nitrogen and oxygen. Elements in compounds combine in specific mass ratios, and since three samples of gas in each case have the same mass ratio, it can be concluded that the elements probably are not combining in a random manner.

Difficulty: 3   Section: 2   Objective: 1

108. Most fresh water in Saudi Arabia is produced by removing salt from sea water. One method involves distillation. Explain how sea water could be purified by distillation, and tell whether it is a chemical or physical process.

Answer:

Answers will vary. Sample answer: Salt water is a mixture, so its components can be separated by physical methods. Distillation involves heating the water, which changes water into steam. When salt water is distilled, steam is condensed back into water, and salt is left behind.

Difficulty: 2   Section: 3   Objective: 2

109. Suppose you were given an unknown liquid and asked to determine if it was an element, a compound, or a mixture. What would you do? How would this help you find out what it was?

Answer:

Answers will vary. Sample answer: I would first try to separate it by using distillation and a centrifuge. If I could separate it this way, I would know that it was a mixture. I would also try to separate it by passing an electric current though it. If I could separate it this way, I would know it was a compound. If I could not separate it at all, I might think it was an element, but I might also need to try other methods of separating it to be sure.

Difficulty: 3   Section: 1, 2, 3   Objective: 1, 1, 1

INTERPRETING GRAPHICS

Use the chart below to answer the following question.

Physical Property	Substance1	Substance 2	Substance 3
Boiling point		2,750°C	2,467°C
Density	$2.702g/cm^2$	$7.874g/cm^2$	
Color	Silvery	Silvery white	
Melting point	660.25°C		660.25°C
Hardness	2.75	4	2.75
Other	Non-magnet		

110. After testing three substances, a scientist has recorded the following data. Are these substances the same or different? How can you tell?

Answer:

Answers will vary. Sample answer: Substances 1 and 3 are probably the same because they have the same melting point, the same amount of hardness, and are nonmagnetic. Substance 2 is different because it has a different density and hardness. It is also a slightly different color.

Difficulty: 3   Section: 1   Objective: 3

Use the graph below to answer the following questions.

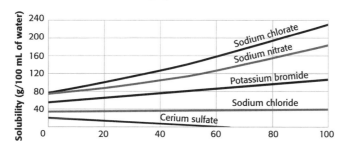

111. Which solid is the most soluble at lower temperatures than at higher temperatures?
    a. sodium chloride   c. potassium bromide
    b. sodium nitrate   d. cerium sulfate

    Answer: D   Difficulty: 2   Section: 3   Objective: 3

112. Which compound's solubility is least affected by temperature changes?
    a. sodium chloride   c. potassium bromide
    b. sodium nitrate   d. cerium sulfate

    Answer: A   Difficulty: 2   Section: 3   Objective: 3

Use the graph below to answer the following questions.

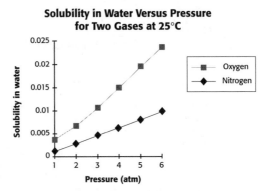

**Solubility in Water Versus Pressure
for Two Gases at 25°C**

113. What is the relationship between pressure and the solubility of oxygen and nitrogen in water?

Answer: As pressure increases, the solubility of oxygen and nitrogen in water increases.

Difficulty: 2   Section: 3   Objective: 3

114. Which gas experiences a greater change in solubility per unit pressure?

Answer:

Oxygen experiences a greater change in solubility per unit pressure. The slope of the line that represents oxygen is steeper.

Difficulty: 2   Section: 3   Objective: 3

CONCEPT MAPPING

115. Use the following terms to complete the concept map below:
pure substances, physical or chemical, chemical, solutions, suspensions, compounds.

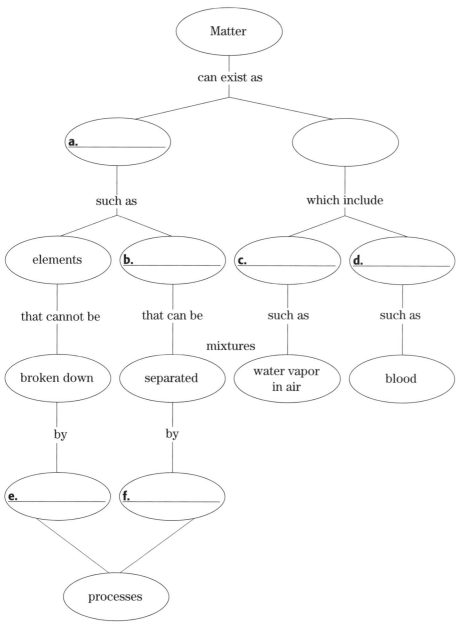

Answer:
a. pure substances, b. compounds, c. solutions, d. suspensions, e. physical or chemical,
f. chemical

Difficulty: 3   Section: 1, 2, 3   Objective: 1, 2; 1, 2, 3; 1, 3, 5

Chapter Resource File

4

Introduction to Atoms

Skills Worksheet

Directed Reading A

Section: Development of the Atomic Theory
THE BEGINNING OF ATOMIC THEORY

_____ 1. The word *atom* comes from the Greek word *atomos*, which means
      a. "dividable."
      b. "invisible."
      c. "hard particles."
      d. "not able to be divided."

_____ 2. Which of the following statements is a part of Democritus's theory about atoms?
      a. Atoms are small, soft particles.
      b. Atoms are always standing still.
      c. Atoms are made of a single material.
      d. Atoms are small particles that can be cut in half again and again.

3. We know that Democritus was right to say that all matter was made up of atoms. So why did people ignore Democritus's ideas for such a long time?

_____

_____

_____

4. The smallest unit of an element that maintains the properties of that element

is a(n) _____.

DALTON'S ATOMIC THEORY BASED ON EXPERIMENTS

_____ 5. Which of the following was NOT one of Dalton's theories?
      a. All substances are made of atoms.
      b. Atoms of the same element are exactly alike.
      c. Atoms of different elements are alike.
      d. Atoms join with other atoms to make new substances.

6. Dalton experimented with different substances. What did his results suggest?

_____

_____

_____

THOMSON'S DISCOVERY OF ELECTRONS

7. In Thomson's experiments with a cathode-ray tube, he discovered that a(n)

_____ charged plate attracted the beam. He concluded

that the beam was made up of particles that have _____
electric charges.

8. The negatively charged subatomic particles that Thomson discovered

are now called _____.

9. In Thomson's "plum-pudding" model, electrons are mixed throughout an

_____.

RUTHERFORD'S ATOMIC "SHOOTING GALLERY"

_____**10.** Before his experiment, what did Rutherford expect the particles to do?
   a. He expected the particles to pass right through the gold foil.
   b. He expected the particles to deflect to the sides of the gold foil.
   c. He expected the particles to bounce straight back.
   d. He expected the particles to become negatively charged.

11. What were the surprising results of Rutherford's gold-foil experiment?

_____

_____

_____

WHERE ARE THE ELECTRONS?

_____**12.** In 1911, Rutherford revised the atomic theory. Which of the following
   is NOT part of that theory?
   a. Most of the atom's mass is in its nucleus.
   b. The nucleus is a tiny, dense, positively charged region.
   c. Positively charged particles that pass close by the nucleus are
      pushed away by the positive charges in the nucleus.
   d. The nucleus is made up of protons and electrons.

13. The center of an atom is a dense region consisting of protons and neutrons

called the _____.

14. What are electron clouds?

_____

Skills Worksheet

Directed Reading A

Section: The Atom
HOW SMALL IS AN ATOM?

_____ **1.** Which of the following statements is true?
     a. A penny has about 20,000 atoms.
     b. A penny has more atoms than Earth has people.
     c. Aluminum is made up of large-sized atoms.
     d. Aluminum atoms have a diameter of about 3 cm.

WHAT'S INSIDE AN ATOM?
Match the correct description with the correct term. Write the letter in the space provided.

_____ **2.** particle of the nucleus that has no electrical charge

_____ **3.** particle found in the nucleus that is positively charged

_____ **4.** particle with an unequal number of protons and electrons

_____ **5.** negatively charged particle found outside the nucleus

_____ **6.** contains most of the mass of an atom

_____ **7.** SI unit used for the masses of atomic particles

a. electron
b. atomic mass unit (amu)
c. nucleus
d. proton
e. ion
f. neutron

HOW DO ATOMS OF DIFFERENT ELEMENTS DIFFER?

8. The simplest atom is the _____ atom. It has one

_____ and one _____.

9. Neutrons in the atom's _____ keep two or more protons from moving apart.

10. If you build an atom using two protons, two neutrons, and two electrons, you

have built an atom of _____.

11. An atom does not have to have equal numbers of _____

and _____.

12. The number of protons in the nucleus of an atom is the

_____ of that atom.

ISOTOPES

_____**13.** Isotopes always have
   a. the same number of protons.
   b. the same number of neutrons.
   c. a different atomic number.
   d. the same mass.

_____**14.** Which of the following is NOT true about unstable atoms?
   a. They are radioactive.
   b. They have a nucleus that always remains the same.
   c. They give off energy as they fall apart.
   d. They give off smaller particles as they fall apart.

_____**15.** What is the mass number of an isotope that has 5 protons, 6 neutrons, and 5 electrons?
   a. 1   **c.** 10
   b. 11   **d.** 16

_____**16.** If carbon has an atomic number of 6, how many neutrons does carbon-12 have?
   a. 12   **c.** 6
   b. 8   **d.** 18

17. Most elements contain a mixture of two or more _____.

18. The weighted average of the masses of all the naturally occurring isotopes of

an element is the _____.

FORCES IN ATOMS

Match the correct definition with the correct term. Write the letter in the space provided.

_____**19.** helps protons stay together in the nucleus

_____**20.** pulls objects toward one another

_____**21.** an important force in radioactive atoms

_____**22.** holds the electrons around the nucleus

a. gravitational force

b. electromagnetic force

c. strong force

d. weak force

Skills Worksheet

Directed Reading B

Section: Development of the Atomic Theory
THE BEGINNING OF ATOMIC THEORY
Circle the letter of the best answer for each question.

1. What does the word atom mean?

   a. "dividable"

   b. "invisible"

   c. "hard particles"

   d. "not able to be divided"

2. Why weren't Democritus's ideas accepted?

   a. Bohr did not agree with his theory.

   b. Dalton proved Democritus wrong.

   c. Aristotle did not agree with his theory.

   d. Rutherford proved Democritus wrong.

From Aristotle to Modern Science

3. What is the smallest particle into which an element can be divided?

   a. a nucleus

   b. a proton

   c. an atom

   d. a neutron

DALTON'S ATOMIC THEORY BASED ON EXPERIMENTS

4. Which of the following ideas was part of Dalton's theories?

   a. All substances are made of atoms.

   b. Atoms can be divided.

   c. Atoms can be destroyed.

   d. Most substances are made of atoms.

Not Quite Correct

Circle the letter of the best answer for each question.

5. What happened in the late 1800s?

    a. Dalton created a new theory.

    b. Dalton disproved his own theory.

    c. Dalton's theory was proved.

    d. Dalton's theory changed.

THOMSON'S DISCOVERY OF ELECTRONS

Read the words in the box. Read the sentences. Fill in each blank with the word or phrase that best completes the sentence.

electrons	particles
cathode-ray tube	positively

6. Thomson experimented with a _____.

7. Thomson discovered that a _____

charged plate attracted the beam.

8. Thomson concluded that the beam was made of

_____ that have negative electric charges.

9. The negatively charged particles Thompson discovered are called

_____.

Like Plums in a Pudding
Circle the letter of the best answer for each question.

10. What did Thomson believe about electrons?

    a. They are mixed throughout an atom.

    b. They are in the center of an atom.

    c. They are positively charged.

    d. They are absent from an atom.

RUTHERFORD'S ATOMIC "SHOOTING GALLERY"
Surprising Results

11. What did Rutherford expect the particles to do?

    a. to pass right through the gold foil

    b. to deflect to the sides of the gold foil

    c. to bounce straight back

    d. to become "blobs" of matter

WHERE ARE THE ELECTRONS?

12. Which of the following statements is NOT true of Rutherford's results?

    a. Some of the particles turned to one side.

    b. some of the particles did not move.

    c. Most of the particles passed through the gold foil.

    d. Some of the particles bounced straight back.

13. What is an atom is made up of?

    a. mostly empty space.

    b. helium.

    c. gold particles.

    d. large particles.

Far From the Nucleus
Circle the letter of the best answer for each question.

14. What did Rutherford believe was in the center of an atom?

  a. an electron

  b. a nucleus

  c. a particle

  d. a proton

BOHR'S ELECTRON LEVELS

15. What did Bohr study?

  a. the way atoms react to light

  b. the size of atoms

  c. the diameter of the nucleus

  d. the division of atoms

16. How did Bohr's model propose that electrons move around the nucleus?

  a. a variety of ways

  b. haphazardly

  c. between the levels

  d. in certain paths

The Modern Atomic Theory

17. What model represents current atomic theory?

  a. electron-cloud model

  b. plum-pudding model

  c. Rutherford's model

  d. Bohr's model

Skills Worksheet

Directed Reading B

Section: The Atom
HOW SMALL IS AN ATOM?
Circle the letter of the best answer for the question.

1. Which of the following statements is true?

    a. A penny has about 20,000 atoms.

    b. A penny has more atoms than the Earth has people.

    c. Aluminum is made up of large-sized atoms.

    d. Aluminum has a diameter of about 3 cm.

WHAT'S INSIDE AN ATOM?
The Nucleus
Read the description. Then, draw a line from the dot next to each description to the matching word.

2. particle with no electrical charge   ●

      a. electron

3. particle that is positively charged   ●

      b. nucleus

      c. proton

4. particle that is negatively charged   ●

      d. neutron

5. contains most of the mass of an atom   ●

HOW DO ATOMS OF DIFFERENT ELEMENTS DIFFER?

Starting Simply

Read the words in the box. Read the sentences. <u>Fill in each blank</u> with the word or phrase that best completes the sentence.

helium	hydrogen	atomic mass unit
neutrons	atomic number	electron

6. The simplest atom is the _____ atom. It

has one proton and one _____.

Now for Some Neutrons

7. If you build an atom using two protons, two neutrons, and two electrons, you have built an atom of

_____.

Building Bigger Atoms

8. An atom does not have to have equal numbers of protons and

_____.

Protons and the Atomic Number

9. The number of protons in the nucleus of an atom is the

_____ of that atom.

10. The SI unit used to express the masses of particles in atoms is

called the _____.

ISOTOPES
Circle the letter of the best answer for each question.

11. What do isotopes always have?

    a. the same number of protons

    b. the same number of neutrons

    c. a different atomic number

    d. the same mass

12. How are isotopes of the same element different?

    a. They have different numbers of protons.

    b. They have different numbers of neutrons.

    c. They have the same number of electrons.

    d. They have different numbers of ions.

Properties of Isotopes

13. Which phrase best describes radioactive isotopes?

    a. They are stable.

    b. They never change.

    c. They are unstable.

    d. They don't produce energy.

Telling Isotopes Apart

14. What is the mass number of an isotope that has 5 protons, 6 neutrons, and 5 electrons?

    a. 1   **c.** 10

    b. 11   **d.** 16

Naming Isotopes

15. Carbon has an atomic number of 6. How many neutrons does carbon-12 have?

    a. 12   **c.** 6

    b. 8   **d.** 18

| Directed Reading B *continued*

Calculating the Mass of an Element

Read the words in the box. Read the sentences. <u>Fill in each blank</u> with the word or phrase that best completes the sentence.

| mass number | atomic mass |

16. The sum of the protons and neutrons in an atom is the

_____.

17. The weighted average of the masses of all the naturally occurring

isotopes of an element is the _____.

FORCES IN ATOMS

| strong force | electromagnetic force |
| weak force | gravitational force |

18. Protons stay together in the nucleus because of

_____.

19. Objects are pulled toward one another because of

_____.

20. An important force in radioactive atoms is

_____.

21. The electrons are held around the nucleus because of

_____.

Vocabulary and Section Summary

Development of the Atomic Theory

VOCABULARY

In your own words, write a definition of the following terms in the space provided.

1. atom

_____

_____

2. electron

_____

_____

3. nucleus

_____

_____

4. electron cloud

_____

_____

SECTION SUMMARY

Read the following section summary.

• Democritus thought that matter is composed of atoms.

• Dalton based his theory on observations of how elements combine.

• Thomson discovered electrons in atoms.

• Rutherford discovered that atoms are mostly empty space with a dense, positive nucleus.

• Bohr proposed that electrons are located in levels at certain distances from the nucleus.

• The electron-cloud model represents the current atomic theory.

Vocabulary and Section Summary

The Atom
VOCABULARY
In your own words, write a definition of the following terms in the space provided.

1. proton

_____

_____

2. atomic mass unit

_____

_____

3. neutron

_____

_____

4. atomic number

_____

_____

5. isotope

_____

_____

6. mass number

_____

_____

7. atomic mass

_____

_____

SECTION SUMMARY

Read the following section summary.

- Atoms are extremely small. Ordinary-sized objects are made up of very large numbers of atoms.

- Atoms consist of a nucleus, which has protons and usually neutrons, and electrons, located in electron clouds around the nucleus.

- The number of protons in the nucleus of an atom is that atom's atomic number. All atoms of an element have the same atomic number.

- Different isotopes of an element have different numbers of neutrons in their nuclei. Isotopes of an element share most chemical and physical properties.

- The mass number of an atom is the sum of the atom's neutrons and protons.

- Atomic mass is a weighted average of the masses of natural isotopes of an element.

- The forces at work in an atom are gravitational force, electromagnetic force, strong force, and weak force.

Skills Worksheet

Section Review

Development of the Atomic Theory
USING KEY TERMS

1. In your own words, write a definition for the term *atom*.

_____

_____

2. Use the following terms in the same sentence: *theory* and *model*.

_____

_____

The statements below are false. For each statement, replace the underlined term to make a true statement.

3. A(n) <u>nucleus</u> is a particle with a negative electric charge.

_____

4. The <u>electron</u> is where most of an atom's mass is located.

_____

UNDERSTANDING KEY IDEAS

_____ **5.** Which of the following scientists discovered that atoms contain electrons?
   a. Dalton
   b. Thomson
   c. Rutherford
   d. Bohr

6. What did Dalton do in developing his theory that Democritus did not do?

_____

_____

7. What discovery demonstrated that atoms are mostly empty space?

_____

_____

| Section Review *continued*

CRITICAL THINKING

8. Making Comparisons Compare the location of electrons according to Bohr's theory and to the current atomic theory.

_____

_____

_____

_____

_____

9. Analyzing Methods How does the design of Rutherford's experiment show what he was trying to find out?

_____

_____

_____

_____

_____

INTERPRETING GRAPHICS

10. What about the atomic model shown below was shown to be incorrect?

_____

_____

_____

_____

_____

Skills Worksheet

Section Review

The Atom

USING KEY TERMS

1. Use the following terms in the same sentence: *proton*, *neutron*, and *isotope*.

_____

_____

Complete each of the following sentences by choosing the correct term from the word bank.

atomic mass unit	atomic number
mass number	atomic mass

2. An atom's _____ is equal to the number of protons in its nucleus.

3. An atom's _____ is equal to the weighted average of the masses of all the naturally occurring isotopes of that element.

UNDERSTANDING KEY IDEAS

_____ **4.** Which of the following particles has no electric charge?
  a. proton   **c.** electron
  b. neutron   **d.** ion

5. Name and describe the four forces that are at work within the nucleus of an atom.

_____

_____

_____

MATH SKILLS

6. The metal thallium occurs naturally as 30% thallium-203 and 70% thallium-205. Calculate the atomic mass of thallium. Show your work below.

| Section Review *continued*

CRITICAL THINKING

7. Analyzing Ideas Why is gravitational force in the nucleus so small?

_____

_____

_____

_____

8. Predicting Consequences Could a nucleus of more than one proton but no neutrons exist? Explain.

_____

_____

_____

_____

INTERPRETING GRAPHICS

9. Look at the two atomic models below. Do the two atoms represent different elements or different isotopes? Explain.

_____

_____

_____

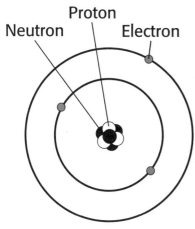 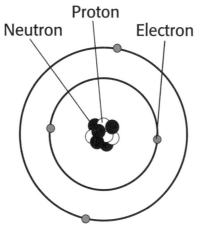

Skills Worksheet

Chapter Review

USING KEY TERMS

The statements below are false. For each statement, replace the underlined term to make a true statement.

1. Electrons have a positive charge.

_____

2. All atoms of the same element contain the same number of neutrons.

_____

3. Protons have no electrical charge.

_____

4. The atomic number of an element is the number of protons and neutrons in the nucleus.

_____

5. The mass number is an average of the masses of all naturally occurring isotopes of an element.

_____

UNDERSTANDING KEY IDEAS

Multiple Choice

_____ 6. The discovery of which particle proved that the atom is not indivisible?
    a. proton   **c.** electron
    b. neutron   **d.** nucleus

_____ 7. How many protons does an atom with an atomic number of 23 and a mass number of 51 have?
    a. 23   **c.** 51
    b. 28   **d.** 74

_____ 8. In Rutherford's gold-foil experiment, Rutherford concluded that the atom is mostly empty space with a small, massive, positively charged center because
    a. most of the particles passed straight through the foil.
    b. some particles were slightly deflected.
    c. a few particles bounced straight back.
    d. All of the above

_____ **9.** Which of the following determines the identity of an element?
   a. atomic number
   b. mass number
   c. atomic mass
   d. overall charge

_____ **10.** Isotopes exist because atoms of the same element can have different numbers of
   a. protons.   **c.** electrons.
   b. neutrons.   **d.** None of the above

Short Answer

11. What force holds electrons in atoms?

_____

_____

12. In two or three sentences, describe Thomson's plum-pudding model of the atom.

_____

_____

_____

Math Skills

13. Calculate the atomic mass of gallium, which consists of 60% gallium-69 and 40% gallium-71. Show your work below.

14. Calculate the number of protons, neutrons, and electrons in an atom of zirconium-90 that has no overall charge and an atomic number of 40. Show your work below.

| **Chapter Review** *continued*

CRITICAL THINKING

15. Concept Mapping Use the following terms to create a concept map:
atom, nucleus, protons, neutrons, electrons, isotopes, atomic number, and
mass number.

16. Analyzing Processes Particle accelerators, are devices that speed up charged particles in order to smash them together. Scientists use these devices to make atoms. How can scientists determine whether the atoms formed are a new element or a new isotope of a known element?

_____

_____

_____

_____

17. Analyzing Ideas John Dalton made a number of statements about atoms that are now known to be incorrect. Why do you think his atomic theory is still found in science textbooks?

_____

_____

_____

_____

18. Analyzing Methods If scientists had tried to repeat Thomson's experiment and found that they could not, would Thomson's conclusion still have been valid? Explain your answer.

_____

_____

_____

_____

| Chapter Review *continued*

INTERPRETING GRAPHICS

Use the diagrams below to answer the questions that follow.

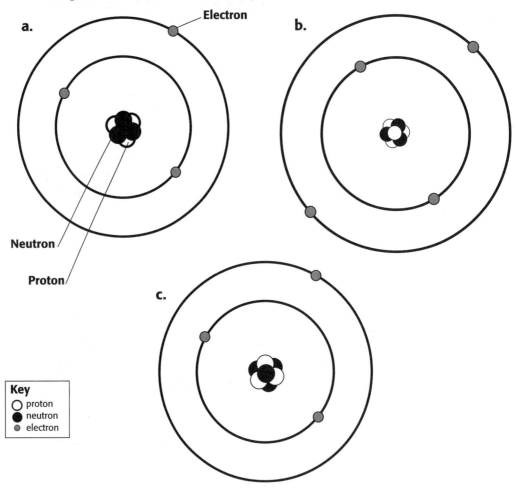

Key
○ proton
● neutron
● electron

19. Which diagrams represent isotopes of the same element?

_____

_____

20. What is the atomic number for A?

_____

_____

21. What is the mass number for B?

_____

_____

Skills Worksheet

Reinforcement

Atomic Timeline

Complete this worksheet after you have finished reading the section "Development of the Atomic Theory."

The table below contains a number of statements connected to major discoveries in the development of atomic theory.

1. In each box, write the name of the scientist(s) associated with the statement. Choose from among the following scientists: Democritus, Rutherford, Thomson, Dalton, Bohr, Schrödinger, and Heisenberg.

2. On a separate sheet of paper, construct a timeline, and label the following: 440 BCE, 1803, 1897, 1909–1911, 1913, and the twentieth century. Cut out the boxes and tape or glue each box at the correct point along the timeline.

A. Most of an atom's mass is in the nucleus.	**B.** There is a small, dense, positively charged nucleus.
C. There are small, negatively charged particles inside an atom.	**D.** Electrons can jump from a path in one level to a path in another level.
E. Atoms of different elements are different.	**F.** He conducted the cathode-ray tube experiment.
G. Atoms are small, hard particles.	**H.** Atoms contain mostly empty space.
I. Atoms are "uncuttable."	**J.** He conducted experiments in combining elements.
K. Electrons travel in certain paths, or energy levels.	**L.** Electron paths cannot be predicted.
M. His theory of atomic structure led to the "plum-pudding" model.	**N.** His model had electrons surrounding the nucleus at a distance.
O. Atoms of the same element are exactly alike.	**P.** Electrons are found in electron clouds, not paths.
Q. All substances are made of atoms.	**R.** Atoms are made of a single material formed into different shapes and sizes.
S. He conducted the gold foil experiment.	**T.** He wanted to know why elements combine in specific proportions.

Skills Worksheet

Critical Thinking

Incredible Shrinking Scientist!

You have received the following E-mail from a friend:

You'll never believe what happened today! My boss, Professor Pat Pending, was accidentally shrunk by her own invention, the "shrinking ray." In order to return her to her normal size, I tried to find her by using a super-high-powered micro-scope. I found the professor near the nucleus of an oxygen atom. Luckily, she was wearing a specially designed suit that carries an electrical charge. As I watched, I noticed something strange: The professor seemed to be traveling outward, as if she were being pushed away from the nucleus. Her lab notebook mentioned that contact must be made with a carbon-14 isotope to reverse the shrinking process. I'll write you tomorrow with an update.

UNDERSTANDING CONCEPTS

1. What was the charge on the professor's suit when she was moving away from the nucleus? How do you know?

_____

_____

_____

2. If the professor had lacked movement toward or away from the nucleus, what would the charge on her suit have been?

_____

_____

_____

3. How might other forces inside the atom affect the professor? Explain your answer.

_____

_____

_____

_____

❙ Critical Thinking *continued*

COMPREHENDING IDEAS

4. How could Professor Pending identify a carbon atom at the subatomic level?

_____

_____

_____

_____

5. How can Professor Pending use the concept of mass number to identify a carbon-14 isotope?

_____

_____

_____

_____

6. How many electrons would be needed to make the carbon-14 isotope a negatively charged ion?

_____

_____

_____

_____

MAKING COMPARISONS

7. The Earth and moon have a relationship that could be compared with the nucleus and electron of a simple atom. Describe the similarities and differences between these relationships. Write your answers below. Discuss your answers in groups.

_____

_____

_____

_____

_____

Section Quiz

Section: Development of the Atomic Theory

Write the letter of the correct answer in the space provided.

_____ **1.** The smallest particle into which an element can be divided and still be the same substance is called a(n)
    a. nucleus.
    b. electron.
    c. atom.
    d. neutron.

_____ **2.** What particle did J. J. Thomson discover?
    a. neutron
    b. electron
    c. atom
    d. proton

_____ **3.** How would you describe the nucleus?
    a. dense, positively charged
    b. large, positively charged
    c. tiny, negatively charged
    d. dense, negatively charged

_____ **4.** Where are electrons *likely* to be found?
    a. the nucleus
    b. electron clouds
    c. mixed throughout an atom
    d. paths, or energy levels

_____ **5.** Dalton believed that
    a. atoms of the same element are exactly alike.
    b. most substances are made of atoms.
    c. atoms of different elements are the same.
    d. atoms can be divided.

Assessment

Section Quiz

Section: The Atom

Match the correct definition with the correct term. Write the letter in the space provided.

_____ **1.** particle of the nucleus with no electrical charge

_____ **2.** negatively charged particle

_____ **3.** keeps a nucleus with two or more protons from flying apart

_____ **4.** subatomic particle that has a positive charge

_____ **5.** pulls objects toward one another

_____ **6.** atom that has the same number of protons as other atoms of the same element do but that has a different number of neutrons

_____ **7.** a charged atom that forms when the numbers of electrons and protons are not equal

_____ **8.** represents the sum of protons in the nucleus of an atom

_____ **9.** enables a neutron to change into a proton and an electron in certain unstable atoms

_____ **10.** the sum of the protons and neutrons in an atom

a. atomic number

b. proton

c. strong force

d. neutron

e. isotope

f. mass number

g. weak force

h. ion

i. electron

j. gravitational force

Assessment

Chapter Test A

Introduction to Atoms

MULTIPLE CHOICE

Write the letter of the correct answer in the space provided.

_____ **1.** What did Democritus, Dalton, Thomson, Rutherford, and Bohr all have in common?
  a. They each identified new elements.
  b. They each identified new isotopes of atoms.
  c. They each contributed to the development of the atomic theory.
  d. They each conducted experiments in which particles collided.

_____ **2.** In Thomson's "plum-pudding" model of the atom, the plums represent
  a. atoms.   **c.** neutrons.
  b. protons.   **d.** electrons.

_____ **3.** An atom of gold with 79 protons, 79 electrons, and 118 neutrons would have a mass number of
  a. 39.   **c.** 197.
  b. 158.   **d.** 276.

_____ **4.** Which of the following has the least mass?
  a. nucleus   **c.** neutron
  b. proton   **d.** electron

_____ **5.** If an isotope of uranium, uranium-235, has 92 protons, how many protons does uranium-238 have?
  a. 92   **c.** 143
  b. 95   **d.** 146

_____ **6.** How did Democritus describe atoms?
  a. large, soft particles
  b. dividable particles
  c. small, hard particles
  d. a single material with one shape and size

_____ **7.** What is the smallest particle into which an element can be divided and still be the same substance?
  a. electron   **c.** proton
  b. neutron   **d.** atom

MATCHING

Match the correct description with the correct term. Write the letter in the space provided.

_____ **8.** particle than cannot be cut

_____ **9.** negatively charged particle discovered by Thomson

_____ **10.** central region of the atom

_____ **11.** region where electrons are likely to be found

_____ **12.** particle in the center of an atom that has no charge

_____ **13.** subatomic particle that has a positive charge

_____ **14.** a unit of mass that describes the mass of an atom or molecule

_____ **15.** the number of protons in the nucleus of an atom

_____ **16.** atom that has the same number of protons but different numbers of neutrons

_____ **17.** the sum of protons and neutrons in an atom

a. atomic number

b. nucleus

c. electron cloud

d. mass number

e. isotope

f. neutron

g. atom

h. electron

i. atomic mass unit (amu)

j. proton

MATCHING

Use the diagram below to answer questions 18 through 21. Write the letter of the correct answer in the space provided.

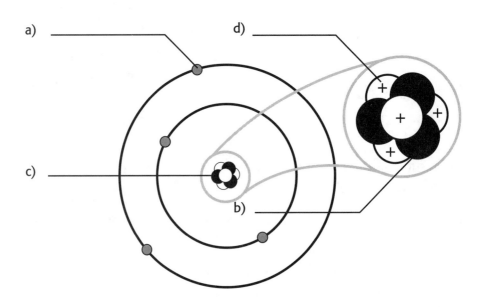

_____ **18.** Which letter refers to the negatively charged particles?

_____ **19.** Which letter refers to the positively charged particles?

_____ **20.** Which letter refers to the particles with no charge?

_____ **21.** Which letter refers to the dense center of the atom?

Name _____ Class _____ Date _____

MULTIPLE CHOICE

Use the figure below to answer the questions 22 and 23. Write the letter of the correct answer in the space provided.

_____22. Who proposed this new model of an atom?
   a. Bohr
   b. Thomson
   c. Rutherford
   d. Democritus

_____23. The raised surfaces show
   a. protons.
   b. electrons.
   c. neutrons.
   d. isotopes.

Assessment

Chapter Test B

Introduction to Atoms

USING KEY TERMS

Use the terms from the following list to complete the sentences below. Each term may be used only once. Some terms may not be used.

atom	atomic number	electron
nucleus	atomic mass	electron cloud
proton	isotope	neutron

1. A positively charged particle in the nucleus of an atom is called

a(n) _____.

2. An atom of an element that has the same number of protons but different

numbers of neutrons is called a(n) _____.

3. The region in an atom that contains most of the mass is called

the _____.

4. The number of protons in an atom determines its _____.

5. The weighted average of all the naturally occurring isotopes of an element is

called the _____.

6. The smallest particle into which an element can be divided and still be the

same substance is a(n) _____.

UNDERSTANDING KEY IDEAS

Write the letter of the correct answer in the space provided.

_____ **7.** What did Bohr, Democritus, Thomson, Dalton, and Rutherford all have
in common?
a. They each identified the electromagnetic force of atoms.
b. They each identified new electron clouds.
c. They each developed ideas about atoms.
d. They each conducted experiments with ions.

_____ **8.** In Thomson's "plum-pudding model" of the atom, the plums represent
      a. atoms.   **c.** neutrons.
      b. protons.   **d.** electrons.

_____ **9.** An atom of carbon with 6 protons, 6 electrons, and 6 neutrons would
have a mass number of
      a. 6.   **c.** 12.
      b. 18.   **d.** 15.

_____ **10.** In an atom, which has the least mass?
      a. nucleus   **c.** neutron
      b. proton   **d.** electron

_____ **11.** If hydrogen-1 has 1 proton, how many protons does hydrogen-2 have?
      a. 2   **c.** 3
      b. 1   **d.** 4

12. How was Bohr's theory of atomic structure similar to the current theory?

_____

_____

_____

_____

_____

13. How was Bohr's theory of atomic structure different from the current theory?

_____

_____

_____

_____

_____

_____

▌Chapter Test B *continued*

14. Describe the difference between atomic number and atomic mass.

_____

_____

_____

15. How are protons in the nucleus of an atom able to stay close to one another even though they have the same charge?

_____

_____

_____

_____

CRITICAL THINKING

16. Long ago, people tried to change inexpensive metals, such as lead, into gold. What fundamental principle of matter did these people fail to understand?

_____

_____

_____

_____

17. The ionosphere is a region of Earth's upper atmosphere. From the name ionosphere, what can you conclude about the gases that make up this region?

_____

_____

_____

_____

18. The approximate composition of naturally occurring magnesium is as follows: 79% magnesium-24, 10% magnesium-25, and 11% magnesium-26. Calculate the atomic mass of magnesium. Show your work.

CONCEPT MAPPING

19. Use the following terms to complete the concept map below:

| charges | density | strong force |
| neutrons | electromagnetic force | |

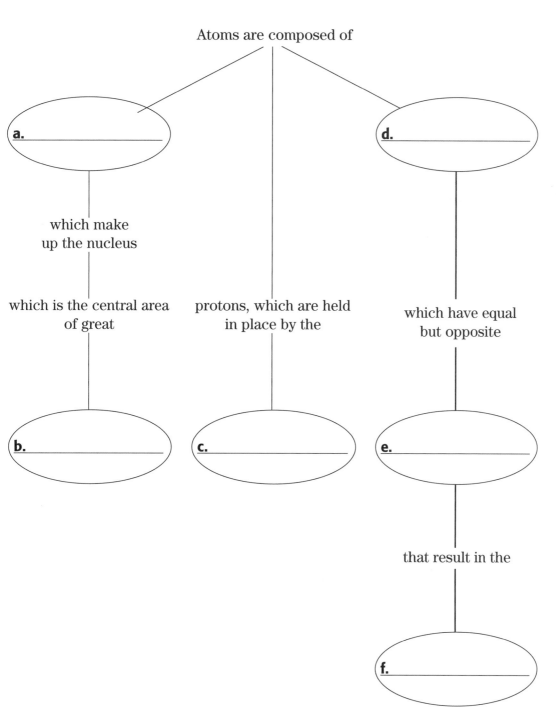

Chapter Test C

Introduction to Atoms
MULTIPLE CHOICE
<u>Circle the letter</u> of the best answer for each question.

1. What was one of Dalton's ideas?

   a. All substances are made of atoms.

   b. Atoms can be divided.

   c. Atoms can be destroyed.

   d. Most substances are made of atoms.

2. What took place in the late 1880s?

   a. Dalton created a new atomic theory.

   b. Dalton disproved his theory.

   c. Dalton's theory was proved.

   d. Dalton's theory was changed.

3. What is the meaning of atom?

   a. "dividable"

   b. "invisible"

   c. "hard particles"

   d. "not able to be divided"

4. Which statement about atoms is true?

   a. A penny has about 20,000 atoms.

   b. Aluminum has large atoms.

   c. A penny has more atoms than Earth has people.

   d. Aluminum has a diameter of about 3 cm.

MULTIPLE CHOICE

Circle the letter of the best answer for each question.

5. Which statement about isotopes is true?

   a. They have the same number of protons.

   b. They have the same number of neutrons.

   c. They have a different atomic number.

   d. They have the same mass.

6. According to Rutherford, what was in the center of an atom?

   a. an electron

   b. a nucleus

   c. a particle

   d. a proton

7. Which phrase describes radioactive isotopes?

   a. They are stable.

   b. They never change.

   c. They are unstable.

   d. They don't produce energy.

8. Which of the following has the least mass in an atom?

   a. nucleus

   b. proton

   c. neuton

   d. electron

MATCHING
Read the description. Then, <u>draw a line</u> from the dot next to each description to the matching word.

9. positively charged particle ●   **a.** electron

10. negatively charged particle ●   **b.** proton

11. uncharged particle ●   **c.** neutron

_____

12. sum of the protons and neutrons ●

13. mass of an atom expressed in atomic mass units ●

14. unit that describes the mass of an atom ●

15. number of protons in the nucleus ●

    a. atomic mass unit

    b. atomic number

    c. mass number

    d. atomic mass

FILL-IN-THE BLANK

Read the words in the box. Read the sentences. <u>Fill in each blank</u> with the word or phrase that best completes the sentence.

electrons	electron-cloud	protons
nucleus	atoms	isotopes

16. Thomson discovered the negatively charged particles called

_____.

17. Rutherford believed that each atom has a(n)

_____ at its center.

18. The current atomic theory includes the

_____ model.

19. All substances are made of _____.

20. Isotopes always have the same number of

_____.

21. Most elements have a mixture of two or more

_____.

strong	gravitational	electromagnetic

22. Protons stay together in the nucleus because of

_____ force.

23. Objects are pulled toward one another by

_____ force.

24. Electrons around the nucleus are held in place by

_____ force.

Assessment

Performance-Based Assessment

OBJECTIVE

Even though we can't see them, electrons are all around us in everything we see and touch. In this activity, you will observe how the charges of electrons interact.

KNOW THE SCORE!

As you work through the activity, keep in mind that you will be earning a grade for the following:

- how well you work with the materials and equipment (20%)
- the quality and clarity of your observations (40%)
- how well you use your observations to answer analysis questions (40%)

Using Scientific Methods

ASK A QUESTION

How do charged objects affect other objects?

MATERIALS AND EQUIPMENT

- two large balloons
- string (1 m)
- water tap
- fluorescent tube

SAFETY INFORMATION

- Wipe up spills right away
- Don't touch broken fluorescent tubes

PROCEDURE

1. Blow up your balloons and tie them off.

2. Tie one end of the string to each of the balloons. Have the group member with the longest, driest hair rub the two balloons in his or her hair for 20 seconds. Then hold the string in the middle with two fingers.

3. What happens when the balloons are brought together?

_____

4. Turn on the water tap partway so the that flow is just a trickle. Recharge one of the balloons with your hair. Hold the balloon next to the water stream.

5. What happens to the stream of water when you bring the balloon near it?

_____

6. Recharge the other balloon. Ask your teacher to dim the lights. Now, holding the tube in the middle, touch the balloon to the fluorescent tube near the tube's end. Describe what happens.

_____

ANALYSIS

7. What happened to the charges of the balloons when you rubbed them in your hair?

_____

_____

8. Based on your observations in Step 2 of the procedure, explain why the two balloons moved as they did.

_____

_____

9. Based on your observations in Step 4 of the procedure, what can you conclude about the electrical charge of the stream of water?

_____

_____

10. What do you think caused the reaction in the fluorescent tube?

_____

_____

11. What does this activity show about the mobility of electrons?

_____

_____

Name _____ Class _____ Date _____

Standardized Test Preparation

READING

Read each of the passages below. Then, answer the questions that follow each passage.

Passage 1 In the Bohr model of the atom, electrons can be found only in certain energy levels. Electrons "jump" from one level to the next level without passing through any of the regions in between. When an electron moves from one level to another, it gains or loses energy, depending on the direction of its jump. Bohr's model explained an unusual event. When electric charges pass through atoms of a gaseous element, the gas produces a glowing light, like in a neon sign. If this light is passed through a prism, a pattern of lines appears, each line having a different color. The pattern depends on the element—neon has one pattern, and helium has another. In Bohr's model, the lines are caused by electron jumps from higher to lower energy levels. Because only certain jumps are possible, electrons release energy only in certain quantities. These "packets" of energy produce the lines that are seen.

_____ **1.** In the Bohr model of the atom, what limitation is placed on electrons?
   A the number of electrons in an atom
   B the electrons' being found only in certain energy levels
   C the size of electrons
   D the speed of electrons

_____ **2.** What causes the colored lines that appear when the light from a gas is passed through a prism?
   F packets of energy released by electron jumps
   G electrons changing color
   H atoms of the gas exchanging electrons
   I There is not enough information to determine the answer.

Standardized Test Preparation *continued*

Passage 2 No one has ever seen a living dinosaur, but scientists have determined the appearance of *Tyrannosaurus rex* by studying fossilized skeletons. Scientists theorize that these extinct creatures had big hind legs, small front legs, a long, whip-like tail, and a mouth full of dagger-shaped teeth. However, theories of how *T. rex* walked have been harder to develop. For many years, most scientists thought that *T. rex* plodded slowly like a big, lazy lizard. However, after studying well-preserved dinosaur tracks and noticing skeletal similarities between certain dinosaur fossils and living creatures like the ostrich, many scientists now theorize that *T. rex* could turn on the speed. Some scientists estimate that *T. rex* had bursts of speed of 32 km/h (20 mi/h)!

_____ **1.** According to this passage, where does most of what we know about the appearance of *Tyrannosaurus rex* come from?

    A fossilized skeletons

    B dinosaur tracks

    C living organisms such as the ostrich

    D living specimens of T. rex

_____ **2.** How did scientists conclude that *T. rex* could probably move very quickly?

    F They measured the speed at which it could run.

    G They compared fossilized *T. rex* tracks with *T. rex* skeletons.

    H They studied dinosaur tracks and noted similarities between ostrich skeletons and *T. rex* skeletons.

    I They measured the speed at which ostriches could run.

│ Standardized Test Preparation *continued*

INTERPRETING GRAPHICS

Use the diagram of the atom below to answer the questions that follow.

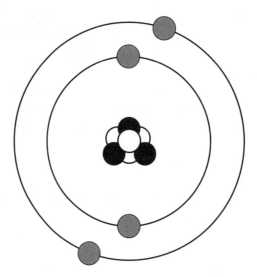

_____ **1.** The black circles in the center of the model represent neutrons. What do the white circles in the center represent?
   A electrons
   B protons
   C nuclei
   D atoms

_____ **2.** What is the mass number of the atom shown in the model?
   F 3
   G 7
   H 9
   I 11

_____ **3.** What is the overall charge of the atom shown in the model?
   A 12
   B 11
   C 0
   D 21

MATH

Read each question below, and choose the best answer.

_____ **1.** Aimee, Mari, and Brooke are 163 cm, 171 cm, and 175 cm tall. Which of the following measurements is a reasonable average height of these three friends?

A 170 cm

B 175 cm

C 255 cm

D 509 cm

_____ **2.** A certain school has 40 classrooms. Most of the classrooms have 25 to 30 students. Which of the following is a reasonable estimate of the number of students that go to this school?

F 40 students

G 100 students

H 1,100 students

I 2,000 students

_____ **3.** Jenna is setting up a fish tank in her room. The tank is the shape of a rectangular prism. The height of the tank is 38 cm, the width is 23 cm, and the length is 62 cm. The tank is filled with water to a point that is 7 cm from the top. How much water is in the tank?

A 44,206 cm^3

B 48,070 cm^3

C 54,188 cm^3

D 64,170 cm^3

_____ **4.** Which of the following is equal to 8^5?

F $8 + 8 + 8 + 8 + 8$

G $5 \times 5 \times 5 \times 5 \times 5 \times 5 \times 5 \times 5$

H 5×8

I $8 \times 8 \times 8 \times 8 \times 8$

Model-Making Lab

Made to Order

Imagine that you are an employee at the Elements-4-U Company, which custom builds elements. Your job is to construct the atomic nucleus for each element ordered by your clients. You were hired for the position because of your knowledge about what a nucleus is made of and your understanding of how isotopes of an element differ from each other. Now, it's time to put that knowledge to work!

OBJECTIVES

Build models of nuclei of certain isotopes.

Use the periodic table to determine the composition of atomic nuclei.

MATERIALS

- periodic table
- plastic-foam balls, blue, 2–3 cm in diameter (6)
- plastic-foam balls, white, 2–3 cm in diameter (4)
- toothpicks (20)

SAFETY

PROCEDURE

1. Use the table below to record your data. Expand the table as needed to include more elements.

Data Collection Table						
	Hydrogen-1	**Hydrogen-2**	**Helium-2**	**Helium-4**	**Beryllium-9**	**Beryllium-10**
Number of protons						
Number of neutrons						
Atomic number						
Mass number						

2. Your first assignment is the nucleus of hydrogen-1. Pick up one proton (a white plastic-foam ball). Congratulations! You have built a hydrogen-1 nucleus, the simplest nucleus possible.

3. Count the number of protons and neutrons in the nucleus, and fill in rows 1 and 2 for this element in the table.

4. Use the information in rows 1 and 2 to determine the atomic number and mass number of the element. Record this information in the table.

Made to Order *continued*

5. Draw a picture of your model.

6. Hydrogen-2 is an isotope of hydrogen that has one proton and one neutron. Using a strong-force connector, add a neutron to your hydrogen-1 nucleus. (Remember that in a nucleus, the protons and neutrons are held together by the strong force, which is represented in this activity by the toothpicks.) Repeat steps 3–5.

7. Helium-3 is an isotope of helium that has two protons and one neutron. Add one proton to your hydrogen-2 nucleus to create a helium-3 nucleus. Each particle should be connected to the other two particles so that they make a triangle, not a line. Protons and neutrons always form the smallest arrangement possible because the strong force pulls them together. Then, repeat steps 3–5.

8. For the next part of the lab, you will need to use information from the periodic table of the elements. Look at the illustration below. It shows the periodic table entry for carbon. You can find the atomic number of any element at the top of its entry on the periodic table. For example, the atomic number of carbon is 6.

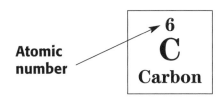

Atomic number

6
C
Carbon

9. Use the information in the periodic table to build models of the following isotopes of elements: helium-4, lithium-7, beryllium-9, and beryllium-10. Remember to put the protons and neutrons as close together as possible— each particle should attach to at least two others. Repeat steps 3–5 for each isotope.

ANALYZE THE RESULTS

1. Examining Data What is the relationship between the number of protons and the atomic number?

_____

2. Analyzing Data If you know the atomic number and the mass number of an isotope, how could you figure out the number of neutrons in its nucleus?

_____

DRAW CONCLUSIONS

3. Applying Conclusions Look up uranium on the periodic table. What is the atomic number of uranium? How many neutrons does the isotope uranium-235 have?

_____

_____

4. Evaluating Models Compare your model with the models of your classmates. How are the models similar? How are they different?

_____

_____

_____

APPLYING YOUR DATA

Combine your model with one that another student has made to create a single nucleus. Identify the element (and isotope) you have created.

_____

_____

Activity

Vocabulary Activity

Atomic Anagrams

After you finish reading the chapter, try this puzzle.

Use the definitions below to unscramble the vocabulary words.

1. weighted average of the mass of all naturally occurring isotopes of the same element

MICTOA SAMS _____

2. the smallest unit of an element that maintains the properties of an element

MOATS_____

3. positively charged particle in the atom

TORPNO _____

4. made up of protons and neutrons

UCSELUN _____

5. particle in the atom that has no charge

TRONUNE_____

6. atoms with the same number of protons but different numbers of neutrons

SOOTPIES_____

7. negatively charged particle in the atom

CLEENROT_____

8. number of protons in a nucleus

MICOTA BRUMEN_____

9. regions where electrons are likely to be found

RENECTOL SCUDLO _____

10. SI unit used to express the mass of atomic particles

TMCOAI SASM NTUI_____

11. sum of protons and neutrons

SAMS BRUNEM _____

Name _____ Class _____ Date _____

SciLinks Activity

Introduction to Atoms

Go to www.scilinks.org. To find links related to atoms, type in the keyword HSM0799. Use the links to answer the following questions about the atom.

Go to www.scilinks.org

Topic: Inside the Atom
SciLinks code: HSM0799

1. If an electron weighed as much as a dime, how much would a proton weigh?

_____

_____

2. How do the masses of protons and neutrons compare?

_____

_____

3. How many naturally occurring kinds of atoms are there?

_____

_____

4. How many atoms have scientists been able to make in labs?

_____

_____

5. In 1968, scientists discovered new particles inside the proton. What are these particles? How many of these particles are in each proton?

_____

_____

6. When did scientists discover the neutron?

_____

7. How many quarks are there in each neutron? In each proton?

_____

8. What holds quarks together?

_____

Performance-Based Assessment

Teacher Notes and Answer Key

PURPOSE
Students demonstrate the stripping of electrons from atoms, repulsion of like charges, attraction of opposites, and electron flow.

Susan Gorman
Northridge Middle School
North Richland Hills, Texas

TIME REQUIRED
One 45-minute class period. Students will need 20 minutes at the activity station and 25 minutes to answer the analysis questions.

RATING
Easy ← 1 2 3 4 → Hard

Teacher Prep–1
Student Set-Up–1
Concept Level–2
Clean Up–1

ADVANCE PREPARATION

Equip each activity station with the necessary materials. Each activity station should have access to a sink with running water.

SAFETY INFORMATION

Wipe up spills immediately. Instruct students not to touch broken fluorescent tubes. Have a disposal container for sharps available in case of fluorescent tube breakage.

TEACHING STRATEGIES

This activity works best in groups of 2–3 students. The balloons in the activity are charged by rubbing them on the students' hair. The reaction of the balloon to the students' hair and to the stream of tap water demonstrates the presence of negative and positive charges. The type of charge affects the balloon's reaction to other materials. The reaction between the balloon and the fluorescent tube illustrates the mobility of electrons.

Performance-Based Assessment *continued*

Evaluation Strategies

Use the following rubric to help evaluate student performance.

Rubric for Assessment

Possible points	Appropriate use of materials and equipment (20 points possible)
20–15	Successfully completes activity; safe and careful handling of materials and equipment; attention to detail; superior lab skills
14–10	Task is generally complete; successful use of materials and equipment; sound knowledge of lab techniques; somewhat unfocused performance
9–1	Attempts to complete tasks yield inadequate results; sloppy lab technique; apparent lack of skill
	Quality and clarity of observations (40 points possible)
40–30	Superior observations stated clearly and accurately; high level of detail
29–20	Accurate observations; moderate level of detail; correct use of units of measurement
19–10	Complete observations, but expressed in unclear manner; may include minor inaccuracies; attempts to use units of measurement include errors or inconsistencies
9–1	Erroneous, incomplete, or unclear observations; lack of accuracy, details, units of measurement
	Explanation of observations (40 points possible)
40–25	Clear, detailed explanation shows superior knowledge of subject
24–15	Adequate understanding of concepts with minor difficulty in expression
14–1	Poor understanding of concepts; explanation unclear or not relevant; substantial factual errors

Assessment

Performance-Based Assessment

OBJECTIVE

Even though we can't see them, electrons are all around us in everything we see and touch. In this activity, you will observe how the charges of electrons interact.

KNOW THE SCORE!

As you work through the activity, keep in mind that you will be earning a grade for the following:

- how well you work with the materials and equipment (20%)
- the quality and clarity of your observations (40%)
- how well you use your observations to answer analysis questions (40%)

Using Scientific Methods

ASK A QUESTION

How do charged objects affect other objects?

MATERIALS AND EQUIPMENT

- two large balloons
- string (1 m)
- water tap
- fluorescent tube

SAFETY INFORMATION

- Wipe up spills right away
- Don't touch broken fluorescent tubes

PROCEDURE

1. Blow up your balloons and tie them off.

2. Tie one end of the string to each of the balloons. Have the group member with the longest, driest hair rub the two balloons in his or her hair for 20 seconds. Then hold the string in the middle with two fingers.

3. What happens when the balloons are brought together?

   The balloons move apart from each other.

4. Turn on the water tap partway so the that flow is just a trickle. Recharge one of the balloons with your hair. Hold the balloon next to the water stream.

5. What happens to the stream of water when you bring the balloon near it?

   The stream of water bends toward the balloon.

❙ Performance-Based Assessment *continued*

6. Recharge the other balloon. Ask your teacher to dim the lights. Now, holding the tube in the middle, touch the balloon to the fluorescent tube near the tube's end. Describe what happens.

The balloon causes a flash of light in the fluorescent tube.

ANALYSIS

7. What happened to the charges of the balloons when you rubbed them in your hair?

The balloons picked up electrons from my hair, which gave them a negative

electric charge.

8. Based on your observations in Step 2 of the procedure, explain why the two balloons moved as they did.

Like charges repel each other, and both of the balloons were negatively

charged.

9. Based on your observations in Step 4 of the procedure, what can you conclude about the electrical charge of the stream of water?

The stream of water must have a positive charge because it is attracted to

the negatively charged balloon.

10. What do you think caused the reaction in the fluorescent tube?

The electrons passed very quickly into the fluorescent tube, which caused

the flash of light.

11. What does this activity show about the mobility of electrons?

Electrons can move from place to place; they are not permanently attached

to atoms.

Made to Order

Teacher Notes and Answer Key

Sharon I. Woolf
Langston Hughes
Middle School
Reston, Virginia

TIME REQUIRED

One 45-minute class period

LAB RATINGS

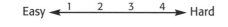

Easy ← 1 2 3 4 → Hard

Teacher Prep–2
Student Set-Up–1
Concept Level–3
Clean Up–1

MATERIALS

The supplies listed are for a pair of students. Foam balls of any color are. acceptable as long as there are two colors. Flexible pipe cleaners may be used instead of toothpicks.

SAFETY CAUTION

• Remind students to review all safety cautions and icons before beginning this lab activity.

PREPARATION NOTES

Before you begin this lab, review the concepts of isotopes, atomic number, and mass number. To create colored balls, use colored markers or spray paint. Alternatively, you can label white balls with "N" or "P." If you prefer to make two-dimensional models, use colored dots (from an office-supply store) to represent the different particles. Reinforce the idea that the particles should be compact—the strong force binds the particles together as tightly as possible.

Name _____ Class _____ Date _____

| Model-Making Lab | DATASHEET FOR CHAPTER LAB |

Made to Order

Imagine that you are an employee at the Elements-4-U Company, which custom builds elements. Your job is to construct the atomic nucleus for each element ordered by your clients. You were hired for the position because of your knowledge about what a nucleus is made of and your understanding of how isotopes of an element differ from each other. Now, it's time to put that knowledge to work!

OBJECTIVES

Build models of nuclei of certain isotopes.

Use the periodic table to determine the composition of atomic nuclei.

MATERIALS

- periodic table
- plastic-foam balls, blue, 2–3 cm in diameter (6)
- plastic-foam balls, white, 2–3 cm in diameter (4)
- toothpicks (20)

SAFETY

PROCEDURE

1. Use the table below to record your data. Expand the table as needed to include more elements.

Data Collection Table						
	Hydrogen-1	Hydrogen-2	Helium-2	Helium-4	Beryllium-9	Beryllium-10
Number of protons						
Number of neutrons						
Atomic number						
Mass number						

2. Your first assignment is the nucleus of hydrogen-1. Pick up one proton (a white plastic-foam ball). Congratulations! You have built a hydrogen-1 nucleus, the simplest nucleus possible.

3. Count the number of protons and neutrons in the nucleus, and fill in rows 1 and 2 for this element in the table.

4. Use the information in rows 1 and 2 to determine the atomic number and mass number of the element. Record this information in the table.

Name _____ Class _____ Date _____

Made to Order continued

5. Draw a picture of your model.

6. Hydrogen-2 is an isotope of hydrogen that has one proton and one neutron. Using a strong-force connector, add a neutron to your hydrogen-1 nucleus. (Remember that in a nucleus, the protons and neutrons are held together by the strong force, which is represented in this activity by the toothpicks.) Repeat steps 3–5.

7. Helium-3 is an isotope of helium that has two protons and one neutron. Add one proton to your hydrogen-2 nucleus to create a helium-3 nucleus. Each particle should be connected to the other two particles so that they make a triangle, not a line. Protons and neutrons always form the smallest arrangement possible because the strong force pulls them together. Then, repeat steps 3–5.

8. For the next part of the lab, you will need to use information from the periodic table of the elements. Look at the illustration below. It shows the periodic table entry for carbon. You can find the atomic number of any element at the top of its entry on the periodic table. For example, the atomic number of carbon is 6.

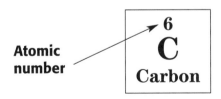

Atomic number

6
C
Carbon

9. Use the information in the periodic table to build models of the following isotopes of elements: helium-4, lithium-7, beryllium-9, and beryllium-10. Remember to put the protons and neutrons as close together as possible— each particle should attach to at least two others. Repeat steps 3–5 for each isotope.

Name _____ Class _____ Date _____

| Made to Order *continued*

ANALYZE THE RESULTS

1. Examining Data What is the relationship between the number of protons and the atomic number?

The number of protons is the same as the atomic number.

2. Analyzing Data If you know the atomic number and the mass number of an isotope, how could you figure out the number of neutrons in its nucleus?

The number of neutrons equals the mass number minus the atomic number.

DRAW CONCLUSIONS

3. Applying Conclusions Look up uranium on the periodic table. What is the atomic number of uranium? How many neutrons does the isotope uranium-235 have?

a. 92

b. 143 neutrons (235 − 92 = 143)

4. Evaluating Models Compare your model with the models of your classmates. How are the models similar? How are they different?

Sample answer: They differ in the way the protons and neutrons are

connected to each other. They are the same in the number of protons and

neutrons that each of the same isotope has, however.

APPLYING YOUR DATA

Combine your model with one that another student has made to create a single nucleus. Identify the element (and isotope) you have created.

If all of the protons and neutrons are used, the isotope created will be

oxygen-20.

Answer Key

Directed Reading A

SECTION: DEVELOPMENT OF THE ATOMIC THEORY

1. D
2. C
3. Aristotle disagreed with Democritus. At the time, Aristotle had more influence on what people thought than Democritus did. Consequently, people believed Aristotle.
4. atom
5. C
6. Dalton's results suggested that elements combine in specific proportions because they are made of single atoms.
7. positively, negative
8. electrons
9. atom
10. A
11. Most of the particles passed right through the gold foil, some of the particles were deflected, and some of the particles bounced straight back.
12. D
13. nucleus
14. Electron clouds are regions inside the atom where electrons are likely to be found.

SECTION: THE ATOM

1. B
2. F
3. D
4. E
5. A
6. C
7. B
8. hydrogen, proton, electron (no particular order for *proton* and *electron*)
9. nucleus
10. helium
11. protons and neutrons (either order)
12. protons
13. A
14. B
15. B
16. C
17. isotopes
18. atomic mass
19. C
20. A
21. D
22. B

Directed Reading B

SECTION: DEVELOPMENT OF ATOMIC THEORY

1. D
2. C
3. C
4. A
5. D
6. cathode-ray tube
7. positively
8. particles
9. electrons
10. A
11. A
12. B
13. A
14. B
15. A
16. D
17. A

SECTION: THE ATOM

1. B
2. D
3. C
4. A
5. B
6. hydrogen, electron
7. helium
8. neutrons
9. atomic number
10. atomic mass unit
11. A
12. B
13. C
14. B
15. C
16. mass number
17. atomic mass
18. strong force
19. gravitational force
20. weak force
21. electromagnetic force

Vocabulary and Section Summary

SECTION: DEVELOPMENT OF THE ATOMIC THEORY

1. atom: the smallest unit of an element that maintains the properties of an element
2. electron: a subatomic particle that has a negative charge
3. nucleus: in physical science, an atom's central region, which is made up of protons and neutrons
4. electron cloud: a region around the nucleus of an atom where electrons are likely to be found

SECTION: THE ATOM

1. proton: a subatomic particle that has a positive charge and that is found in the nucleus of an atom
2. atomic mass unit: a unit of mass that describes the mass of an atom or molecule
3. neutron: a subatomic particle that has no charge and that is found in the nucleus of an atom
4. atomic number: the number of protons in the nucleus of an atom; the atomic number is the same for all atoms of an element
5. isotope: an atom that has the same number of protons (or the same atomic number) as other atoms of the same element do but that has a different number of neutrons (and thus a different atomic mass)
6. mass number: the sum of the numbers of protons and neutrons in the nucleus of an atom
7. atomic mass: the mass of an atom expressed in atomic mass units

Section Review

SECTION: DEVELOPMENT OF THE ATOMIC THEORY

1. Sample answer: the smallest part of an element that has the properties of that element
2. electron
3. nucleus
4. B

5. He performed experiments and drew conclusions from them to develop his theory.
6. Rutherford's gold foil experiment, in which he observed that most of the positively charged particles he aimed at a piece of gold foil went straight through
7. Bohr suggested that electrons could only move around the nucleus in certain paths. They could jump between these paths, but not stay between them.
8. Bohr's theory held that electrons can only travel in certain paths around the nucleus. The current atomic theory is that electrons travel in regions where they are *likely* to be found.
9. Rutherford placed a surface behind the gold foil, which would glow where the positively charged particles hit it. This shows that he was trying to find out where the particles went after hitting the gold foil.
10. that electrons are mixed throughout an atom

SECTION: THE ATOM

1. Sample answer: Different isotopes have the same number of protons, but different numbers of neutrons.
2. atomic number
3. atomic mass
4. B
5. Gravitational force acts between objects based on their mass. Electromagnetic force attracts objects of opposite electric charge, and repels objects of the same electric charge. The strong force holds the protons and neutrons of atomic nuclei together. The weak force plays a role in radioactive decay.
6. $(0.30 \times 203 \text{ amu}) + (0.70 \times 205 \text{ amu}) = 204.4 \text{ amu}$
7. Because the masses of nuclear particles are so small.
8. No; without neutrons, two protons brought into close contact would repel each other.
9. The two atoms shown are different elements; they have different numbers of protons.

Chapter Review

1. Protons
2. protons
3. Neutrons
4. mass number
5. atomic mass
6. C
7. A
8. D
9. A
10. B
11. electromagnetic force
12. Sample answer: The plum-pudding model describes the atom as a lump of positively charged material with negatively charged particles throughout. The positively charged material is like the pudding, and electrons are like plums in it.
13. $(0.60 \times 69$ amu$) + (0.40 \times 71$ amu$) = 69.8$ amu
14. number of protons = atomic number = 40
    number of neutrons = mass number–atomic number = 50
    number of electrons = number of protons = 40
15. An answer to this exercise can be found at the end of the teacher edition.
16. Scientists must determine the atomic number, or the number of protons, in the newly formed nucleus. The nucleus is that of a new element only if the number of protons is different from all known elements.
17. Sample answer: Dalton's atomic theory was the first one based on experimental evidence. It helps show how a theory develops as new information is discovered.
18. No; the results of an experiment must be repeatable to be considered valid.
19. A and C
20. 3
21. 7

Reinforcement

A. Rutherford, 1909–1911
B. Rutherford, 1909–1911
C. Thomson, 1897
D. Bohr, 1913
E. Dalton, 1803
F. Thomson, 1897
G. Democritus, 440 BCE
H. Rutherford, 1909–1911
I. Democritus, 440 BCE
J. Dalton, 1803
K. Bohr, 1913
L. Schrödinger and Heisenberg, twentieth century
M. Thomson, 1897
N. Rutherford, 1909–1911
O. Dalton, 1803
P. Schrödinger and Heisenberg, twentieth century
Q. Dalton, 1803
R. Democritus, 440 BCE
S. Rutherford, 1909–1911
T. Dalton, 1803

Critical Thinking

1. Because the nucleus is positively charged, the suit also must have been positively charged to create this repulsion.
2. Her suit would have had a neutral charge.
3. Answers will vary according to the forces students discuss. Sample answer: If her suit was positively charged, then the electromagnetic force would pull her toward the electrons in the atom.
4. Knowing that the atomic number of carbon is six, Professor Pending could look for an atom with six protons in its nucleus.
5. An atom's mass number is equal to its protons plus its neutrons. All carbon atoms have six protons. Carbon-14 would have six protons and eight neutrons. Professor Pending could use this characteristic to identify the correct atom.
6. A negatively charged ion has more electrons than protons. Therefore, the ion would require at least seven electrons.

7. The orbit of the moon can be compared with the movement of an electron. They both travel around objects with greater masses. They differ with respect to the forces that cause their motion. The moon orbits Earth because of gravity. The motion of an electron around a nucleus is a result of electromagnetism.

Section Quizzes

SECTION: DEVELOPMENT OF THE ATOMIC THEORY

1. C
2. B
3. A
4. B
5. A

SECTION: THE ATOM

1. D
2. I
3. C
4. B
5. J
6. E
7. H
8. A
9. G
10. F

Chapter Test A

1. C
2. D
3. C
4. D
5. A
6. C
7. D
8. G
9. H
10. B
11. C
12. F
13. J
14. I
15. A
16. E
17. D
18. A
19. D
20. B
21. C

22. B
23. B

Chapter Test B

1. proton
2. isotope
3. nucleus
4. atomic number
5. atomic mass
6. atom
7. C
8. D
9. C
10. D
11. B
12. Bohr's theory and the current theory both have electrons traveling in orbits around a central nucleus.
13. In Bohr's theory, the electrons move only in definite paths. Current atomic theory expresses the position of electrons in terms of the probability that electrons will be found in regions of the atom called electron clouds.
14. The atomic number is the number of protons in an atom. Atomic mass is the sum of the number of protons and neutrons in an atom of a particular isotope.
15. Protons can stay close to one another inside the nucleus of an atom due to the strong force. Although the electromagnetic force causes particles with the same charge to repel each other, the strong force is greater than the electromagnetic force at close distances.
16. These people did not understand that elements, such as lead and gold, are divided into smaller particles called atoms. Each atom of an element is composed of a unique number of protons, neutrons, and electrons. Atoms cannot be created or destroyed. Therefore, it is not possible to simply convert one metal into another.
17. The ionosphere must contain ions, which are electrically charged particles. To be charged, the numbers of electrons and protons in the particles must not be equal.
18. $(0.79 \times 24) + (0.10 \times 25) + (0.11 \times 26) = 24.32$ amu

CONCEPT MAPPING

19. **a.** neutrons, **b.** density, **c.** strong force,
    d. electrons, **e.** charges,
    f. electromagnetic force

Chapter Test C

1. A
2. D
3. D
4. C
5. A
6. B
7. C
8. D
9. B
10. A
11. C
12. C
13. D
14. A
15. B
16. electrons
17. nucleus
18. electron-cloud
19. atoms
20. protons
21. isotopes
22. strong
23. gravitational
24. electromagnetic

Standardized Test Preparation

READING

Passage 1
1. B
2. F

Passage 2
1. A
2. H

INTERPRETING GRAPHICS

1. B
2. G
3. D

MATH

1. B
2. H
3. A
4. I

Vocabulary Activity

1. atomic mass
2. atoms
3. proton
4. nucleus
5. neutron
6. isotopes
7. electron
8. atomic number
9. electron clouds
10. atomic mass unit
11. mass number

SciLinks Activity

1. It would weigh as much as a gallon of milk.
2. The masses are almost the same.
3. 90
4. about 25
5. quarks, three
6. 1932
7. three in each neutron and proton
8. Particles called gluons hold quarks together.

Lesson Plan

Section: Development of the Atomic Theory

Pacing

Regular Schedule	with lab(s): N/A	without lab(s): 1 day
Block Schedule:	with lab(s): N/A	without lab(s): 0.5 day

Objectives

1. Describe some of the experiments that led to the current atomic theory.

2. Compare the different models of the atom.

3. Explain how the atomic theory has changed as scientists have discovered new information about the atom.

National Science Education Standards Covered

UCP 2: Evidence, models, and explanation

SAI 2: Understandings about scientific inquiry

HNS 1: Science as a human endeavor

HNS 2: Nature of science

HNS 3: History of science

KEY
SE = Student Edition   **TE** = Teacher's Edition
CRF = Chapter Resource File

FOCUS *(5 minutes)*

_ **Chapter Starter Transparency** Use this transparency to introduce the chapter.

_ **Bellringer, TE** Have students write what they think a statement by Democritus means.

_ **Bellringer Transparency** Use this transparency as students enter the classroom and find their seats.

_ **Reading Strategy, SE** Have students create an outline of the section, using section headings.

MOTIVATE *(10 minutes)*

_ **Activity, Photographic Dots, TE** Have students use a magnifying lens to examine newspaper photographs. **(GENERAL)**

TEACH *(20 minutes)*

_ **Reading Strategy, Making a Prediction, TE** Ask students to predict whether Democritus's theory is correct or even partly correct. **(GENERAL)**

_ **Discussion, Dalton Discussion, TE** Using diagrams, discuss how Dalton's atomic theory explains his observations. (**GENERAL**)

_ **Group Activity, Scientist Flashcards, TE** Have students create flash cards that connect the scientists in this section with their accomplishments. (**BASIC**)

_ **Activity, Static Electricity, TE** Have students complete a static electricity activity. (**GENERAL**)

_ **Discussion, Influences on Atomic Theory, TE** Have students write a paragraph about the person they believe had the greatest impact on present-day atomic theory. (**GENERAL**)

_ **Connection Activity Literature, The Shrinking Man, TE** Read excerpts of *The Shrinking Man* to students. (**GENERAL**)

_ **Directed Reading A/B, CRF** These worksheets reinforce basic concepts and vocabulary presented in the lesson. (**BASIC/SPECIAL NEEDS**)

_ **Vocabulary and Section Summary, CRF** Students write definitions of key terms and read a summary of section content. (**GENERAL**)

_ **Reinforcement, CRF** This worksheet reinforces key concepts in the chapter. (**GENERAL**)

_ **SciLinks Activity, Inside the Atom, SciLinks code HSM0799, CRF** Students research Internet resources related to atoms. (**GENERAL**)

_ **Teaching Transparency, Thomson's Cathode-Ray Tube Experiment** Use this graphic to help students understand the experiment that led to the discovery of electrons.

_ **Teaching Transparency, Rutherford's Gold-Foil Experiment** Use this graphic to help students understand the experiment that led to Rutherford's revision of the atomic theory.

CLOSE *(10 minutes)*

_ **Reteaching, Table of Atomic Discoveries, TE** Construct a table that summarizes the discoveries of the scientists covered in this section. (**BASIC**)

_ **Homework, Theories of Atomic Structure, TE** Have students write a paragraph explaining why making and using models of scientific discoveries are important. (**GENERAL**)

_ **Section Review, SE** Students answer end-of-section vocabulary, key ideas, and critical thinking, and interpreting graphics questions. (**GENERAL**)

_ **Section Quiz, CRF** Students answer 5 objective questions about atoms. (**GENERAL**)

_ **Quiz, TE** Students answer 3 questions about atoms. (**GENERAL**)

_ **Alternative Assessment, TE** Students role-play scientists or philosophers discussed in this section. (**GENERAL**)

Lesson Plan

Section: The Atom

Pacing

Regular Schedule   **with lab(s):** 2 days   **without lab(s):** 1 day

Block Schedule: **with lab(s):** 1 days   **without lab(s):** 0.5 day

Objectives

1. Describe the size of an atom.

2. Name the parts of an atom.

3. Describe the relationship between numbers of protons and neutrons and atomic number.

4. State how isotopes differ.

5. Calculate atomic masses.

6. Describe the forces within an atom.

National Science Education Standards Covered

PS 1c: Chemical elements do not break down during normal laboratory reactions involving such treatments as heating, exposure to electric current, or reaction with acids. There are more than 100 known elements that combine in a multitude of ways to produce compounds, which account for the living and nonliving substances that we encounter.

KEY	
SE = Student Edition	**TE** = Teacher's Edition
CRF = Chapter Resource File	

FOCUS (*5 minutes*)

_ **Bellringer, TE** Ask students if they believe the definition of the atom is still correct in light of the discovery of particles that are smaller than atoms.

_ **Bellringer Transparency** Use this transparency as students enter the classroom and find their seats.

_ **Reading Strategy, SE** Have students create a concept map, using important terms from the section.

MOTIVATE (*10 minutes*)

_ **Discussion, The Atomic Scale, TE** Discuss the number of atoms in a penny. (GENERAL)

TEACH *(65 minutes)*

_ **Activity, TE** Have advanced learners research the contributions of Japanese scientists. **(ADVANCED)**

_ **Connection Activity, Math, TE** Have students determine how many gold atoms it would take to measure the width of a dollar bill. **(GENERAL)**

_ **Connection to Earth Science, TE** Show students the arrangement of gold atoms in a sample of gold. **(GENERAL)**

_ **Connection Activity, Math, TE** Have students calculate the diameter of an atom that has a nucleus the size of a penny. **(GENERAL)**

_ **Connection Activity, Real World, TE** Tell students about the development of the Atomic Energy Commission. **(GENERAL)**

_ **Reading Strategy, Atomic Diagrams, TE** Have students create and label diagrams of several different atoms in their science journals. **(GENERAL)**

_ **Guided Practice, Atomic Numbers and the Elements, TE** Have students use the periodic table to find the atomic numbers of different elements. **(GENERAL)**

_ **Connection to Paleontology, TE** Tell students about carbon dating. **(GENERAL)**

_ **Chapter Lab, Made to Order, SE** Students build models of nuclei of certain isotopes and use the periodic table.

_ **Directed Reading A/B, CRF** These worksheets reinforce basic concepts and vocabulary presented in the lesson. **(BASIC/SPECIAL NEEDS)**

_ **Vocabulary and Section Summary, CRF** Students write definitions of key terms and read a summary of section content. **(GENERAL)**

_ **Critical Thinking, CRF** Ask students to fill out the worksheet about the incredible shrinking scientist. **(ADVANCED)**

CLOSE *(10 minutes)*

_ **Reteaching, Descriptions of Atomic Structure, TE** Have students write a simple description of an atom. **(BASIC)**

_ **Section Review, SE** Students answer end-of-section vocabulary, key ideas, math, critical thinking, and interpreting graphics questions. **(GENERAL)**

_ **Section Quiz, CRF** Students answer 10 objective questions about atoms. **(GENERAL)**

_ **Quiz, TE** Students answer 3 questions about atoms. **(GENERAL)**

_ **Alternative Assessment, TE** Students create a concept map using key terms from the section. **(GENERAL)**

Lesson Plan

End of Chapter Review and Assessment

Pacing

Regular Schedule   **with lab(s):** N/A   **without lab(s):** 2 days

Block Schedule: **with lab(s):** N/A   **without lab(s):** 1 day

---

KEY

SE = Student Edition   **TE** = Teacher's Edition

CRF = Chapter Resource File

_ **Chapter Review, SE** Students answer end-of-chapter vocabulary, key ideas, critical thinking, and graphics questions. **(GENERAL)**

_ **Vocabulary Activity, CRF** Students review vocabulary terms by completing an atomic anagram activity. **(GENERAL)**

_ **Concept Mapping Transparency** Use this graphic to help students review key concepts.

_ **Chapter Test A/B/C, CRF** Assign questions from the appropriate test for chapter assessment. **(GENERAL/ADVANCED/SPECIAL NEEDS)**

_ **Standardized Test Preparation, SE** Students answer reading comprehension, math, and interpreting graphics questions in the format of a standardized test. **(GENERAL)**

_ **Test Generator, One-Stop Planner.** Create a customized homework assignment, quiz, or test using the HRW Test Generator program. **(GENERAL)**

Introduction to Atoms

MULTIPLE CHOICE

1. The smallest particle into which an element can be divided and still be the same substance is called a(n)
   a. nucleus.   c. atom.
   b. electron.   d. neutron.
   Answer: C   Difficulty: 1   Section: 1   Objective: 3

2. What particle did J. J. Thomson discover?
   a. neutron   c. atom
   b. electron   d. proton
   Answer: B   Difficulty: 1   Section: 1   Objective: 1

3. How would you describe the nucleus?
   a. dense, positively charged   c. tiny, negatively charged
   b. large, positively charged   d. dense, negatively charged
   Answer: A   Difficulty: 1   Section: 1   Objective: 2

4. Where are electrons likely to be found?
   a. the nucleus   c. mixed throughout an atom
   b. electron clouds   d. paths, or energy levels
   Answer: B   Difficulty: 1   Section: 1   Objective: 3

5. Dalton believed that
   a. atoms of the same element are exactly alike.
   b. most substances are made of atoms.
   c. atoms of different elements are the same.
   d. atoms can be divided.
   Answer: A   Difficulty: 1   Section: 1   Objective: 2

6. What did Democritus, Dalton, Thomson, Rutherford, and Bohr all have in common?
   a. They each identified new elements.
   b. They each identified new isotopes of atoms.
   c. They each contributed to the development of the atomic theory.
   d. They each conducted experiments in which particles collided.
   Answer: C   Difficulty: 1   Section: 1   Objective: 3

7. In Thomson's "plum-pudding" model of the atom, the plums represent
   a. atoms.   c. neutrons.
   b. protons.   d. electrons.
   Answer: D   Difficulty: 1   Section: a1   Objective: 3

8. An atom of gold with 79 protons, 79 electrons, and 118 neutrons would have a mass number of
   a. 39.   c. 197.
   b. 158.   d. 276.
   Answer: C   Difficulty: 1   Section: 2   Objective: 5

9. Which of the following has the least mass?
   a. nucleus   c. neutron
   b. proton   d. electron
   Answer: D   Difficulty: 1   Section: 2   Objective: 1

10. If an isotope of uranium, uranium-235, has 92 protons, how many protons does uranium-238 have?

a. 92
b. 95
c. 143
d. 146

Answer: A   Difficulty: 2   Section: 2   Objective: 4

11. How did Democritus describe atoms?

a. large, soft particles
b. dividable particles
c. small, hard particles
d. a single material with one shape and size

Answer: C   Difficulty: 1   Section: 1   Objective: 3

12. What is the smallest particle into which an element can be divided and still be the same substance?

a. electron
b. neutron
c. proton
d. atom

Answer: D   Difficulty: 1   Section: 1   Objective: 1

13. What did Bohr, Democritus, Thomson, Dalton, and Rutherford all have in common?

a. They each identified the electromagnetic force of atoms.
b. They each identified new electron clouds.
c. They each developed ideas about atoms.
d. They each conducted experiments with ions.

Answer: C   Difficulty: 1   Section: 1   Objective: 3

14. In Thomson's "plum-pudding model" of the atom, the plums represent

a. atoms.
b. protons.
c. neutrons.
d. electrons.

Answer: D   Difficulty: 1   Section: b1   Objective: 2

15. An atom of carbon with 6 protons, 6 electrons, and 6 neutrons would have a mass number of

a. 6.
b. 18.
c. 12.
d. 15.

Answer: C   Difficulty: 2   Section: 2   Objective: 5

16. In an atom, which has the least mass?

a. nucleus
b. proton
c. neutron
d. electron

Answer: D   Difficulty: 1   Section: 2   Objective: 1

17. If hydrogen-1 has 1 proton, how many protons does hydrogen-2 have?

a. 2
b. 1
c. 3
d. 4

Answer: B   Difficulty: 2   Section: 2   Objective: 4

18. What was one of Dalton's ideas?

a. All substances are made of atoms.
b. Atoms can be divided.
c. Atoms can be destroyed.
d. Most substances are made of atoms.

Answer: A   Difficulty: 1   Section: 1   Objective: 2

19. What took place in the late 1880s?

a. Dalton created a new atomic theory.
b. Dalton disproved his theory.
c. Dalton's theory was proved.
d. Dalton's theory was changed.

Answer: D   Difficulty: 1   Section: 1   Objective: 3

20. What is the meaning of atom?

a. "dividable"
b. "invisible"
c. "hard particles"
d. "not able to be divided"

Answer: D   Difficulty: 1   Section: 1   Objective: 3

21. Which statement about atoms is true?
    a. A penny has about 20,000 atoms.
    b. Aluminum has large atoms.
    c. A penny has more atoms than Earth has people.
    d. Aluminum has a diameter of about 3 cm.
    Answer: C   Difficulty: 1   Section: 2   Objective: 1

22. Which statement about isotopes is true?
    a. They have the same number of protons.
    b. They have the same number of neutrons.
    c. They have a different atomic number.
    d. They have the same mass.
    Answer: A   Difficulty: 1   Section: 2   Objective: 4

23. According to Rutherford, what was in the center of an atom?
    a. an electron   c. a particle
    b. a nucleus   d. a proton
    Answer: D   Difficulty: 1   Section: 1   Objective: 2

24. Which phrase describes radioactive isotopes?
    a. They are stable.   c. They are unstable.
    b. They never change   d. They don't produce energy..
    Answer: C   Difficulty: 1   Section: 2   Objective: 4

25. Which of the following has the least mass in an atom?
    a. nucleus   c. neuton
    b. proton   d. electron
    Answer: D   Difficulty: 1   Section: c2   Objective: 1

COMPLETION

Use the terms from the following list to complete the sentences below.

atom   atomic number
nucleus   atomic mass
proton   isotope
electron   electron cloud
neutron

26. A positively charged particle in the nucleus of an atom is called a(n)

    _____.
    Answer: proton   Difficulty: 1   Section: 2   Objective: 2

27. An atom of an element that has the same number of protons but different numbers of
    neutrons is called a(n) _____.
    Answer: isotope   Difficulty: 1   Section: 2   Objective: 4

28. The region in an atom that contains most of the mass is called _____.
    Answer: nucleus   Difficulty: 1   Section: 1   Objective: 2

29. The number of protons in an atom determines its _____.
    Answer: atomic number
                            Difficulty: 1   Section: 2   Objective: 3

30. The weighted average of all the naturally occurring isotopes of an element is called the

    _____.
    Answer: atomic mass
                            Difficulty: 1   Section: 2   Objective: 5

31. The smallest particle into which an element can be divided and still be the same substance is a(n) _____ .

    Answer: atom   Difficulty: 1   Section: 1   Objective: 1

Use the terms from the following list to complete the sentences below.

    electrons   electron-cloud
    nucleus   atoms
    isotopes   protons

32. Thomson discovered the negatively charged particles called _____ .

    Answer: electrons   Difficulty: 1   Section: 1   Objective: 3

33. Rutherford believed that each atom has a(n) _____ at its center.

    Answer: nucleus   Difficulty: 1   Section: 1   Objective: 3

34. The current atomic theory includes the _____ model.

    Answer: electron cloud

                       Difficulty: 1   Section: c1   Objective: 2

35. All substances are made of _____ .

    Answer: atoms   Difficulty: 1   Section: 1   Objective: 1

36. Isotopes always have the same number of _____ .

    Answer: protons   Difficulty: 1   Section: 2   Objective: 4

37. Most elements have a mixture of two or more _____ .

    Answer: isotopes   Difficulty: 1   Section: 2   Objective: 4

Use the terms from the following list to complete the sentences below.

    strong   electromagnetic
    gravitational

38. Protons stay together in the nucleus because of _____ force.

    Answer: strong   Difficulty: 1   Section: 2   Objective: 6

39. Objects are pulled toward one another by _____ force.

    Answer: gravitational

                       Difficulty: 1   Section: 2   Objective: 6

40. Electrons around the nucleus are held in place by _____ force.

    Answer: electromagnetic

                       Difficulty: 1   Section: 2   Objective: 6

    electrons   forces
    atoms   electron clouds
    isotopes   neutrons
    protons

41. In 1803 John Dalton proposed that all substance are made of _____ .

    Answer: atoms   Difficulty: 1   Section: 1   Objective: 3

42. In 1897 the British scientist J. J. Thomson discovered _____ , the negatively charged particles in the atom.

    Answer: electrons   Difficulty: 1   Section: 1   Objective: 1

43. Twentieth-century scientists believe electrons are found in regions called

    _____ .

    Answer: electron clouds

                       Difficulty: 1   Section: 1   Objective: 3

44. Neutrons and _____ each have a mass of about 1 amu.
    Answer: protons   Difficulty: 1   Section: 2   Objective: 1

45. The pushes and pulls between objects are called _____.
    Answer: forces   Difficulty: 1   Section: 2   Objective: 6

46. Because their mass is so small, _____ are not included in an atom's mass number.
    Answer: electrons   Difficulty: 1   Section: 2   Objective: 5

47. Isotopes have different numbers of _____.
    Answer: neutrons   Difficulty: 1   Section: 2   Objective: 4

48. Atoms that are _____ of each other are always the same element.
    Answer: isotopes   Difficulty: 1   Section: 2   Objective: 4

49. A charged particle is called a (an) _____.
    Answer: ion   Difficulty: 1   Section: 2   Objective: 3

nucleus	atom
mass number	atomic
number	ion

50. The sum of the protons and neutrons in an atom is called the _____.
    Answer: mass number
                        Difficulty: 1   Section: 2   Objective: 5

51. Around 440 BCE, Democritus proposed the idea of a (an) _____, a particle that could not be cut in half.
    Answer: atom   Difficulty: 1   Section: 1   Objective: 3

52. In 1911 Ernest Rutherford proposed that each atom has a (an) _____, a tiny, extremely dense, positively charged region.
    Answer: nucleus   Difficulty: 1   Section: 1   Objective: 1

53. Most of the atom's mass is found in the _____.
    Answer: nucleus   Difficulty: 1   Section: 2   Objective: 2

54. All atoms of an element have the same _____.
    Answer: atomic number
                        Difficulty: 1   Section: 2   Objective: 3

55. A hydrogen atom with one proton in its nucleus has a (an) _____ of one.
    Answer: atomic number
                        Difficulty: 1   Section: 2   Objective: 3

SHORT ANSWER

56. How was Bohr's theory of atomic structure similar to the current theory?
    Answer:
    Bohr's theory and the current theory both have electrons traveling in orbits around a central nucleus.
    Difficulty: 1   Section: 1   Objective: 2

57. How was Bohr's theory of atomic structure different form the current theory?
    Answer:
    In Bohr's theory, the electrons move only in definite paths. Current atomic theory expresses the position of electrons in terms of the probability that electrons will be found in regions of the atom called electron clouds.
    Difficulty: 1   Section: 1   Objective: 2

58. Describe the difference between atomic number and atomic mass.
    Answer:
      The atomic number is the number of protons in an atom. Atomic mass is the sum of the number of protons and neutrons in an atom of a particular isotope.
    Difficulty: 2   Section: 2   Objective: 3, 5

59. How are protons in the nucleus of an atom able to stay close to one another even though they have the same charge?
    Answer:
      Protons can stay close to one another inside the nucleus of an atom due to the strong force. Although the electromagnetic force causes particles with the same charge to repel each other, the strong force is greater than the electromagnetic force at close distances.
    Difficulty: 1   Section: 2   Objective: 6

60. Compare protons and neutrons.
    Answer:
      Protons are positively charged particles in the nucleus of an atom. Neutrons are particles in the nucleus of an atom that have no charge.
    Difficulty: 2   Section: 2   Objective: 2

61. Put the following atomic models in the proper sequence: Rutherford's model, electron-cloud model, "plum-pudding" model, Bohr's model.
    Answer:
      "plum-pudding" model, Rutherford's model, Bohr's model, electron-cloud model
    Difficulty: 2   Section: 1   Objective: 3

62. How does the current model of the atom differ from Bohr's model?
    Answer:
      Bohr believed electrons traveled in definite paths. The current model says that the exact path of an electron cannot be predicted.
    Difficulty: 2   Section: 1   Objective: 2

63. What happens if the number of electrons and protons are not equal?
    Answer:
      It becomes a charged particle called an ion.
    Difficulty: 1   Section: 2   Objective: 6

64. What is the effect of electromagnetic force?
    Answer:
      Objects that have the same charge repel each other and objects with the opposite charge attract each other. The electromagnetic force holds the electrons around the nucleus.
    Difficulty: 2   Section: 2   Objective: 6

65. What would happen to a nucleus containing two or more protons if the strong force was absent?
    Answer:
      The nucleus would fly apart.
    Difficulty: 2   Section: 2   Objective: 6

66. Calculate the number of neutrons in carbon-12.
    Answer: 6   Difficulty: 2   Section: 2   Objective: 4

67. If the diameter of an atom is 100,000 miles, what is the diameter of its nucleus?
    Answer: 1 mile   Difficulty: 2   Section: 2   Objective: 1

68. Is it possible to have carbon atoms with different numbers of protons? Explain.

    Answer:
       No. All atoms of an element have the same atomic number, the number of protons in
       the nucleus of an atom.

    Difficulty: 2   Section: 2   Objective: 3

69. What three things happen to radioactive atoms after a certain amount of time?

    Answer:
       They spontaneously fall apart. As they fall apart, they give off smaller particles as well
       as energy.

    Difficulty: 1   Section: 2   Objective: 4

70. What error did Thomson find in Dalton's atomic theory?

    Answer:
       Thomson discovered that atoms are made of smaller parts.

    Difficulty: 1   Section: 1   Objective: 1

71. What is the name for Thomson's model of the atom?

    Answer:
       the "plum-pudding" model

    Difficulty: 1   Section: 1   Objective: 3

72. What is the current model of the atom called?

    Answer:
       the electron-cloud model

    Difficulty: 1   Section: 1   Objective: 3

73. What is an atom's mass number equal to?

    Answer:
       the total number of protons and neutrons in that atom

    Difficulty: 1   Section: 2   Objective: 5

74. How is the atomic mass of an element calculated?

    Answer:
       by taking a weighted average of the mass numbers of the isotopes of that element

    Difficulty: 1   Section: 2   Objective: 5

75. How do isotopes differ from one another?

    Answer:
       in the number of neutrons they have

    Difficulty: 1   Section: 2   Objective: 4

MATCHING

    a. atomic number   f. mass number
    b. proton   g. weak force
    c. strong force   h. ion
    d. neutron   i. electron
    e. isotope   j. gravitational force

76. ____ particle of the nucleus with no electrical charge

    Answer: D   Difficulty: 1   Section: 2   Objective: 2

77. ____ negatively charged particle

    Answer: I   Difficulty: 1   Section: 2   Objective: 2

78. ____ keeps a nucleus with two or more protons from flying apart

    Answer: C   Difficulty: 1   Section: 2   Objective: 6

79.   subatomic particle that has a positive charge
   Answer: B   Difficulty: 1   Section: 2   Objective: 2
80. ____ pulls objects toward one another
   Answer: J   Difficulty: 1   Section: 2   Objective: 6
81. ____ atom that has the same number of protons as other atoms of the same element do
   but that has a different number of neutrons
   Answer: E   Difficulty: 1   Section: q2   Objective: 4
82. ____ a charged atom that forms when the numbers of electrons and protons are not equal
   Answer: H   Difficulty: 1   Section: 2   Objective: 6
83. ____ represents the sum of protons in the nucleus of an atom
   Answer: A   Difficulty: 1   Section: 2   Objective: 3
84. ____ enables a neutron to change into a proton and an electron in certain unstable atoms
   Answer: G   Difficulty: 1   Section: 2   Objective: 6
85. ____ the sum of the protons and neutrons in an atom
   Answer: F   Difficulty: 1   Section: 2   Objective: 5

   a. atomic number   f. neutron
   b. nucleus   g. atom
   c. electron cloud   h. electron
   d. mass number   i. atomic mass unit (amu)
   e. isotope   j. proton

86. ____ particle than cannot be cut
   Answer: G   Difficulty: 1   Section: 1   Objective: 3
87. ____ negatively charged particle discovered by Thomson
   Answer: H   Difficulty: 1   Section: 1   Objective: 1
88. ____ central region of the atom
   Answer: B   Difficulty: 1   Section: 1   Objective: 1
89. ____ region where electrons are likely to be found
   Answer: C   Difficulty: 1   Section: 1   Objective: 2
90. ____ particle in the center of an atom that has no charge
   Answer: F   Difficulty: 1   Section: 2   Objective: 2
91. ____ subatomic particle that has a positive charge
   Answer: J   Difficulty: 1   Section: 2   Objective: 2
92. ____ a unit of mass that describes the mass of an atom or molecule
   Answer: I   Difficulty: 1   Section: 2   Objective: 5
93. ____ the number of protons in the nucleus of an atom
   Answer: A   Difficulty: 1   Section: 2   Objective: 3
94. ____ atom that has the same number of protons but different numbers of neutrons
   Answer: E   Difficulty: 1   Section: 2   Objective: 4
95. ____ the sum of protons and neutrons in an atom
   Answer: D   Difficulty: 1   Section: 2   Objective: 3

   a. electron   c. neutron
   b. proton

96. ____ positively charged particle
   Answer: proton   Difficulty: 1   Section: 2   Objective: 2
97. ____   negatively charged particle
   Answer: electron   Difficulty: 1   Section: 2   Objective: 2
98. ____ uncharged particle
   Answer: neutron   Difficulty: 1   Section: 2   Objective: 2
   a. atomic mass unit   c. mass number
   b. atomic number   d. atomic mass

99.   sum of the protons and neutrons
        Answer: C   Difficulty: 1   Section: 2   Objective: 5
100. ____ mass of an atom expressed in atomic mass units
        Answer: D   Difficulty: 1   Section: 2   Objective: 5
101. ____ describes the mass of an atom
        Answer: A   Difficulty: 1   Section: 2   Objective: 5
102. ____ number of protons in the nucleus
        Answer: B   Difficulty: 1   Section: 2   Objective: 3

ESSAY

103. Long ago, people tried to change inexpensive metals, such as lead, into gold. What fundamental principle of matter did these people fail to understand?
     Answer:
       These people did not understand that elements, such as lead and gold, are divided into smaller particles called atoms. Each atom of an element is composed of a unique number of protons, neutrons, and electrons. Atoms cannot be created or destroyed. Therefore, it is not possible to simply convert one metal into another.
     Difficulty: 3   Section: 1   Objective: 1, 2

104. The ionosphere is a region of Earth's upper atmosphere. From the name ionosphere, what can you conclude about the gases that make up this region?
     Answer:
       The ionosphere must contain ions, which are electrically charged particles. To be charged, the numbers of electrons and protons in the particles must not be equal.
     Difficulty: 3   Section: 2   Objective: 3, 6

PROBLEMS

105. The approximate composition of naturally occurring magnesium is as follows: 79% magnesium-24, 10% magnesium-25, and 11% magnesium-26. Calculate the atomic mass of magnesium. Show your work.
     Answer:
       $(0.79 \times 24) + (0.10 \times 25) + (0.11 \times 26) = 24.32$ amu
     Difficulty: 2   Section: 2   Objective: 5

INTERPRETING GRAPHICS

Use the diagram below to answer the following four questions.

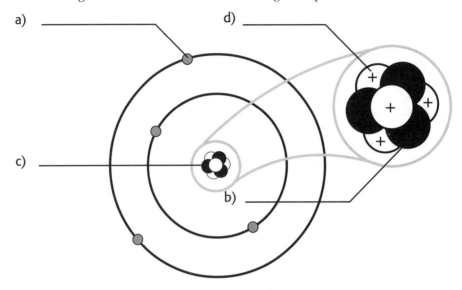

106. Which letter refers to the negatively charged particles?
    Answer: B   Difficulty: 1   Section: 2   Objective: 2

107. Which letter refers to the positively charged particles?
    Answer: A   Difficulty: 1   Section: 2   Objective: 2

108. Which letter refers to the particles with no charge?
    Answer: D   Difficulty: 1   Section: 2   Objective: 2

109. Which letter refers to the dense center of the atom?
    Answer: C   Difficulty: 1   Section: 2   Objective: 2

Use the figure below to answer the following two questions.

110. Who proposed this new model of an atom?
    a. Bohr   c. Rutherford
    b. Thomson   d. Democritus
    Answer: B   Difficulty: 1   Section: 1   Objective: 2

111. The raised surfaces show
    a. protons.   c. neutrons.
    b. electrons.   d. isotopes.
    Answer: B   Difficulty: 1   Section: 1   Objective: 3

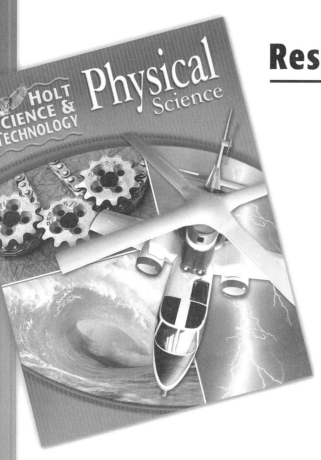

Physical Science

HOLT SCIENCE & TECHNOLOGY

The Periodic Table

CHAPTER 5

| Skills Worksheet)

Directed Reading A

Section: Arranging the Elements

1. Why do you think scientists might have been frustrated by the organization of the elements before 1869?

_____

_____

_____

_____

_____

_____

DISCOVERING A PATTERN

_____ **2.** Which arrangement of elements did Mendeleev find produced a repeating pattern of properties?
   a. by increasing density
   b. by increasing melting point
   c. by increasing shine
   d. by increasing atomic mass

3. When something occurs or repeats at regular intervals, it is called

_____ .

4. Mendeleev's table, which shows elements' properties following a pattern that

repeats every seven elements, is called the _____ .

5. How was it possible that Mendeleev was able to predict the properties of elements that no one knew about?

_____

_____

_____

_____

_____

_____

CHANGING THE ARRANGEMENT

_____ **6.** How did Moseley solve the problem of the elements that did not fit the pattern according to their properties?

    a. He rearranged the elements by atomic mass.

    b. He discovered protons, neutrons, and electrons.

    c. He disproved the periodic law.

    d. He determined the elements' atomic number and then arranged them by atomic number.

7. When the repeating chemical and physical properties of elements change periodically with the elements' atomic numbers, it is called the

_____.

PERIODIC TABLE OF THE ELEMENTS

_____ **8.** Which information is NOT included in each square of the periodic table in your text?

    a. atomic number   **c.** melting point

    b. chemical symbol   **d.** atomic mass

9. How can you tell on the periodic table that carbon is a solid at room temperature?

_____

_____

_____

THE PERIODIC TABLE AND CLASSES OF ELEMENTS

10. Elements are classified as metals, nonmetals, or metalloids according to their

_____.

11. The number of _____ in the outer energy level of an atom helps determine which category an element belongs in.

12. How can the zigzag line on the periodic table help you?

_____

_____

_____

13. Most elements are _____, which can be found to the left of the zigzag line on the periodic table.

14. Most metals are _____, which means that they can be drawn into thin wires.

15. Most metals are _____ at room temperature.

16. Most metals are malleable. What does this mean?

_____

_____

17. What metal is flattened into sheets that are made into cans and foil?

_____

18. What elements are found to the right of the zigzag line on the periodic table?

_____

19. Semiconductors, also called _____, are the elements that border the zigzag line on the periodic table.

DECODING THE PERIODIC TABLE

_____**20.** Which elements often share properties?
- **a.** those in a period
- **b.** those in a group
- **c.** those with the same color
- **d.** those in a horizontal row

_____**21.** The physical and chemical properties of the elements change
- **a.** within a group.
- **b.** within a family.
- **c.** across each period.
- **d.** across each group.

22. For most elements, the _____ has one or two letters, with the first letter always capitalized.

23. Horizontal rows of elements on the periodic table are called

_____.

24. Vertical columns of elements on the periodic table are called

_____, or _____.

25. Some elements, such as _____, are named after

scientists. Others, such as _____, are named after places.

Skills Worksheet

Directed Reading A

Section: Grouping the Elements

_____ 1. What gives elements in a family or group similar properties?
   a. the same atomic mass
   b. the same number of protons in their nuclei
   c. the same number of electrons in their outer energy level
   d. the same number of total electrons

GROUP 1: ALKALI METALS

_____ 2. Which of the following is NOT true of alkali metals?
   a. They can be cut with a knife.
   b. They are usually stored in water.
   c. They are the most reactive of all the metals.
   d. They can easily give away their outer electron.

3. Metals that share both physical and chemical properties are called

_____.

GROUP 2: ALKALINE-EARTH METALS

4. Atoms of _____ have two outer-level electrons.

5. What are two products made from calcium compounds?

_____

_____

_____

6. In what way does calcium help you?

_____

_____

_____

7. Name three alkaline-earth metals besides calcium.

_____

_____

_____

| Directed Reading A *continued*

GROUPS 3–12: TRANSITION METALS

_____ **8.** Which of the following characteristics does NOT describe transition
metals?
  a. They are good conductors of thermal energy.
  b. They are more reactive than alkali and alkaline-earth metals.
  c. They have one or two electrons in the outer energy level.
  d. They are denser than elements in Groups 1 and 2.

9. Metals that are less reactive than alkali metals and alkaline-earth metals are

called _____.

10. How is mercury different from other transition metals?

_____

_____

11. Two rows of transition metals are placed at the bottom of the periodic table

to save space. Elements in the first row are called _____.

Elements in the second row are called _____.

12. Which lanthanide forms a compound that enables you to see red on a
computer screen?

_____

13. Which actinide is used in some smoke detectors?

_____

GROUP 13: BORON GROUP

14. Why did Emperor Napoleon III of France use aluminum dinnerware?

_____

_____

15. What are some of the uses of aluminum?

_____

_____

_____

▍Directed Reading A *continued*

GROUP 14: CARBON GROUP

16. The metalloids _____ and _____,
both in Group 14, are used to make computer chips.

17. What are three compounds of carbon that are necessary for living things on Earth?

_____

18. The hardest material known is _____.

19. What are some of the uses of diamond?

_____

_____

20. What form of carbon is used as a pigment?

_____

GROUP 15: NITROGEN GROUP

21. Nitrogen is a _____ at room temperature.

22. Each element in the Nitrogen Group has _____ electrons
in the outer level.

23. Nitrogen from the air can react with what element to make ammonia for fertilizer?

_____

GROUP 16: OXYGEN GROUP

24. How is oxygen different from the other four elements in Group 16?

_____

_____

25. The element _____ can be found as a yellow solid in
nature and is used to make sulfuric acid.

26. Why is oxygen important?

_____

_____

_____

GROUP 17: HALOGENS

27. The atoms of _____ need to gain only one electron to have a complete outer level.

28. What important use do the halogens iodine and chlorine have in common?

_____

_____

29. Halogens combine with most metals to form _____, such

as _____.

30. How does chlorinating water help protect people?

_____

_____

_____

GROUP 18: NOBLE GASES

_____**31.** Which of the following statements about noble gases is NOT true?
  a. They are colorless and odorless at room temperature.
  b. They have a complete set of electrons in their outer energy level.
  c. They normally react with other elements.
  d. All of them are found in Earth's atmosphere in small amounts.

32. The atoms of _____ have a full set of electrons in their outer level.

33. The low _____ of helium makes blimps and weather balloons float.

HYDROGEN

_____**34.** Which of the following statements about hydrogen is NOT true?
  a. It is useful as rocket fuel.
  b. It is the most abundant element in the universe.
  c. Its physical properties are closer to those of nonmetals than to those of metals.
  d. It has two electrons in its outer energy level.

Skills Worksheet

Directed Reading B

Section: Arranging the Elements

Circle the letter of the best answer for each question.

DISCOVERING A PATTERN

1. How did Mendeleev arrange the elements?

   a. by increasing density

   b. by increasing melting point

   c. by increasing shine

   d. by increasing atomic mass

Periodic Properties of the Elements

2. What does periodic mean?

   a. happening at regular intervals

   b. happening almost never

   c. happening twice

   d. happening once or twice

3. Mendeleev's pattern repeated after how many elements?

   a. every two elements

   b. every three elements

   c. every seven elements

   d. every five elements

Predicting Properties of Missing Elements

4. How did Mendeleev predict the properties of missing elements?

   a. by making the properties up

   b. by comparing the properties of found elements

   c. by using the pattern he found

   d. by not following the pattern

CHANGING THE ARRANGEMENT
<u>Circle the letter</u> of the best answer for each question.

5. What does the periodic law say about the properties of elements?

  a. They change with atomic mass.

  b. They change with atomic number.

  c. They change with mass number.

  d. They change when the isotope changes.

6. How many elements discovered since 1914 follow the periodic law?

  a. all of them

  b. about half of them

  c. none of them

  d. every seventh element

PERIODIC TABLE OF THE ELEMENTS

7. What is NOT included in each square of the periodic table in your text?

  a. atomic number

  b. chemical symbol

  c. melting point

  d. atomic mass

8. What color indicates an element is a solid?

  a. red

  b. blue

  c. green

  d. yellow

THE PERIODIC TABLE AND CLASSES OF ELEMENTS

Read the words in the box. Read the sentences. <u>Fill in each blank</u> with the word or phrase that best completes the sentence.

| nonmetal | semiconductors | metals | metalloids |

9. Most of the elements in the periodic table are

_____ .

10. More than half of the _____ are gases at

room temperature.

11. The atoms of _____ have about half of a

complete set of electrons in their outer energy level.

12. Metalloids are also called _____ .

DECODING THE PERIODIC TABLE
Each Element Is Identified by a Chemical Symbol

| mendelevium | chemical symbol | californium |

13. Elements such as _____ are named after

scientists.

14. Elements such as _____ are named after

places.

15. For most elements, the _____ has one or

two letters.

Rows Are Called *Periods*

Circle the letter of the best answer for each question.

16. What is each horizontal row called?

   a. group

   b. family

   c. period

   d. property

17. How do you read periods?

   a. from top to bottom

   b. from bottom to top

   c. from left to right

   d. from right to left

18. How do the physical and chemical properties of the elements change?

   a. within a group

   b. within a family

   c. across each period

   d. across each group

Columns Are Called *Groups*

19. What is another name for *group*?

   a. period

   b. family

   c. element

   d. electron

20. Which elements usually have the same properties?

   a. those in a period

   b. those in a group

   c. those with the same color

   d. those in a horizontal row

Skills Worksheet)

Directed Reading B

Section: Grouping the Elements
Circle the letter of the best answer for each question.

1. What do atoms of elements in a group have that makes their properties similar?

    a. the same atomic mass

    b. the same number of protons

    c. the same number of outer level electrons

    d. the same total number of electrons

2. At the atomic level, what makes elements reactive?

    a. having a filled outer level

    b. exchanging or sharing electrons

    c. having the same number of electrons

    d. having the same number of protons

GROUP 1: ALKALI METALS

3. Look at the chart. What is the symbol for potassium?

    a. Li

    b. K

    c. Cs

    d. Fr

4. How are the alkali metals similar?

    a. They are very reactive.

    b. They have few uses.

    c. They are so hard they cannot be cut.

    d. They are often stored in water.

| Directed Reading B *continued*

GROUP 2: ALKALINE-EARTH METALS
Circle the letter of the best answer for each question.

5. What is true about all of the alkaline-earth metals?

   a. They are have low density.

   b. They are less reactive than alkali metals are.

   c. They have three outer level electrons.

   d. They have few uses.

6. Look at the chart. Which element is not an alkaline-earth metal?

   a. magnesium

   b. calcium

   c. barium

   d. sodium

GROUPS 3–12: TRANSITION METALS

7. Groups are read from top to bottom. What elements are in Group 3?

   a. Sc, Ti, V, Mn

   b. V, Nb, Ta, Db

   c. Sc, Y, La, Ac

   d. La, Hf, Ta, W

Properties of Transition Metals
Circle the letter of the best answer for each question.

8. How would you describe most transition metals?

   a. poor conductor of electric current

   b. dull

   c. good conductor of thermal energy

   d. low density and melting points

Lanthanides and Actinides

9. What word best describes the lathanides?

   a. radioactive

   b. unstable

   c. reactive

   d. dull

10. What word best describes the actinides?

   a. radioactive

   b. stable

   c. shiny

   d. reactive

Directed Reading B *continued*

Read the words in the box. Read the sentences. <u>Fill in each blank</u> with the word or phrase that best completes the sentence.

reactive	oxygen	hydrogen
aluminum	tin	carbohydrates

GROUP 13: BORON GROUP

11. All elements in the Boron Group are_____

and solid at room temperature.

12. The most common element in the Boron Group is

_____ which is used to make airplane parts.

GROUP 14: CARBON GROUP

13. Compounds of carbon, such as proteins, fats, and

_____, are necessary for life on Earth.

14. The symbol Sn stands for the metal _____.

GROUP 15: NITROGEN GROUP

15. Nitrogen can react with _____ to

make ammonia.

GROUP 16: OXYGEN GROUP

16. In order for a substance to burn, it needs

_____.

| Directed Reading B *continued*

GROUP 17: HALOGENS

Circle the letter of the best answer for each question.

17. What is made when a halogen reacts with a metal?

    a. a salt

    b. a compound

    c. a nonmetal

    d. an electron

GROUP 18: NOBLE GASES

18. Look at the chart. How many nonmetals are in Group 18?

    a. three

    b. six

    c. four

    d. eight

19. Look at the chart. What element does the symbol Kr represent?

    a. argon

    b. helium

    c. neon

    d. krypton

20. What element helps light bulbs last longer?

    a. neon

    b. krypton

    c. argon

    d. xenon

HYDROGEN

Circle the letter of the best answer for each question.

21. What is the symbol for hydrogen?

    a. Hy

    b. K

    c. H

    d. Hi

22. Which word or words describe hydrogen?

    a. colorless gas

    b. unreactive

    c. high density

    d. very rare

23. Where is hydrogen located on the periodic table?

    a. in Group 1

    b. in Group 18

    c. above Group 1

    d. below Group 1

Skills Worksheet

Vocabulary and Section Summary

Arranging the Elements
VOCABULARY
In your own words, write a definition of the following terms in the space provided.

1. periodic

_____

_____

2. periodic law

_____

_____

3. period

_____

_____

4. group

_____

_____

SECTION SUMMARY
Read the following section summary.

- Mendeleev developed the first periodic table by listing the elements in order of increasing atomic mass. He used his table to predict that elements with certain properties would be discovered later.

- Properties of elements repeat in a regular, or periodic, pattern.

- Moseley rearranged the elements in order of increasing atomic number.

- The periodic law states that the repeating chemical and physical properties of elements relate to and depend on elements' atomic numbers.

- Elements in the periodic table are classified as metals, nonmetals, and metalloids.

- Each element has a chemical symbol.

- A horizontal row of elements is called a *period*.

- Physical and chemical properties of elements change across each period.

- A vertical column of elements is called a *group* or *family*.

- Elements in a group usually have similar properties.

Skills Worksheet

Vocabulary and Section Summary

Grouping the Elements

VOCABULARY

In your own words, write a definition of the following terms in the space provided.

1. alkali metal

_____

_____

2. alkaline-earth metal

_____

_____

3. halogen

_____

_____

4. noble gas

_____

_____

SECTION SUMMARY

Read the following section summary.

• Alkali metals (Group 1) are the most reactive metals. Atoms of the alkali metals have one electron in their outer level.

• Alkaline-earth metals (Group 2) are less reactive than the alkali metals are. Atoms of the alkaline-earth metals have two electrons in their outer level.

• Transition metals (Groups 3–12) include most of the well-known metals and the lanthanides and actinides.

• Groups 13–16 contain the metalloids and some metals and nonmetals.

• Halogens (Group 17) are very reactive nonmetals. Atoms of the halogens have seven electrons in their outer level.

• Noble gases (Group 18) are unreactive nonmetals. Atoms of the noble gases have a full set of electrons in their outer level.

• Hydrogen is set off by itself. Its properties do not match the properties of any one group.

Skills Worksheet

Section Review

Arranging the Elements
USING KEY TERMS

1. In your own words, write a definition for the term *periodic*.

_____

_____

UNDERSTANDING KEY IDEAS

_____ **2.** Which of the following elements should be the best conductor of electric current?

a. germanium

b. sulfur

c. aluminum

d. helium

3. Compare a period and a group on the periodic table.

_____

_____

4. What property did Mendeleev use to position the elements on the periodic table?

_____

_____

5. State the periodic law.

_____

_____

CRITICAL THINKING

6. Identifying Relationships An atom that has 117 protons in its nucleus has not yet been made. Once this atom is made, to which group will element 117 belong? Explain your answer.

_____

_____

_____

_____

| Section Review *continued*

---

7. Applying Concepts Are the properties of sodium, Na, more like the properties of lithium, Li, or magnesium, Mg? Explain your answer.

_____

_____

_____

_____

INTERPRETING GRAPHICS

8. The image below shows part of a periodic table. Compare the image below with the similar part of the periodic table in your book.

1	**1** **H** 1.0079 水素	
2	**3** **Li** 6.941 リチウム	**4** **Be** 9.01218 ベリリウム
3	**11** **Na** 22.98977 ナトリウム	**12** **Mg** 24.305 マグネシウム
	19 **K**	**20** **Ca**

(additional columns: **21** **Sc**, **22** **Ti**)

_____

_____

_____

_____

Section Review

Grouping the Elements
USING KEY TERMS

Complete each of the following sentences by choosing the correct term from the word bank.

      noble gas   alkaline-earth metal
      halogen   alkali metal

1. An atom of a(n) _____ has a full set of electrons in its outermost energy level.

2. An atom of a(n) _____ has one electron in its outermost energy level.

3. An atom of a(n) _____ tends to gain one electron when it combines with another atom.

4. An atom of a(n) _____ tends to lose two electrons when it combines with another atom.

UNDERSTANDING KEY IDEAS

_____ **5.** Which group contains elements whose atoms have six electrons in their outer level?
      a. Group 2   **c.** Group 16
      b. Group 6   **d.** Group 18

6. What are two properties of the alkali metals?

_____

_____

7. What causes the properties of elements in a group to be similar?

_____

_____

8. What are two properties of the halogens?

_____

_____

9. Why is hydrogen set apart from the other elements in the periodic table?

_____

_____

10. Which group contains elements whose atoms have three electrons in their outer level?

_____

_____

INTERPRETING GRAPHICS

11. Look at the model of an atom below. Does the model represent a metal atom or a nonmetal atom? Explain your answer.

_____

_____

_____

CRITICAL THINKING

12. Making Inferences Why are neither the alkali metals nor the alkaline-earth metals found uncombined in nature?

_____

_____

_____

_____

13. Making Comparisons Compare the element hydrogen with the alkali metal sodium.

_____

_____

_____

_____

Skills Worksheet)

Chapter Review

USING KEY TERMS

Complete each of the following sentences by choosing the correct term from the word bank.

group	period	alkali metals
halogens	alkaline-earth metals	noble gases

1. Elements in the same vertical column on the periodic table belong to the

same _____.

2. Elements in the same horizontal row on the periodic table belong to the

same _____.

3. The most reactive metals are _____.

4. Elements that are unreactive are called _____.

UNDERSTANDING KEY IDEAS

Multiple Choice

_____ **5.** Mendeleev's periodic table was useful because it
   a. showed the elements arranged by atomic number.
   b. had no empty spaces.
   c. showed the atomic number of the elements.
   d. allowed for the prediction of the properties of missing elements.

_____ **6.** Most nonmetals are
   a. shiny.
   b. poor conductors of electric current.
   c. flattened when hit with a hammer.
   d. solids at room temperature.

_____ **7.** Which of the following items is NOT found on the periodic table?
   a. the atomic number of each element
   b. the name of each element
   c. the date that each element was discovered
   d. the atomic mass of each element

_____ **8.** Which of the following statements about the periodic table is false?
   a. There are more metals than nonmetals on the periodic table.
   b. Atoms of elements in the same group have the same number of electrons in their outer level.
   c. The elements at the far left of the periodic table are nonmetals.
   d. Elements are arranged by increasing atomic number.

_____ **9.** Which of the following statements about alkali metals is true?
  a. Alkali metals are generally found in their uncombined form.
  b. Alkali metals are Group 1 elements.
  c. Alkali metals should be stored underwater.
  d. Alkali metals are unreactive.

_____ **10.** Which of the following statements about elements is true?
  a. Every element occurs naturally.
  b. All elements are found in their uncombined form in nature.
  c. Each element has a unique atomic number.
  d. All of the elements exist in approximately equal quantities.

Short Answer

11. How is Moseley's basis for arranging the elements different from Mendeleev's?

_____

_____

12. How is the periodic table like a calendar?

_____

_____

Math Skills

Examine the chart of the percentages of elements in the Earth's crust below. Then, answer the questions that follow.

46.6% O
1.6% Other
2.0% Mg
2.6% K
2.8% Na
3.6% Ca
5.0% Fe
8.1% Al
27.7% Si

13. Excluding the "Other" category, what percentage of the Earth's crust are alkali metals?

_____

14. Excluding the "Other" category, what percentage of the Earth's crust are alkaline-earth metals?

_____

| **Chapter Review** *continued*

CRITICAL THINKING

15. Concept Mapping Use the following terms to create a concept map:
periodic table, elements, groups, periods, metals, nonmetals, and metalloids.

▍Chapter Review *continued*

16. **Forming Hypotheses** Why was Mendeleev unable to make any predictions about the noble gas elements?

_____

_____

_____

_____

17. **Identifying Relationships** When an element that has 115 protons in its nucleus is synthesized, will it be a metal, a nonmetal, or a metalloid? Explain your answer.

_____

_____

_____

_____

18. **Applying Concepts** Your classmate offers to give you a piece of sodium that he found on a hiking trip. What is your response? Explain.

_____

_____

_____

_____

19. **Applying Concepts** Identify each element described below.

   a. This metal is very reactive, has properties similar to those of magnesium, and is in the same period as bromine.

_____

_____

_____

_____

   b. This nonmetal is in the same group as lead.

_____

_____

_____

Chapter Review *continued*

INTERPRETING GRAPHICS

20. Study the diagram below to determine the pattern of the images. Predict the missing image, and draw it. Identify which properties are periodic and which properties are shared within a group.

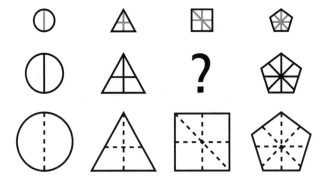

_____

_____

_____

_____

Skills Worksheet

Reinforcement

Placing All Your Elements on the Table

Complete this worksheet after you have finished reading the section "Grouping the Elements."

You can tell a lot about the properties of an element just by looking at the element's location on the periodic table. This worksheet will help you better understand the connection between the periodic table and the properties of the elements. Follow the directions below, and use crayons or colored pencils to color the periodic table at the bottom of the page.

1. Color the square for hydrogen yellow.

2. Color the groups with very reactive metals red.

3. Color and label the noble gases orange.

4. Color the transition metals green.

5. Using black, mark the zigzag line that shows the position of the metalloids.

6. Color the metalloids purple.

7. Use blue to color all of the non-metals that are not noble gases.

8. Color the metals in Groups 13–16 brown.

9. Circle and label the actinides in yellow.

10. Circle and label the lanthanides in red.

11. Circle and label the alkali metals in blue.

12. Circle and label the alkaline-earth metals in purple.

13. Circle and label the halogens in green.

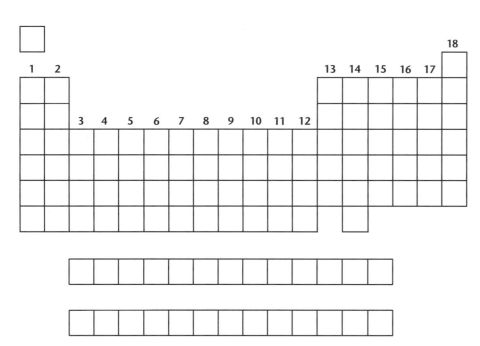

▌Reinforcement *continued*

Answer the following questions using the periodic table on the previous page.

14. The alkaline-earth metals react similarly because they all have the same number of electrons in their outer energy level. Which group contains the alkaline-earth metals?

_____

15. How many electrons are in the outer energy level of the atoms of alkaline-earth metals?

_____

16. Hydrogen is in a different color than the rest of the elements in Group 1. Give an example of how hydrogen's characteristics set it apart from other Group 1 elements.

_____

_____

17. What is the name of the group of unreactive nonmetals that includes argon?

_____

18. Except for the metalloids, what do all of the elements on the right side of the zigzag line have in common?

_____

_____

Imagine you are a scientist who has just discovered a new element. The element has an atomic number of 113, and it has three electrons in the outer energy level of each atom.

19. Where would you place this new element in the periodic table?

_____

20. Which element would have properties most similar to the new element?

_____

21. What name would you suggest for this new element?

_____

_____

Skills Worksheet

Critical Thinking

A Solar Solution

While searching the Internet for new science products, you come across a bulletin board advertising the following items. Use your knowledge of the periodic table of elements to review the following advertisement for accuracy:

Acme Science Products

• **NEW AND IMPROVED "ACME SALT"** —100% sodium. Because it is found in nature, it is 100% PURE.

• **NEW!** Experimental electrical wire made entirely of sulfur. Get yours while supplies last.

• **ELIMINATE WATER BILLS** by using the new "Acme Thirst Buster 2" water system. With an electric spark, it combines oxygen and hydrogen to create your own water supply at home.

• The Acme **"EVERLAST LIGHT BULB"** will burn twice as long as other bulbs because it is filled with oxygen.

• Acme has discovered **A BRAND NEW ELEMENT.** Find out more on our home page!"

EVALUATING INFORMATION

1. What is wrong with the Acme salt ad?

_____

_____

_____

_____

DEMONSTRATING REASONED JUDGMENT

2. Would buying sulfur electric wire be a wise choice? Explain.

_____

_____

_____

_____

_____

_____

| Critical Thinking *continued*

PREDICTING CONSEQUENCES

3. Do you think that using electricity to combine oxygen and hydrogen in your home could cause a problem?

_____

_____

_____

_____

4. Would the Acme "Everlast Light Bulb" last longer than an ordinary bulb? Explain.

_____

_____

_____

_____

COMPREHENDING IDEAS

5. Acme claims to have discovered a new element. How can you determine if this claim is true?

_____

_____

_____

_____

6. How would you go about classifying this new element?

_____

_____

_____

_____

Name _____ Class _____ Date _____

Assessment

Section Quiz

Section: Arranging the Elements

Write the letter of the correct answer in the space provided.

_____ 1. *Periodic* means
   a. happening at regular intervals.
   b. happening very rarely.
   c. happening frequently.
   d. happening three or four times a year.

_____ 2. Periodic law states that
   a. elements are either gases, solids, or liquids.
   b. mercury is a liquid at room temperature.
   c. properties of elements change periodically with the elements'
     atomic numbers.
   d. some elements only stay in a liquid state for short periods.

_____ 3. Each vertical column on the periodic table is called a(an)
   a. period.
   b. group.
   c. element.
   d. property.

_____ 4. The elements to the right of the zigzag line on the period table are
   called
   a. nonmetals.
   b. metals.
   c. metalloids.
   d. conductors.

_____ 5. Most metals are
   a. solid at room temperature.
   b. bad conductors of electric current.
   c. dull.
   d. not malleable.

Section Quiz

Section: Grouping the Elements

Match the correct description with the correct term. Write the letter in the space provided.

_____ **1.** metals that are so reactive that in nature they are found only combined with other elements

_____ **2.** metals that have two outer-level electrons

_____ **3.** shiny, reactive metals, some of which are used to make steel

_____ **4.** elements whose atoms are radioactive

_____ **5.** very reactive nonmetals

_____ **6.** unreactive nonmetals that do not react with other elements under normal conditions

_____ **7.** metals in Groups 3–12 that do not give away their electrons as easily as atoms of Groups 1 and 2

_____ **8.** the most common element in Group 13, the Boron Group

_____ **9.** nonmetal that forms a wide variety of compounds, such as proteins, fats, and carbohydrates

_____ **10.** an element that is necessary for substances to burn

a. aluminum

b. transition metals

c. lanthanides

d. oxygen

e. actinides

f. carbon

g. halogens

h. alkali metals

i. alkaline-earth metals

j. noble gases

Assessment

Chapter Test A

The Periodic Table
MULTIPLE CHOICE
Write the letter of the correct answer in the space provided.

_____ **1.** Most of the elements in the periodic table are
    a. metals.
    b. metalloids.
    c. gases.
    d. nonmetals.

_____ **2.** Mendeleev arranged the elements by
    a. density.
    b. melting point.
    c. appearance.
    d. increasing atomic mass.

_____ **3.** The horizontal row on the period table is called a(n)
    a. group.
    b. family.
    c. period.
    d. atomic number.

_____ **4.** Which one of the following tells the physical state of an element at room temperature?
    a. the atomic number
    b. the color of the chemical symbol
    c. the atomic mass
    d. the element name

_____ **5.** How do the physical and chemical properties of the elements change?
    a. within a group
    b. across each period
    c. within a family
    d. across each group

_____ **6.** What is necessary for substances to burn?
    a. hydrogen
    b. oxygen
    c. helium
    d. carbon

_____ **7.** Transition metals are
   a. good conductors of thermal energy.
   b. more reactive than alkali metals.
   c. not good conductors of electric current.
   d. used to make aluminum.

_____ **8.** The elements' properties follow a pattern that repeats every
   a. 7 elements.
   b. 5 elements.
   c. 14 elements.
   d. 10 elements.

_____ **9.** The vertical column of elements on the periodic table is called a(n)
   a. period.
   b. semiconductor.
   c. atomic mass.
   d. group.

MATCHING

Match the correct description with the correct term. Write the letter in the space provided.

_____ **10.** These metals react with water to form hydrogen.

_____ **11.** This metal, part of the Boron Group, is used for aircraft parts.

_____ **12.** This is important to most living things.

_____ **13.** Cement and chalk are compounds of this.

_____ **14.** Some of these reactive metals are used to make steel.

_____ **15.** Chlorine and iodine are these.

_____ **16.** This is a colorless, odorless gas.

_____ **17.** Diamond and soot are forms of this.

_____ **18.** This makes up about 80% of the air we breathe.

_____ **19.** Light bulbs last longer when they are filled with this gas.

a. aluminum

b. argon

c. halogens

d. nitrogen

e. oxygen

f. alkali metals

g. calcium

h. carbon

i. hydrogen

j. lanthanides

MULTIPLE CHOICE

Use the figure below to answer questions 20–22.

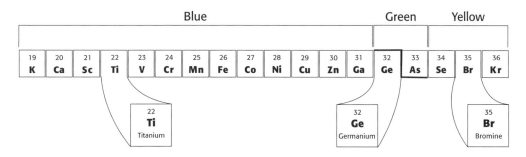

_____**20.** Which of the following elements is the most metallic?
  a. K
  b. Kr
  c. Fe
  d. Cu

_____**21.** Which of these elements is the least metallic?
  a. V
  b. Zn
  c. Co
  d. Se

_____**22.** Which element group has all nonmetals?
  a. K, Ca, Sc
  b. Se, Br, Kr
  c. V, Cr, Mn
  d. As, Se, Br

MULTIPLE CHOICE

Refer to the figure below to answer questions 23 and 24.

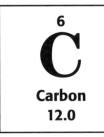

_____ **23.** The number beneath carbon indicates the
   a. atomic number.
   b. atomic mass.
   c. chemical symbol.
   d. element name.

_____ **24.** The number at the top is the
   a. atomic number.
   b. element name.
   c. atomic mass.
   d. chemical symbol.

Assessment

Chapter Test B

The Periodic Table

USING KEY TERMS

Use the terms from the following list to complete the sentences below. Each term may be used only once. Some terms may not be used.

halogens	periodic law	period
periodic	group	noble gases
alkali metals	alkaline-earth metals	actinide

1. The days of the week are _____ because they repeat in the same order every seven days.

2. A rule that states that repeating chemical and physical properties of elements change periodically with the atomic number of the elements is the _____.

3. Iodine and chlorine are examples of _____.

4. Pure _____ are often stored in oil to keep them from reacting with water and oxygen.

5. Atoms of _____ have two outer-level electrons.

6. Each up-and-down column of elements on the periodic table is called a(n) _____.

UNDERSTANDING KEY IDEAS

Write the letter of the correct answer in the space provided.

_____ **7.** What element makes up about 20% of the air we breathe?
　　a. nitrogen　　　　　　**c.** oxygen
　　b. bromine　　　　　　**d.** sulfur

_____ **8.** Mendeleev found that the elements' properties followed a pattern that repeated every
　　a. 7 elements.　　　　　**c.** 14 elements.
　　b. 5 elements.　　　　　**d.** 10 elements.

_____ **9.** The groups of elements that do not have individual names are called the
　　a. transition metals.　　**c.** alkaline-earth metals.
　　b. alkali metals.　　　　**d.** nonmetals.

_____**10.** The carbon group has two metalloids, both of which are used to make
    a. dinnerware.
    b. foil.
    c. cans.
    d. computer chips.

_____**11.** Diamond and soot are very different, yet both are natural forms of
    a. carbon.
    b. nickel.
    c. boron.
    d. copper.

_____**12.** What element is used to make the most widely used compound in the chemical industry?
    a. sulfur
    b. tellurium
    c. selenium
    d. polonium

13. State the periodic law, which is the basis for the periodic table.

_____

_____

_____

_____

_____

_____

14. Explain why hydrogen is unique.

_____

_____

_____

_____

_____

15. What generalizations can you make about transition metals?

_____

_____

_____

_____

_____

_____

CRITICAL THINKING

16. Compare the lanthanides and the actinides.

_____

_____

_____

_____

_____

_____

_____

_____

17. Carbon forms many important compounds. Could life exist without carbon? Explain your answer.

_____

_____

_____

_____

_____

_____

_____

_____

18. How does the unreactivity of noble gases make them useful?

_____

_____

_____

_____

_____

CONCEPT MAPPING

19. Use the following terms to complete the concept map below:

nonmetals   metals   solids

gases   shiny   metalloids

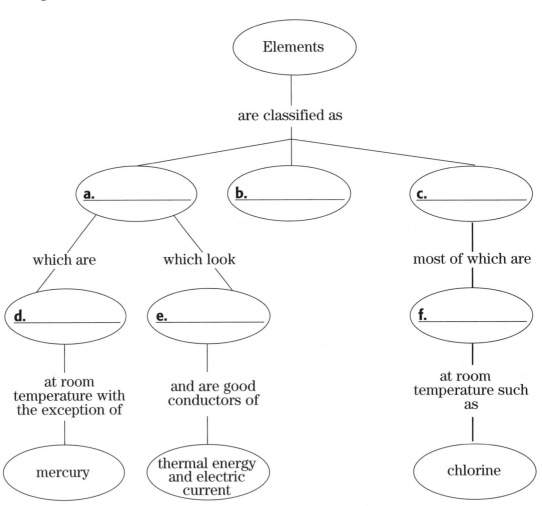

Chapter Test C

The Periodic Table
MULTIPLE CHOICE
Circle the letter of the best answer for each question.

1. What are most of the elements in the periodic table?

    a. metals

    b. metalloids

    c. precious metals

    d. nonmentals

2. How did Mendeleev group the elements?

    a. by density

    b. by melting point

    c. by appearance

    d. by increasing atomic mass

3. Mendeleev's pattern repeated after how many elements?

    a. every seven elements

    b. every three elements

    c. every five elements

    d. every two elements

4. How would you describe most metals?

    a. They are easily shattered.

    b. They are bad conductors of electric current.

    c. They are dull.

    d. They can be drawn into thin wires.

Circle the letter of the best answer for each question.

5. How many of the recently discovered elements follow periodic law?

a. none of them

c. all of them

b. every eighth element

d. half of them

6. What are the left-to-right rows on the periodic table?

a. periods

b. families

c. properties

d. groups

7. Which of the following is a property of alkali metals?

a. They are so hard they cannot be cut.

b. They are very reactive.

c. They are stored in water.

d. They have few uses.

8. When a halogen reacts with a metal, what is formed?

a. a salt

b. a compound

c. a nonmetal

d. an electron

9. What helps light bulbs last longer?

a. krypton

b. xenon

c. argon

d. neon

MATCHING

Read the description. Then, <u>draw a line</u> from the dot to the matching word.

10. group made up of six nonmetals ●   **a.** semiconductor

11. another name for metalloid ●   **b.** mendelevium

12. element named after a scientist ●   **c.** noble gases

13. element named after a state ●   **d.** californium

---

14. word meaning "group" ●

15. word describing actinides ●   **a.** radioactive

16. word describing hydrogen ●   **b.** shiny

17. word describing most transition ●   **c.** colorless
metals   **d.** shiny

FILL-IN-THE-BLANK

Read the words in the box. Read the sentences. <u>Fill in each blank</u> with the word or phrase that best completes the sentence.

aluminum	silicon	oxygen
carbohydrates	hydrogen	

18. In the Boron Group, the most common element

is _____.

19. Proteins, fats, and _____, which are

compounds of carbon, are necessary for life on Earth.

20. Nitrogen and _____ can be combined to

make ammonia.

21. Germanium and _____ are used to make

computer chips.

22. A substance needs _____ to burn.

Name _____ Class _____ Date _____

Performance-Based Assessment

OBJECTIVE

You've read about the periodic table. Now you will have a chance to observe the chemical properties of elements in action! In this activity you will cause a reaction between the iron in steel wool and the oxygen in the air.

KNOW THE SCORE!

As you work through the activity, keep in mind that you will be earning a grade for the following:

- how you work with materials and equipment (30%)
- the quality and clarity of your observations (40%)
- how you use the periodic table to explain those observations (30%)

Using Scientific Methods

ASK A QUESTION

What will happen when iron in steel wood reacts with the air?

MATERIALS AND EQUIPMENT

- graduated cylinder
- protective gloves
- vinegar
- small bowl

- fine steel wool, 0000 grade
- watch or clock
- thermometer
- rubber band

SAFETY INFORMATION

- Do not touch broken thermometers.
- Wear safety goggles.

FORM A HYPOTHESIS

1. Describe the steel wool before the reaction.

_____

_____

TEST THE HYPOTHESIS

2. Use the graduated cylinder to measure 50 mL of vinegar. Pour the vinegar into the bowl.

3. Place the steel wool in the vinegar and leave it there for 2 minutes.

| Performance-Based Assessment *continued*

4. With a gloved hand, remove the steel wool from the vinegar.

5. Wrap the steel wool around the thermometer. Use a rubber band to hold the steel wool in place.

6. Record the thermometer's starting temperature.

_____

7. Keep the steel wool around the thermometer for 10 minutes.

8. Record the thermometer's ending temperature.

_____

ANALYZE THE RESULTS

1. Describe the steel wool after the reaction in Step 3.

_____

_____

2. Record the thermometer's starting temperature.

_____

3. Record the thermometer's ending temperature.

_____

4. List the two changes that you observed or measured after the reaction.

_____

5. Use the locations of iron and oxygen in the periodic table to explain the change in the steel wool's appearance.

_____

_____

DRAW CONCLUSIONS

6. What would you expect to see if you put steel wool in a chamber filled with chlorine gas? Explain.

_____

_____

_____

Performance-Based Assessment *continued*

7. What would you expect to see if you put the steel wool in a chamber filled with neon gas? Explain.

_____

_____

_____

_____

8. Iron is a transition metal. List two common properties of transition metals.

_____

_____

_____

_____

Standardized Test Preparation

READING

Read each of the passages below. Then, answer the questions that follow each passage.

Passage 1 Napoleon III (1808–1873) ruled as emperor of France from 1852 to 1870. Napoleon III was the nephew of the famous French military leader and emperor Napoleon I. Early in his reign, Napoleon III was an <u>authoritarian</u> ruler. France's economy did well under his dictatorial rule, so the French rebuilt cities and built railways. During the 1850s and 1860s, Napoleon III used aluminum dinnerware because aluminum was more valuable than gold. Despite his wealth and French economic prosperity, Napoleon III lost public support and popularity. So, in 1860, he began a series of reforms that allowed more individual freedoms in France.

_____ **1.** What is the meaning of the word *authoritarian* in the passage?
   A controlling people's thoughts and actions
   B writing books and stories
   C being an expert on a subject
   D being very wealthy

_____ **2.** Which of the following statements best describes why Napoleon III probably changed the way he ruled France?
   F He was getting old.
   G He was unpopular and had lost public support.
   H He had built as many railroads as he could.
   I He used aluminum dinnerware.

_____ **3.** According to the passage, in what year did Napoleon III die?
   A 1808
   B 1873
   C 1860
   D 1852

Passage 2 Named after architect Buckminster Fuller, buckyballs resemble the geodesic domes that are characteristic of the architect's work. Excitement over buckyballs began in 1985, when scientists projected light from a laser onto a piece of graphite. In the soot that remained, researchers found a completely new kind of molecule! Buckyballs are also found in the soot from a candle flame. Some scientists claim to have detected buckyballs in space. In fact, one suggestion is that buckyballs are at the center of the condensing clouds of gas, dust, and debris that form galaxies.

_____ **1.** Which of the following statements correctly describes buckyballs?
  A They are a kind of dome-shaped building.
  B They are shot from lasers.
  C They were unknown before 1985.
  D They are named for the scientist who discovered them.

_____ **2.** Based on the passage, which of the following statements is an opinion?
  F Buckyballs might be in the clouds that form galaxies.
  G Buckyballs are named after an architect.
  H Scientists found buckyballs in soot.
  I Buckyballs are a kind of molecule.

_____ **3.** According to the passage, why were scientists excited?
  A Buckyballs were found in space.
  B An architect created a building that resembled a molecule.
  C Buckyballs were found to be in condensing clouds of gas that form galaxies.
  D A new kind of molecule was found.

▌Standardized Test Preparation *continued*

INTERPRETING GRAPHICS

Use the image of the periodic table below to answer the questions that follow.

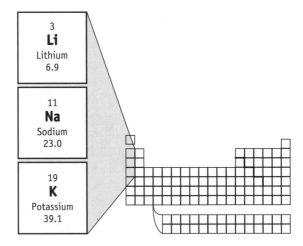

_____ **1.** Which of the following statements is correct for the elements shown?
    A Lithium has the greatest atomic number.
    B Sodium has the least atomic mass.
    C Atomic number decreases as you move down the column.
    D Atomic mass increases as you move down the column.

_____ **2.** Which of the following statements best describes the outer electrons in atoms of the elements shown?
    F The atoms of each element have 1 outer-level electron.
    G Lithium atoms have 3 outer-level electrons, sodium atoms have 11, and potassium atoms have 19.
    H Lithium atoms have 7 outer-level electrons, sodium atoms have 23, and potassium atoms have 39.
    I The atoms of each element have 11 outer-level electrons.

_____ **3.** The elements featured in the image belong to which of the following groups?
    A noble gases
    B alkaline-earth metals
    C halogens
    D alkali metals

| Standardized Test Preparation *continued*

MATH

Read each question below, and choose the best answer.

_____ **1.** Elvira's house is 7.3 km from her school. What is this distance expressed in meters?

    A 0.73 m

    B 73 m

    C 730 m

    D 7,300 m

_____ **2.** A chemical company is preparing a shipment of 10 g each of four elements. Each element must be shipped in its own container that is completely filled with the element. Which container will be the largest?

Element	Density (g/cm^3)	Mass (g)
Aluminum	2.702	10
Arsenic	5.727	10
Germanium	5.350	10
Silicon	2.420	10

    F the container of aluminum

    G the container of arsenic

    H the container of germanium

    I the container of silicon

_____ **3.** Arjay has samples of several common elements. Each element has a unique atomic mass (expressed in amu). Which of the following lists shows the atomic masses in order from least to greatest?

    A 63.55, 58.69, 55.85, 58.93

    B 63.55, 58.93, 58.69, 55.85

    C 55.85, 58.69, 58.93, 63.55

    D 55.85, 63.55, 58.69, 58.93

Model-Making

Create a Periodic Table

You probably have classification systems for many things in your life, such as your clothes, your books, and your CDs. One of the most important classification systems in science is the periodic table of the elements. In this lab, you will develop your own classification system for a collection of ordinary objects. You will analyze trends in your system and compare your system with the periodic table of the elements.

OBJECTIVES

Classify objects based on their properties.

Identify patterns and trends in data.

MATERIALS

- bag of objects
- balance, metric
- meterstick

- paper, graphing (2 sheets)
- paper, 3 × 3 cm squares (20)

PROCEDURE

1. Your teacher will give you a bag of objects. Your bag is missing one item. Examine the items carefully. Describe the missing object in as many ways as you can. Be sure to include the reasons why you think the missing object has the characteristics you describe.

_____

_____

_____

2. Lay the paper squares out on your desk or table so that you have a grid of five rows of four squares each.

3. Arrange your objects on the grid in a logical order. (You must decide what order is logical!) You should end up with one blank square for the missing object.

4. Record a description of the basis for your arrangement.

_____

_____

5. Measure the mass (g) and diameter (mm) of each object, and record your results in the appropriate square. Each square (except the empty one) should have one object and two written measurements on it.

Create a Periodic Table *continued*

6. Examine your pattern again. Does the order in which your objects are arranged still make sense? Explain.

_____

_____

7. Rearrange the squares and their objects if necessary to improve your arrangement. Record a description of the basis for the new arrangement.

_____

_____

8. Working across the rows, number the squares 1 to 20. When you get to the end of a row, continue numbering in the first square of the next row.

9. Copy your grid below. In each square, be sure to list the type of object and label all measurements with appropriate units.

ANALYZE THE RESULTS

1. Constructing Graphs On a separate piece of paper make a graph of mass (y-axis) versus object number (x-axis). Label each axis, and title the graph.

2. Constructing Graphs Now make a graph of diameter (y-axis) versus object number (x-axis).

Create a Periodic Table *continued*

DRAW CONCLUSIONS

3. Analyzing Graphs Discuss each graph with your classmates. Try to identify any important features of the graph. For example, does the graph form a line or a curve? Is there anything unusual about the graph? What do these features tell you? Record your answers.

_____

_____

_____

_____

_____

4. Evaluating Models How is your arrangement of objects similar to the periodic table of the elements found in this textbook? How is your arrangement different from that periodic table?

_____

_____

_____

_____

5. Making Predictions Look again at your prediction about the missing object. Do you think your prediction is still accurate? Try to improve your description by estimating the mass and diameter of the missing object. Record your estimates.

_____

_____

_____

_____

6. Evaluating Methods Mendeleev created a periodic table of elements and predicted characteristics of missing elements. How is your experiment similar to Mendeleev's work?

_____

_____

_____

Quick Lab

Conduction Connection

MATERIALS

- cup, plastic-foam
- graphite, mechanical pencil lead
- water, hot
- wire, copper, bare

SAFETY INFORMATION

PROCEDURE

1. Fill a **plastic-foam cup** with **hot water**.

2. Stand a **piece of copper wire** and a **graphite lead** from a mechanical pencil in the water.

3. After 1 min, touch the top of each object. Record your observations.

_____

_____

_____

4. Which material conducted thermal energy the best? Why?

_____

_____

Activity

Vocabulary Activity

Bringing It to the Periodic Table

After you finish reading the chapter, try the following puzzle.

On the next page is a partially filled-in quotation by Dmitri Mendeleev. Fill in the term described by each clue below. Then put the numbered letters into the corresponding squares on the next page to find out what Mendeleev said. The answers to questions 9–11 are chemical symbols.

1. states that the properties of elements are periodic functions of their atomic numbers

— — — — — — — —   — — —
59   16   27 40 24   41

2. column or family in the periodic table

— — — — —
19 35 58

3. any element in Groups 3–12

— — — — — — — — — — — — — —
31   14   43   55 18   7 33 10

4. elements in Group 1

— — — — — — — — — — — —
17   22   48   8   36   11

5. having a regular, repeating pattern

— — — — — — — —
52   15   25   28 23

6. metals with two electrons in the outer energy level

— — — — — — —-— — — — —
51   50   20 42   54   2

7. a row of elements

— — — — — — —
61 6 26   56

8. elements that don't react readily with other elements

— — — — — — — — — —
29   49   62   44   64

9. atomic number 9

—
13

Vocabulary Activity *continued*

10. atomic number 39

$\overline{}$
57

11. atomic number 54

$\overline{}$ $\overline{}$
47   63

12. elements having properties of metals and nonmetals

___ ___ ___ ___ ___ ___ ___ ___ ___ ___
39   46   37   5   12

13. the first rows of transition metals at the bottom of the periodic table

___ ___ ___ ___ ___ ___ ___ ___ ___ ___ ___
          1   9   34   4

14. the most abundant element in the universe

___ ___ ___ ___ ___ ___ ___
          21   38   3

15. group containing iodine and chlorine

___ ___ ___ ___ ___ ___ ___ ___
32   60   30   53   45

MENDELEEV'S QUOTATION:

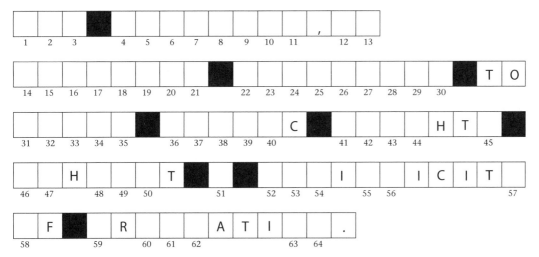

Name _____ Class _____ Date _____

SciLinks Activity

THE PERIODIC TABLE

Go to www.scilinks.org. To find links related to the periodic table, type in the keyword HSM1125. Then, use the links to answer the following questions about the periodic table.

Go to www.scilinks.org

Topic: Periodic Table
SciLinks code: HSM1125

1. What is gold? Write a description that includes its degree of ductility and malleability, its color, its classification (metal, metalloid, nonmetal), and three general uses.

_____

_____

_____

2. What unit of measurement is used to weigh gold?

_____

_____

3. What are some common uses for boron?

_____

_____

_____

4. How is astatine produced? What element is it most similar to?

_____

_____

5. Which two elements were discovered in the 1990s?

_____

_____

6. Name the rare Earth element that was discovered in 1789 and named for the planet Uranus. What is it used for?

_____

_____

_____

Performance-Based Assessment

Teacher Notes and Answer Key

PURPOSE

Students produce an oxidation reaction and observe its effects. Students then use their knowledge of the periodic table to explain the reaction.

Rebecca Ferguson
Northridge Middle School
North Richland Hills, Texas

TIME REQUIRED

One 45-minute class period. Students will need 20 minutes to perform the procedure and 25 minutes to answer the analysis questions.

RATING

Easy  Hard

Teacher Prep–2
Student Set-Up–1
Concept Level–2
Clean Up–2

ADVANCE PREPARATION

Equip each activity station with the necessary materials. You may choose to copy the periodic table for students' use during this activity.

SAFETY INFORMATION

Use plastic bowls, if available. Use alcohol thermometers rather than mercury thermometers. Instruct students not to touch broken thermometers. Have a disposal container for sharps available in case of thermometer breakage. Perform this activity in a well-ventilated area. All students should wear safety goggles. Mop up spills immediately.

TEACHING STRATEGIES

This activity works best in groups of 2–3 students. The reaction of the iron in the steel wool with the oxygen in the air is classified as an oxidation-reduction (redox) reaction. The iron is the reducing agent that gives up its electrons. The oxygen in the air is the oxidizing agent that accepts electrons. The acid in vinegar facilitates the transfer of electrons by enhancing the conductivity of the moisture left on the steel wool. The two products of this reaction are iron (III) oxide (rust) and heat.

Evaluation Strategies

Use the following rubric to help evaluate student performance.

Rubric for Assessment

Possible points	Appropriate use of materials and equipment (30 points possible)
30–20	Successfully completes activity; safe and careful handling of materials and equipment; attention to detail; superior lab skills
19–10	Task is generally complete; successful use of materials and equipment; sound knowledge of lab techniques; somewhat unfocused performance; mild neglect of safety measures
9–1	Attempts to complete tasks yield inadequate results; unsafe lab technique; apparent lack of skill
	Quality and clarity of observations (40 points possible)
40–30	Superior observations stated clearly and accurately; high level of detail; correct use of units of measurement
29–20	Accurate observations; moderate level of detail; correct use of units of measurement
19–10	Complete observations, but expressed in unclear manner; may include minor inaccuracies; attempts to use units of measurement include errors or inconsistencies
9–1	Erroneous, incomplete, or unclear observations; lack of accuracy, details, units of measurement
	Explanation of observations (30 points possible)
30–20	Clear, detailed explanation shows superior knowledge of the periodic table
19–10	Adequate understanding of periodic table concepts with minor difficulty in expression
9–1	Poor understanding of the periodic table; explanation unclear or not relevant to periodic table; substantial factual errors

Assessment

Performance-Based Assessment

OBJECTIVE

You've read about the periodic table. Now you will have a chance to observe the chemical properties of elements in action! In this activity you will cause a reaction between the iron in steel wool and the oxygen in the air.

KNOW THE SCORE!

As you work through the activity, keep in mind that you will be earning a grade for the following:

- how you work with materials and equipment (30%)
- the quality and clarity of your observations (40%)
- how you use the periodic table to explain those observations (30%)

Using Scientific Methods

ASK A QUESTION

What will happen when iron in steel wood reacts with the air?

MATERIALS AND EQUIPMENT

- graduated cylinder
- protective gloves
- vinegar
- small bowl

- fine steel wool, 0000 grade
- watch or clock
- thermometer
- rubber band

SAFETY INFORMATION

- Do not touch broken thermometers.
- Wear safety goggles.

FORM A HYPOTHESIS

1. Describe the steel wool before the reaction.

   Sample answer: The steel wool looks like metallic cotton. The color is gray

   or dark silver.

TEST THE HYPOTHESIS

2. Use the graduated cylinder to measure 50 mL of vinegar. Pour the vinegar into the bowl.

3. Place the steel wool in the vinegar and leave it there for 2 minutes.

| **Performance-Based Assessment** *continued*

4. With a gloved hand, remove the steel wool from the vinegar.

5. Wrap the steel wool around the thermometer. Use a rubber band to hold the steel wool in place.

6. Record the thermometer's starting temperature.

The starting temperature is 24°C.

7. Keep the steel wool around the thermometer for 10 minutes.

8. Record the thermometer's ending temperature.

The ending temperature is 30°C.

ANALYZE THE RESULTS

1. Describe the steel wool after the reaction in Step 3.

The parts of the steel wood that were soaked in vinegar appear rusty. The

color changed from gray to orange.

2. Record the thermometer's starting temperature.

The starting temperature is 24°C.

3. Record the thermometer's ending temperature.

The ending temperature is 30°C.

4. List the two changes that you observed or measured after the reaction.

Rust appeared and the temperature of the steel wood rose by 6°C.

5. Use the locations of iron and oxygen in the periodic table to explain the change in the steel wool's appearance.

Iron is a reactive transition metal. Oxygen belongs to a group of reactive

elements. The iron and oxygen reacted with one another, forming rust.

DRAW CONCLUSIONS

6. What would you expect to see if you put steel wool in a chamber filled with chlorine gas? Explain.

The steel wool would rust very quickly. Chlorine is more reactive than

oxygen.

Performance-Based Assessment *continued*

7. What would you expect to see if you put the steel wool in a chamber filled with neon gas? Explain.

The steel wool and neon would not react. Neon is a noble gas and is

therefore nonreactive.

8. Iron is a transition metal. List two common properties of transition metals.

Answers will vary. Sample answer: good conductors of thermal energy and

electric current, high density, high melting point, less reactive than alkali

metals and alkaline-earth metals, silver-colored.

Model Making

Create a Periodic Table

Teacher Notes and Answer Key

TIME REQUIRED

One to two 45-minutes class periods

Norman Holcomb
Marion Elementary School
Maria Stein, Ohio

RATING

Easy ◄——1——2——3——4——► Hard

Teacher Prep–3
Student Set-Up–1
Concept Level–3
Clean Up–1

MATERIALS

The materials listed for this lab are for each group of 2–4 students. For each group of students, assemble a collection of 20 objects (five sets of four objects). You should provide a bag containing 19 of these objects. A recommended collection of objects includes sets of coins (penny, nickel, dime, quarter), sets of buttons that are similar but vary in diameter, and washers that vary in diameter. Other objects, such as nuts, bolts, and paper circles, will work and are easily obtainable. The difference in masses should be large enough for a beam balance to detect. Ideally, each set (one column on the table) should be of the same material and thickness and vary only in diameter.

PREPARATION NOTE

You may have students prepare the 20 squares of paper, but the lab will go faster if the squares are prepared ahead of time.

Name _____ Class _____ Date _____

| Model-Making | DATASHEET FOR CHAPTER LAB |

Create a Periodic Table

You probably have classification systems for many things in your life, such as your clothes, your books, and your CDs. One of the most important classification systems in science is the periodic table of the elements. In this lab, you will develop your own classification system for a collection of ordinary objects. You will analyze trends in your system and compare your system with the periodic table of the elements.

OBJECTIVES

Classify objects based on their properties.

Identify patterns and trends in data.

MATERIALS

- bag of objects
- balance, metric
- meterstick
- paper, graphing (2 sheets)
- paper, 3 × 3 cm squares (20)

PROCEDURE

1. Your teacher will give you a bag of objects. Your bag is missing one item. Examine the items carefully. Describe the missing object in as many ways as you can. Be sure to include the reasons why you think the missing object has the characteristics you describe.

_____

_____

_____

2. Lay the paper squares out on your desk or table so that you have a grid of five rows of four squares each.

3. Arrange your objects on the grid in a logical order. (You must decide what order is logical!) You should end up with one blank square for the missing object.

4. Record a description of the basis for your arrangement.

_____

_____

5. Measure the mass (g) and diameter (mm) of each object, and record your results in the appropriate square. Each square (except the empty one) should have one object and two written measurements on it.

Name _____ Class _____ Date _____

| Create a Periodic Table *continued*

6. Examine your pattern again. Does the order in which your objects are arranged still make sense? Explain.

_____

_____

7. Rearrange the squares and their objects if necessary to improve your arrangement. Record a description of the basis for the new arrangement.

_____

_____

8. Working across the rows, number the squares 1 to 20. When you get to the end of a row, continue numbering in the first square of the next row.

9. Copy your grid below. In each square, be sure to list the type of object and label all measurements with appropriate units.

ANALYZE THE RESULTS

1. Constructing Graphs On a separate piece of paper make a graph of mass (*y*-axis) versus object number (*x*-axis). Label each axis, and title the graph.

2. Constructing Graphs Now make a graph of diameter (*y*-axis) versus object number (*x*-axis).

| Create a Periodic Table *continued*

DRAW CONCLUSIONS

3. Analyzing Graphs Discuss each graph with your classmates. Try to identify any important features of the graph. For example, does the graph form a line or a curve? Is there anything unusual about the graph? What do these features tell you? Record your answers.

Answers will vary. The primary feature is the repeating pattern of increases.

This pattern in the first graph indicates the periodic nature of the mass of

the items. This pattern in the second graph indicates the periodic nature of

the diameter of the items.

_____

4. Evaluating Models How is your arrangement of objects similar to the periodic table of the elements found in this textbook? How is your arrangement different from that periodic table?

Answers will vary. Similarities include repeating patterns (such as mass)

across the table. Differences may include no consistent family traits and no

chemical properties associated with position in the table.

_____

5. Making Predictions Look again at your prediction about the missing object. Do you think your prediction is still accurate? Try to improve your description by estimating the mass and diameter of the missing object. Record your estimates.

Answers will vary, depending on the student's original prediction. Accept all

reasonable answers. (You may wish to provide the students with the missing

object so they can further evaluate their prediction.)

_____

6. Evaluating Methods Mendeleev created a periodic table of elements and predicted characteristics of missing elements. How is your experiment similar to Mendeleev's work?

This experiment is similar in that a pattern was identified that helped to

identify characteristics of a missing object.

_____

Name _____ Class _____ Date _____

Conduction Connection

MATERIALS

- cup, plastic-foam
- graphite, mechanical pencil lead
- water, hot
- wire, copper, bare

SAFETY INFORMATION

PROCEDURE

1. Fill a **plastic-foam cup** with **hot water**.

2. Stand a **piece of copper wire** and a **graphite lead** from a mechanical pencil in the water.

3. After 1 min, touch the top of each object. Record your observations.

_____

_____

_____

4. Which material conducted thermal energy the best? Why?

The wire conducted thermal energy better than the pencil lead did. The wire

is made of the metal copper; pencil lead is made of graphite, a form of the

nonmetal carbon. Metals conduct thermal energy better than nonmetals do.

Answer Key

Directed Reading A

SECTION: ARRANGING THE ELEMENTS

1. Answers will vary. Sample answer: Scientists might have been frustrated because the elements weren't organized and therefore their properties couldn't be predicted.
2. D
3. periodic
4. periodic table of the elements
5. Mendeleev was able to predict the properties of unknown elements by using the pattern of properties in the periodic table.
6. D
7. periodic law
8. C
9. Chemical symbols are color-coded on the periodic table according to state. The color of the chemical symbol for carbon is red, which corresponds to a solid.
10. properties
11. electrons
12. Answers will very. Sample answer: The zigzag line can help me recognize which elements are metals, which are nonmetals, and which are metalloids.
13. metals
14. ductile
15. solid
16. It means that most metals can be flattened with a hammer and will not shatter.
17. aluminum
18. nonmetals
19. metalloids
20. B
21. C
22. chemical symbol
23. periods
24. groups, families
25. mendelevium, californium

SECTION: GROUPING THE ELEMENTS

1. C
2. B
3. alkali metals
4. alkaline-earth metals
5. cement and chalk
6. Answers will vary. Sample answer: Calcium is an important part of a compound that keeps your bones and teeth healthy.
7. Accept three from this list: beryllium, magnesium, strontium, barium, and radium.
8. B
9. transition metals
10. Answers will vary. Sample answer: Mercury is in a liquid state at room temperature. The other transition metals are solids at room temperature.
11. lanthanides, actinides
12. europium
13. americium
14. Answers will vary. Sample answer: Aluminum was considered more valuable than gold.
15. Answers will vary. Sample answer: Aluminum is used in making aircraft parts, lightweight automobile parts, foil, cans, and siding.
16. silicon, germanium
17. proteins, fats, and carbohydrates
18. diamond
19. Answers will vary. Sample answer: used as a jewel and on cutting tools, such as saws, drills, and files.
20. soot
21. gas
22. five
23. hydrogen
24. Answers will vary. Sample answer: Oxygen is a gas at room temperature. The other four elements are solids.
25. sulfur
26. Answers will vary. Sample answer: Oxygen, which makes up about 20% of air, is important to most living things. It is also necessary for substances to burn.
27. halogens
28. Both are used as disinfectants.
29. salts, sodium chloride

30. Answers will vary. Sample answer: Chlorinating water helps protect people from many diseases by killing the organisms that cause the diseases.

31. C

32. noble gases

33. density

34. D

Directed Reading B

SECTION: ARRANGING THE ELEMENTS

1. D

2. A

3. C

4. C

5. B

6. A

7. C

8. A

9. metals

10. nonmetals

11. metalloids

12. semiconductors

13. mendelevium

14. californium

15. chemical symbol

16. C

17. C

18. C

19. B

20. B

SECTION: GROUPING THE ELEMENTS

1. C

2. B

3. B

4. B

5. A

6. D

7. A

8. C

9. C

10. A

11. reactive

12. aluminum

13. carbohydrates

14. tin

15. hydrogen

16. oxygen

17. A

18. B

19. D

20. C

21. C

22. A

23. C

Vocabulary and Section Summary

SECTION: ARRANGING THE ELEMENTS

1. periodic: describes something that occurs or repeats at regular intervals

2. periodic law: the law that states that the repeating chemical and physical properties of elements change periodically with the atomic numbers of the elements

3. period: in chemistry, a horizontal row of elements in the periodic table

4. group: a vertical column of elements in the periodic table; elements in a group share chemical properties

SECTION: GROUPING THE ELEMENTS

1. alkali metal: one of the elements of Group 1 of the periodic table (lithium, sodium, potassium, rubidium, cesium, and francium)

2. alkaline-earth metal: one of the elements of Group 2 of the periodic table (beryllium, magnesium, calcium, strontium, barium, and radium)

3. halogen: one of the elements of Group 17 of the periodic table (fluorine, chlorine, bromine, iodine, and astatine); halogens combine with most metals to form salts

4. noble gas: one of the elements of Group 18 of the periodic table (helium, neon, argon, krypton, xenon, and radon); noble gases are unreactive

Section Review

SECTION: ARRANGING THE ELEMENTS

1. Sample answer: *Periodic* means "happening in a regular repeating pattern."

2. C

3. A period in the periodic table is a horizontal row of elements. A group is a vertical column of elements.

4. atomic mass

5. The repeating chemical and physical properties of elements change periodically with the atomic numbers of the elements.

6. halogen; Element 117 has 117 protons. So, it would fall under astatine in the periodic table.

7. lithium; Sodium and lithium are in the same group, so their properties should be more alike than the properties of sodium and magnesium are.

8. The periodic table has the same shape, atomic numbers, and chemical symbols. The names of the elements are in a different language (Japanese).

SECTION: GROUPING THE ELEMENTS:

1. noble gas
2. alkali metal
3. halogen
4. alkaline-earth metal
5. C
6. Answers may vary but could include that they have one electron in their outer level; are very reactive; are soft, silver-colored, and shiny; and have a low density.
7. having the same number of electrons in the outer level of their atoms
8. Answers may vary but could include that they have seven electrons in their outer level, are very reactive, conduct electric current poorly, react violently with alkali metals to form salts, and are never found uncombined in nature.
9. The properties of hydrogen do not match the properties of any single group.
10. boron group (Group 13)
11. metal; The model shows two electrons in the outer level, so the atom represented is most likely a metal.
12. They are so reactive that they react with water or oxygen in the air.
13. Both hydrogen and sodium have one electron in their outer level. Atoms of both elements give away one electron when joining with other atoms. However, hydrogen is a nonmetal and is a gas at room temperature, whereas sodium is a solid metal at room temperature.

Chapter Review

1. group
2. period
3. alkali metals
4. noble gases
5. D
6. B
7. C
8. C
9. B
10. C
11. Moseley arranged elements by increasing atomic number. Mendeleev arranged elements by increasing atomic mass.
12. Both are periodic. The periodic table has repeating properties of elements. The calendar has repeating days and months.
13. 5.4% (sodium and potassium)
14. 5.6% (magnesium and calcium)
15. An answer to this exercise can be found at the end of the teacher's edition.
16. Mendeleev could make predictions only about elements where there were clear gaps in his table. Because no noble gases were known at the time, there were no obvious gaps in the table and no way that he could have known that a whole column was missing.
17. metal; it will be located below the metal bismuth to the left of the zigzag
18. I would tell my classmate that he didn't find sodium. Sodium is very reactive and cannot be found uncombined in nature. Sodium would react with oxygen and water in the air and form a compound.
19. a. calcium
    b. carbon
20. Periodic properties are the order of the shapes and the number of lines inside the shape. The properties shared in a group are the shape and the color of the lines inside the shape.

Reinforcement

PLACING ALL YOUR ELEMENTS ON THE TABLE

1.–13. Make sure that students have colored the table properly.

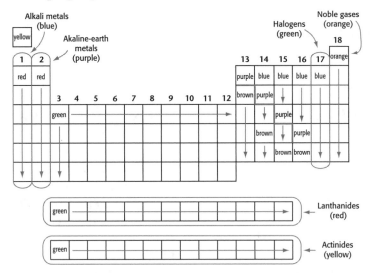

14. They are in Group 2.

15. 2

16. Answers will vary. Sample answer: The alkali metals are solids, while hydrogen is a gas at room temperature.

17. They are called the noble gases.

18. B

19. Group 13

20. C

21. Accept all answers.

Critical Thinking

1. Answers will vary. Sample answer: Sodium is not found by itself naturally. Because of its reactivity, sodium always combines with other elements.

2. Answers will vary. Sample answer: No; sulfur, a nonmetal, is a poor conductor of heat and energy. An electrical current could not travel along sulfur wire.

3. Answers will vary. Sample answer: Yes; an explosion would result. Hydrogen reacts explosively when combined with oxygen in this manner.

4. Answers will vary. Sample answer: No; the oxygen in the "Everlast Light Bulb" would react with the heating filament and cause it to burn out more quickly than a light bulb filled with a nonreactive gas, such as argon.

5. Answers will vary. Sample answer: If the substance could not be broken down any further and if its chemical and physical properties were not identical to any other element, the claim would be true.

6. Answers will vary. Sample answer: The element would be classified according to its chemical and physical properties.

Section Quizzes

SECTION: ARRANGING THE ELEMENTS

1. A
2. C
3. B
4. A
5. A

SECTION: GROUPING THE ELEMENTS

1. H
2. I
3. C
4. E
5. G
6. J
7. B
8. A
9. F
10. D

Chapter Test A

1. A
2. D
3. C
4. B
5. B
6. B
7. A
8. A
9. D
10. F
11. A
12. E
13. G
14. J
15. C
16. I
17. H
18. D
19. B
20. A
21. D
22. B
23. B
24. A

Chapter Test B

1. periodic
2. periodic law

3. halogens
4. alkali metals
5. alkaline-earth metals
6. group
7. C
8. A
9. A
10. D
11. A
12. A
13. Answers will vary. Sample answer: The periodic law states that chemical and physical properties of elements are periodic, repeating functions of the elements' atomic numbers. This is why elements in vertical groups of the periodic table share similar properties.
14. Answers will vary. Sample answer: The properties of hydrogen do not match the properties of any single group.
15. Answers will vary. Sample answer: Transition metals tend to be shiny and to conduct thermal energy and electric current well.
16. Answers will vary. Sample answer: The lanthanides and actinides are transition metals. The lanthanides are shiny, reactive metals. The actinides are radioactive.
17. Answers will vary. Sample answer: Life could not exist without carbon. Carbon forms compounds such as proteins, fats, and carbohydrates that are necessary for living things on Earth.
18. Answers will vary. Sample answer: When light bulbs are filled with argon, they last longer. Argon is unreactive and so does not react with the metal filament in a light bulb. The low density of helium makes blimps and weather balloons float.
19. **a.** metals; **b.** metalloids; **c.** nonmetals; **d.** solids; **e.** shiny; **f.** gases

Chapter Test C

1. A
2. D
3. A
4. D
5. C
6. A
7. B

8. A

9. C

10. C

11. A

12. B

13. D

13. D

14. D

15. A

16. C

17. B

18. aluminum

19. carbohydrates

20. hydrogen

21. silicon

22. oxygen

Standardized Test Preparation

READING

Passage 1

1. A

2. G

3. B

Passage 2

1. C

2. F

3. D

INTERPRETING GRAPHICS

1. D

2. F

3. D

MATH

1. D

2. I

3. C

Vocabulary Activity

1. periodic law

2. group

3. transition metal

4. alkali metals

5. periodic

6. alkaline-earth

7. period

8. noble gases

9. F

10. Y

11. Xe

12. metalloids

13. lanthanides

14. hydrogen

15. halogens

Mendeleev's Quotation: The elements, if arranged according to their atomic weights, exhibit a periodicity of properties.

SciLinks Activity

1. Answers will vary. Sample answer: Gold is a heavy, yellow, metallic chemical element. It is a precious metal with a high degree of ductility and malleability. It is used in the manufacture of jewelry, electronics, and coins.

2. the troy ounce

3. Answers will vary. Sample answer: Gold circuits ar used in the electronic sensors that operate airbags. These sensors ensure that airbags operate without failing, saving many lives each year.

4. Astatine is produced by bombarding bismuth with alpha particles. It is most similar to iodine.

5. Ununnilium (Uuu) was discovered in 1994. Darmstatium (Ds), which was temporarily called Ununbium (Uub) was discovered in 1996.

6. Uranium was discovered in 1789 and named for the planet Uranus. It is used as fuel for nuclear reactors.

Lesson Plan

Section: Arranging the Elements

Pacing

Regular Schedule:	**with lab(s):** 2 days	**without lab(s):** 1 day
Block Schedule:	**with lab(s):** 1 day	**without lab(s):** 0.5 day

Objectives

1. Describe how Mendeleev arranged elements in the first periodic table.

2. Explain how elements are arranged in the modern periodic table.

3. Compare metals, nonmetals, and metalloids based on their properties and on their location in the periodic table.

4. Describe the difference between a period and a group.

National Science Education Standards Covered

UCP 1: Systems, order, and organization

SAI 2: Understandings about scientific inquiry

SPSP 5: Science and technology in society

HNS 1: Science as a human endeavor

HNS 2: Nature of science

HNS 3: History of science

PS 1b: Substances react chemically in characteristic ways with other substances to form new substances (compounds) with different characteristic properties. In chemical reactions, the total mass is conserved. Substances often are placed in categories or groups if they react in similar ways; metals is an example of such a group.

KEY

SE = Student Edition   **TE** = Teacher's Edition
CRF = Chapter Resource File

FOCUS (*5 minutes*)

_ **Chapter Starter Transparency** Use this transparency to introduce the chapter.

_ **Bellringer, TE** Have students determine patterns that can be established with a deck of cards.

_ **Bellringer Transparency** Use this transparency as students enter the classroom and find their seats.

_ **Reading Strategy, SE** Have students create a mnemonic device to remember the difference between groups and periods.

MOTIVATE (10 minutes)

_ **Demonstration, Grouping, TE** Ask the class to group student volunteers based on lists of characteristics. (**GENERAL**)

TEACH (65 minutes)

_ **Activity, Element Sampling, TE** Have students identify and list characteristics of samples of various elements. (**GENERAL**)

_ **Using the Figure, TE** Tell students that the color scheme on the periodic table will be continued throughout the book. (**GENERAL**)

_ **Activity, Looking for Gaps, TE** Have students consider the progression of atomic mass across the periodic table. (**ADVANCED**)

_ **Research, TE** Have students find out if any new elements have been synthesized since this book has been published. (**GENERAL**)

_ **Connection to History, TE** Tell students about the early steps that led to the creation of the modern periodic table. (**GENERAL**)

_ **Quick Lab, Conduction Connection, SE** Students determine whether graphite or copper conducts thermal energy the best. (**GENERAL**)

_ **Activity, Element Game, TE** Have students make a memory game to practice learning element names and symbols. (**BASIC**)

_ **Directed Reading A/B, CRF** These worksheets reinforce basic concepts and vocabulary presented in the lesson. (**Basic/Special Needs**)

_ **Vocabulary and Section Summary, CRF** Students write definitions of key terms and read a summary of section content. (**GENERAL**)

_ **Teaching Transparency, The Periodic Table of the Elements** Use this graphic to help students understand the organization of the periodic table.

_ **Chapter Lab, Create a Periodic Table, SE** Students create a periodic table using ordinary objects. (**GENERAL**)

_ **Datasheet for Chapter Lab, Create a Periodic Table, CRF** Students use the datasheet to complete the Chapter Lab. (**GENERAL**)

CLOSE (10 minutes)

_ **Reteaching, TE** Reinforce the meanings of the terms malleable and brittle.

_ **Section Review, SE** Students answer end-of-section vocabulary, key ideas, critical thinking, and interpreting graphics questions. (**GENERAL**)

_ **Section Quiz, CRF** Students answer five objective questions about the elements on the periodic table. (**GENERAL**)

_ **Quiz, TE** Students answer three questions about the elements on the periodic table. (**GENERAL**)

Lesson Plan

Section: Grouping the Elements

Pacing

Regular Schedule:	**with lab(s):** N/A	**without lab(s):** 1 days
Block Schedule:	**with lab(s):** N/A	**without lab(s):** 0.5 day

Objectives

1. Explain why elements in a group often have similar properties.

2. Describe the properties of the elements in the groups of the periodic table.

National Science Education Standards Covered

ST 2: Understandings about science and technology

PS 1b: Substances react chemically in characteristic ways with other substances to form new substances (compounds) with different characteristic properties. In chemical reactions, the total mass is conserved. Substances often are placed in categories or groups if they react in similar ways; metals is an example of such a group.

PS 3e: In most chemical and nuclear reactions, energy is transferred into or out of a system. Heat, light, mechanical motion, or electricity might all be involved in such transfers.

> **KEY**
> **SE** = Student Edition   **TE** = Teacher's Edition
> **CRF** = Chapter Resource File

FOCUS *(5 minutes)*

_ **Bellringer, TE** Have students determine the characteristics of several animals and tell how determining the characteristics of elements can help them tell the elements apart.

_ **Bellringer Transparency** Use this transparency as students enter the classroom and find their seats.

MOTIVATE *(10 minutes)*

_ **Discussion, TE** Discuss cookie ingredients, comparing them with ingredients for the universe—the periodic table of the elements. **(GENERAL)**

TEACH (20 minutes)

_ **Reading Strategy, SE** Have students read the section silently and, in pairs, summarize what they've read.

_ **Using the Figure, Group Trends, TE** Have students describe how lithium should react with water.

_ **Cultural Awareness, TE** Explain the Arabic origins of alkali metals. **(GENERAL)**

_ **Connection to Life Science, TE** Explain the importance of calcium to health. **(GENERAL)**

_ **Connection to History, Canning, TE** Describe the development of food preservation through canning. **(GENERAL)**

_ **Using the Figure, Allotropes, TE** Explain allotropes to students. **(GENERAL)**

_ **Connection Activity History, Sulfur, TE** Have students write a report, make a poster, or prepare a presentation on the uses of sulfur prior to 1777. **(ADVANCED)**

_ **Cultural Awareness, The Curies, TE** Tell students about the accomplishments of the Curies. **(GENERAL)**

_ **Connection to Astronomy, TE** Have students research how elements may be created or changed in violent celestial reactions. **(GENERAL)**

_ **Directed Reading A/B, CRF** These worksheets reinforce basic concepts and vocabulary presented in the lesson. **(Basic/Special Needs)**

_ **Vocabulary and Section Summary, CRF** Students write definitions of key terms and read a summary of section content. **(GENERAL)**

_ **Reinforcement, CRF** This worksheet reinforces key concepts in the chapter. **(BASIC)**

_ **Critical Thinking, CRF** Ask students to fill out the worksheet about new science products found on an advertisement. **(ADVANCED)**

_ **SciLinks Activity, The Periodic Table, SciLinks code HSM1125, CRF** Students research Internet resources related to gold. **(GENERAL)**

CLOSE (10 minutes)

_ **Reteaching, TE** Teach students a game to help them remember the properties of the groups on the periodic table. **(GENERAL)**

_ **Section Review, SE** Students answer end-of-section vocabulary, key ideas, interpreting graphics, and critical thinking questions. **(GENERAL)**

_ **Section Quiz, CRF** Students answer ten objective questions about the elements on the periodic table. **(GENERAL)**

_ **Quiz, TE** Students answer three questions about the elements on the periodic table. **(GENERAL)**

_ **Alternative Assessment, TE** Students will prepare a concept map of the periodic table. **(GENERAL)**

Lesson Plan

End of Chapter Review and Assessment

Pacing

Regular Schedule:	**with lab(s):** N/A	**without lab(s):** 1 day
Block Schedule:	**with lab(s):** N/A	**without lab(s):** 0.5 day

> **KEY**
> **SE** = Student Edition   **TE** = Teacher's Edition
> **CRF** = Chapter Resource File

_ **Chapter Review, SE** Students answer end-of-chapter vocabulary, key ideas, critical thinking, and graphics questions. (**GENERAL**)

_ **Vocabulary Activity, CRF** Students review chapter vocabulary terms by completing a quotation puzzle. (**GENERAL**)

_ **Chapter Test A/B/C, CRF** Assign questions from the appropriate test for chapter assessment. (**General/Advanced/Special Needs**)

_ **Performance-Based Assessment, CRF** Assign this activity for general level assessment for the chapter. (**GENERAL**)

_ **Standardized Test Preparation, CRF** Students answer reading comprehension, math, and interpreting graphics questions in the format of a standardized test. (**GENERAL**)

_ **Test Generator, One-Step Planner** Create a customized homework assignment, quiz, or test using HRW Test Generator program.

The Periodic Table

MULTIPLE CHOICE

1. *Periodic* means
   a. happening at regular intervals.   c. happening frequently.
   b. happening very rarely.   d. happening three or four times a year.
   Answer: A   Difficulty: 1   Section: 1   Objective: 1

2. Periodic law states that
   a. elements are either gases, solids, or liquids.
   b. mercury is a liquid at room temperature.
   c. properties of elements change periodically with the elements' atomic numbers.
   d. some elements only stay in a liquid state for short periods.
   Answer: C   Difficulty: 1   Section: 1   Objective: 2

3. Each vertical column on the periodic table is called a(an)
   a. period.   c. element.
   b. group.   d. property.
   Answer: B   Difficulty: 1   Section: 1   Objective: 4

4. The elements to the right of the zigzag line on the period table are called
   a. nonmetals.   c. metalloids.
   b. metals.   d. conductors.
   Answer: A   Difficulty: 1   Section: 1   Objective: 3

5. Most metals are
   a. solid at room temperature.   c. dull.
   b. bad conductors of electric current. d. not malleable.
   Answer: A   Difficulty: 1   Section: 1   Objective: 3

6. Most of the elements in the periodic table are
   a. metals.   c. gases.
   b. metalloids.   d. nonmetals.
   Answer: A   Difficulty: 1   Section: 1   Objective: 3

7. Mendeleev arranged the elements by
   a. density.   c. appearance.
   b. melting point.   d. increasing atomic mass.
   Answer: D   Difficulty: 1   Section: 1   Objective: 1

8. The horizontal row on the period table is called a(n)
   a. group.   c. period.
   b. family.   d. atomic number.
   Answer: C   Difficulty: 1   Section: 1   Objective: 4

9. Which one of the following tells the physical state of an element at room temperature?
   a. the atomic number   c. the atomic mass
   b. the color of the chemical symbol   d. the element name
   Answer: B   Difficulty: 1   Section: 1   Objective: 2

10. How do the physical and chemical properties of the elements change?
    a. within a group   c. within a family
    b. across each period   d. across each group
    Answer: B   Difficulty: 1   Section: 1   Objective: 2

11. What is necessary for substances to burn?
    a. hydrogen
    b. oxygen
    c. helium
    d. carbon
    Answer: B   Difficulty: 1   Section: 2   Objective: 2

12. Transition metals are
    a. good conductors of thermal energy.
    b. more reactive than alkali metals.
    c. not good conductors of electric current.
    d. used to make aluminum.
    Answer: A   Difficulty: 1   Section: 2   Objective: 2

13. The elements' properties follow a pattern that repeats every
    a. 7 elements.
    b. 5 elements.
    c. 14 elements.
    d. 10 elements.
    Answer: A   Difficulty: 1   Section: 1   Objective: 1

14. The vertical column of elements on the periodic table is called a(n)
    a. period.
    b. semiconductor.
    c. atomic mass.
    d. group.
    Answer: D   Difficulty: 1   Section: 1   Objective: 4

15. What element makes up about 20% of the air we breathe?
    a. nitrogen
    b. bromine
    c. oxygen
    d. sulfur
    Answer: C   Difficulty: 1   Section: 2   Objective: 2

16. Mendeleev found that the elements' properties followed a pattern that repeated every
    a. 7 elements.
    b. 5 elements.
    c. 14 elements.
    d. 10 elements.
    Answer: A   Difficulty: 1   Section: 1   Objective: 1

17. The groups of elements that do not have individual names are called the
    a. transition metals.
    b. alkali metals.
    c. alkaline-earth metals.
    d. nonmetals.
    Answer: A   Difficulty: 1   Section: 2   Objective: 2

18. The carbon group has two metalloids, both of which are used to make
    a. dinnerware.
    b. foil.
    c. cans.
    d. computer chips.
    Answer: D   Difficulty: 1   Section: 2   Objective: 2

19. Diamond and soot are very different, yet both are natural forms of
    a. carbon.
    b. nickel.
    c. boron.
    d. copper.
    Answer: A   Difficulty: 1   Section: 2   Objective: 2

20. What element is used to make the most widely used compound in the chemical industry?
    a. sulfur
    b. tellurium
    c. selenium
    d. polonium
    Answer: A   Difficulty: 1   Section: 2   Objective: 2

21. What are most of the elements in the periodic table?
    a. metals
    b. metalloids
    c. precious metals
    d. nonmentals
    Answer: A   Difficulty: 1   Section: 1   Objective: 3

22. How did Mendeleev group the elements?
    a. by density
    b. by melting point
    c. by appearance
    d. by increasing atomic mass
    Answer: D   Difficulty: 1   Section: 1   Objective: 1

23. Mendeleev's pattern repeated after how many elements?
    a. every seven elements
    b. every three elements
    c. every five elements
    d. every two elements
    Answer: A   Difficulty: 1   Section: 1   Objective: 1

24. How would you describe most metals?
    a. They are easily shattered.
    b. They are bad conductors of electric current.
    c. They are dull.
    d. They can be drawn into thin wires.
    Answer: D   Difficulty: 1   Section: 1   Objective: 3

25. How many of the recently discovered elements follow periodic law?
    a. none of them
    b. every eighth element
    c. all of them
    d. half of them
    Answer: C   Difficulty: 1   Section: 1   Objective: 2

26. What are the left-to-right rows on the periodic table?
    a. periods
    b. families
    c. properties
    d. groups
    Answer: A   Difficulty: 1   Section: 1   Objective: 4

27. Which of the following is a property of alkali metals?
    a. They are so hard they cannot be cut.
    b. They are very reactive.
    c. They are stored in water.
    d. They have few uses.
    Answer: B   Difficulty: 1   Section: 2   Objective: 2

28. When a halogen reacts with a metal, what is formed?
    a. a salt
    b. a compound
    c. a nonmetal
    d. an electron
    Answer: A   Difficulty: 1   Section: 2   Objective: 2

29. What helps light bulbs last longer?
    a. krypton
    b. xenon
    c. argon
    d. neon
    Answer: C   Difficulty: 1   Section: 2   Objective: 2

COMPLETION

Use the terms from the following list to complete the sentences below.

halogens
period
group
alkali metals
actinide

periodic law
periodic
noble gases
alkaline-earth metals

30. The days of the week are _____ because they repeat in the same order every seven days.
    Answer: periodic   Difficulty: 1   Section: 1   Objective: 1

31. A rule that states that repeating chemical and physical properties of elements change periodically with the atomic number of the elements is the _____.
    Answer: periodic law Difficulty: 1   Section: 1   Objective: 2

32. Iodine and chlorine are examples of _____.
    Answer: halogens   Difficulty: 1   Section: 2   Objective: 2

33. Pure _____ are often stored in oil to keep them from reacting with water and oxygen.

   Answer: alkali metals

   | Difficulty: 1 | Section: 2 | Objective: 2 |

34. Atoms of _____ have two outer-level electrons.

   Answer: alkaline-earth metals

   | Difficulty: 1 | Section: 2 | Objective: 2 |

35. Each up-and-down column of elements on the periodic table is called a(n) _____.

   Answer: group   Difficulty: 1   Section: 1   Objective: 4

Use the terms from the following list to complete the sentences below.

   aluminum   silicon
   oxygen   carbohydrates
   hydrogen

36. In the Boron Group, the most common element is _____.

   Answer: aluminum   Difficulty: 1   Section: 2   Objective: 1

37. Proteins, fats, and _____, which are compounds of carbon, are necessary for life on Earth.

   Answer:
      carbohydrates

   Difficulty: 1   Section: 2   Objective: 2

38. Nitrogen and _____ can be combined to make ammonia.

   Answer: hydrogen   Difficulty: 1   Section: 2   Objective: 2

39. Germanium and _____ are used to make computer chips.

   Answer: silicon   Difficulty: 1   Section: 2   Objective: 2

40. A substance needs _____ to burn.

   Answer: oxygen   Difficulty: 1   Section: 2   Objective: 2

Use the terms from the following list to complete the sentences below.

   elements   periodic
   periodic law   group
   period   alkali
   transition

41. When something is _____, it occurs or repeats at regular intervals.

   Answer: periodic   Difficulty: 1   Section: 1   Objective: 1

42. Mendeleev's table became known as the periodic table of the _____.

   Answer: elements   Difficulty: 1   Section: 1   Objective: 1

43. All of the more than 30 elements discovered since 1914 follow the _____.

   Answer: periodic law Difficulty: 1   Section: 1   Objective: 2

44. Properties such as conductivity and reactivity change gradually from left to right in each _____.

   Answer: period   Difficulty: 1   Section: 1   Objective: 4

45. A family is also called a _____.

   Answer: group   Difficulty: 1   Section: 1   Objective: 4

46. Because they are so reactive, _____ metals are found only combined with other elements in nature.
    Answer: alkali   Difficulty: 1   Section: 2   Objective: 2

47. The elements in Groups 3–12 are known as _____ metals.
    Answer: transition   Difficulty: 1   Section: 2   Objective: 1

Use the terms from the following list to complete the sentences below.

    alkali   transition
    lanthanides   alkaline-earth
    metalloidshalogens
    actinides

48. Sodium and potassium are _____ metals.
    Answer: alkali   Difficulty: 1   Section: 2   Objective: 1

49. Some of the _____, the shiny, reactive transition metals, are used to make steel.
    Answer: lanthanides Difficulty: 1   Section: 2   Objective: 2

50. All the atoms of _____ are unstable.
    Answer: actinides   Difficulty: 1   Section: 2   Objective: 2

51. Chlorine and bromine are examples of _____.
    Answer: halogens   Difficulty: 1   Section: 2   Objective: 1

52. Semiconductors, also known as _____, have some properties of metals and some properties of nonmetals.
    Answer: metalloids   Difficulty: 1   Section: 1   Objective: 3

53. The _____ metals are shiny and have one or two electrons in their outer level.
    Answer: transition   Difficulty: 1   Section: 2   Objective: 2

54. Magnesium, calcium, and barium are _____ metals.
    Answer:
       alkaline-earth
                         Difficulty: 1   Section: 2   Objective: 1

SHORT ANSWER

55. State the periodic law, which is the basis for the periodic table.
    Answer:
       Answers will vary. Sample answer: The periodic law states that chemical and physical properties of elements are periodic, repeating functions of the elements' atomic numbers. This is why elements in vertical groups of the periodic table share similar properties.
    Difficulty: 1   Section: 1   Objective: 2

56. Explain why hydrogen is unique.
    Answer:
       Answers will vary. Sample answer: The properties of hydrogen do not match the properties of any single group.
    Difficulty: 1   Section: 2   Objective: 2

57. What generalizations can you make about transition metals?

 Answer:
 Answers will vary. Sample answer: Transition metals tend to be shiny and to conduct thermal energy and electric current well.

 Difficulty: 1   Section: 2   Objective: 1

58. Who was Henry Moseley and what did he determine?

 Answer:
 Answers will vary. Sample answer: He was a British scientist who determined the number of protons—the atomic number—in an atom.

 Difficulty: 1   Section: 1   Objective: 2

59. What is periodic law?

 Answer:
 Answers will vary. Sample answer: Periodic law states that the repeating chemical and physical properties of elements change periodically with the atomic numbers of the elements.

 Difficulty: 1   Section: 1   Objective: 2

60. What does it mean when a chemical symbol is red?

 Answer:
 It means that the element is a solid at room temperature.

 Difficulty: 1   Section: 1   Objective: 2

61. Each element has two numbers. What is the top number? What is the bottom number?

 Answer:
 Top: atomic number; bottom: atomic mass

 Difficulty: 1   Section: 1   Objective: 2

62. What are three characteristics of metals?

 Answer:
 Answers will vary. Sample answer. Most metals are solid at room temperature, have few electrons in their outer energy level, and are shiny. Other possible answers: Most metals are ductile, good conductors of electric current and thermal energy, and are malleable.

 Difficulty: 1   Section: 1   Objective: 3

63. How would you describe boron?

 Answer:
 Answers will vary. Sample answer: Boron is a metalloid that is almost as hard as a diamond, but is also very brittle. At high temperatures, it is a good conductor of electric current.

 Difficulty: 1   Section: 1   Objective: 3

64. What are three characteristics of nonmetals?

 Answer:
 Answers will vary. Sample answer: Atoms of nonmetals have an almost complete set of electrons in their outer level. Nonmetals are not malleable or ductile. Other possible answers: Nonmetals are not shiny and are poor conductors of thermal energy and electric current.

 Difficulty: 2   Section: 1   Objective: 3

65. What is sodium chloride and what is it used for?

 Answer:
 Sodium chloride is table salt. It is used to flavor food.

 Difficulty: 1   Section: 2   Objective: 2

66. What are three alkaline-earth metals?

    Answer:
    Answers will vary. Sample answer: beryllium, magnesium, and calcium. Other
    possible answers: strontium, barium, and radium.

    Difficulty: 1   Section: 2   Objective: 1

67. How would you describe the elements that are listed after plutonium, which is element
    94?

    Answer:
    Answers will vary. Sample answer: These elements do not occur in nature. They are
    made in laboratories. Other possible answers: They are radioactive, or unstable, and
    their atoms can change into atoms of another element.

    Difficulty: 1   Section: 2   Objective: 2

68. What does the periodic law state?

    Answer:
    The chemical and physical properties of elements are periodic functions of their
    atomic numbers.

    Difficulty: 1   Section: 1   Objective: 2

69. Using the periodic table, which elements are in the same group as oxygen?

    Answer:
    sulfur, selenium, tellurium, and polonium

    Difficulty: 1   Section: 1   Objective: 2

70. List five elements whose symbols don't seem to come from their English names; for
    example, Fe is iron.

    Answer:
    Others include K—potassium, Na—sodium, W—tungsten, Cu—copper, Ag—silver,
    and Au—gold.

    Difficulty: 1   Section: 1   Objective: 4

71. Using the periodic table, determine which two groups have highly reactive metals.

    Answer:
    on the left, Groups 1 and 2

    Difficulty: 2   Section: 2   Objective: 1

72. What are the actinides? What is one characteristic of all actinides?

    Answer:
    the elements that follow actinium with atomic numbers 90–103; they are all radioactive

    Difficulty: 1   Section: 2   Objective: 2

73. Of the gases oxygen, argon, chlorine, and neon, which would be the two most chemically
    reactive?

    Answer:
    oxygen and chlorine; argon and neon are in Group 18, the noble gases, which are very
    unreactive

    Difficulty: 3   Section: 2   Objective: 2

MATCHING

a. aluminum	f. carbon
b. transition metals	g. halogens
c. lanthanides	h. alkali metals
d. oxygen	i. alkaline-earth metals
e. actinides	j. noble gases

74. ___ metals that are so reactive that in nature they are found only combined with other elements

Answer: H   Difficulty: 1   Section: 2   Objective: 2

75. ___ metals that have two outer-level electrons

Answer: I   Difficulty: 1   Section: 2   Objective: 2

76. ___ shiny, reactive metals, some of which are used to make steel

Answer: C   Difficulty: 1   Section: 2   Objective: 2

77. ___ elements whose atoms are radioactive

Answer: E   Difficulty: 1   Section: 2   Objective: 2

78. ___ very reactive nonmetals

Answer: G   Difficulty: 1   Section: 2   Objective: 2

79. ___ unreactive nonmetals that do not react with other elements under normal conditions

Answer: J   Difficulty: 1   Section: 2   Objective: 2

80. ___ metals in Groups 3–12 that do not give away their electrons as easily as atoms of Groups 1 and 2

Answer: B   Difficulty: 1   Section: 2   Objective: 1

81. ___ the most common element in Group 13, the Boron Group

Answer: A   Difficulty: 1   Section: 2   Objective: 1

82. ___ nonmetal that forms a wide variety of compounds, such as proteins, fats, and carbohydrates

Answer: F   Difficulty: 1   Section: 2   Objective: 2

83. ___ an element that is necessary for substances to burn

Answer: D   Difficulty: 1   Section: 2   Objective: 2

a. aluminum	f. alkali metals
b. argon	g. calcium
c. halogens	h. carbon
d. nitrogen	i. hydrogen
e. oxygen	j. lanthanides

84. ___ These metals react with water to form hydrogen.

Answer: F   Difficulty: 1   Section: 2   Objective: 2

85. ___ This metal, part of the Boron Group, is used for aircraft parts.

Answer: A   Difficulty: 1   Section: 2   Objective: 2

86. ___ This is important to most living things.

Answer: E   Difficulty: 1   Section: 2   Objective: 2

87. ___ Cement and chalk are compounds of this.

Answer: G   Difficulty: 1   Section: 2   Objective: 2

88. ___ Some of these reactive metals are used to make steel.

Answer: J   Difficulty: 1   Section: 2   Objective: 2

89. ___ Chlorine and iodine are these.

Answer: C   Difficulty: 1   Section: 2   Objective: 2

90. ___ This is a colorless, odorless gas.

Answer: I   Difficulty: 1   Section: 2   Objective: 2

91. ___ Diamond and soot are forms of this.
   Answer: H   Difficulty: 1   Section: 2   Objective: 2
92. ___ This makes up about 80% of the air we breathe.
   Answer: D   Difficulty: 1   Section: 2   Objective: 2
93. ___ Light bulbs last longer when they are filled with this gas.
   Answer: B   Difficulty: 1   Section: 2   Objective: 2

   a. semiconductor   c. noble gases
   b. mendelevium   d. californium

94. ___ group made up of six nonmetals
   Answer: C   Difficulty: 1   Section: 2   Objective: 2
95. ___ another name for metalloid
   Answer: A   Difficulty: 1   Section: 1   Objective: 2
96. ___ element named after a scientist
   Answer: B   Difficulty: 1   Section: 1   Objective: 2
97. ___ element named after a state
   Answer: D   Difficulty: 1   Section: 1   Objective: 2

   a. radioactive   c. colorless
   b. shiny   d. shiny

98. ___ word meaning "group"
   Answer: C   Difficulty: 1   Section: 1   Objective: 4

99. ___ word describing actinides
   Answer: A   Difficulty: 1   Section: 2   Objective: 2

100. ___ word describing hydrogen
   Answer: C   Difficulty: 1   Section: 2   Objective: 2

101. ___ word describing most transition metals
   Answer: B   Difficulty: 1   Section: 2   Objective: 2

ESSAY

102. Compare the lanthanides and the actinides.
   Answer:
      Answers will vary. Sample answer: The lanthanides and actinides are transition
      metals. The lanthanides are shiny, reactive metals. The actinides are radioactive.
   Difficulty: 2   Section: 2   Objective: 2

103. Carbon forms many important compounds. Could life exist without carbon? Explain
   your answer.
   Answer:
      Answers will vary. Sample answer: Life could not exist without carbon. Carbon forms
      compounds such as proteins, fats, and carbohydrates that are necessary for living
      things on Earth.
   Difficulty: 3   Section: 2   Objective: 2

104. How does the unreactivity of noble gases make them useful?
   Answer:
      Answers will vary. Sample answer: When light bulbs are filled with argon, they last
      longer. Argon is unreactive and so does not react with the metal filament in a light
      bulb. The low density of helium makes blimps and weather balloons float.
   Difficulty: 2   Section: 2   Objective: 2

INTERPRETING GRAPHICS

Use the figure below to answer the following questions.

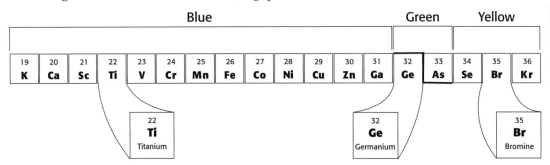

105. Which of the following elements is the most metallic?
   a. K
   b. Kr
   c. Fe
   d. Cu

   Answer: A   Difficulty: 1   Section: 1   Objective: 2

106. Which of these elements is the least metallic?
   a. V
   b. Zn
   c. Co
   d. Se

   Answer: D   Difficulty: 1   Section: 1   Objective: 2

107. Which element group has all nonmetals?
   a. K, Ca, Sc
   b. Se, Br, Kr
   c. V, Cr, Mn
   d. As, Se, Br

   Answer: B   Difficulty: 1   Section: 1   Objective: 3

Refer to the figure below to answer the following questions.

108. The number beneath carbon indicates the
   a. atomic number.
   b. atomic mass.
   c. chemical symbol.
   d. element name.

   Answer: B   Difficulty: 1   Section: 1   Objective: 2

109. The number at the top is the
   a. atomic number.
   b. element name.
   c. atomic mass.
   d. chemical symbol.

   Answer: A   Difficulty: 1   Section: 1   Objective: 2

CONCEPT MAPPING

110. Use the following terms to complete the concept map below:

nonmetals   metals
solids   gases
shiny   metalloids

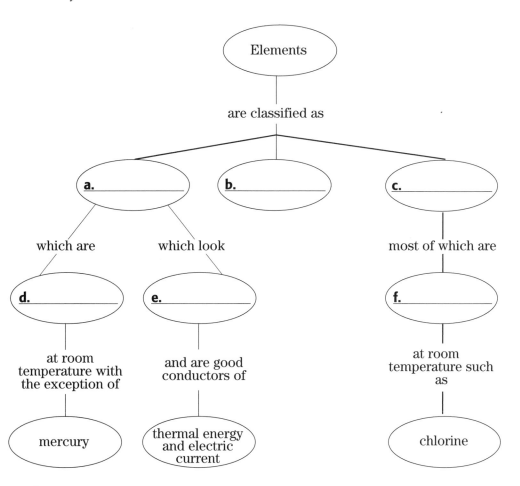

Answer:
a. metals; b. metalloids; c. nonmetals; d. solids; e. shiny; f. gases

Difficulty: 3   Section: 1   Objective: 2

Chapter 1
The Properties of Matter

TEACHING TRANSPARENCIES
Differences Between Mass and Weight
Examples of Chemical Changes

ADDITIONAL TRANSPARENCIES
Chapter Starter Transparency
Bellringer Transparencies
Concept Mapping Worksheet
Concept Mapping Transparency
Concept Mapping Transparency Answer Key

The Properties of Matter   **CONCEPT MAPPING TRANSPARENCY**

Use the following terms to complete the concept map below:
weight, milliliters, mass, cubic centimeters, matter, motion, volume, gravity

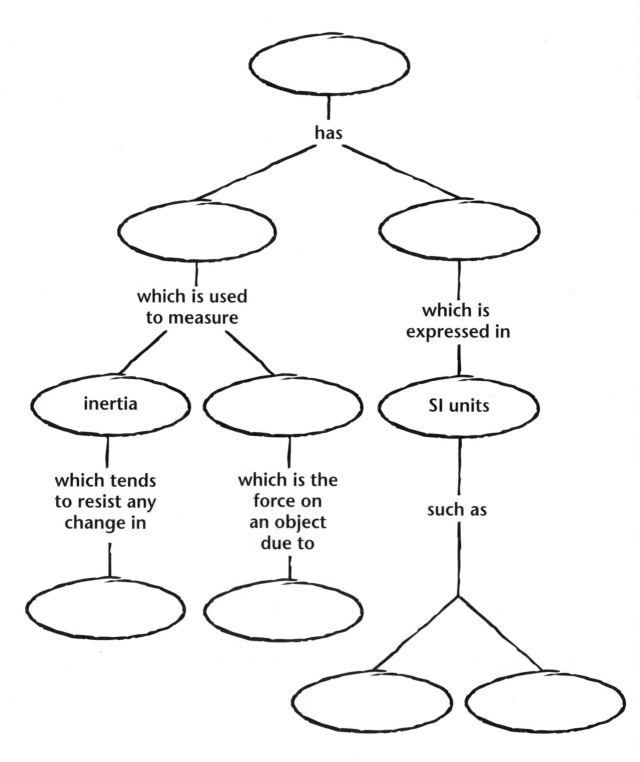

Chapter 2
States of Matter

TEACHING TRANSPARENCIES
Models of a Solid, a Liquid, and a Gas
Boyle's Law; Charles's Law
Changing the State of Water

ADDITIONAL TRANSPARENCIES
Chapter Starter Transparency
Bellringer Transparencies
Concept Mapping Worksheet
Concept Mapping Transparency
Concept Mapping Transparency Answer Key

CHAPTER 2

Use the following terms to complete the concept map below:

changes of state, melting, vaporization, liquid, condensation, states of matter, solid

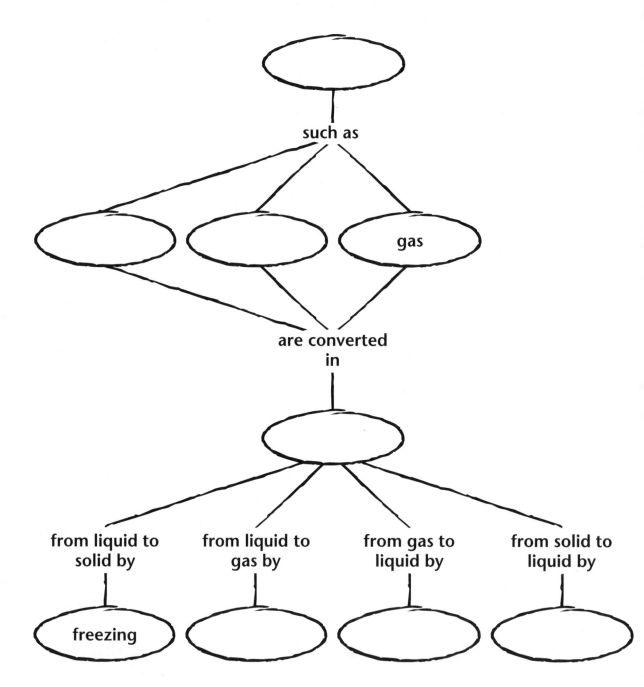

such as

gas

are converted
in

from liquid to
solid by

from liquid to
gas by

from gas to
liquid by

from solid to
liquid by

freezing

Chapter 3
Elements, Chemicals, and Mixtures

TEACHING TRANSPARENCIES

The Three Major Catagories of Elements
Separation of a Mixture
Solubility Graph

ADDITIONAL TRANSPARENCIES

Chapter Starter Transparency
Bellringer Transparencies
Concept Mapping Worksheet
Concept Mapping Transparency
Concept Mapping Transparency Answer Key

Elements, Compounds, and Mixtures   **CONCEPT MAPPING TRANSPARENCY**

Use the following terms to complete the concept map below:
mixture, colloid, filter, element, suspension, solution, compound

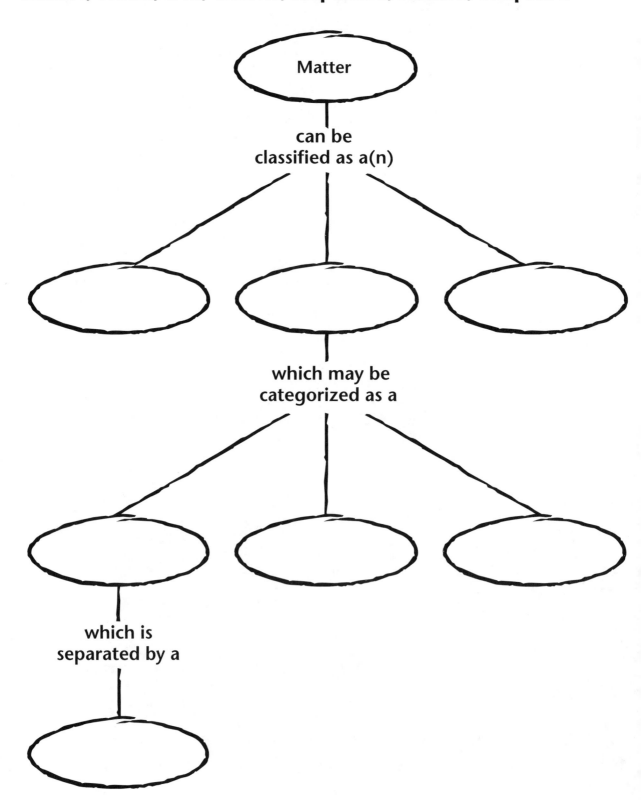

Chapter 4
Introduction to Atoms

TEACHING TRANSPARENCIES
Thomson's Cathode-Ray Tube Experiment
Rutherford's Gold-Foil Experiment
Parts of an Atom
Forces in the Atom

ADDITIONAL TRANSPARENCIES
Chapter Starter Transparency
Bellringer Transparencies
Concept Mapping Worksheet
Concept Mapping Transparency
Concept Mapping Transparency Answer Key

Use the following terms to complete the concept map below:
a nucleus, mass number, isotopes, protons, atoms, electrons, atomic number

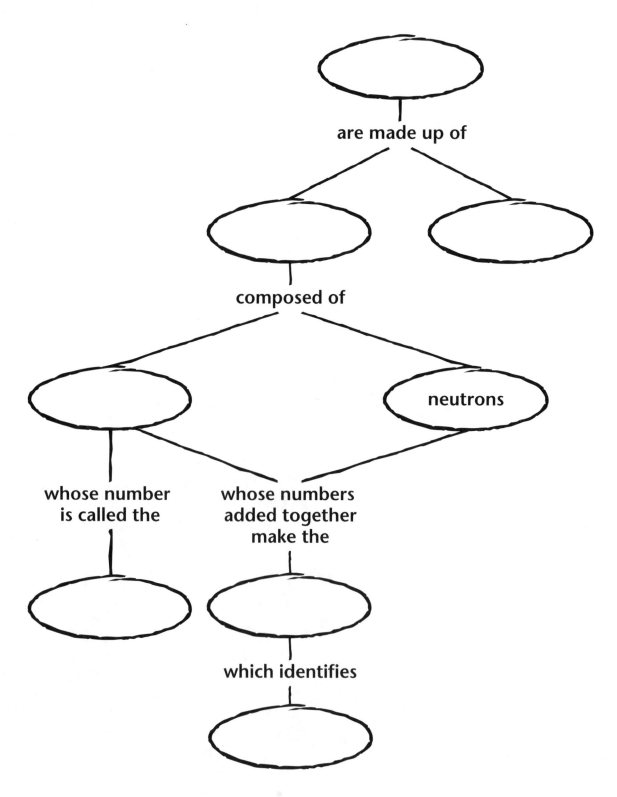

Chapter 5
The Periodic Table

TEACHING TRANSPARENCIES
The Periodic Table of the Elements

ADDITIONAL TRANSPARENCIES
Chapter Starter Transparency
Bellringer Transparencies
Concept Mapping Worksheet
Concept Mapping Transparency
Concept Mapping Transparency Answer Key

Use the following terms to complete the concept map below:
elements, periods, metals, electrons, nonmetals, periodic table, families

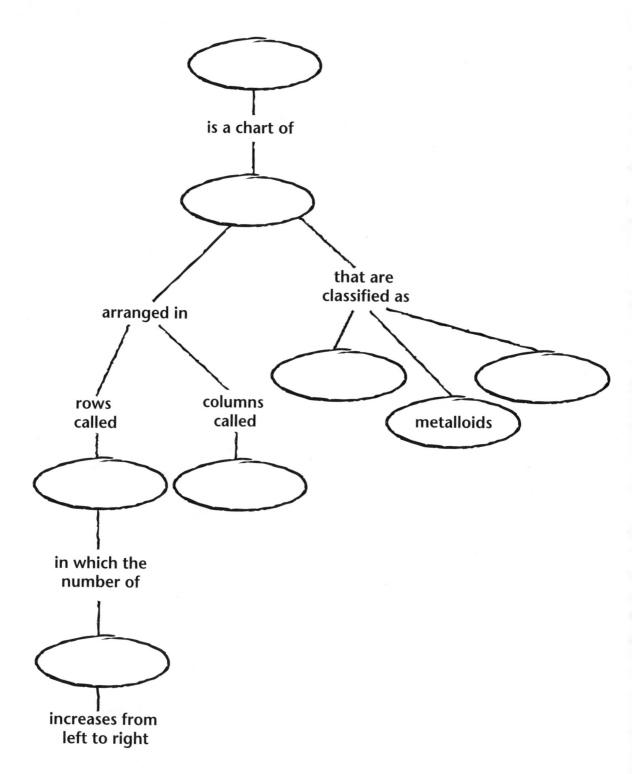

is a chart of

arranged in

that are
classified as

rows
called

columns
called

metalloids

in which the
number of

increases from
left to right